Mapping your
THESIS

The comprehensive manual
of theory and techniques for
masters and doctoral research

Barry White

ACER Press

First published 2011
by ACER Press, an imprint of
Australian Council *for* Educational Research Ltd
19 Prospect Hill Road, Camberwell
Victoria, 3124, Australia

www.acerpress.com.au
sales@acer.edu.au

Edited by Susannah Burgess
Cover design, text design and typesetting by ACER Project Publishing
Cover image: Compass © Shutterstock/Andris Tkacenko;
World globe © Shutterstock/Anton Balazh
Illustration (page 21): Joseph Jastrow
Printed in Australia by BPA Print Group

National Library of Australia Cataloguing-in-Publication data:

Author: White, Barry, 1946-

Title: Mapping your thesis : the comprehensive manual of theory and
                 techniques for masters and doctoral research / Barry White.

ISBN: 9780864318237 (pbk.)

Notes: Includes bibliographical references and index.

Subjects: Dissertations, Academic--Technique Rhetoric.
                 Authorship--Technique.

Dewey Number: 808.066378

Foreword

Over the past decade I have accumulated 72 texts from national and international authors on a range of topics relating to graduate research education and training and have been a co-editor of three texts with Professor Terry Evans of Deakin University. Some of these works consider the nature of the research question while others focus on argumentation, thesis structure, research methods and the process of supervision. There are also a number of texts which take as their foci aspects of the research process, such as ways to manage a period of graduate study, the necessary steps in the building and maintaining of relationships with supervisors, and strategies to ensure that personal health issues do not have a deleterious impact on family and personal relationships.

Some works are sole and others are co-authored or co-edited with contributions from leading researchers, educators, Deans and Directors of Graduate Research and from successful recent graduates. All these texts are replete with 'nuggets' of expertise and wisdom gleaned from long years of direct engagement and participation in the field of graduate research education and training and all make valuable and thoughtful contributions. These texts are intended for current candidates and those recently graduated, supervisors, senior research educators or administrators.

Mapping Your Thesis departs from many of these approaches in a number of ways.

First, at 350+ pages and 279 references this is a formidable sole-authored work and the first of its type and design to be authored by a New Zealand academic. Second, it is equally suitable as a reference and resource text for either candidate or supervisor. Third, it is a text that may serve as a key resource for a semester unit or formal university training program for either candidates and/or supervisors during group discussions or independent non-discipline specific readings. Fourth, functioning as a compendium, the 13 chapters provide a methodical 'drilling down' and analysis of each of the sub-parts of the thesis; from ontology, epistemology and axiology, interdisciplinarity and title development through to the results, discussion section and examination of the thesis. Lastly, the text interweaves the scope, intent, intellectual rigor and contribution required for both the master's and doctoral degree, and thus provides for candidates (for either degree) and supervisors comprehensive and dispassionate arguments as to what must be fulfilled for a successful outcome.

The first three chapters serve as a thorough theoretical grounding for potential candidates in the process of researching their subject domain, creating the intellectual boundaries in which to 'nest' their research premises. These chapters will engage readers at a high level of erudition and the scholarly tone and close attention to detail provide for the potential applicant a primer in the quality, depth of language and intellectual preparation required for a comprehensive research proposal.

Having personally led multiple workshops and training sessions over the years, I welcome the opportunity (all too rare) to engage candidates actively, within the first six months of their candidature, in discussion about the core conceptual underpinnings of their research. *Mapping Your Thesis* provides the impetus and argues the necessity for candidates to initially grapple with a number of fundamental starting points such as genre, explicit method, implicit theory, linguistic nuance within their specific discipline and the nature of interdisciplinary research.

My observation I suspect is partly due to a combination of factors: variable approaches to undergraduate research training, candidate language and culture, variations within disciplines, structure of the particular university research training model and resultant expectations, and supervisor knowledge and skill. It is also no doubt a reflection of the degree to which candidates are exposed early in their candidature to regular rigorous debates characteristic of models of intensive and structured doctoral education programs most often found in countries in North America and Europe. Also, the prevailing emphasis, particularly within Australian universities, on completion rates and financial incentives no doubt leads to some sacrifice of candidate time required to read widely, think dispassionately and to ponder, muse and debate often and deeply about such matters.

Without doubt one of the key contributions of *Mapping Your Thesis* is that it seeks to engage and lead both candidate and supervisor in a systematic, diligent and persevering way to consider both the master's and doctoral thesis as pinnacles of individual and collective achievement. It is an inspiring work that has no doubt required of the author sustained passion, precision and relentless determination.

Mapping Your Thesis represents a substantial contribution to the growing field of works now emerging from Australian and New Zealand scholars and I have no doubt that this text will make a sustained and lasting contribution to the theory and practice of graduate research education.

Carey Denholm PhD FACE, MAPS
Adjunct Professor
Former Dean of Graduate Research
University of Tasmania
Registered Psychologist

Contents

Acknowledgements

Beggar that I am, I am even poor in thanks.

(Shakespeare, Hamlet, 2.2.271–2)

Like diamonds, all books, to one degree or another, are flawed. I take full responsibility for the flaws in this book. However, without assistance the flaws would have been far more numerous. As in the case of Hamlet, this brief acknowledgement does little to settle the debt of gratitude I owe to those who so freely gave support and advice. Without the support of my former colleagues, Irina Filatova and Mandy Goedhals, I would not even have been able to start the project. Without the ongoing support of Emmanuel Manalo, Michael Ward, David Thompson and my long-suffering wife Althea, I would not have been able to bring it to completion. Special thanks go to Marion Blumenstein and Susan Carter. Marion gave invaluable advice on statistics and, in addition, constructed the table and line graph in the Results chapter. Susan's assiduous reading of most of the chapters in the book greatly improved the quality of the writing in them.

Dedication

To Lara,
with lots of love

Midway in our life's journey, I went astray
from the straight road and woke to find myself
in a dark wood. How shall I say
what wood that was! I never saw so drear,
so rank, so arduous a wilderness!
Its very memory gives a shape to fear.
Death could scarce be more bitter than that place!
But since it came to good, I will recount
all that I found revealed there...

(Dante, *The Divine Comedy, Inferno,* Canto 1)

Preface

The question of changes in philosophical fashions is not only distressing because it frustrates our unconscious desire for stable and reassuring paradigms; it is also a puzzling phenomenon because we are not equipped for reconnecting the sequence of theoretical stances which characterise our intellectual history… And yet, however common the turnover in intellectual fashions, we somehow tend to believe that it will not happen again.

(Fiumara, 1995, p.41)

1 RESEARCH CATEGORIES

1. Because change in philosophic fashion will happen again this book is necessarily ephemeral. It can only claim, therefore, to offer passing insight into the current state of ongoing conversations on theory and its impact on how knowledge is conceptualised and expressed. Because ongoing the conversations have neither clearly defined beginnings nor endings. They are thus metaphor for fluidity. This is important because both masters' and doctoral theses by research, from an historical perspective, are relatively recent emergences from this fluidity. Inherently, therefore, they are subject to evolution. How they have evolved and the consequences of the process are central for they inform both the book's purpose and structure. But as emergences subject to different evolutionary processes, theses lack homogeneity both between and within national systems. Masters' and doctoral theses also differ from one another. This is not a given: they were once equivalents.[1] But, from a contemporary perspective, each varies from the other in terms of scale, purpose and the kinds of skills and knowledge they are required to demonstrate. This lack of homogeneity and equivalence is the context within which the purpose of this book has been defined: it is to raise awareness of, and provide grist for reflection on, the critical choices research and thesis writing currently involves. It is descriptive and discursive but not prescriptive. How can it be anything other in the face of the general diversity of theses and in their particular idiosyncrasies? Tolstoy said happy families were all alike, while each unhappy one is unhappy in its own way (cited in Taleb, 2007, p.185). In this sense theses resemble unhappy families and in this sense too free decisions will need to be made: the application of a simple rule is not a free decision; it is only when they endure the undecidable that decisions become free (Derrida J. cited in Schostak, 2006, p.137).[2]

Genre knowledge

2. Reflecting a mere sequence of the more recent of the theoretical stances characterising Western intellectual history, disciplines too are novel and evolving conceptualisations. They were not originally conceived as such. In the intellectual environment of the eighteenth and nineteenth centuries they were regarded as accreted slices of knowledge legitimised by the laws of a rational universe. Such was the strength of scientism during this period that research writing throughout the disciplines sought to be minimally expressive in order to present phenomena and opinions as objectively as possible. In this environment writing could, thus, be construed as an unfortunate necessity (Golden-Biddle & Locke, 1997). But it was the very success of disciplines so conceived that served to undermine this perception for each discipline, in tandem with changes in intellectual fashion, developed specific discourses to both represent and privilege particular ways of thinking. Instead of a generalised skill writing in research came to be construed as a transformative process of acculturation: the manner of writing, the works and views referred to and the issues addressed a reflection of the disciplinary and theoretic perspectives of the time.

3. This is genre knowledge best learned through immersion rather than by analysing its conventions (Peck MacDonald, 1994). The writing of it tends to be resistant to acts of authorial ingenuity (Dillon, 1991). Were this not the case it would fail to fulfil one of the requirements of disciplinarity; in the context of particular disciplines and theoretic approaches to research genre knowledge is situated knowledge. Its mode of communication needs to be readily understood by individuals from a wide range of other cultures but who share membership of the same disciplinary culture. This is the universal in university. But, in an institutional setting, disciplines become destabilised when confronted with new understandings and different sets of social needs. It is thus no accident that the growth during the late twentieth century of the networks linking an increasingly fragmented yet interdependent global society have led the purposes of research to become more diffuse and the number of legitimised 'ways of knowing' to increase (Newman, Ridenour, Newman & DeMarco, 2003). It is, therefore, also no accident that qualitative, mixed methods and interdisciplinary research, individually and collectively, also reflect complexity and ambiguity. This is necessarily the case for they arose from and were a response to an environment where judgements need to be made within increasingly multiplied and often conflicting frames of reference (Roland, 2006) and where expert knowledge is undeterminable by facts and dependent on arguable assumptions (Dillon, 1991).

Conceptual constructs

4. This is the current environment in which theses need to be written and it posed a number of challenges for a book of this kind. The response explains its structure. Running as a leitmotif throughout is the notion that no conceptual construct can be complete unto itself: concepts can only be defined in terms of their dynamic relations with other constructs. Words, for example, need other words if the subtle meanings of each are to be defined. In the same way the definition of any discipline requires the existence of other disciplines. To this extent all disciplines are interdisciplinary also to this extent they are non-homogeneous. Similar logic applies to methodological approaches to research, the discreteness of each dependent upon its relation to the others. It is in this context that the three broad methodological categories informing the discussion in this book were adopted for didactic purposes only: at no time are they considered autonomies. Their inherent slipperiness is particularly apparent in the term adopted for one of them, exegetic research. First used in a theological context and later broadened to include non-biblical literature, exegesis is critical explanation or analysis of obscure or symbolic text. But, while exegesis draws meaning from text eisegesis imposes meaning. Assuming we cannot read innocently where then does exegesis stop and eisegesis start? Is it, moreover, valid to compare them in this linear fashion? Is not their relationship far more complex? In a deconstructive sense the concepts not only need each other if their meanings are to be understood, they also undermine each other. This too is the manner in which the relationship between each of the other methodological categories that inform the discussion in this book, qualitative and empirical research, should be understood. But, while the former is broadly recognisable as naturalistic, interpretive and grounded in the lived experiences of people, the use of the latter rather than the more usual term quantitative research requires explanation.

Empirical vs empiricism

5. Fundamental to the methodology of the sciences is the testing of hypotheses and theories by observation rather than by logic, reasoning or intuition alone. The methodology derives from the Classical period where practitioners of empirical medicine doubted theories and relied instead on past experience to inform their treatments (Taleb, 2007). However, it was only in the seventeenth century that John Locke formulated the philosophical doctrine of empiricism. In doing so, as is inevitable in doctrinal philosophy, he applied a number of arguable assumptions. Primary among these was the concept of the human mind not only as a *tabula rasa* upon which experience subsequently is imprinted

but also as functioning independent of the body. Mind/body dualism was not peculiar to Locke; the concept stretched all the way back to Plato. But it is assumptions such as these that make empiricism less acceptable today than it was three centuries ago. It is for this reason that the term empirical in the book should not be confused with empiricism. However, because the etymology of empirical lies in Classical practice its interpretation is also exposed to contemporary criticism. The empirics, for example, trusted experience in inverse proportion to their trust in reason and they had good reason for doing so. Nonetheless, despite the baggage of its heritage, the term empirical more accurately represents the process of contemporary scientific methodology than does the clumsy term quantitative. This explains its use in the book.

How do methodologies and disciplines relate?

6. Now, if exegetic, empirical and qualitative approaches to research are not distinct they ought to be able to relate to each other. The same logic applies to academic disciplines. But how do methodologies relate to each other? How do disciplines relate to each other? And how do methodologies and disciplines each relate to the other? Such questions require us to establish what methodology is and what disciplines are. If this does not sound immediately relevant to your research bear in mind that critical self-awareness of the founding assumptions of academic discourse is highly valued in a research student (Dillon, 1991). A twelfth century monk explains why:

Some things are worth knowing on their own account; but others, although apparently offering no return for our trouble, should not be neglected, because without them the former cannot be thoroughly mastered.

(Willmann, 1907, np)

So let's start with methodology.

2 METHODOLOGY

1. There is a distinction between a research strategy and a research method. Surveys, case studies, experiments, action research and grounded theory, for example, are strategies implemented using questionnaires, interviews, observation, document analysis or a wide range of other methods (Denscombe, 2001). Each of these methods, in turn, can be applied in multiple ways. There are, for example, many types of interviews and many ways in which observation might be undertaken. A number of these, or techniques for applying them, have come to be associated with empirical, exegetic or qualitative approaches: random sampling and the use of control groups in empirical research and ethnographic and narrative

interviews, for example, in qualitative approaches. There is, however, no intrinsic link binding the theory and assumptions explaining empirical, exegetic or qualitative research to particular methods or techniques[3] (Greens & Caracelli, 2003). Instead, what makes methods or techniques appropriate to, or 'right' for, a particular research setting is, instead, the extent to which they have been justified in the context of the purpose of the research, in the context of the technical attributes of each method or technique, and in the context of the theory and assumptions explaining empirical, exegetic or qualitative approaches. In order to be accepted as legitimate in particular research settings all methods, therefore, need a logical justification. This is what constitutes the concept methodology and explains why all theses, implicitly or explicitly, have a methodology and why that methodology permeates every aspect of a thesis.

2. Methodology is not, however, a recipe; it does not tell you just what to do. Rather, it acts as a guide about what to pay attention to, what difficulties to expect, and how to approach problems (Wenger, 1998, p.9). The need for such a guide is apparent in the contemporary debate on global warming. When research findings differ we have no single Archimedian point from which a single decisive view can be produced:

> *…no way of peeking round the corner, looking over our own shoulders, asking God and discovering what the temperature really is, or what it really once was, independently of the techniques of observation that are on trial. We can soldier on, perhaps with new theories and techniques, if we can discover them, and that is all.*

(Blackburn, 2005, p.57)

3. Method and methodology, therefore, are interrelated concepts and yet distinct from each other. Because all methods need a justification it thus follows that the rationale and theoretic assumptions that underlie research need to be understood.

Thinking abstractly

4. But understanding is not an end in itself. Instead, it is a means to enable researchers to participate in the ongoing debates about the nature and purpose of what they do. The benefits of doing so are substantial for every aspect of the thesis will be informed by an ability to read, write and think at a deeper conceptual level. In this sense all research shares the goal of making researchers think abstractly (Morse & Richards, 2002). This explains why examiners, particularly in the humanities and social sciences, often pay significant attention not only to the methodology underpinning a thesis but also to the justification provided for its adoption. Unless clearly thought through this attention can be particularly disconcerting during a *viva voce* (living voice) examination:

Inasmuch as choice always favours X in favour of Y, questions about the choice of theory and/or method can therefore be among the meanest: 'You chose to work with Freud rather than Lacan—why?' The fact that most research projects could be approached effectively, if with different results, using many other theories and methods makes this a particularly terrifying category of question for the candidate to prepare for and I am aware of many poor candidates who have come out of vivas declaring: 'He just went on and on about X and why I hadn't used his work/ that approach.'

(Pearce, 2005, p.73)

Methodology reflected in each chapter

5. It is logical, therefore, that the manner in which methodology permeates a thesis in its entirety should be reflected in the chapters of this book. Thus, in chapter one the theoretic assumptions underpinning the concept methodology are explained and chapter two indicates how methodological approach affects how interdisciplinary research is conceived and applied. Chapter three illustrates how methodology influences the topic chosen, the questions posed or hypotheses proposed and the manner in which the title of the thesis, and the thesis itself, is constructed. Methodology also, as will be seen in chapter four, influences the selection of supervisor/s. In chapters five and six the manner in which methodological approach guides the expression of thought in writing is discussed, and chapters seven, eight and nine show that the explanatory context for both the introduction to the thesis and the review of the literature/discourses will be provided by that perspective. Chapter ten explains why the methods chosen to conduct the research are a direct consequence of the theoretic approach or approaches adopted. Because all that follows in a thesis and in the book is a logical consequence of the issues discussed in these chapters it can, therefore, be seen that methodology is of fundamental importance to the manner in which a particular research undertaking, from the outset, has been designed.

3 RESEARCH DESIGN

1. Research design is the logic that links methodology to specific strategies and methods. The term, in other words, refers to the coherence of the methods used and the overall manner in which data is collected and analysed in order to provide sufficient and suitable evidence to fulfil the objectives of a research undertaking (Manalo & Trafford, 2004). A sound research design thus reflects a clear understanding of what needs to done and how it ought to be done. Without these sets of understandings there can be no confidence that

the research has been properly conducted. Therefore, because the soundness of the research design adopted is fundamental to the success of a thesis the design will need to be fully justified and explained. The manner in which the design is conceived and expressed in empirical, qualitative and exegetic theses will, however, differ.

Empirical design: explicit method, implicit theory

2. Empirical researchers deal with objects and concepts that have measurable attributes. Meaning, therefore, is implicitly derived from theory and explicitly by observation, measurement and experiment. Because the results of this work are, to one degree or another, considered generalisable, empirical research is nomothetic (to generalise and derive predictive laws that explain measurable phenomena). This means that empirical researchers are usually able to approach research undertakings with a significant body of generalised findings and observations. In consequence they are also usually able, from the outset, to establish a significant degree of focus and, thus, to implement a systematic, linear process of adopting a particular design and implementing the necessary procedures. From this perspective methods are defined as sets of techniques or modes of enquiry applied in a systematic way so as to enable other researchers to establish the reliability and objectivity of what has been accomplished and to validate the process by replicating it. In order to enable them more easily to do so there needs to be 'full disclosure'. In empirical theses, therefore, a detailed explanation of how the data were derived and analysed will be provided in a devoted methods section or sections. (Doctoral theses might have a number of methods sections.)

Qualitative design: explicit method, explicit theory

3. However, in qualitative research there is a close and explicit relationship between theory and method. This is because qualitative researchers do not seek to describe pre-existing facts about the world but, rather, how individuals construct the character of their own worlds (Oakley, 1999). Because it seeks to interpret and explore social and cultural and, therefore, conceptual phenomena that defy objective measurement qualitative research is idiographic; meaning is explained as specific, subjective and contingent. For this reason qualitative researchers, apart from methodological theory, have few generalised findings and observations upon which to rely when they begin their research. This has a number of immediate effects on the manner in which research design is conceived and methods are applied. First, because the process is of necessity more research led than in the case of empirical undertakings, it cannot be considered *a priori* as linear: the

movement forward is not comfortably and logically visible (Meloy, 2002). This can be seen in the following advice provided by a supervisor to a student beginning research for a qualitative thesis: 'talk to everyone about everything and write down everything you observe and see what emerges as interesting. Don't worry about having an analytic framework at this point' (Meloy, 2002, p.57). The second effect is linked to this need to keep strategic options open. Method is not, as in empirical research, seen as procedure, technique or mode of enquiry to be applied in a systematic way, but as sets of flexible approaches whose application needs to be logically grounded in the context of the research as it proceeds: '... I realized the futility of searching for the "right" grounded theory method and instead focused attention on crafting an interpretive logic of justification for my grounded theory' (Grubs, 2006, p.81). Third, the relationship between theory and method in qualitative research is not only explicit but, at times, so close as to allow one to merge with the other. Most qualitative approaches, for example, require researchers to be both phenomenological[4] and ethnographic.[5] But each of these theoretic approaches also constitutes a discrete method. Coupled with the subjective need for qualitative researchers to be both reflexive (self-referential) instruments and, together with their research participants, actors in the research narrative, the manner in which both methods and research design are conceived and discussed in qualitative theses will, therefore, differ from the manner in which they are conceived and discussed in empirical theses. While some of the former will have a devoted methods section or sections where the synergy between theory and methods are established, others, because of the particular needs of their subject matter, will be more idiosyncratically constructed with discussion of the methods, theory and the literature in which they are enmeshed running through the narrative of the thesis as a whole. The collective consequence of the idiosyncratic subjectivity inherent in the processes of qualitative research is that the coherence of the research design of qualitative theses cannot be measured against the same criteria applied to empirical theses. While the criteria of *credibility*, *dependability* and *confirmability*, are applied in the former *validity, reliability* and *objectivity* are, instead, applied in the latter.[6] It can thus be seen that differing methodological positions have different textual outcomes. In this sense language use is epistemic: it is consciously directed to the knowledge making purposes of a particular methodological approach (Peck MacDonald, 1994).

Exegetic design: implicit method, explicit theory

4. In empirical theses where the choice of method is implicitly contingent upon theory and in qualitative theses where the choice of method is explicitly

contingent on theory, the justification for and explanation of the conceptual framework of each thesis will be presented in the introduction and literature review and the explanation of how that framework was applied will be in the methods section/s of all empirical theses and in some qualitative theses. (It is for this reason that the section in which the methods are discussed should not be called methodology but methods or any other term appropriate to the specific needs of the research undertaken: procedures, for example.) Even when qualitative theses do not have an explicit methods section or sections, there will, nonetheless, be an explicit discussion in the narrative justifying the application of particular methods as the need to do so arises. However, in exegetic research the choice of theoretic approach is often so explicit and the methods adopted in consequence so implicit that discussion of the relationship between them is entirely neglected. Thus, while history has long cultivated methodological self-consciousness through historiography, it is quite common for researchers in, for example, English literature, to claim their work is essentially without method (Pearce, 2005).

5. This is a missed opportunity because, even though obscure, the relationship between theory and method in exegetic theses, as is the case in all approaches to research, is important. A decision, for example, to write in either the first or third person might be a consequence of theoretic approach and could, therefore, 'be a methodological choice that will affect the outcome of the thesis as much as the initial choice of theorist' (cited in Pearce, 2005, p.53). There is, in fact, an entire discourse on the use in research narratives of the authorial voice (Garman, 2006). The wording of the title of a thesis is methodological for alternative wording might result in a different interpretation of the research. Is it possible to read objectively?

A highly educated, privileged, middle-class person may position the texts/readers of popular romance in a highly condescending way, for example. Anyone, or anything, that is liable to being made into an 'other' in humanities research thus becomes a methodological issue.

(Thody, 2006, p.141)

Methodology in this sense is very practical because it not only frames the theories and methods adopted but also the manner in which we justify our actions to ourselves and to each other (Wenger, 1998). But, having established that methodological approach exerts a formative influence upon the manner in which researchers conceive, design and express their work, it is also necessary to establish why this so. Why do individual researchers need to adopt a methodological approach at all? The answer, in brief, is that all research rests upon assumption: the assumption of what is considered to be real and true.

ENDNOTES

1 In medieval Europe the distinction between masters' (*Magister Artium*) and doctoral degrees (*Licentia Doctorandi*) signified the tradition to which particular universities belonged. Those aligned with the University of Bologna conferred doctorates and those aligned, as were Oxford and Cambridge, with the University of Paris, conferred masters' degrees. Both degrees, because they conferred the right to teach at a university, fulfilled the same function (Simpson, 1983).

2 Numbered paragraphs were a feature of the 1823 edition of Jeremy Bentham's *Introduction to the Principles of Morals and Legislation*. In this bible of Utilitarianism the purpose of doing so, as in the case of the Christian Bible, was utility. This explains the use of numbered text here.

3 Close definition makes methods and techniques more specific to particular approaches to research. Unlike a randomised controlled trial, for example, a trial is not specific to empirical research.

4 A phenomenological study seeks to describe rather than explain phenomena as perceived by participants who experienced them. Researchers, thus, need to limit preconceptions. This process, *epoché*, is common to most approaches to qualitative research.

5 The term derives from cultural anthropology from which it also draws the concept 'funds of knowledge', the strategic and cultural resources that each community possesses. Ethnographic studies tend to be unstructured, dialogic, long–term, field–based explorations of cultures, methods being secondary to strategies for participation in the field. The approach, as in most qualitative studies, emphasises naturalness and the need for thick description.

6 *Credibility* is the extent to which a researcher's interpretations are rooted in the constructions of a participant or literary work. *Dependability* is the extent to which interpretation has been made distinct from the material researched. *Confirmability*, the extent to which it has been made possible for other researchers to confirm what has been done, is a criterion adopted by some exegetic and qualitative researchers but, because it bears a close resemblance to objectivity, is rejected by others. For a discussion of *validity, reliability* and *objectivity* see below.

CHAPTER 1

Appearance and Reality

You do look, my son, in a moved sort,
As if you were dismayed. Be cheerful, sir.
Our revels now are ended. These our actors,
As I foretold you, were all spirits, and
Are melted into air, into thin air.
And, like the baseless fabric of this vision,
The cloud-capped towers, the gorgeous palaces,
The solemn temples, the great globe itself—
Yea, all which it inherit—shall dissolve
And, like this insubstantial pageant faded,
Leave not a rack behind. We are such stuff
As dreams are made on, and our little life
Is rounded with a sleep.

(Shakespeare, *The Tempest*, 4.1.165–177)

1.1 TRUTH

1. It appears self-evident that research should be a search for 'truth' rather than an attempt to verify 'untruth' (Cryer, 2006, p.85). Truth in this context is not connected to the tradition in Roman and medieval law that torture is an acceptable determinant of truth: 'Torture is the inquiry after truth by means of torment' (Fiumara, 1995, p.50). Nor is it a question of integrity. It is rather a worry 'that however sincere and careful we are, we are trapped in partial or perspectival or outright illusory and fictional views, with little or no chance of realizing our plight' (Blackburn, 2005, p.xvi). So, in this context, is the distinction between 'truth' and 'untruth' self-evident? Without such a distinction, how are truths to be generated and supported? (Garman, 2006). What, for that matter, counts as research? Is it a search for knowledge? The answer to this, at least, appears to be self-evident for knowledge in Latin is *scientia* and, in the West between the late sixteenth and mid-twentieth century, science was the name of the most respectable kind of knowledge (Lakatos, 1978).

However, contemporary science is but one among several ways of 'knowing'. While intellectual and moral purposes have always been linked (Rowland, 2006), an explicit relationship is no longer drawn between research and knowledge. Knowledge might just as easily be coupled instead with liberation, emancipation, expressive art or programmatic politics (Newman et al., 2003). Many feminist scholars, for example, have chosen qualitative approaches, such as participatory action research, for a particular programmatic purpose: as emancipatory practice to make the voices of the marginalised heard (Brannen, 2005) and, in doing so, bring to light new forms of knowledge; in this case 'suppressed knowledge' (Rowland, 2006).

Correspondence theory

2. Just as the purpose of research has become more diffuse since the mid-twentieth century so too have the truth claims and, therefore, the basis for legitimacy upon which research rests. This is evident in the contemporary distinction between 'data' and 'representation' a distinction reflecting the oldest of the binary oppositions in metaphysics[1]: that between reality and appearance (Rorty, 1999). The use of the term data implies an objective reality independent of the observer. This is reflected in Aristotle's statement: 'To say of what is that it is, or of what is not that it is not, is true' (cited in Blackburn & Simmons, 2005, p.1). This is the correspondence theory of truth. Because the mind is considered a mirror accurately reflecting reality, the truth or falsity of a statement can be determined by the extent to which it corresponds with that reality: data thus are qualities or elements that reflect a measurable reality. The problem is that it is impossible to determine if a belief or description accurately represents the world as it exists independent of thought (Linn, 1996):

...even the idea of a 'resemblance' between an idea and something that is not an idea seems preposterous: how does our idea of solid things resemble them? How does our idea of spatial distance resemble spatial distance?

(Blackburn, 2005, p.141)

There is also the 'etcetera problem'. Complete descriptions are needed if the requirements of correspondence are to be met but this is not possible because an etcetera clause has to be used to permit any description to be brought to a close. All that is possible, therefore, are incomplete descriptions (Hart, 2005). Besides, given fact is inferential. For example, the apparently factual statement 'electrons have a negative charge' requires knowledge of the inferences that support the statement and, thus, requires a significant understanding of physics (Blackburn & Simmons, 2005). Given fact also depends upon perspective:

...my car is a vastly different model for me compared to a mechanic, a marketing man or an environmentalist. In other words, 'the Earth', 'humankind' even 'my car' indicate a heterodoxy of position and intention, not a correspondential mapping of object space and information space.

(Smith & Jenks, 2006, p.126)

That the mind is not a mirror is apparent in the following extract by the anthropologist Claude Levi-Strauss:

...either I can be like some traveller of the olden days, who was faced with a stupendous spectacle, all, or almost all, of which eluded him, or worse still, filled him with scorn and disgust; or I can be a modern traveller, chasing after the vestiges of a vanished reality. I lose on both counts, and more seriously than may at first appear, for, while I complain of being able to glimpse no more than the shadow of the past, I may be insensitive to the reality as it is taking shape at this very moment, since I have not reached the stage of development at which I would be capable of perceiving it. A few hundred years hence, in this same place, another traveller, as despairing as myself, will mourn the disappearance of what I might have seen, but failed to see. I am subject to a double infirmity: all that I perceive offends me, and I constantly reproach myself for not seeing as much as I should.

(Cited in Blackburn, 2005, p.207)

Coherence theory

3. In the context of these extracts does the following characterisation of objectivity by a team of researchers make sense? 'We understood the biases we brought to the research as individuals and as a team. We could, therefore, take care to minimize the impact of our biases on the data collected' (Golden-Biddle & Locke, 1997, p.78). Acceptance that to a greater or lesser degree reality is constructed rather than given is a reflection of coherence theory. Because what we perceive as reality is filtered by our assumptions, each of us sees reality differently. Coherence theory, therefore, entirely or partially rejects any distinction between what is known and the knower of it. This approach interprets truth as the extent to which a statement 'coheres to' or reflects a set of propositions that seek to explain, or to represent, that reality. Where coherence theorists differ is whether there is one reality, one truth, which can be known with a reasonable degree of probability or whether there are many truths the veracity of each only ascertainable relative to the knower. The danger in regard to the latter is collapse into complete relativism.[2] Nonetheless, correspondence theorists and those coherence theorists who subscribe to one reality can use the term data in the sense that it corresponds

with, or in so far as currently can be ascertained, coheres to, one reality. Constructivists, instead, use the term 'representation'.

Materialists and Solipsists

4. Reduced to a crude linear continuum there are two extremes of thought in regard to the relationship between reality and appearance and, thus, to the nature of truth. At one end are the Materialists who, because they hold that matter is the only thing that can truly be said to exist, argue that all phenomena must be the result of the interaction of material things: real phenomena have single explanations and, therefore, a unified set of laws underlies nature. Truth, from this perspective, is realisable in an independent, objective, single reality. At the other extreme are the thinkers who can broadly be categorised as Solipsists. They argue that there is no logical link between the mental and the physical because the only knowledge that we can be certain of is that contained in our own thoughts: this is summed up in Descartes' 'I think therefore I am' or, more eloquently in Coleridge's description of Hamlet: 'for ever occupied with the world within him, and abstracted from external things' (cited in Akroyd, 2002, p.435). Under these conditions all we can do is infer the thoughts of others and hope to understand them by analogy with our own. But, because knowledge requires greater justification than mere inference and analogy, knowledge of anything outside the mind is unjustified. This denial of a reality independent of the mind makes objectivity simply a 'view from nowhere' and subjectivity the key to the relative truths revealed in multiple constructed realities. Now, while scientific hypotheses are constructed so as to allow the possibility of refutation, the beauty of Materialism and Solipsism is that neither can logically be refuted.

1.2 ASSUMPTION

1. How are we to come to terms with these contradictions? The ancient Greeks tried 'witnessing'. On special occasions accredited individuals witnessed events to later attest, in appropriate but awkwardly structured language, what had taken place:

   We who now address you here, were there then, and we witnessed there then what we are about to tell you here now in order that you here and we here may all talk here now and in the future about how what happened there then affects us here.

   (Schostak, 2006, p.14)

   There can be no simple relationship between account and event for attempting to control adds to the sources of distortion by reducing the complexity of what is being witnessed (Schostak, 2006). The same dilemma applies to closed system analysis in behavioural research. The methodological aim here is to isolate key variables by carefully defined and operationalised concepts.[3] It also explains the variety of procedures to standardise interviews to facilitate comparison and quantification (Schostak, 2006). Where, though, does this leave the researcher? Well, in the first instance, it means a willingness to refrain from reconciling contradiction but, instead, to seek the productiveness implicit in it. The exercise of doing so is akin to the realisation of one's own error: it creates a space for new knowledge (Rowland, 2006). In the second it means acceptance that assumptions, mental models of the nature, limits and certainty of knowledge, will inform the kinds of research questions asked, the approaches adopted and the results produced (Greene & Caracelli, 2003). Assumptions about the nature of research account, for example, for the implied objective disengagement of the American Psychological Association's (APA) preference for use of the past tense in research writing and for the subjectivity implicit in the Modern Languages Association's (MLA) preference for the present tense. What a thesis writer's assumptions are, therefore, particularly in exegetic or qualitative theses, will need to be indicated in the introductory chapter: 'While aware of postmodernist debate over issues of objectivity and historical realism, this thesis will balance skepticism with some confidence about an empirical approach to the past' (Thompson, 2002, p.1).

Vocabulary

2. As has already become apparent assumptions also influence the terminology used in a thesis. Vocabulary is an important indicator of where researchers, consciously or otherwise, have positioned themselves theoretically. This is because language, like knowledge, is not simply 'transparent', reflecting an objective reality. It is, instead, as an inevitable consequence of its socially constructed, communicative function, a constitutive force reflecting a particular view of reality (Grubs, 2006). In a thesis an empirical researcher, for example, will use the term 'investigator' rather than the qualitative 'explorer'. Empirical researchers will also use the term 'literature review' because it reflects the nomothetic tendency of empiricism: the researcher is able to come to the research question with an established body of generalisable knowledge situated in the existing literature. A qualitative researcher, however, might instead use the term 'review of the discourses' because it reflects the idiographic tendency of constructivism: literature is not a body of generalised knowledge but part of an ongoing, context specific debate joined as and when the needs of the research require it. Words might

also reveal a position in a thesis discussion long before that position has been made explicit: the use of 'global warming', for example, as opposed to 'climate change'.

Nonlinearity

3. Based on the assumption events have causes the word 'because' is central to language. Do events have causes? They might for the concept is productive. But how do we know when we have a cause? Does the statement 'X always follows Y' mean Y causes X? Not necessarily. Does day cause night? The statement 'X must be followed by Y' means only that we observe and, therefore, infer that X must follow Y. Inference is not, though, an empirical concept so the question must be 'under what conditions is it plausible to infer that an observed relationship is causal?' (Punch, 2006, p.49). In an experiment variables might be controlled in order to identify single causes. But confounding variables, as in any social setting, will exert an influence. Because it is not possible, in any setting, to possess all relevant information the possible causes of any event are infinite (Taleb, 2007). 'History is opaque. You see what comes out, not the script that produces events, the generator of history. There is a fundamental incompleteness in your grasp of such events' (Taleb, 2007, p.8). The problem here is butterflies. One flapping its wings might cause a tornado on the other side of the world.[4] But this only makes sense if all other variables are excluded. Attempting to trace the cause of a tornado back to the butterfly illustrates the difficulty. The mathematician Henri Poincaré was the first to introduce the concept 'nonlinearity': small effects can have significant consequences. This, and because all factors work together, is the reason why it is not possible to take all possible causes of an event into account (Taleb, 2007). The word 'because', therefore, is no more than an inference arbitrarily splitting and falsifying the infinitely rich flux of events (Blackburn, 2005).

Measurement

4. Nonetheless, despite Poincaré's insights, linearity remains in some contexts a viable concept. If the laws of motion were nonlinear, no sane astronaut would be willing to be blasted into space (Lewin, 2001). This is at least one of the reasons explaining why in the sciences natural phenomena are usually more amenable to categorisation and measurement than is human behaviour. There are also others:

…biological structure transforms over millennia and eons, and is thus sufficiently stable to lend itself to the assumptions of analytic science. By contrast, other phe-

nomena, such as a culture's symbolic tools, not only evolve more quickly, but are also subject to very different sets of influences. Analytic methods are not just inadequate, but inappropriate for making sense of such dispersed, rapidly changing, and intricately entangled sets of phenomena.

(Davis, 2008, p.57)

It is for this reason that students in the sciences often consider the role of assumption in research as mere distraction. Let's, therefore, first establish a point of principle. Can we doubt the assumption that it is possible to measure precisely the quantity of a tangible substance or the length of a visible object? Well, consider the length of the hypotenuse of a right-angled isosceles triangle. If the square of the hypotenuse is equal to the sum of the squares of the opposite sides then, where these sides are each one unit in length, $\sqrt{2}$ is the length of the hypotenuse. (Together with *pi* the first of the irrational numbers to be discovered, $\sqrt{2}$ expressed as a fraction is one followed by an infinite number of decimal places.) This means that although apparently amenable on paper to objective measurement, no one can ever claim to have measured precisely the length of the hypotenuse of such a triangle. Even bearing in mind that it is we who impose the structure of the number system[5] on objects we wish to measure, the assumption that it is possible to measure precisely the quantity of a tangible substance or the length of a visible object is incorrect.

5. Now it is readily acknowledged that this example is double-edged: while illustrating the limits of objective measurement the example also implies these limits are utterly inconsequential. *Ipso facto* the entire debate about the role of assumption on an individual's ability to perceive an objective reality is also inconsequential and, thus, irrelevant to the natural sciences. But wait, the mere measurement of tangible quantities and lengths or operationally defined concepts are not what constitute science; measurements are only part of a much more elaborate process. What is considered important to measure, what—consciously or subconsciously—is ignored or assumed, how results are reconstituted and given meaning are what constitutes science. The foundational theories of contemporary evolutionary biology which until recently have given primacy to the role of DNA in the evolutionary process are, for example, being shaken by a reassessment of the relatively minor role until recently attributed to RNA. New perspectives are changing long-held assumptions about what ought to be researched and how it ought to be researched. Thus, while numbers register support for or departure from theory 'with an authority and finesse that no qualitative technique can duplicate' (Sharrock & Read, 2002, p.180) they are also unavoidably interpretive figures as they are produced through theoretical understandings

of what is to be counted (Schoenberger, 2001). This is the meaning behind Einstein's apocryphal statement: 'Everything that's countable doesn't necessarily count; what counts isn't necessarily countable' (cited in Rowland, 2006, p.119).

Etic and emic

6. The role of assumption is enhanced in investigations of human behaviour because, unlike the case in the natural sciences, such behaviour defies categorisation into easily measured variables. The question of what constitutes social reality explains the ongoing attempts by researchers in the more empirical of the social sciences (psychology, for example) to limit the role of assumption by identifying, defining and categorising the etic (universal) features of human behaviour in order to create more easily controlled variables so as better to understand the emic (local): 'My dissertation advisor instilled in me the importance of transforming basic observational (etic) data into categories that are culturally meaningful (emic data)' (Meloy, 2002, p.69). While some social sciences tend to be more empirical than others all are overwhelmingly entangled with theoretic issues (Sharrock & Read, 2002). This is why they are called 'social' sciences. But reducing, as in the natural sciences, the object of investigation to dependent and independent variables also removes it from context. After having conducted a carefully controlled investigation the unresolved problem then becomes to recontextualise the findings: to what extent is it valid to say that the decontextualised variables, the proxy, represent the inherent complexity of the natural setting? 'The critical issue in every measurement, therefore, is how well the proxy represents the phenomenon of interest' (Dent, 2005, p.258).

7. That this is a problem, that interpretation is inevitably demanded, that simplification might facilitate comprehension of part at the expense of the whole, is indicated by the growing list of measures of validity in empirical research. Nonetheless, to retain a sense of perspective, dissecting complex systems to study how the parts relate to the whole is the basis for much of what we know about nature (Lewin, 2001). But the limitations of analytic methods (from the Greek *analusis* meaning dissolve) have become increasingly apparent for complex systems are more than a sum of their parts: an ant colony is more than a collection of ants.[6] It is the distinction between complicated (a sum of its parts) and complex (more than a sum of its parts) that explains why a major imperative in both exegetic and qualitative research is the endeavour to retain context: to constantly search for ways to retain as much of the naturalness of the text or of the research setting as possible. In qualitative research, for example, an open-ended interview is considered more 'natural' than an open-

ended questionnaire. But, how natural is an open-ended interview? Is it less or more natural than an ethnographic interview, a narrative interview or a focus group? Ironically, it is often the case that the more natural the method the more ethically problematic it becomes to use the research material. In any event, no matter how natural the method the researcher has to intervene by selecting and writing the material and it is here that the real challenge to naturalness lies (Thody, 2006).

1.3 ONTOLOGY, EPISTEMOLOGY AND AXIOLOGY

1. The problem of using part to reflect a greater whole confronts all researchers. It is no surprise then that it is the fundamental ontological problem of Western metaphysics: what constitutes the greater whole? What, in other words, is reality and how do we relate to it? (Ontology is that aspect of metaphysics devoted to the study of what is taken to be real, the suffix 'ology' meaning 'the study of'. Epistemology[7] is the study of what can be taken as true, and axiology the study of what can be regarded as of value. Each is obviously deeply enmeshed with the others.) Addressing these questions raises an immediate problem: because ontology, epistemology and axiology are conceptual schemes how are they to be understood? This brings us back to the problem of language: because it is a constitutive force reflecting a particular view of reality, there can be no such thing as an external point of view to language. There is no possibility, thus, of standing back and comparing a particular concept with a particular reality or of separating two conceptual approaches and comparing the one with the other (Sharrock & Read, 2002). This is why these concepts lie at the core of philosophic debate.

Legitimate knowledge

2. Now, it is important to recognise that many sources of authority are at play when a thesis is being researched and written. Each of these, with varying degrees of legitimacy, will claim to certify what counts as acceptable knowledge (Garman, 2006). But, as will be seen, one of the necessary, though often difficult tasks is to draw a distinction between institutional sources of authority and those that lie largely within an individual's own control. It is acknowledged that non-theorising is an impenetrable act 'so fighting it requires fighting one's own self' (Taleb, 2007, p.64): to apply a noun without a subconscious accompanying adjective is very difficult. But one's conscious theoretic perspective, one's assumptions (in so far as they can be accessed), should fall into the category of individual control for they ought not to be a consequence of having merely been learned from others. They should,

instead, be a consequence of grappling, in concert with others, with one's own preconceptions and assumptions about what counts as legitimate knowledge (Garman & Piantanida, 2006). Fortunately, the wheel does not need to be reinvented, others have been there before; for over two millennia in fact.

Plato

3. In the West the need for philosophy arose from the attempt by Socrates in the fifth century BCE to establish a way of thinking that could establish truly universal claims everyone would intuitively accept as both moral and truthful. On the assumption we all share an inborn faculty of reason the practice of dialectic he believed would support this and, in doing so, make us both virtuous and knowledgeable (Rorty, 1999). Socrates was not, thus, a dogmatist. Showing that one can admit the authority of truth without supposing that one possesses it he questioned and questioned but never dictated (Blackburn, 2005). It was, however, Plato (c427–c347 BCE) student of Socrates and teacher of Aristotle, who established the foundations of Western philosophy by attempting to relate the establishment of truth with the emerging certainties of mathematics expressed through geometry, music and poetry.

4. Plato was an idealist; his concern was not with the material but with ideas. The motivation for his concern was a question that, as yet, remains unresolved: how does consciousness emerge from matter? (Is life entirely explicable by the laws of mechanics, physics, and chemistry?) Plato's response was to argue that although matter obeys physical laws life, and thus consciousness, is a vital force (thus beyond human comprehension) infused into mere material (Lewin, 2001). This also means that Truth, because it is an idea, is also independent of us. This belief resulted in a set of philosophical distinctions, appearance-reality, which dominated Western philosophy until the mid-twentieth century. It was this distinction that allowed Plato to provide the Socratic project of establishing universal claims with philosophic structure. Decide where you position yourself on the issue of appearance-reality by providing, presuming it were possible to do so, a definition of a table, a definition that covers all possible tables. Which has the greater claim to reality, the essential, metaphysical table of the definition or the approximation perceived to be a table?

5. In support of the former contention Plato argued there are universal essences (a definition might be described as an essence) that we all apply to the particulars of what we see in order to recognise it as, in this case, an approximation of a table. Plato argued that these universals were Forms: distinct but mind independent, immaterial, eternal entities that exist in an abstract realm. (An example is a number, any number. They appear to exist

objectively and independently of our thoughts but do not exist in space and time. If they are independent of us mathematics can be said to have been discovered rather than created [Stanford Encyclopedia].) Because Plato believed that life has a pre-bodily state where knowledge of the Forms is first acquired (what today is called innate knowledge) learning is a process of being brought to an awareness, of being reminded, of the Forms (Rowland, 2006). This explains the meaning of the Greek word for truth *a-letheia*, as unforgetting or disclosure (Crusius, 1991). (Reading dramatic texts, for example, can disclose tacit knowledge of the depth of our emotions.) In this context Forms, because of their role as referents or universal concepts, allow us by intellectual inference alone to recognise (to 'instantiate') 'tableness' as a table. Their function, in other words, is to make the phenomenal world intelligible. The process is what Plato called turning the soul around, so rather than being concerned with the body the 'eye of the soul' instead, would gaze upon the *eidos*, the immaterial Forms, the invisible world of universal truths (Fiumara, 1995).

6. This visual metaphor has played a determinative role in Western intellectual history. For example, Martin Luther in the sixteenth century admonished parishioners 'to tear the eyes out of their reason' if they wanted to be good Christians (Rumana, 2000, p.5). In contemporary terms we refer to 'insight' and we use the word theory that derives from the Greek verb *teorein*, to see (Fiumara, 1995). Plato knew that the world of the senses is stable enough for us to describe, but he also knew that we mistake what changes slowly for permanence: 'as far as any rose could remember, no gardener had ever died' (Blackburn, 2005, p.101). In contrast to the eternal world of the Forms sensory descriptions could only achieve the status of *doxa*, or opinions. This remains a contemporary issue: 'universal change is hostile to stable understanding. Science must proceed by finding the permanent among the impermanent' (Blackburn, 2005, p.99). Plato did not, therefore, doubt the existence of a reality, but for him it was extrasensory.

Aristotle

7. Aristotle, however, strongly objected to Plato's notion of Forms arguing that nothing can be both one thing and, at the same time, have things in common with every other individual thing it instantiated. Aristotle therefore revised the theory of Forms by eliminating their independence from perceived concrete entities. So, whereas for Plato particular physical objects are instantiated by abstract universals, Aristotle considered all objects, animate and inanimate, to be composed of both potential and form. A piece of wood, for example, has the potential to become a carving and a seed a tree. Potential,

because it is latent, lacks reality for it is both without shape or purpose. What activates potential is its essence: in the case of these examples, the ideas of a woodcarver or the blueprint within a seed. It is essence that allows potential to achieve form and, thus, reality.[8] The fact that essence precedes reality explains Aristotle's assumption of eternal goals towards which everything should aim. This means that individuals only become complete, most godlike, by actualising their innate purpose (Rumana, 2000). It is in this sense that Aristotle's ideas are teleological.[9]

8. As in the case of Plato's Forms, therefore, Aristotle's potential and essence are both immaterial and abstract. But, unlike Plato's Forms, Aristotle's essence uses potential to achieve concrete reality and, thus, provides material for empirical observation. Whereas Plato argued that only universal ideas could define specific realities Aristotle argued that it was specific, observed realities that could define universal ideas. While Plato, therefore, helped provide an explanation of how the universal features of particular things are established by being modelled after universal archetypes, Aristotle helped explain how universal concepts can be derived from the study of particular things. For this reason Aristotle, observational scientist as much as philosopher can be considered the founding figure of Western empiricism.

9. The differences between Plato and Aristotle had a significant impact on the intellectual history of the West. For two millennia, for example, a divide separated perceptions of the natural world. Aristotelian mechanists argued that living organisms are simply machines completely explicable by the laws of mechanics, physics, and chemistry. Platonists, on the other hand, while agreeing that living organisms obeyed physical laws insisted that life was something extra, a vital force breathed into mere material. By its nature, therefore, life was beyond scientific analysis (Lewin, 2001).

Scholasticism

10. Nonetheless, the appeal of the ideas of both Plato and Aristotle to early Christianity lay in the theological struggle not only to establish the ontological status of Christ but also the relationship between mind, soul and body. Plato's concept of pure and complete universals had obvious appeal in explaining the nature of the divine and of the relation between body and soul: the former as shadow and the latter as eternal. The influence of Plato's metaphor of the 'eye of the soul' can be seen, for example, in St Paul's words: 'Now we see through a glass darkly, but then we shall see face to face' (Blackburn, 2005, p.81). However, Plato's argument that universals existed as independent entities obviously had less appeal. Later medieval theologians, St Thomas Aquinas among the most prominent, while retaining these aspects

of Plato's universals adapted some of Aristotle's ideas to make more explicit the link between body and soul. God's plan for humanity was, they believed, accessible to reason (Rumana, 2000). As opposed to the fundamentalist concern with revealed theology and its emphasis on faith alone, their concern was with rational theology in order to make Christianity a greater force for social justice. Thus, while the soul continued to be seen as Form existing independently of the body, its potential, when activated by divine essence, could only be realised within the body. This fusion of Platonic, Aristotelian and eschatological (an end time: judgement day) Catholic thinking into Scholasticism enabled new ways of thinking about the world.

1.4 REASON

1. The logical consequence during the sixteenth and seventeenth century when these new ways of thinking were applied outside the authoritarian framework of the church was Humanism: a belief that Christian faith required a commitment to the search for truth and morality not through tradition or authority but through the application of reason alone. In this sense reason was liberating for its application could free humanity from its passions and its history. The logical consequence was individualism: 'man [sic] in the image of God' (Smith & Jenks, 2006, p.59). There was also a less logical consequence: Realism. Reflecting their historical legacy of opposition to an absolutist theology, Realists sought with Foundationalism, the idea that knowledge must be founded on concrete certainty, to establish a new science which would permit the same level of confidence which medieval theologians had expressed in their belief in a reality ontologically independent of the senses.

Descartes

2. Most expressive of the 'foundation' metaphor is René Descartes' rationalist treatise *Meditations*. In it he made what, in terms of contemporary philosophy, was a daring move (Rumana, 2000). Although implicitly reliant on Plato's dualism of mind and body he explicitly rejected the methods of earlier philosophers when he applied reason to doubt his own thoughts until he could find one about which he could absolutely be certain:

…judging that I was liable to error as anyone else, I rejected as being false all the reasonings I had hitherto accepted as proofs…But immediately afterwards I became aware that, while I decided thus to think that everything was false, it followed necessarily that I who thought thus must be something; and observing that this truth: I think, therefore I am, was so certain and so evident that all

the most extravagant suppositions of the skeptics were not capable of shaking it, I judged that I could accept it without scruple as the first principle of the philosophy I was seeking.

(Cited in Schostak, 2006, p.37)

Unfortunately for Descartes his concept c*ogito ergo sum* (I think therefore I am) was firmly shaken by sceptics primarily because it relied upon the postulation of God to prove the existence of other consciousnesses (Schostak, 2006) and because it could not explain how mind and body (which, like Plato, he considered ontologically discrete entities), interact. Nonetheless, the application of reason, an essence fundamentally detached from its surroundings (Linn, 1996), to establish objective facts upon which incontrovertible knowledge could be built proved extraordinarily seductive for most of the next three centuries. At the beginning of the twentieth century, for example, Bertrand Russell began his *Problems of Philosophy* with the question: 'Is there any knowledge which is so certain that no reasonable man could doubt it?' Despite his conclusion once again that the answer is 'no' (Linn, 1996, p.12) the survival of the idea of mind and body as separate entities is implicit in the criteria that some universities apply to measure standards attained by research students. 'They should, for example, demonstrate ability to…as though ability to demonstrate and knowledge of how to apply that ability are distinct from each other' (Rowland, 2006, p.48).

Newton

3. Perhaps the primary reason for the allure of the power of reason is the attraction of the concept of an ordered universe. One without the other would, in fact, make little sense (Linn, 1996). Mathematics is a language apparently capable of precise definition in a way not possible in a language of words and it was in this sense that Galileo spoke of mathematics as the language of the universe: phenomena can be decomposed analytically and treated mathematically as though the sum of their parts (Smith & Jenks, 2006).

Numbers go about as far as we can go in shearing away detail. When we talk of numbers, nothing is left of shape, or color, or mass, or anything else that identifies an object, except the very fact of its existence.

(Holland, 1998, p.23)

It was Newton who through the powers of mathematical calculation and empirical observation, appeared in his 1687 work *The Mathematical Principles of Natural Philosophy* to have deciphered God's ultimate laws explaining how the universe functioned (Lakatos, 1978, p.3).

For Newton, the universe was rationalistic, deterministic and of clockwork order; effects were functions of causes, small causes (minimal initial conditions) produced small effects (minimal and predictable) and large causes produced large effects. Predictability, causality, patterning, control, universality, linearity, continuity, stability, objectivity, all contributed to the view of the universe as an ordered mechanism in an albeit complicated equilibrium, a rational, closed, controllable and deterministic system susceptible to comparatively straightforward scientific discovery and laws.

(Morrison, 2008, p.19)

Together with John Locke's argument that the human mind was not contaminated by original sin but is a *tabula rasa* upon which external reality is the most formative influence, Newton's work vindicated the belief that there is one science about one determinate[10] world and that an individual is capable of objectively seeing that one world as it 'really' is. Objectivism is an epistemological notion that meaning exists apart from consciousness:

A tree in a forest exists objectively, regardless of its being seen and categorized. Its 'tree-ness' is intrinsic to it as an object. When seen by humans its tree-ness is available for them to see empirically, categorize as such and take to be a tree.

(Hart, 2005, p.409)

Positivism

4. The guiding principle of a tightly deductive science with precise concepts and rules, together with the discovery and elaboration of further empirically established scientific laws during the course of the nineteenth century, appeared to make the power of Realist science unassailable for, with its unparalleled achievements, only it could claim to have successfully characterised reality (Sharrock & Read, 2002, p.16). Positivism, a philosophy most clearly enunciated by Auguste Comte in the eighteen fifties, appeared to crown this achievement for it extended the methods and attitudes of Realist science to all fields of human knowledge: rationality and objectivity in both the sciences and the humanities are both desirable and achievable, cumulative facts are therefore what count as knowledge and the history of civilisation is a history of progress. Modernism had been born, its claim to superior knowledge a function of its discourse of representation.

5. Ironically, though, the ideas of a number of the most influential thinkers of the nineteenth century were to prove disruptive of this perception of Modernism and sent it in an unexpected direction. This should not have come as a surprise for Romanticism's emphasis on subjective experience,

Friedrich Nietzsche's 'will to power', Charles Darwin's blurring of the distinction between animal and human, and Karl Marx's revolutionary socialism which replaced human rationality as the driving force of history with the rationality of economics, made it apparent that an assault upon Realism had been running as an undercurrent to its most dramatic scientific and engineering achievements. This was also reflected in the fine arts with impressionism's and later abstract expressionism's rejection of objective assessment in favour of subjective response. It was also reflected in the cultural movements irrationalism and aestheticism which, though embracing the progressive potential of modernism, de-emphasised rationality and considered disruption a necessary means to undermine traditional class and gender relations in Europe.

6. The dawn of the twentieth century provided additional impetus to these trends. On the one hand Freud, Adler and Jung showed that objectivity was not a personal attribute to be set aside by choice: perception, instead, was unavoidably filtered by experience. As Nietzsche had argued drawing a distinction between facts and values was, therefore, a fallacious dichotomy. On the other hand, Einstein's $e=mc^2$ undermined Newtonian certainties: time was now relative and reality a function of the interaction of energy, mass and velocity. These new insights and exposure to the cataclysmic consequences of primal nationalism in two world wars undermined what little faith remained in humans as rational beings. It also exposed the fundamental contradiction that had, from the outset, confounded Realism: if history is progressive and experience an open-ended process, what we know today is less than we will know tomorrow and much less than we (individually and collectively) will know in the distant future. Yet Realists claimed that on the basis of present experience they were capable of recognising laws of nature that would apply not only in the face of experience gained in the distant future but also for all eternity. Their claim to have been lifted above the flow of history proved to be unsustainable.

7. Clearly Realism produced extraordinary results: the problem was overconfidence in what could be represented and analysed (Richardson, 2005). Gone, therefore, were the foundations of Realism: an objective external world, a progress-driven cybernetic and, perhaps most important of all, Humanism. Positing the centrality of the human subject Humanism privileged humanity, isolated it and made it unique; a prime characteristic of the 'humanities' (Smith & Jenks, 2006). This, though, is a perception uninformed by Darwin. When so informed the replacement in importance of agency by structure[11] led to the disappearance of Humanism's central concept of the unitary-autonomous person (Craig, 2003). Such has been the change that a contemporary hypothesis proposes that humanity both uses

and is used by cognition. Far from cognition making us the independent agents of modernism, cognition as a self-organising agent might, therefore, merely be parasitical on us (Smith & Jenks, 2006).

Post-positivism

8. Although Realism briefly survived in attenuated form as Logical Empiricism, philosophic thinking in the second half of the twentieth century has been dominated by Post-positivism. This is a broad rubric that, in a particular sense, applies to those who acknowledge the criticism of Realism but, nonetheless defend some of its positions (generally called Critical Realists), and in a broader sense includes those who reject Realism in its entirety (generally called Constructivists). Thus, while Critical Realists continue to consider science as an empirical process because it depends upon evidence observable by the senses, they acknowledge that interest laden, power laden, and value laden social issues unavoidably influence those senses (Mertens, 2003, p.137). But, without a conviction of the universality of reason, the conviction that lay at the heart of the eighteenth century Enlightenment and of nineteenth century Modernism, reason for Critical Realists lacks univocal meaning. Richard Rorty illustrates this when he wrote:

...consider the principle 'Thou shalt not kill'. This is admirably universal, but is it more or less rational than the principle 'Do not kill unless one is a soldier defending his or her country, or is preventing a murder, or is a state executioner, or a merciful practitioner of euthanasia?' I have no idea whether it is more or less rational, and so do not find the term 'rational' useful in this area.

(Cited in Schostak, 2006, p.124)

One of the reasons why reasonable individuals can hold incompatible beliefs based on the same data is because reason is culture bound (Taleb, 2007):

The Supreme Court of Belgium in a judgment of 11 November 1889 justified the inadmissibility of women to the bar in spite of the absence of any law to this effect, affirming that 'if the legislature had not excluded women from the bar by a formal disposition it was because it was too self-evident an axiom to state, that the service of justice was reserved to men'.

(Dillon, 1991, p.101)

Reason by the standards of another culture can, thus, be unreasonable. Even the very concept reason can act to our detriment. Before knowledge of bacteria, for example, many surgeons in the West rejected the practice of hand washing because, despite a meaningful decrease in hospital deaths, the connection between the two could not reasonably be explained. This is why the classical empirics attempted, in so far as possible, to practise medicine without relying on reason: they wanted to benefit from chance observations. Their methods have been revived in contemporary evidence-based medicine (Taleb, 2007). However, beliefs held without the application of reason can be equally dangerous:

No real belief, however trifling and fragmentary it may seem, is ever truly insignificant; it prepares us to receive more of its like, confirms those which resembled it before, and weakens others; and so gradually it lays a stealthy train in our inmost thoughts, which may some day explode into overt action.

(Cited in Blackburn, 2005, p.5)

1.5 CRISIS OF LEGITIMACY

1. Where then does this leave the concepts reason and truth? This question is the basis of the 'legitimation crisis' in contemporary thought: the apprehension that there may be nothing upon which thought and action can be secured (Bernstein, 1983). The responses have been varied. There are those who argue that the attainment of one truth, the ultimate law explaining the universe, is theoretically possible, but who also concede this is of little practical consequence because its attainment might take longer than the time allotted to the human species. And, on the other hand, are those quantum physicists who argue that the indeterminism of the quantum world makes it possible for there to be many worlds and, therefore, many truths (*The Economist*, 14 July 2007, p.84). (Quantum mechanics also makes it difficult to define what is meant by physical reality. Is, for example a quantum—a 'packet'—of light 'real'?). Epistemological pluralism (a belief that there is not one but multiple competing truths about the world) is not, therefore, peculiar to the humanities and the more theoretical of the social sciences (anthropology and sociology, for example). But because they, as in the case of theoretical physics, deal primarily with conceptual issues it is with them that the approach is most commonly associated. In this context epistemological pluralism is associated with pragmatism, cultural relativism, and conceptual relativism. (The first holds that truth is a function of our interests: something is true relative to its success in achieving those interests. The second holds that because different cultures see the world differently so too will their concepts of truth also differ. Conceptual relativists argue that the very nature of concepts permits the co-existence of mutually exclusive perceptions and truths.) While Critical Realists pursue the ideal of 'probable truth', Constructivists, because reality is seen as constructed in discourse

communities, see truth as multiple. Constructivists do not, therefore, claim their research portrayals correspond to a general reality. They strive, instead, for a reflexive (self-analytical), coherent description that provides readers an insight into uniquely constructed realities (Garman, 2006).

Popper

2. The temptation to substitute *persuasive* for *true* and *believe* for *know* (Dillon, 1991, p.6) is, however, resisted by Critical Realists:

Knowing that we are fallible, that what stands the test today may well fail to do so tomorrow or in the next century, does not prevent us, or even exempt us, from making and defending claims to truth here and now.

(Moisio, 2007, p.x)

How to set about doing so remains the problem. Its nature is illuminated by the behaviour of turkeys. Because they learn backwards their learning might have negative value: their confidence in the affection a farmer apparently feels for them grows each time they are fed, their confidence in fact is at its height when risk of slaughter is at its highest (Taleb, 2007). This is the 'problem of induction': the possibility of a disconfirming case, irrespective of the weight of confirmatory evidence, makes induction a probabilistic exercise. The inverse, though, means we know what is wrong with a lot more confidence than we know what is right. This explains Karl Popper's hypothetico-deductive model: we get closer to the truth by negative instances than by verification (Taleb, 2007).

3. The origin of the model lay in Popper's admiration for the theories of Einstein: they showed the conditions by which they could be disproved rather than confirmed (Hart, 2005). Therefore, to draw a distinction between scientific and non-scientific statements, Popper adopted the concept falsifiability. In place of truth, this concept allows a scientific proposition to be considered 'contingently true' if it has the potential to be shown false. This applied equally to propositions in mathematics. Here a proof is a demonstration, generally involving an assumption expressed in natural language, as opposed to the language of mathematics, that a proposition is necessarily true. Because mathematical equations, like the mind, do not have empirical existence a mathematical proof, therefore, is a logical, not an empirical, argument. Thus, although it was acknowledged that Freudian psychoanalysis was able logically to explain behaviour it was not considered able to predict behaviour. Therefore, because it was unable to make predictions that might be shown false, psychoanalysis could not be considered scientific. In 1974 evolutionary biology was also put on notice for Popper:

…had come to the conclusion that Darwinism is not a testable scientific theory but a metaphysical research programme… [because]…natural selection did not appear to be testable in the ways genuine science necessitated.

(Yang, 2008, p.213)

But, because Marx and Engels' revolutionary socialism did make novel forecasts the process of history would eventually justify or negate it could, until proven otherwise, be considered scientific: hence the name scientific socialism. From Popper's perspective, therefore, progress in science was the cumulative addition of justified forecasts: the length of time a theory is not falsified is testament to its robustness and power to explain and predict (Hart, 2005). It is only in the context, therefore, of the provisionality of unfalsified theories that it is possible for Critical Realists in the natural sciences to regard empirically established theories as determinist and for those in the more empirical of the social sciences to regard them as probabilist.[12] It is also only in this context that each might use the word 'fact' for, no matter how objective facts appear to be, they only exist as facts in the context of unfalsified theory.

1.6 PARADIGMS

1. As illustrated by the cases of psychoanalysis and revolutionary socialism the arbitrariness of falsifiability indicates the problem of applying determinate rules to draw distinctions between truth and untruth. It was for this reason that Thomas Kuhn (1922–1996), physicist and historian of science, introduced the concept of a paradigm: an exemplar open to differing interpretations (Bernstein, 1983). Because, he argued, the theories of Newton and Einstein were not on a continuum but incommensurable[13], applying Popper's model of predictive success to each had little meaning: Einstein was not more 'scientific' than Newton for each was defining what being 'scientific' meant (Rorty, 1999). Science was not, therefore, the progressive refining of a single interpretation but was constituted by a succession of paradigms (Crusius, 1991) each of which in its own way was progressive. Progressive is usually understood to mean evolution towards a goal. But this is a teleological interpretation implying that science is moving toward 'truth'. Kuhn's notion of progress was, rather, evolution from. In this sense his idea of progress was Darwinian: 'In natural selection, changes in organisms occur…not because they are better in any absolute sense, but because they fit better within the environmental constraints' (Peck MacDonald, 1994, p.29).

2. As used by Kuhn and, subsequently by others, paradigm has taken on multiple meanings. In a general sense, it is a culturally embedded discourse practice, and therefore neither inviolate nor unchanging: a 'framework for thinking' about how valid research ought to be conducted (Greene & Caracelli, 2003). In a particular sense, though, Kuhn attempted to restrict the concept to mean those founding ideas, the 'exemplary achievements', of, for example, Galileo, Newton and Einstein, around which subsequent scientific revolutions (paradigm shifts) were built (Sharrock & Read, 2002). It is in this context that he used the Gestalt switch, a conversion that makes everything look different, as an analogy to illustrate that paradigms are rivals in the sense that scientists can accept as valid either the prevailing paradigm, Newton's physics for example, or its proposed alternative, Einstein's. They cannot, however, simultaneously accept both. Neither, he argued, can they engage in reversion (Sharrock & Read, 2002). Once, for example, persuaded by the evidence that Einstein's explanation of the foundational laws of physics had greater validity than Newton's, an individual could no longer go back and see the world as he or she had done prior to the new insights. So to this extent, although helpful, the Gestalt shift analogy is misleading.

Born to be refuted

3. But the problem of incommensurability is that paradigms, in either a general or specific sense, are not authoritarian frameworks of thought that recognise no valid alternatives (Sharrock & Read, 2002). This must necessarily be the case for, although they have a core of coherent assumptions, paradigms are characteristically complex constructions with undigested anomalies and dimensions that do not enjoy the same degree of coherence (Greene & Caracelli, 2003). This must also be so for the simple reason that the concept of a paradigm is an attempt 'to capture the complexity of nature within a simple scheme' in order to show how science works (Sharrock & Read, 2002,

p.135). It is inevitable, therefore, that the complexity of nature will always overflow that scheme. However, the irony is that the fact that paradigms have anomalies, that there are some things they cannot do, complements the fact that there are many more things they can do (Sharrock & Read, 2002). This is because, while providing scientists an explanatory framework within which to conduct their work, paradigms also provide a rich source of new problems. To this extent, a paradigm is 'a challenge—the challenge is to make it work as well as it can' (Sharrock & Read, 2002, p.35). But the further irony is that because no paradigm can claim to offer a solution to all of the problems it confronts, there will always be a need to overthrow it. To this extent all paradigms are born to be refuted for they carry within them the seeds of their own ultimate rejection (Sharrock & Read, 2002). It is in this sense that those individuals responsible for 'paradigm shifts' were rarely consciously attempting to overturn the received wisdom. They were, instead, trying to solve a problem within the paradigm. It was only after having run out of possible solutions that they began to seek answers beyond the paradigm's boundaries (Sharrock & Read, 2002). Before he developed heliocentrism, Copernicus, for example, spent most of his life working within the Ptolemaic paradigm (Sharrock & Read, 2002).

Far from equilibrium

4. One danger of explaining 'paradigm shifts' in this way is that it creates the impression they are the function of a single set of insights by one individual the consequences of which are immediately apparent both to that individual and to others as well.[14] This, though, is not the case. First, new paradigms emerge from the matrix of the prior system; they are not produced *de novo* (Sharrock & Read, 2002). Second, some theories in the previous paradigm are carried over to the new. Newton's laws of gravity, for example, still apply. Third, the amount of work required to interrogate and elaborate a paradigm to the point at which valid criticism of it becomes possible is significant; in some cases taking centuries (Sharrock & Read, 2002). Fourth, the process of interrogation and elaboration, logically, is the result of the efforts of many individuals. It is the accumulated results of this combined effort that provides sufficient evidentiary and conceptual mass for a tipping point, a potential breakthrough, to take place. In this respect paradigms reflect complexity theory: driven by differential energy 'far from equilibrium' complex systems are the structures most likely to exhibit new patterns of self-organisation (Smith & Jenks 2006). The theory of evolution, therefore, was itself a product of evolution (Smith & Jenks, 2006). It is no wonder then that many individuals have the simultaneous opportunity to make the breakthrough (Phillips & Pugh, 2005). The fact that

one individual appears to anticipate the others is usually a consequence of their ability creatively to combine and elaborate the new ideas and to express them accessibly (Sharrock & Read, 2002).

Not immediately recognisable

5. Another danger of seeing paradigm change as a sudden 'shift' of perception is that it creates the impression that new paradigms are immediately recognisable as such.

At the end of the year in which Darwin and Wallace presented their papers on evolution by natural selection that changed the way we view the world, the president of the Linnean Society, where the papers were presented, announced that the society saw 'no striking discovery,' nothing in particular that could revolutionize science.

(Taleb, 2007, p.167)

This lack of recognition is explained by the nature of paradigms: they are not simply collections of conjectures that, through a process of trial and error, are open to clear acceptance or rejection. The Ptolemaic system, for example, is complex, credibly explaining planetary motion and Newton's four laws at the centre of his hypothesis are:

…tenaciously protected from refutation by a vast 'protective belt' of auxiliary hypotheses. And, even more importantly, the research programme also has a 'heuristic', that is, powerful problem-solving machinery, which, with the help of sophisticated mathematical techniques, digests anomalies and even turns them into positive evidence.

(Lakatos, 1978, p.4)

When new theories defy accommodation in the overall framework it is not necessarily easy to see that a paradigm's core explanatory function has been brought into question. This explains why Kuhn felt Popper's concept of Falsification could be misleading for evidence that appears to falsify an existing paradigm may turn out to be accounted for by adjusting or modifying the paradigm without abandoning it (Bernstein, 1983). It is the complex nature of their construction that makes the transition from one paradigm to the next characteristically slow. Einstein, for example, despite receiving a Nobel Prize for early work on quantum mechanics, devoted much of his later career to a vain defence of Newton's scientific determinism: 'God,' Einstein said in response to Werner Heisenberg's Uncertainty Principle, 'does not play dice with the universe. God, it turns out, is an inveterate gambler' (Hawking, nd, np).

6. There is also another reason why the shift from one paradigm to another is often slow. This is because paradigms, as a result of their inherent conceptual complexity, necessarily constitute intellectual cultures. As such 'they are fundamentally embedded in the socialization of their adherents: a way of life rather than simply a set of technical and procedural differences' (Oakley, 1999, p.155). At one level the reluctance to abandon a way of life can be attributed to a tendency common to the human condition: belief perseverance (Taleb, 2007). Tolstoy, for example, observed:

> *...most men [sic]...can seldom accept even the simplest and most obvious truths if it can be such as would oblige them to admit the falsity of conclusions which they have delighted in explaining to colleagues, which they have proudly taught to others, and which they have woven, thread by thread, into the fabric of their lives.*

(Cited in Hersch & Moss, 2004, p.6)

When, in other words, people's identities are at stake, passions run deep (Becher & Trowler, 2001). It is also because they are 'embedded in the socialisation of their adherents' that the conduct of rational and conclusive debate about conceptual differences becomes difficult. The tribunal that sat in judgement on Galileo, for example, required justification of new beliefs in old terms (Rorty, 1999). Because each party to these debates premises their argument upon principles the other contests they talk, as politicians so often do, past one another.

1.7 THE LINGUISTIC TURN

1. The characteristics of language facilitate this process. On the one hand it is not genetic and, therefore, hard-wired into us. If it were it would not need to be learned but it would also need to be rudimentary and incapable of versatile development (Smith & Jenks, 2006). On the other it is not the slippery device described by Humpty Dumpty: "'When I use a word," Humpty Dumpty said, in a rather scornful tone, "it means just what I choose it to mean, neither more nor less"' (Carroll, L. chap. vi). Used in this way language would cease to convey any meaning at all. There are, therefore, generally accepted rules governing the use of language in order for it to become an effective channel of communication. Nonetheless, the amorphous nature of our concepts means that despite these rules language inevitably falsifies what it is trying to capture. It is not possible, in other words, to speak correctly of anything that 'is always becoming and never is' (Blackburn, 2005, p.103). This applies equally to ourselves: 'Moment by moment we become, however imperceptibly, altered selves...we are complex beings, always under construction...' (Kerwin, 2008, p.12).

Structuralism

2. In the early nineteen sixties the anthropologist Claude Lévi-Strauss rejected the then current representationalist view that words derive their meaning from correspondence with 'real' objects. On the basis of his own research and that of Ferdinand de Saussure he argued, instead, that meaning is derived from the manner in which language is structured. All cultures, in this view, are systems of communication in which the structural relationships of the constituent elements of each system can be identified. The explanation for this, he believed, lay in the resemblance of the functioning of the human mind to that of mathematical equations: through binary opposition (male/female, good/evil) the mind divides meanings into sub-classes on a hierarchical basis (male prior to female, good prior to evil), then divides each of these further thereby creating a system of 'relations' (Hart, 2005). By studying these classifications and the relations between them Lévi-Strauss believed much could be learnt about how we think.

Post-structuralism

3. By the mid-nineteen sixties, however, a number of prominent thinkers, Roland Barthes, Michel Foucault and Jacques Derrida among them, broke with Structuralism. The fundamental reason for doing so was their belief that the methodology of the approach was itself culturally conditioned and, therefore, subject to bias and misinterpretation. This break had two immediate implications for the interpretation of text. First, while Structuralists believed that texts could only be interpreted on the basis of the social and cultural heritage of an author, Post-structuralists held that the reader's society and culture played as much, if not a dominant role. Second, while Structuralists considered the hierarchical positioning of classes of meaning as an essential quality of the relationship between them, Post-structuralists saw the relationship as only providing an illusion that texts have a singular meaning. The relationship was instead, they believed, symptomatic of a system of dominance and dependency in need of exposure. The only way to do so was to identify the assumptions underlying such systems.

Barthes

4. These views were made explicit in 1968 when Barthes published 'The Death of the Author'. In it he argued that as soon as language is written a distance develops between it and the author.

   Writing preserves discourse over time and allows...wide distribution over space. The inevitable result is some degree of alienation, as texts speak to a situation and an audience that no longer exist.

   (Crusius, 1991, p.3)

Drawing on interior consciousness the spoken word, thus, is immediate and transparent while the written word becomes unanchored (Peters, 2008). Therefore, because any text can have multiple possible meanings, the meaning the author apparently intended is secondary to the meaning the reader actually perceives. The metaphorical event 'The Death of the Author' was for this reason also 'The Birth of the Reader'. But the reason texts are not univocal is also because the concept of a reader as singular entity is a fictional construct. Instead, individuals comprise not only conflicting tensions and knowledge claims (class and gender for example) but have concepts that both shape and are shaped by language: 'Whenever we perceive the world as we do, we easily overlook that we behave in a way to perceive it as such and that the world is part of the loop created by our language, beliefs and desires' (Fiumara, 1995, p.91). Texts are also not univocal because language is always a web of meaning rather than literal interpretation. Take, for example, the word 'trust', it is inherently vague yet central to our lives. So, because each written or spoken word gives rise to complex matrices of meanings and because people change as their ideas change, the interpretive process is never complete. It is, in other words, endlessly deferred.

Derrida

5. It was Derrida, also in the late 1960s, who introduced an approach to illustrate clearly that the source of the meanings of spoken or written words is so irreducibly complex as to be, in effect, unfathomable. In doing so he introduced into popular parlance the term 'deconstruction'. His initial proposition was that, from an historical perspective, Western philosophy could only be understood as a series of failed attempts to establish a firm base upon which true propositions could be derived. These points of origin, be they either Plato's Forms or Modernism's rationality, in order to function as such were considered entirely self-sufficient and non-corporeal: they simply existed in each philosophy as a permanent presence. But, Derrida argued, to be understood each presence needs an absence: a comparison with what it is not. 'Good', for example, is only meaningful in the presence of 'evil'. This comparison, though, is not between independent constructs:

…the 'otherness' which is excluded to maintain the myth of a pure and uncontaminated original presence is actually constitutive of that which presents itself as such. We could say that the 'thing' that makes 'good' possible (i.e. 'evil') is the very 'thing' that also undermines it and makes it impossible. It is this strange 'logic' to which Derrida sometimes refers as 'deconstruction'.

(Biesta, 2008, p.x)

This is the way language functions: it offers meanings (the perfect love, for example) the material world can never fulfil. Meaning is split, therefore, between the real and ideal, between absence and presence (Schostak, 2006).

Nietzsche

6. The basis for these beliefs had already been established in the late nineteenth century when Friedrich Nietzsche proposed that 'the world can be justified only as an aesthetic phenomenon' (Linn, 1996, p.21). Having rejected both Realism and metaphysics he was the first Western philosopher to give primacy to the role of language in the development of thought. This had implications for the concept of truth. If truth was a function of language there could not have been truth prior to language. This is a perception with which the Christian Bible seems in accord: 'In the beginning was the Word and the Word was with God, and the Word was God' (John 1:1)... 'And the Word became flesh, and dwelt among us...' (John 1:14). In this context truth is absolute but, from Nietzsche's perspective, truth is never independent and absolute but dependent and historical: it is always truth for someone (Crusius, 1991). These ideas were taken further during the first half of the twentieth century by John Dewey and Ludwig Wittgenstein and in the second by Martin Heidegger, Hans-Georg Gadamer and Richard Rorty. Both Derrida and Gadamer were significantly influenced by the abstruse work of Heidegger. But while Derrida was the initiator of deconstruction, Gadamer was pivotal in the development of philosophical hermeneutics. As can be expected from their frame of reference each of these approaches to understanding the meaning of language is intimately related but understanding how they relate to each other is subject to ongoing debate.

Gadamer

7. To what extent are we free? To be entirely free is to be another God. Instead the circumscribed freedom we enjoy 'was won for us by the totality of the evolutionary process' (Smith & Jenks, 2006, p.13). Ironically though it was this process that made us social beings, an attribute that limits our cognitive freedom. Central to philosophic hermeneutics is our internalisation of the norms of the society into which we are 'thrown' long before we have the capacity to reflect critically on those norms (Crusius, 1991): we are 'embedded in, and entwined with, our world, not simply contained within it' (Dall'Alba, 2009, p.35). Society, in consequence, makes us to a greater extent than we make it. Also in consequence our self-identity, a 'sedimentation' of the past, is more a product of what we have forgotten about that past than what we remember (Crusius, 1991). One of the implications of our 'thrownness' is

that we subconsciously pre-interpret everything we encounter. We cannot, therefore, be objective observers because our vocabulary and conceptual schemes predispose us to see things in a particular way (Crusius, 1991): '…the traditions of which we are part tend to be taken for granted and are not transparent to us: the fish is the last to discover water' (Dall'Alba, 2009, p.37).

8. But 'predispose' implies plasticity; an ability to a degree to reconfigure, relearn and reprogramme (Smith & Jenks, 2006). How then, in this light, are we to assess truth claims? How should we address the pivotal question: 'When should I change my mind?' (Crusius, 1991, p.88). The answer, Gadamer argued, is non-eristic dialogue. A dialogue, in other words, in which listening and talking are acts of sculpting and being sculpted (Schostak, 2006), where something is made in common: 'Not "in me" or "in you," but rather "in the between", via the exchange itself' (Crusius, 1991, p.38). This view has two immediate implications. The first is that communication is no longer considered simply a mechanical process conveying ideas that have prior and independent existence. It is seen, instead, as a cooperative process modifying the thinking of each participant (Biesta, 2008): '…we are, in our very being, persuaders and interpreters, beings immersed in language and dwelling in a world both made and revealed by language' (Crusius, 1991, p.9). The second is that 'truth' is seen as permanently tensive. Thus commitment to any idea is considered over-commitment and there is wariness of any idea that impedes its own criticism (Crusius, 1991). It is in this context that constructive dialogue is preparatory to the development of what the Ancient Greeks called *phronesis* (practical judgement)[15]: the ability of an 'experienced person' to choose a prudent course amid the contingencies of daily life (Crusius, 1991). Such has been the influence of phronesis that it was included as one of the four cardinal virtues of Western Christendom: temperance, prudence, fortitude and justice.

Rorty

9. Both Derrida and Gadamer's conceptions deny the existence of a norm through which truth can be derived: that there is nothing in general to say about truth in general, just a piecemeal construction of particular truths (Blackburn & Simmons, 2005, p.6.). This perspective accords with Richard Rorty's view that 'our sense of objectivity is not a matter of corresponding to objects, but of getting together with other subjects—there is nothing to objectivity except intersubjectivity' (Linn, 1996, p. 31). He did not, therefore, deny:

…that there is an objective universe which is as it is regardless of how we describe it. What is being denied is that it makes sense to talk about something else which is also objective and called truth.

(Linn, 1996, p.32)

Because there was no need, thus, for a metaphysical theory of truth he considered the Platonic Tradition to have outlived its usefulness: '…the value of cooperative human inquiry has only an ethical base, not an epistemological or metaphysical one' (Rumana, 2000, p. 77). Rorty, therefore, dissolved rather than solved the problem of truth and, in doing so not only repudiated the basis of the entire Western philosophical tradition but also the need for philosophy itself (Blackburn & Simmons, 2005, p.4).

1.8 CONCLUSION

1. Research approaches arising from different epistemological foundations do not necessarily stand in mutual contradiction: not only can they be compared in multiple ways their shared continuities are often as significant as their differences. The porosity of the shifting boundaries between them make it inevitable that when a methodology is adopted (*Among the concepts this thesis will explore will be…* or *Inspired by discourse theory I argue that…*) a debate about the elements that constitute paradigms and theories within and across methodological boundaries is being explicitly entered:

   While there is no consensus on the manner for combining different theoretic approaches in such a way as to ensure valid inferences, some researchers (Fielding and Townsend 2004; Givens 2002) have recently begun to specify criteria that apply to…research.

Philosophy as praxis

2. While the thrust of the argument has been that what is taken to be real (ontology), what is taken to be true (epistemology) and what is taken to be of value (axiology) lie at the heart of both learning about and conducting research—that without scholarly apparatus, the strategic necessity of theory, research stands in danger of being insufficiently 'problematized'—it is equally important to place the argument in context. Because not all research is explicitly linked to theory it is readily conceded that not all theses need to be introduced with speculation, metaphysical or otherwise, about the nature of truth and reality. It is also true that, just as the process of research evolves, so too does the nature of theory and philosophy. There was a trend, particularly in the humanities, in Western universities in the nineteen seventies and eighties to see particular theories, theories not formally taught but which students were expected to know, as dogma. Instead of shedding partial light, the jargon of theory stifled debate. It was the ebbing of this trend to which the term 'the death of Theory' (Theory in the uppercase) applies (Benton, 2005). (A relieved academic who had been a student at the

time wrote: 'I want to know where Theory is buried so I can dance on its grave' (Benton, 2005, np).

3. A more sustained historical trend, though, has been to consider philosophy analytical, rather than speculative and transcendent. Wittgenstein indicates the reason why:

    ... we have got onto slippery ice where there is no friction and so in a certain sense the conditions are ideal, but also, just because of that, we are unable to walk. We want to walk: so we need friction. Back to the rough ground!

    (McCormack, 2008, p.850)

    Philosophy, therefore, as praxis: of putting theoretical knowledge into practice. (The equivalent in qualitative research is *reflexive practice.*) Karl Marx, for example, felt that philosophy's validity was in how it informed action. This was, however, a restatement of an approach familiar to the ancient Hebrews and the later Romans. Psalm 34.8, for example, advises believers to 'Taste and see that the Lord is good'. Here 'taste' means 'understanding learned from experience' for in Hebrew *ta'am* means both taste and reason and in Latin *sapid* is to have taste and *sapere* is to be wise. It is in this context therefore, that the point of the argument in this chapter has been that, to a greater or lesser degree, a discussion of pertinent theory, in all theses, in all disciplines, provides historical perspective and indicates an understanding of the debates about issues of importance to the area of research. The extent to which there is explicit need to engage with theory will be up to each thesis writer to decide in the context of their own research. It is a decision, though, that is best made with a sound prior understanding of the theory involved. A tepid or uninformed foray into the debate, particularly by qualitative and exegetic researchers, risks evoking a critical response from thesis examiners: 'Much more reading and conceptualization needs to be done' (Lovat, Holbrook, Bourke, Dally, Hazel, 2002, p.14) or: 'Serious misunderstanding of theory' (Lovat et al., 2002, p.14). Should a researcher, on the other hand, simply decide that in their case theory does not apply they will be abdicating to others the right fully to situate and give meaning to what has been achieved.

4. The benefits of a full and informed involvement in the debate are, thus, substantial. Not only will every aspect of the thesis be informed by the researcher's ability to read, write and think at a deeper conceptual level, but he or she will also be able to pose, and provide informed responses to, questions central to their research. For example: 'To what extent does contingency shape our understandings?'[16] They will, in addition, also cease to identify themselves according to the topic of their research. As in the case of most professional

researchers they will, instead, identify themselves by their methodological orientation (Bastalich, nd). The most important consequence of this will be a research design for the thesis that is not only both coherent and effective but also, perhaps, innovative.

ENDNOTES

1 Metaphysics is a branch of philosophy primarily concerned with explaining reality as an intellectual construct. In this instance the prefix 'meta' means 'to transcend' the physical.

2 Relativism: the belief that concepts are not dependent for their meaning on absolutes but on other concepts.

3 Operationalising a concept enables measurement by linking it to empirical indicators.

4 Another butterfly flapping its wings might have no consequential effect for in complex systems slight differences in initial conditions produce different, and unpredictable, outcomes.

5 Irrational numbers are one of the reasons explaining attempts since the nineteenth century to create artificial logical languages to formalise logical and mathematical relationships.

6 Complexity is not an objective characteristic but a description of phenomena within fabrics of relationships (Fioretti & Visser, 2004). The reason why complexity defies simplification is because it is not compressible: the information non-linear processes contain lies not in individual members but in their transformational patterns of interaction. It is these interactions that enable collectives to exceed the summed capacity of their members (Davis & Sumara, 2006).

7 Ancient Greeks made a distinction between technë and epistemë. At schools of empirical medicine, for example, students were taught technë (craft) not epistemë (theory).

8 Because in Aristotelian thought a definition was considered a statement of the essence of a thing, a distinction had to be drawn between *nominal* and *real* essence. We understand, for example, the meaning of the word 'ghost' but do we know the real nature of ghosts? A definition of a ghost, therefore, will be nominal not real.

9 Directed towards a final result. In contemporary theology 'intelligent design' is a teleological argument.

10 The mathematician and astronomer Marquis de Laplace was the originator of the term determinism: every event is causally determined and at any instant can have only one possible outcome.

11 Agency is the ability of an organism, in this case, individuals, to act independently. Structures are the factors, class, religion and gender for example, that influence the

ability of humans to act independently. Agents can only operate through structures and structures evolve through the action of agents.

12 Probabilism: the belief that in the absence of certainty probability can be accepted as a valid criterion.

13 Fundamentally incompatible: inches, for example, compared with litres.

14 The discoveries of Galileo, Newton and Einstein are obvious examples of this perception. The one exception is quantum mechanics where at least seven individuals are usually considered responsible for developing and elaborating the necessary insights.

15 Aristotle distinguished between *phronesis* and *sophia*. The latter, usually translated as 'wisdom', involves deliberation concerning universal truths.

16 Lack of citation in this and in examples on the following pages indicate author constructions.

CHAPTER 2

Interdisciplinarity

My work is in line with those who welcome the standard distinction between explaining exact phenomena and interpreting elusive occurrences but do not conceptually use distinctions as irreducible dichotomies. Discreteness and continuity can thus be viewed as complementary concepts emerging against a background of linguistic evolution in which there could be no sharp division between metaphorical and literal language.

(Fiumara, 1995, p.72)

2.1 INTRODUCTION

1. If disciplines are creatures of their time, what time is this reference to? Although arising from classical idealism and medieval scholasticism the concept of disciplines as discrete intellectual and administrative entities was a product of eighteenth century Realism and nineteenth century Positivism: knowledge was the product of a tightly deductive process requiring the application of precise rules, facts and categories. 'When these ideas and crisp constructs inhabit our minds, we privilege them over other less elegant objects, those with messier and less tractable structures' (Taleb, 2007, p.xxv). The result was a prescriptive taxonomy of knowledge, rigid norms stabilised and protected by universities to whom disciplines owed their very existence.

2. Classification is a necessary condition for human cognition but classification only works when it is not seen as definitive and when the advantages of simplification outweigh the loss from view of complex interrelationships (Smith & Jenks, 2006). It was in this context that the growth during the twentieth century of the networks linking an increasingly fragmented yet interdependent global society served to destabilise the established categories of knowledge (Smith & Jenks, 2006). This was also the context in which philosophic thinking during the second half of the twentieth century came to be dominated by the twin pillars of Post-positivism: Critical Realism and Constructivism. Despite their differences in other respects each of these perspectives were

drawn together with the acknowledgement by the former and the embrace by the latter of the idea that observation is both interest and power laden (Mertens, 2003). Both the process of deduction and the concept of rules and facts became, therefore, either suspect or were rejected entirely and faith in the metanarrative (an encompassing explanatory schema) of disciplinary study shaken (Rowland, 2006). In this environment where existing classifications of knowledge became open to interrogation earlier claims by academics to exceptionalism because of the special significance of disciplinary knowledge no longer found a sympathetic audience (Bechcr & Trowler, 2001).

3. This explains why it is no accident that since the mid-twentieth century the purposes of research have become more diffuse and the number of 'ways of knowing' has increased (Newman et al., 2003, p.172). It is, therefore, also no accident that qualitative, mixed methods and interdisciplinary research, individually and collectively, also reflect complexity and ambiguity for they all arose from and were a response to an environment where judgements need to be made within increasingly multiplied and often conflicting frames of reference (Rowland, 2006). This also explains why qualitative, mixed methods and interdisciplinary research are also not, as most Positivist research was, 'problem' based. The difficulty with 'problem' is that it connotes a bounded question and an encapsulated answer. In doing so it does profound injury to the complex-system, open-endedness of each of these approaches.

2.2 THE DRIVERS AND FACILITATORS OF INTERDISCIPLINARITY

1. Research as complex system oriented and, thus, interdisciplinary, is therefore a creature of its time. Now, it can be argued that the concept interdisciplinarity is not new. A Roman writer in the first century CE, for example, wrote:

The inexperienced may wonder at the fact that so many various things can be retained in the memory; but as soon as they observe that all branches of learning have a real connection with, and a reciprocal action upon, each other, the matter will seem very simple…

(Willmann, 1907, np).

But such statements arose within specific historical contexts where learning and knowledge had very different meanings and purposes from those of today. Nonetheless, the thrust of the statement that understanding requires an integration of information aligns with the logic explaining interdisciplinary research. In this sense then, it is not new. What is new though, and what has resulted in the identification of interdisciplinarity as a discrete phenomenon, is its purposefulness. This is both a consequence of the complex forces that drove the emergence of Post-modernism and of the new insights and technologies that facilitated its development. During the Second World War, for example, it was discovered that joint operations analysis groups could tackle complex tactical and strategic issues and get useful answers (Alhadeff-Jones, 2008). In turn the later concept of sustainability moved beyond narrow indicators of economic efficiency to include social justice and political regulation (Thompson Klein, 2004). It is also worth bearing in mind that an important contributor to qualitative research gaining traction as a methodological approach was the introduction in the late nineteen-fifties of the first light, portable tape-recorders.

2. In the same way interdisciplinarity as a research approach gained traction with the growth in sophistication of information technology. Internet search engines, for example, cluster information through criteria that ignore disciplines, and the increased carrying capacity of databases has broadened their initially discipline-defined contents. It is also the case that the increase in the volume of material that information technology makes accessible has made it increasingly difficult for any individual to evaluate that material adequately.

The Library of Congress in Washington contains about seven thousand works on Shakespeare—twenty years' worth of reading if read at the rate of one a day… the number keeps growing. Shakespeare Quarterly, *the most exhaustive of bibliographers, logs about four thousand serious new works—books, monographs, and other studies—every year.*

(Bryson, 2008, p.20)

It is doubtful, therefore, if any Shakespeare scholar can ever claim to be entirely up-to-date on the relevant literature. On the other hand, information technology has made researchers less dependent on the libraries of their home institutions and, by collapsing our sense of space and time (Rowland, 2006), has allowed widely dispersed individuals to construct online research communities. Not only, therefore, has the sharing of common goals been made much easier, but the cost of doing so has been reduced significantly (Dunham, 2005). In addition, computer modelling and simulation techniques specifically designed to address complex, non-linear questions have become the norm in science, architecture and engineering (Princeton University, 2005). (Prior to electronic computing individuals like Newton were limited to what could be done with pen and paper. Thus, although often aware of nonlinearity, they were required to use linear approximations [Davis & Sumara, 2005].) But technology not only facilitates interdisciplinary research it can also reconfigure entire categories of thought. Electronic information technology is not, for example, symbiotic with literature and its values in the way that mechanical print is.[1] Computers, for example, 're-introduce oral characteristics into writing; linearity to connectivity; fixity to fluidity; and passivity to interactivity' (Peters, 2008, p.827). The concept 'literature' as a discrete cultural category oriented to the printed book might with time, therefore become simply one category among many for social and intellectual communication (Craig, 2003).

2.3 UNIVERSITIES AND INTERDISCIPLINARITY

1. It is in the context of these drivers and facilitators that, internationally, university administrators have made a commitment to promote interdisciplinarity in both teaching and research. What started, therefore, in Western universities during the nineteen-seventies as a means to undermine entrenched social and institutional practices from the bottom up[2] has since become top down institutional practice (Kwa, 2002). Again, as in the case of the emergence of disciplines, this reordering of both the processes and structures of learning and knowledge creation raises the issue of social power. Academics at universities often have dual identities: they not only teach and conduct research but many, if not most, are to some degree actively involved in aspects of the administration and management of the institution. To this extent although managers and academic staff at contemporary universities represent separate cultures they are cultures that reflect the identity conflict of those involved (Rowland, 2006). But, until the mid-twentieth century the distinction between senior management and teaching staff at universities was less distinct than it is today. Academics in full-time, senior management positions would often return to research work during the course of their careers. Since that time, however, both the number and size of universities has grown and their technological sophistication has increased. Not only, therefore, has the cost and complexity of running universities gone up but so too has the need for a specialised cadre of managers to run them. A role in management has, in consequence, become for some academics an attractive alternate career path. But this is not the only distinction from past practice.

2. With operating budgets often rivalling in size those of large corporations, the primary tasks of contemporary high-level university managers is not only to administer but also to promote efficiency, economy and market responsiveness (Becher & Trowler, 2001). They have, in other words, become 'corporatised'. This has meant an increasing remoteness from academic practices, the adoption of language that has it roots in industrial production—*outputs, enhanced research capacity*—and a tendency to expect senior academics to speak on behalf of management rather than to remind management of academic values (Roland, 2006, p.76). In an environment of competitiveness, scarce resources, new costs and unpredictable fluctuations in enrolments it has also

meant that senior management has had to exercise increased pragmatism in its dealings with donors in the corporate and state sectors (Becher & Trowler, 2001). These sources of revenue have, in turn, developed a pragmatic interest in interdisciplinarity because the complexity of the issues confronting them invariably cuts across a wide range of disciplines (Schoenberger, 2001). So, despite change being a normal condition for disciplinary cultures and for universities as institutions, a disjuncture has nonetheless developed between the disciplinary structure of universities and those who, in relation to those institutions, exercise power in contemporary society. Shifts in power, in other words, means redefinition of what counts as useful knowledge.

3. Managers of contemporary universities thus face dilemmas similar to those confronting university administrators in the late eighteenth and early nineteenth centuries: how to adapt one system of learning and knowledge construction to another. Because it is not an either/or dilemma this is no simple task. Disciplines undoubtedly perform a useful administrative function: they are, for example, a bulwark against unnecessary duplication of teaching and research. In some areas, because they so effectively delimit the objects and methodologies of research and crystallise differences between fields (Reynolds, 2001), disciplines or their subsets also appear to produce optimal outcomes. Part of the need for disciplines lies within the word itself:

Only when you are so familiar with the elements (building blocks) of your discipline that you no longer have to think about how they are combined, do you enter the creative phase… If you play the piano and have to concentrate on fingering, you will not hear the flow of the music, the 'long line'. Local concerns drive out global perceptions, and so it is with other disciplines.

(Holland, 1998, p.212)

It has, though, become increasingly apparent that disciplinary categories are often obstacles preventing desirable research and learning outcomes. The inertia of established disciplines, the tendency in academia to default to disciplinary positions (Wall & Shankar, 2008) and the current reward system at universities does not, however, always permit a clear recognition that disciplines might constitute obstacles (Sperber, 2005):

The very qualities that make a community an ideal structure for learning—a shared perspective on a domain, trust, a communal identity, long-standing relationships, an established practice—are the same qualities that can hold it hostage to its history and its achievements. The community can become an ideal structure for avoiding learning.

(Wenger et al., 2002, p.141)

Is there, or should there be, a happy medium where disciplinarity and interdisciplinarity co-exist in uneasy alliance? The latter continually probing the interstices and the former considering further inroads 'a deeply disturbing trend which needs to be understood and resisted if it is not to undermine the whole enterprise' (Rowland, 2006, p.14). 'The explanation for this "drawing a line in the sand" lies not in fear of transgression but of what is considered a necessary consequence of a lack of disciplinary engagement: entropy (an increase in disorderliness)' (Rowland, 2006).

4. It is for this reason that coexistence in uneasy alliance, the apparent current consensus, necessarily privileges disciplines. Hence the term 'interdisciplinarity' and hence also the conception of it as a trade-off of depth for breadth: 'we cannot have interdisciplinarity unless we sustain strong individual disciplines as well… We cannot afford to generate large numbers of graduate scientists who know a bit of everything but nothing properly' (The Royal Society, 2005, np). Indicative of this binary approach has been the establishment at many universities of interdisciplinary research clusters and the organisation of related discipline into 'schools.' Many have also introduced general education programs into undergraduate degree courses in order 'to produce graduates with flexibility (and) critical thinking skills and an appreciation and understanding of fields outside of their usual area of study…' (University of Auckland, 2004b, np). But, while the public discourse explaining these initiatives usually emphasise the benefits of interdisciplinarity—that it brings fresh perspectives, provides new tools and techniques, and integrates conceptual models—in private, misgivings and frustrations are commonly expressed (Sperber, 2005). The source of much of this disquiet—and implicitly discontent with 'coexistence in uneasy alliance'—lies, as in the case of the concept 'discipline' itself, with the problem of definition. One representative university report, alluding to this, cautioned that 'it is possible that across the University there is not a shared understanding of what interdisciplinarity entails or a common approach to enable its development' (University of Auckland, 2004a, np.).

2.4 DEFINING INTERDISCIPLINARITY

1. The problem is that interdisciplinarity is a generic term used to encompass all approaches to interdisciplinary research as both concept and applied process. As such it has become so overloaded with 'linguistic freight' that it is in danger of becoming meaningless. Nonetheless, the fact that it is 'saturated with meaning' requires that meaning to be unpacked if the concept is to be understood (Manathunga, Lant & Mellick, 2006, p.366). But, to what extent is it meaningful to define particular approaches to interdisciplinarity when the approach is explicitly based on rejection of compartmentalisation?

Nondisciplinarity and postdisciplinarity

2. On the premise that all disciplines are so fragmented that to define any subject field as a discipline is arbitrary, one possible response is to reject the term interdisciplinarity entirely (Thompson Klein, 1994). Some who do so prefer instead nondisciplinarity. But doing so not only ignores the social, intellectual and institutional reality of disciplines but also homogenises them. Literary studies and physics, for example, differ from one another not only in regard to what is done but also in regard to how what is done is conceptualised. They also, therefore, differ in regard to how they are conceived as disciplines. Postdisciplinarity (or neodisciplinarity), however, rather than rejecting the reality of disciplines seeks, instead, to problematise and combine them into more fluid, conceptually open categories. Gender studies, for example, encompass elements from, amongst others, literary studies, economics, history, sociology, anthropology and philosophy. In the same way cognitive science, communication studies and critical discourse analysis also flexibly encompass a broad range of disciplinary fields. But, while each of the disciplinary elements constituting these flexible new structures are there for a reason, each element is not necessarily there for the same reason. Depending on the outcome the consequences of the resulting differences between them can either be considered a significant advantage or an acute problem (Craig, 2003).

Protodisciplinarity

3. On the other hand, protodisciplinarians tend to be far more focused. While also attempting to integrate disciplines, they see as the end result the emergence of another discrete, acknowledged discipline. Those involved are usually in outcomes-based disciplines. Researchers currently, for example, in physics, chemistry and engineering might well coalesce in a discipline of nanotechnology, while some biologists, psychologists, linguists, computer scientists and engineers might come together in a discipline of machine learning.

Multidisciplinarity

4. In contrast to post- and protodisciplinarity, multidisciplinarity is not integrative. Instead, the interdisciplinary process is seen as additive: disciplinary perspectives are simply contrasted, no explicit attempt being made to alter them. A course on climate change, for example, might include the juxtaposition of different disciplinary perspectives. The task of synthesis is left to individuals to make. Alternatively, researchers from different disciplines might contribute to a common project, but the analytical

processes are kept separate and the resulting knowledge claims only circulated within the separate domains of each discipline (MacMynowski, 2007). Pluridisciplinarity constitutes a subset of multidisciplinarity. While the latter might involve a juxtaposition of unrelated disciplines, pluridisciplinarity involves a juxtaposition only of those considered mutually related: mathematics, physics and astronomy for example, or, alternatively, history, anthropology and sociology. Cross-disciplinarity is also a subset of multidisciplinarity. The difference between the two, however, is subtler than that between pluridisciplinarity and multidisciplinarity. Instead of merely being juxtaposed, disciplinary perspectives, instead, are co-opted in order to permit one to illustrate an aspect of the other. A course on medieval architecture, for example, might include inputs by historians of medieval history. Superficially at least, therefore, multidisciplinarity and its subsets, because they are additive not integrative, are marked by lack of controversy. But this is true at one level only: while a course or research undertaking might be regarded as multidisciplinary, individuals cannot be considered as such for personal integration of the learning or research material, to one degree or another is inevitable. It is also possible, because of misconceptions by the parties involved, for an interdisciplinary endeavour to be considered by one party as postdisciplinary and by the other as multidisciplinary. In the new field of medical humanities, for example, those from the humanities might see their role as reappraising medicine while those in medicine might consider the purpose of the humanities as additive, as 'softening' medical practice (Rowland, 2006).

Transdisciplinarity

5. In contrast to multidisciplinarity, transdisciplinarity goes beyond juxtaposition or illustration. It might, for example, involve the wholesale application of one discipline's theories, concepts or methods to another. Economics, for example, has been mathematised (Becher & Trowler, 2001) and holistic medicine is a consequence of the application of the philosophy of holism to medicine (Thompson Klein, 1994). Alternatively transdisciplinarity might explicitly contest the self-definition of particular disciplines by bringing different assumptions and theories, indigenous knowledge for example, into critical engagement with those definitions. To this extent transdisciplinarity is also critical interdisciplinarity, for differences in perspective and practices emerge when one explanatory framework is contrasted with another (Rowland, 2006). This is indicative of a core feature of interdisciplinarity: while all research has the potential to be subversive, interdisciplinary research can, according to the extent to which it is instrumental or critical

in its orientation, explicitly be made so. While a necessary tension exists between them, the former will be instrumental to the solution of specific problems while a critical orientation might contain explicit radical and intellectual challenges to social and institutional practices (Rowland, 2002). A particular aspect of interdisciplinary medical research, for example, could be instrumental to the solution of a particular medical condition. On the other hand, because it might have involved aspects of 'alternative medicine', it could also bring into question conventional views of how medical research, as a whole ought to be conducted. Transdisciplinarity is not, though, necessarily an imposition on a discipline. It might, in the first instance, apply in those cases where individuals, particularly those within broadly defined disciplinary fields, reorient their work in accordance with the commitments of a socially more powerful discipline: geographers, for example, becoming economic geographers (Schoenberger, 2001). It might also apply where one discipline's theories or concepts are adopted in other disciplines (Rowland, 2006). Complexity theory, formerly the preserve of mathematics and physics has, for example, been appropriated as an explanatory mechanism by a wide variety of disciplines.

2.5 DISCIPLINARY PERMEABILITY

1. Economics and sociology are social sciences and both have traditional cores of seminal works. Economists, however, tend to argue less about the nature and purpose of their discipline than do sociologists (Becher & Trowler, 2001). This is primarily a consequence of the greater empirical coherence of economics relative to sociology. (It has been argued, though, that economics is a sub-discipline of sociology because the economic system is part of the social system [Sawyer, 2005].) Nonetheless, each, in common with the other social sciences and with the humanities, deals in its fundamentals with abstractions. Because abstractions, irrespective of whether they are operationalised or not, are less amenable to measurement than material objects the theoretic constructs of the social sciences and humanities cannot be stabilised to the same extent as is possible in the natural sciences. This is particularly apparent in philosophy that, as watchdog of critical thinking, has duties beyond those of other disciplines (Taleb, 2007). However, an academic in philosophy complained that:

   [we]…seem to be lacking the most elementary lingua franca to discuss our field in general [and] the most rudimentary notion of a set of problems that are common to the discipline…

   (Cited in Becher & Trowler, 2001, p.116).

Academics in the natural sciences secure in their assumptions about the law-like nature of the systems they study tend, thus, to be more confident in their disciplinary status than do academics in the social sciences and humanities (Rowland, 2002). But, to interpret this statement as valorising the natural sciences is to adopt them as a vantage point from which to view the social sciences and humanities. It may well be that academics in these disciplines do not seek convergences of opinion and do not, therefore, place the same value on the stability of their theoretic constructs as do those in the natural sciences (Peck MacDonald, 1994).

Contestation within disciplines

2. Nonetheless, it remains the case that in the humanities and social sciences, more than in the natural sciences, contestation about the 'essential structures' of a discipline is central to its claim to be a discipline. It is not simply interdisciplinarity, therefore, that represents a possible site of contestation; contestation also takes place within disciplines (Rowland, 2006). The backgrounds and interests, for example, of educational researchers tend to be diverse (Davis & Sumara, 2005). Architects deal with a complex, evolving mix of both natural and cultural forces and, in consequence, the discipline is subject to constant pressure to redefine itself. The head of a department of architecture remarked: 'Architecture is a discipline in which the question "What is architecture?" must always be a valid and live question. Once we stop asking that question the discipline is dead' (Rowland, 2006, p.96). But neither are some natural sciences immune to tension over their standing as autonomous disciplines. The discovery of DNA, for example, was a veritable 'cognitive revolution' that in the 1970's reconfigured traditional demarcations between physics, chemistry , and biology (Thompson Klein, 2004). The molecular biologist Francis Crick, one of the discoverers of DNA, went so far as to argue that the ultimate aim 'was to explain all biology in terms of physics and chemistry' (Yang, 2008, p.213). But only three orders of magnitude, the distinction between atomic nuclei and electrons, make physics distinct from chemistry. It is this relationship that explains why the laws of physics constrain the laws of chemistry. It is also in this sense that it has been argued that chemistry is reducible to physics (Holland, 1998).[3]

Synoptic disciplines

3. However, because their theoretic constructs are generally more permeable than those of the natural sciences, disciplines in the social sciences and humanities ought to be more amenable to interaction with one another. The implications of a weaker disciplinary self-confidence on interdisciplinary research are,

however, unpredictable. Individuals in disciplines with a weaker status might, for instance, be prepared to yoke themselves together conceptually and methodologically in order to present a false united front to outsiders (Schoenberger, 2001); in effect making their discipline less permeable. Others, though, might be encouraged to seek collaborative relationships (Rowland, 2002). The latter is more likely in those disciplines that regard themselves as 'synoptic': those that because of their internal diversity are peculiarly open to other disciplines. While all disciplines import aspects of other fields to clarify their own perspectives some are particularly open to other disciplines. Education, for example, is a net importer of theory: '…the domain has a rather startling trade deficit. One rarely encounters the insights of educators or educational researchers in academic literatures outside the field' (Davis & Sumara, 2006, p.165). Anthropologists, sociologists and historians, too, frequently become 'licensed rustlers' who poach stock and purloin crops from neighbours (Becher & Trowler, 2001, p.45). They also poach and purloin from each other. In the 1980s there was recurring concern by some historians that the influence of social anthropology and sociology, by emphasising the importance of the 'hidden' and 'underlying' above the observable, was leading the discipline astray (Peck MacDonald, 1994, p.83). This was countered, however, by the argument that these influences were a natural function of history's significant internal interdisciplinarity:

…there is no exclusive preferred form for the writing of history and…no single group in history and no one aspect of the past—the social, the political, the cultural, the economic—is inherently more important, or more essential, or more relevant than others.

(Levine, 1993, p.12)

4. Disciplines like history, anthropology, sociology and geography can be regarded as 'synoptic' because of the comprehensive nature of their areas of investigation. Other disciplines, such as computer studies, physics and mathematics, might also be regarded as such because they incorporate 'languages of concordance' that enable them to 'harmonise their endeavours' between each other (Thompson Klein, 1994). Even theoretic contiguity between individuals within separate disciplines might serve to make disciplines 'synoptic'. It could, for example, be argued that a Marxist economist and a Marxist literary theorist have more in common than a Marxist economist and a neo-classical economist (Rowland, 2002). The point is most disciplines encompass a diversity of research styles and epistemological characteristics and the discourse communities in which academics function are frequently more stable than the disciplines to which academics belong (Peck MacDonald, 1994). A mechanical engineer, for example, remarked: 'I have more

in common with the mathematicians who study fluid mechanics than I have with other engineers who study combustion—though combustion is my main research topic' (Becher & Trowler, 2001, p.65). From this perspective, therefore, distinctions between disciplines often reflect administrative convenience rather than issues of intellectual substance (Fiumara, 1995).

2.6 COMMUNICATING BETWEEN ASYMMETRIC DISCIPLINES

1. A discipline is a 'community of practice' in the sense that it consists of individuals who derive their academic identity from the practices they share with other individuals in that discipline. It is important to recognise, though, that communities of practice constitute a community not because every person in it believes the same thing. Working together creates differences as well as similarities. In fact rebellion as a form of participation 'often reveals a greater commitment than does passive conformity' (Wenger, 1998, p.77). What makes a community of practice a community are the resources it creates for negotiating communal meaning (Wenger, 1998). Thus, because a sense of self is not *expressed* by language but, instead, is created by language (Linn, 1996), the vocabulary and literature of a community of practice are central to its cultural identity. A 'community of interest', on the other hand, involves members of separate 'communities of practice' coming together because of a shared interest. An interdisciplinary team or network is an example. The differences between the two types of communities explain why it is logical to expect that a 'community of interest' will confront greater communication problems than a 'community of practice' (Bowker & Star, 1999). Because shared synoptic elements imply some disciplines are more related than others (Gilbert, nd) it is also logical to expect that in such disciplines these common elements will come to the fore in interdisciplinary undertakings in which each is involved and thus facilitate communication between them. But, interdisciplinary challenges that involve disciplines with minimal overlap have greater disciplinary breadth. In cases where, for example, approaches premised on Critical Realism in the natural sciences need to be integrated with those premised on Constructivism in the social sciences, a common vocabulary will need to be developed if any meaningful communication is to take place (Gilbert, nd). But the possible rewards for such development are significant for the most valuable innovations in interdisciplinary work are often a consequence of the integration of distinct, strongly articulated perspectives (Rowland, 2006).

2. If disciplines reflect different cultures each with its own system of meaning, they must also reflect different kinds of thinking. This is why the language of another culture can be studied but, if one is not part of that culture, meaning

can be illusive (Schoenberger, 2001). For this reason the question becomes: 'Is it possible to combine different kinds of thinking into one form of understanding?' (Ceroni, 2006, p.129). Is it possible, in other words, that some disciplines are commensurable while others are not? Because some disciplines represent different systems of belief and because it is not possible to set aside ones beliefs in order to see the world through the eyes of an individual with another system of belief, the answer at first glance must be 'yes'. But, belief systems are necessarily complex conceptual constructions some of which are more accessible than others and none of which can claim to be pure. For these reasons it can be argued that:

...alternative cultures are not to be thought of on the model of alternative geometries. Alternative geometries are irreconcilable because they have axiomatic structures, and contradictory axioms. They are designed to be irreconcilable. Cultures are not so designed, and do not have axiomatic structures.

(Rorty cited in Rumana, 2000, p.79)

Because difference is not total, mutual understanding cannot be engulfed. Religion and science, for example, might appear to be incommensurable but both, in fact, pursue the same quest, the quest for truth. They do, though, ask different questions. Science asks, 'how'? Religion asks what is arguably the more interesting question, 'why'? Thus, because truth claims cannot be vindicated by the nature of their relationship with a mind-independent reality (Rorty, 1999), the communicative task is to find resources in language to enable communication between individuals with fundamentally different schema.

Ordinary words used specially

3. Ironically, it is not usually specialist disciplinary terms that give rise to misunderstanding. More often it is ordinary words used specially (Rowland, 2003). For example 'equilibrium' in ordinary usage 'suggests stability, "business as usual", but in thermodynamics it is associated with entropy. "Heat death" is a postulated, eventual equilibrium. Not so much "business as usual" as "end of business"' (Smith & Jenks, 2006, p.82). The differing meanings of words reflect, therefore, fundamental shifts in thinking: language, in other words, constitutes the knowledge making (Peck MacDonald, 1994). This can also be seen in the contradictory meanings words take when used to convey the generalised concepts of the social sciences and the particularising focus of history on change over time. In the social sciences, for example, abstract nouns such as 'process', 'pattern', 'system', 'organisation', and 'structure' suggest permanence, while conceptual nouns such as 'peasant' and 'community' appear to have concrete referents. To historians, however, they are abstractions attached both to time and place (Peck MacDonald, 1994). It is also the case

that words fundamental to all research have multiple meanings: evidence, knowledge, fact, objective, research, validity and truth. The capacity of these terms to confuse is a consequence both of differing epistemological perspectives of how each ought to be interpreted and of their common meaning when used in colloquial conversation. On the one hand, words have a specific meaning and, on the other, a general meaning. Individuals from particular disciplines might have a shared understanding of the specific meaning while individuals from other disciplines will only share the general meaning. Each could, thus, talk past the other unaware they are divided by a common vocabulary. In other words disciplines may appear commensurable because they share a common vocabulary but the different discourses embodied in that vocabulary can have quite different mechanisms to convey meaning (Li, 1995).

Genre

4. The emergence of a vocabulary with meanings common to individuals from different disciplinary cultures can only take place as the research undertaking itself proceeds (Thompson Klein, 1994). Self-consciously directed toward shaping the knowledge-making purposes of a disciplinary community, language in this context is epistemic and, therefore, uses genres: fields of meaning that organise verbal and non-verbal discourses. As such they are semiotic structures that both enable and restrict meaning. 'Uses' is apposite in this context rather than 'belongs' because the reality and truths genres create, like disciplines themselves, are not fixed and stable but relate to an economy of genres, their complexity a consequence of the complexity of that relation (Frow, 2006). Genres, like disciplines, are thus complex systems: open and dynamic and partly constituting each other while at the same time maintaining their own coherence. While this coherence provides a rationale for the investigation of individual difference between complex systems like genres and disciplines, a focus on their dynamism and openness makes it possible to interpret and evaluate the novel outcomes precipitated by their interaction as they iteratively emerge (Mason, 2008). It is in this context that the concept of a 'boundary object' becomes apposite for it means that words with different meanings, while having the potential to divide, can also serve as common points of reference around which intersecting communities can develop a common understanding (Bowker & Star, 1999). In this sense a boundary connects and disconnects.

When a boundary object serves multiple constituencies, each has only partial control over the interpretation of the object…[thus]…using an artifact as a boundary object requires processes of coordination and translation between each form of partial jurisdiction.

(Wenger, 1998, p.108)

Emergence

5. A core element in interdisciplinary communication is emergence for it permits a mediating vocabulary to emerge between diverse disciplines incrementally and collaboratively through the integrative acts implicit in the interdisciplinary research process itself (Thompson Klein, 1994). It does this by contributing towards change: new insights born as a result of language change become catalysts for sparking new ideas and novel insights (EPA STAR, 2001). In this sense emergence reflects the evolutionary nature of language (Fiumara, 1995). It is also in this sense not coincidental that emergence is also a core element in complexity theory: given a significant degree of complexity in a particular environment, or critical mass, new properties and behaviours emerge that are not contained in the essence of the constituent elements, or able to be predicted from a knowledge of initial conditions (Mason, 2008). Understanding how this process takes place in language requires insight into the importance of metaphor.

2.7 METAPHOR

1. The need for imperative clarity requires technical language to be denotative, that is, directive. This is essential for precision in empirical undertakings and for empirical researchers to reach agreement with one another. It is for this reason that denotative writing leaves little room for metaphor (Reynolds, 2001). There is, though, a price to be paid: 'An "excessive" propensity for literal meanings may ultimately be detrimental to the life of language inasmuch as it becomes increasingly detached from the immense complexity of human interactions' (Fiumara, 1995, p.54). But the language of interdisciplinary work (and of ordinary life) because it is required to provide insight into different meaning systems needs, instead, to be connotative, that is, to imply a meaning that goes beyond literal translation. Literal here meaning not what cannot be: a uniform and conceptually closed interpretation of a word. It means, instead, the distinction individuals draw between familiar and unfamiliar vocabularies and theories (Reason, 2003). This is to invoke a model of categorisation by prototype: we tend to work from what we know best in an *ad hoc* negotiation of unfamiliar experiences rather than by employing a formal grid that can be applied indifferently (Frow, 2006). In doing so the substantive point is invoked that it is possible to compare concepts in multiple ways. Metaphor, the etymology of which lies in the words 'to transfer' or 'to carry across', performs this connotative function more effectively than does simile. Whereas the latter merely involves the comparison of one thing with another ('as brave as a lion'), the former constructs the possibilities available for meaning by

invoking one meaning system to clarify an apparently unrelated system: a 'startling mistake', for example. Thus, in order to inspire insight metaphor has two meanings, one literally false and the other metaphorically true (Fiumara, 1995): 'that Juliet is the sun is, perhaps, figuratively true; but since it is only figuratively true, it's of no astronomical interest' (Foder, 2009, np). To attempt to understand the unknown we must, therefore, resort to concepts we do know: 'a configuration half-perceived, a relationship faintly grasped, or a concept newly emergent must be, first, named metaphorically' (Fiumara, 1995, p.12). This explains why the role of metaphor in understanding is ubiquitous and essential (Richardson, 2005).

Definition by prototype

2. The difference between denotative and connotative language is reflected in the difference between locution and illocution. The former is the factual aspect of speech. The latter is metaphoric. Both construction and construal illocution, therefore, 'produces something in the saying' (Fiumara, 1995, p.118). Silencing, the deprivation of an individual's illocutionary potential, forces intuitions to remain concrete, insufficiently mentalised (Fiumara, 1995).

Granting permission to address their 'superiors' metaphorically would be comparable to recognizing slaves' capacity to migrate from one epistemic context to another, while their 'own' (imposed) vocabulary is confined to producing self-confirming prophecies supporting the social epistemology from which it emanates

(Fiumara, 1995, p.2)

With no empirical relationship with a 'reality' words themselves are like metaphors: by disconnecting a particular word from a particular thing talking about things in general becomes possible. School as a concept only becomes possible, for example, when it does not relate to any given school (Schostak, 2006). Nonetheless, a given school provides a subconscious prototype to typify what we understand by schools, or birds, in general:

We take a robin or a sparrow to be more central to that category than an ostrich… classes defined by prototypes have a common core and then fade into fuzziness at the edges.

(Frow, 2006, p.54)

It is at these edges where metaphor enacts its transformational function. In doing so the 'fuzziness' inherent in the process means metaphors cannot map onto the concepts they seek to describe exactly. It is seeking to comprehend where concept and metaphor do not overlap that allows a phenomenon to be explored (Wallace & Wray, 2006). This can be seen in the differences between a boat and any other floating object. Some of the relationships between them are contradictory while others are not. 'The discrepancies are, as it were, kept together by the similarities so that an area is created which is suitable for mental "leaps", generating links' (Fiumara, 1995, p.114).

Generative connections

3. In each instance metaphor utilises a concrete and commonly understood meaning, the analogue or 'source' domain, to donate meaning to a more important but obscurely understood and elusive 'target' domain. Metaphor, in other words, is both reductive account and analogy in the sense that it is an argument from one particular to another particular. It is also both a cognitive process and a linguistic expression reflecting that process. What facilitates a donation of meaning from the source to the target domain is the asymmetry between them. Asymmetry, in fact, is inscribed into the mechanics of metaphor: argument is war is very different from war is argument (Reynolds, 2001). But, in order for metaphor to construct the possibilities available for meaning, there need to be utilisable points of contact between the 'target' and 'source' domains. It is in this context that the metaphor of a 'field', as in 'field of research,' becomes so useful. In a linear sense a 'field' implies a flat surface with finite boundaries where change in one part will, because of its implied connectedness result in changes elsewhere in the field.

4. It is the ability to recognise the points of contact that constitute a 'field of research,' and to understand the nature of the relationship between them, that permits a researcher fully to explore the possibilities of interdisciplinary research. When conceived as a connecting or uniting power this recognition of the capacity of a 'source' and 'target' domain to be responsive to one another (Booth et al., 2000) is, essentially, an act of imagination (Fiumara, 1995): a creative act that requires an ability to reveal generative connections hidden from other observers: major developments in human understanding usually occur when new and previously unnoticed associations are made between seemingly disparate phenomena (Davis & Sumara, 2006, p.76). Drawing associations is the ability, in other words, to recognise how change in one discipline might have implications for another, but apparently unrelated, discipline. How new insights in physics, for example, might provide new theories and analytic tools for use in English literature (Reynolds, 2001). In this sense interdisciplinary work is at its most difficult when it involves disciplines with very different conceptual constructs. But, when metaphor is used as a communicative common denominator, it can also be these undertakings that prove to be the most productive. This is why metaphor construction is a higher order metacognitive[4] skill (Manathunga et al., 2006): both imaginative rationality (Sheard, 2006) and connubial procreation (Fiumara, 1995).

5. But why, in the example of physics and English literature, should the former be the 'source' domain and the latter the 'target' domain? In this instance because physics is better able to stabilise its theoretic constructs than English literature the relationship between the two disciplines reflects the asymmetry of the concrete and the elusive in metaphor. It is not surprising therefore, that structured and more concrete disciplines like physics will more often be a source of metaphors for a less structured discipline like English literature than the other way around. However, where structured disciplines become less confident, in the case of physics in regard to ethical issues for example, then the relationship might well be reversed. Thus, when the first atomic device was detonated in 1945 the physicist, Robert Oppenheimer, did not turn to his own discipline for a metaphor to express his awe and misgiving. He quoted, instead, from a literary work, the Bhagavad-Gita: 'Now I am become Death, the destroyer of worlds' (Wikipedia).

Figurative and literal

6. Metaphors might be new and entirely innovative or worn out into literalness. In such expressions, for example, as the 'wings of a building' or the 'branches of science' the figurative has entirely disappeared into the literal (Fiumara, 1995). In one sense dead metaphors, because they have become literal, are the most successful. But that some metaphors traverse the qualitative gradient from figurative to literal means the boundaries between metaphor and literalness are temporary, shifting and interwoven (Fiumara, 1995, p.37). Literal and metaphoric, denotative and connotative, locution and illocution should, therefore, be considered complex dualities rather than mere dichotomies: 'Just as life requires both stability and change so language as an evolving process is required to be both literal and metaphoric' (Fiumara, 1995, p.15).

2.8 HEURISTIC AND HERMENEUTIC

1. It is apparent that metaphor is more than analogy, a mere comparison. It is, instead, a device that allows complex processes to be explored and, in doing so, allows understanding to be shaped. The method of exploration, looking at a process already seen through one metaphoric frame in terms of another (Fiumara, 1995), can be seen, for example, in the decisions that need to be made when deciding which of the following metaphors is most appropriate to explain the manner in which genes control the development of an embryo: a blueprint (a builder builds a house by placing bricks in positions specified by the blueprint); a recipe (a cook makes a cake not by placing crumbs and currants in specified positions but by putting ingredients through specified procedures); or an origami (a process that follows a sequence of folding instructions) (Dawkins, 2005, p.426).

Seen from this perspective metaphor is a mutation caused by, but not the product of, reason (Linn, 1996). But it can also be seen that isolated from one another, metaphors have their limitations. This is apparent in a 'field of research' where a vision is evoked of a flattened and easily surveyed surface connecting various points around its boundary (Booth et al., 2000). The relationship between epistemologically distinct frameworks of knowledge is not, though, flat and easily surveyed. The metaphors applied, therefore, will need to be extended and elaborated as understanding of the phenomena under investigation deepens. In this sense the layers of metaphor used during the course of an investigation will provide a history of the manner in which insights were developed. It is also in this sense that the heuristic at the heart of metaphor construction is revealed.

Heuristic

2. As a noun 'heuristic'[5] is a device (a metaphor, story, cartoon or graph, for example), constructed in such a way as to capture the essence of a complex concept. As an adjective it describes a series of creative and rational processes to develop interpretive conceptualisations that are thought provoking but not prescriptive (Stabile, 2006). In this case, though, the model of rationality is shifted from that which seeks determinate rules to one that emphasises the role of exemplars and judgemental interpretation (Bernstein, 1983). Thus, because they are both creative and rational, these processes (in this instance metaphor construction) are not discrete and linear but provisionally distinct and iterative, each iteration or act of creative synthesis adding a new layer of complexity and understanding (Stabile, 2006). These layers, thus, are a form of identity construction for both complexity and understanding, in changing what we know, also changes who we are (Land, Meyer & Smith, 2008).

Hermeneutic

3. Reconciling asymmetric research approaches in an interdisciplinary research undertaking is not, therefore, a response to a question that implies disciplines are binary constructs: this, for example, is how researchers in English literature approach the issue and this is how they do it in physics, how then do we reconcile these approaches? (Booth, Rogers & AgInsight, 2000). Instead, the construction of metaphor requires a 'to and fro' movement between the parts and the whole: a cycle of differentiation, clarification, and synthesis that reflexively builds linked patterns and layers of understanding of the tools and theories that need to be explained and understood (MacMynowski, 2007). This, in essence, is the process of hermeneutics[6]: an attempt to establish a 'community of understanding' through a dialectic progression from one context to another (Booth et al., 2000). It involves, in other words, the cultivating, in so far as it

is possible, of an ability to understand something from someone else's point of view: to understand understanding itself. The dialectic of the progression is not instrumental: dialectic in the Platonic sense of 'turning the soul around…so the eye of the soul…travels the road of inquiry…and proceeds to the first principle itself' (Rumana, 2000, p.3). Because the meaning of what is to be understood cannot be exhausted hermeneutic dialectic is viewed instead as an ongoing conversation reflective of the fundamentally dialogical character of society.

2.9 CONCLUSION

1. These perspectives have a number of important implications. First, all scientific theorising, in the broadest sense of the term, requires an attitude of provisionality and systematic doubt to remain self-critical (Dillon, 1991). Second, an ethnographic approach to the development of understanding is implicitly encouraged. In the context of disciplines genre knowledge is situated knowledge, best comprehended, therefore, through immersion, rather than by being taught. It is, in other words, by entering the disciplinary conversation, rather than analysing its conventions, that interdisciplinary understanding develops (Peck MacDonald, 1994). Third, *discontinuity* is replaced with *simultaneity*. Because complexity rests on an understanding of phenomena as part of a fabric of relations there can be 'no simple idea, because a simple idea…is always inserted, to be understood, in a complex system of thoughts and experiences' (Alhadeff-Jones, 2008, p.68). There can be no distinction, therefore, between knower and knowledge or, because discourses—as is the case with disciplines—only have meaning in relation to each other, no discourse or discipline that stands alone (Davis, 2008). This is a reflection of the intrinsic nature of complex systems: closed systems in equilibrium die; complex systems need disequilibria in order to survive. As such they are emergences, produced not only from their constituting order, but also from the disorder characterising the relations among their components (Alhadeff-Jones, 2008). Fourth, insights emerging from hermeneutic dialectic are organising knowledge in the sense that they contribute to a reordering of the totality of understanding. In this sense also they are an implicit critique of disciplinary modes of organising knowledge (Alhadeff-Jones, 2008). Fifth, the processes of hermeneutics indicate how abstractions guide interpretation of particulars and how interpretation of particulars, in turn, helps form further abstractions. All academic knowledge making, therefore, is a consequence of interplay between both induction and deduction (Peck MacDonald, 1994), poetry and rationality:

If we look carefully at how creative, eminent scientists describe their own work, we find [a world] which uses logical analysis as a critical tool in the refinement of ideas, but which often begins in a very different place, where imagery, metaphor and analogy…are proponent.

(Bargar & Duncan, 1982, cited in Cryer, 2006, p.204)

It is in this sense that perceptions of cognition that deny imagination a central role in the constitution of reality need to be revised for 'metaphoric thinking is as fundamental as inductive and deductive reasoning in formulating hypotheses, providing explanations, forming categories, generating predictions, and guiding behaviour' (Fiumara, 1995, p.10). This is not an implication that there are no important differences between disciplines in the humanities and the social and natural sciences. It is an implication, instead, that distinctions between disciplines should no longer be drawn in phallogocentric terms, such as hard and soft (Linn, 1996). These distinctions valorise a particular view of academic work because they are grounded in the values of that view (Peck MacDonald, 1994). Nonetheless, sixth, epistemic knowledge is suspect because by positing a common ground founded upon a common rationality it seeks an end point—common agreement—within the episteme and, thus, the end of intellectual exchange (Dillon, 1991). This stems from the Platonic and humanist attempt to establish an unshakeable ground of certain knowledge. The assumption, thus, that on all issues of disagreement consensus can be achieved through reasoned argument is denied. In the absence of absolutes, we are left with 'the conversation that we ourselves are' (Crusius, 1991, p.8): the notion of conversation conducted in the hope of reaching agreement or at least fruitful disagreement so long as the conversation can be sustained. In the hermeneutic tradition, therefore, conversation replaces argument for, because it has no agenda, it lacks an internal tendency toward resolution or closure (Dillon, 1991). Conversation, thus, is considered an end in itself:

…as soon as one sees one's self as making rather than finding—as a proposer of rules rather than a discoverer of facts—one realizes the possibility of alternative rules, and of a plurality of interpretations of any proposed rule. This realization permits one to engage, for the first time, in genuine dialogue.

(Rorty cited in Rumana, 2000, p.9)

Seventh, the move away from epistemic knowledge and the remodeling of rationality has shifted the focus of knowledge making away from abstract logicality to community and process instead:

…the process whereby a community of practitioners gives reasons for its choices, carries on negotiation and persuasion within the community, and selects some problems and solutions as superior to others on the basis of shared…understandings.

(Peck MacDonald, 1994, p.13)

53

Eighth, that the use of knowledge as a verb, as a perception of it as an ongoing, evolving process, is more appropriate than its implied fixity and separateness from the knower when used as a noun (Reason, 2003).

2. Disciplines are communities of practice committed to the regulative ideal of developing norms through rational consensus (Bernstein, 1983). This explains their appeal: By conforming to the norms, individuals can get perfect strangers to take their words seriously, even to cite them, and sometimes to assent (Dillon, 1991). However, it also explains the limitation of those norms: knowledge is inseparable from social practice, the practice of justifying one's assertions to the community. But, because reason, rather than being the dominant voice, is only one of those that vie for an individual's attention, even the results of rational consensus are arguments rather than demonstrations (Dillon, 1991). It is in this context that Rorty writes:

For my anti-hierarchical purposes, I find it helpful to say, with Kuhn, that whether or not individual practitioners are aware of it, they are trained to and rewarded for solving intricate puzzles—be they instrumental, theoretical, logical, or math- ematical—at the interface between their phenomenal world and their community's beliefs about it.

(Rorty, 1999, p.187)

It is in this sense too that the dichotomy between objectivism and relativism becomes pernicious (Bernstein, 1983) and epistemological claims to universality become suspect. Hermeneutics, however, has ontological significance and, thus, a claim to universality precisely because from its perspective to be rational is to be willing to refrain from epistemology, from thinking that there is a special set of terms in which all contributions to the knowledge making conversation should be put (Dillon, 1991). It is, instead, a process, a complex of virtuous attitudes:

…the ability to listen and 'decenter', and thus dialogically to enter the lifeworld of the other; a passion for the openness and endlessness of the conversation; an orien- tation toward a sense of wonder; and a sense of the provisionality and limitations of any practice however successful…

(Dillon, 1991, p.140)

Disciplinary perspectives and practices might, therefore, be asymmetrical but, because they are part of social practice, cannot be incommensurable. In fact, just as metaphor construction draws part of its strength from its inscribed asymmetry, so hermeneutics generates its greatest creative energy when communicating between asymmetric disciplines. This communication through metaphor is, however, of a special kind, it is holistic, iterative and allusive, each step 'more like grasping a proverb, catching an allusion, seeing a joke…

than it is like achieving communion' (Bernstein, 1983, p.95). Metaphor thus, by its very nature, lacks precision; it is instead its originality that enables individuals to see things differently. This explains why metaphor construction is a higher order metacognitive skill (Manathunga et al., 2006). It also explains why Rorty sees metaphor rather than reason or truth as lying at the root of intellectual history:

A sense of human history as the history of successive metaphors would let us see the poet, in the generic sense of the maker of new worlds, the shaper of new languages, as the vanguard of the species.

(Cited in Linn, 1996, p.48)

It is also in this sense, therefore, that metaphor can be considered in evolutionary terms as a useful mutation enduring only so long as a particular environment is receptive to it. But, because language cannot ground itself as literal, at no time is anything being accurately represented: all metaphor can do is provide insight into the complexities generated by earlier metaphors (Linn, 1996).

2.10 BECOMING AN INTERDISCIPLINARY RESEARCHER

1. In view of these perspectives what, therefore, is needed in order to conduct interdisciplinary research successfully? While disciplinary 'transcendence does not necessarily mean cutting oneself off from the ground where one stands, but rather widening one's horizons' (cited in Wall & Shankar, 2008, p.552) the dominant perception of interdisciplinary research is one of a trade-off of depth for breadth. Current research indicates that while most students believe their employment prospects, at least in the public or private sectors, will be enhanced as a consequence of undertaking interdisciplinary research, they tend to be anxious about not becoming an expert in a single discipline (Manathunga et al., 2006). This is understandable when it is borne in mind that students will be submitting their thesis to the usually discipline specific department in which they are registered. When thoughtfully applied a secure disciplinary base is, though, entirely compatible with particular approaches to interdisciplinary work:

The freedom to work on our specific projects, within the standards and expectations set out by our academic departments, mediated the inevitable conflict and dissension that arises within some transdisciplinary working groups that are trying to meet the expectations of particular disciplines within a singular research project.

(Wall & Shankar, 2008, p.557)

Intercultural competence

2. In addition to a secure disciplinary base the second need is willingness and ability to unpack and interrogate the meaning and implications of interdisciplinarity in the context of the requirements of particular research undertakings and in the context of the disciplines involved. The need to do so is obviously necessary to the adequate conduct of the work but, in addition, it is likely that the examiners of the thesis will expect a discussion explaining and justifying the approach to interdisciplinary research adopted. If the university attended has an interdisciplinary research education program the opportunity to attend should be taken for these programs often use locally tailored strategies to enhance the skills needed in interdisciplinary research. (Some programs, for example, use research portfolios that identify and document the achievement of key interdisciplinary research attributes while others use regular focus group meetings to explore students' interdisciplinary research projects and to address common challenges they confront [Manathunga, 2006].) Possibly the biggest advantage to be gained from such programs, though, is a change in one's attitude. A researcher reporting on an interdisciplinary research education program wrote that students start 'with enormous stereotypes about the other disciplines, which are broken down during their studies together' (Manathunga et al., 2006, p.374). Students themselves reported that adopting a 'critical stance toward each of our original disciplines made us more open and willing to learn from other disciplines' (Wall & Shankar, 2008, p.556). These changes in attitude point to a key aspect of interdisciplinary learning: it is not simply a cognitive process it also has an emotional/social dimension as well (Manathunga, 2006). What is required, therefore, in addition to the attributes mentioned above, are listening skills, intercultural competence, pro-activeness, a high tolerance for being confused and a realisation that the boundaries to be crossed are not necessarily disciplinary, more usually they are personal, for the accustomed way of doing things and the usual way of seeing things often need to change.

Supervising interdisciplinary research

3. The trend for the completion of masters' and doctoral theses within shorter timeframes can make it extremely difficult to gain broad-based knowledge of interdisciplinary fields (Pearson et al., 2009). In addition, because of its diverse and sometimes unorthodox nature, students who undertake interdisciplinary research often have more difficulty finding appropriate thesis supervisors than do those whose research is discipline based. From a supervisor's perspective the supervision of interdisciplinary research is usually more time consuming than would otherwise be the case. This is due, on the one hand,

to the additional, and sometimes considerable, administrative work involved and, on the other, to the personal skills they need to develop in order both to facilitate interdisciplinary research and assess the results. Not only, therefore, will supervisors need to create a protected space for intellectual experiment by the research student (Schoenberger, 2001), but as facilitator the primary supervisor, in particular, will need to possess the attributes of an effective team leader so as to ensure that each member of the team has a common understanding of what the research is about and is prepared to contribute to the common pool. If this is not the case interdisciplinary researchers might find themselves in the following invidious position: 'Currently I have three supervisors—each a specialist in a related area but all hesitate to comment when it comes to issues not related enough' (pers. comm.).

4. So, in order to function effectively as a team both student and supervisors will need not only to develop a realistic understanding of their own strengths and weaknesses in regard to the issues under investigation but will also need to take especial care to maintain open lines of communication between each other. This, however, is not easily done for different disciplines reflect different sets of interests and priorities and, therefore, different formulations of what constitutes a research question or problem.

An engineer, an architect and an ecologist might have very different ideas about what constitutes a good bridge, or an appropriate bridge in a particular situation. Thus we might say that from an engineering point of view, or from an ecological point of view, this or that is a preferable design.

(Rowland, 2006, p.22)

This explains why supervisors of interdisciplinary projects need to be effective brokers, a task that requires enough legitimacy to influence practice but which is yielding enough to be inclusive of different perspectives (Wenger, 1998). It also often requires the ability to resolve conflict. More usually though it requires acceptance that tensions will be ongoing and that the real talent of brokerage is to maintain an acceptable and productive level of coexistence (Wenger, 1998).

The pros and cons

5. The number of journals devoted to interdisciplinary research is growing. However, with only a few exceptions, they have yet to match the prestige and impact of the most esteemed of the discipline based-journals (Rowland, 2006). Thus, in effect, the academic literature remains divided by disciplinary boundaries. This poses two immediate difficulties for interdisciplinary researchers. First, they often as a result have to rely on personal networks

in other disciplines in order to know where to access research material. Establishing these networks is one of the reasons why interdisciplinary studies often involve longer start-up times than those that are discipline based. Second, submitting articles for publication (as might also be the case with research grant applications) has the potential to become problematic because not only might it be necessary to obtain comments from more reviewers on smaller aspects of the submission than would usually be the case, but the idiosyncratic definitions of interdisciplinarity the reviewers employ will inevitably influence their approach to the submission.

6. These issues are of obvious concern to all interdisciplinary researchers but should be of particular concern to those planning a career in academe: not only is it often difficult to gain recognition in a home discipline for work published in other fields but, from a disciplinary perspective their publication record might appear incoherent (Manathunga et al., 2006). Because this can negatively impact prospects for tenure or promotion, all researchers undertaking interdisciplinary work should consider carefully whether moving away from a core discipline might strengthen or, alternatively, weaken career outcomes (Manathunga, 2006). However, having pointed to the dangers of interdisciplinarity, it is important to keep the potential benefits in mind. Look at one of the greatest achievements of twentieth-century science: Crick and Watson were not molecular biologists. If they had been they might not have dared think outside the discipline and propose their model for DNA (Cryer, 2006).

ENDNOTES

1 Print-on-demand books remain in digital form until ordered. The consequent decrease in costs has helped to increase the number of specialist titles available thus facilitating disciplinary specialisation.

2 Influenced by Foucault, Critical theorists argued that disciplinary institutions like prisons or universities function by sanctioning what they define as normal behaviour and by proscribing what they consider deviant. Thus, by questioning the concept 'discipline' they sought to undermine the entrenched social and institutional practices that moulded universities and the society in which they were situated (Kwa, 2002).

3 Because relational properties are acquired during interactions between members, collectives can exceed the summed capacity of those members (Davis & Sumara, 2006). This explains how biological can emerge from chemical and psychological from biological (Emmeche et al., 1997). It is in this sense also that emergences from complexity are irreducible to the initial conditions that gave rise to them. Thus though the laws of chemistry are constrained by the laws of physics as are

biological processes constrained by the laws of chemistry, chemistry is not reducible to physics and neither is biology reducible to chemistry (Mason, 2008).

4   The ability to reason about one's own thinking.

5   The term heuristic is derived from the Greek heurisco meaning 'I find.' A heuristic method of education is one, like Plato's, that encourages learners to discover knowledge through their own actions.

6   The principles of hermeneutics offer insight into the role of exegesis: the latter is analysis of text, the former the methods and theory underlying the analysis.

CHAPTER 3

Title Development

Contrary to the formal scholastic framework that assumes that the problem is given and clear, and the solution just has to be calculated, the problem is only fully defined when the solution is created. They are dialectically linked—mutually constituted.

(Adapted from Booth et al., 2000, p.31)

3.1 INTRODUCTION

1. Thesis writers will not be present when examiners assess their work. For this reason the thesis must speak as eloquently as possible on the researcher's behalf. However, the external examiners will first see the title of the thesis, together with the abstract, in the letter from the university officially inviting them to take on the task of examining. So, the need to start influencing examiners positively precedes their receipt of the actual thesis; the task, instead, rests with the title and abstract. This is why the abstract is best written thoughtfully throughout the thesis writing process rather than as a hurried afterthought. This will not only help ensure that the abstract accurately reflects the contents of the thesis, it will also help to retain focus when the thesis is being written because thinking about the abstract requires a precise distillation of what the thesis is about. It will become, in other words, a 'rolling synopsis' (Dunleavy, 2003). Nonetheless, irrespective of how well the abstract has been written the primary signaller to the examiners of what has been done in a thesis remains the title.

2. Readers and listeners tend to be most heavily influenced by what comes first and by what comes last. So the title can significantly influence an examiner's implicit and explicit assumptions about a thesis. He or she might be influenced by the clarity of the title or the lack thereof; by the difficulty or ease of the task undertaken; by its originality or lack thereof; by the recognition of issues currently, or likely to be, of importance, in dispute or controversial; and by the amount of information imparted: research boundaries, for example,

or methodology and method. Because the title of the thesis needs to speak clearly and say so much it is likely to be one of the last things revised. This is particularly the case in theses with a significant exegetic or qualitative component because in these approaches the focus of the work often needs to be constructed and refined as the research proceeds.

3.2 THE 'OPENNESS' OF RESEARCH

1. Reported within a framework of valid assumptions and aimed primarily at problem solving or hypothesis testing empirical research tends to be deductive—to derive particulars from general principles. In exegetic and qualitative approaches, on the other hand, assumptions need to be established within the confines of carefully elaborated contexts. Assumptions tend to be exploratory and, thus, inductive—an argument supported by premises that only provide sufficient evidence to indicate the conclusion is *unlikely* to be false. It has already been established that epistemologically distinct research approaches do not necessarily stand in mutual contradiction to one another. Because shared continuities are often as significant as their differences, all approaches to research apply both induction and deduction. Nonetheless, the generalised knowledge that empirical researchers bring to a research undertaking usually permits deduction to be applied from the outset while the more exploratory tendencies of exegetic and qualitative research means that induction will predominate. These differences can be seen in the following thesis titles:

   - Empirical: *Designing Efficient Parallel Algorithms for Graph Problems* (Liang, 1997). The argument implicit in this title is that current parallel algorithms, as applied to graph problems (the context), are inefficient. A very specific focus, therefore, is provided by use of the word 'efficient'.
   - Exegetic: *The Rhetoric of Adolescent Fiction: The Pedagogy of Reading Practices in South Australian Secondary English Classes* (Van der Hoeven, 2002). The key theoretic issue has been placed prior to the colon while the analytic focus (The Pedagogy of Reading Practices) and the context or the 'boundary' of the research ('South Australian Secondary English Classes') are placed after the colon. Because the focus is on a theoretic issue it must, inevitably, be less sharp than in the case above. It is also, for this reason, apparent why colons are so infrequently used in this manner in the titles of empirical theses—the issues with which they deal tend to be explicit rather than theoretic.
   - Qualitative: *Exploring what the doing does… A poststructural analysis of nurses' subjectivity in relation to pain* (Price, 2000). Although structured in a way similar to the example immediately above, it is significantly more open-ended: rather

than an investigation of a clearly defined theoretic issue, this is an exploration, through a particular method within a defined context, of a concept.

What does 'research led' mean?

2. Words in a title that imply exploration such as *discover*, *understand* or *describe* usually indicate qualitative studies. So too do those that imply theory development as opposed to theory testing. Words in a title implying explanation or correlation, such as *determinants*, *variables*, *factors*, *why*, *a comparison of* or *the relationship between* usually signal empirical studies (Creswell & Plano Clark, 2007, p.91). Their brevity also usually signals empirical titles. The APA reference manual, for example, recommends ten to twelve words (2010, p.23). However, despite the apparent difference in the degree of focus between them, empirical, exegetic and qualitative researchers all lay equal claim to being 'research led': to be flexible when confronted with new developments in research direction and outcome. The fact they are all equally able to do so is explained by their different perspectives about what being 'research led' means.

3. Empirical research rests on the assumption that when the correct measuring instruments are used phenomena, to a significant degree, can be quantified, measured and explained. This approach, therefore, is *normative*: insights or norms amenable to generalisation can be developed. Because these insights or norms might then assist in the incremental construction of patterns of understanding, empirical research is also theory and law stating or *nomothetic*. In consequence, new research questions can be constructed and hypotheses tested empirically in the light of a growing body of established theory and law. This means that empirical researchers are usually able to identify their research question clearly at the outset. Look, for example, at the thesis title: *What is the nature of the flow field between two eccentric rotating cylinders in the presence of a slotted sleeve?* (Hird, 1997). There is already a body of established knowledge explaining the nature of each of the identified elements and how they behave in particular contexts. This knowledge permits the research undertaking to establish the clarity of its focus: how the elements behave together. This explains the irony inherent in empirical work: its nomethetic tendency permits researchers to restrict their focus in order to provide a wealth of detail (Sharrock & Read, 2002). It is, therefore, the ability to identify a research question or to establish a hypothesis with a significant degree of clarity at the start of a research undertaking that differentiates students engaged in empirical research from those involved in exegetic or qualitative research. For the latter two, the titles of their theses need to be constructed. What, though, is a title?

3.3 THE RELATIONSHIP BETWEEN TOPIC, TITLE, THESIS AND HYPOTHESIS

1. A *topic* indicates a theme or an area of discussion. For example, *Celtic tradition* or *Cold desert environments*. When there is only a topic, therefore, the definition of what constitutes relevant research material will inevitably be less focused, and the subsequent search for it less efficient than would be the case if there were a specific title. This is because a *title* indicates the particular aspect of a *topic* that is to be discussed. For example, *The Role of Bees in Celtic tradition* or *The Effects of Temperature Variation upon the Feeding Habits of Dromedary Camels (Camelus dromedarius) in Cold Desert Environments*. A title can be expressed in a variety of ways:

    *   as a question: *Perceptions of higher education: does culture matter?*;
    *   as an exploration: *Monuments in a Freirean framework*;
    *   as a statement: *Why young drivers are accident prone*;
    *   as an investigation: *The Social Determination of Quality: a Theoretical and Empirical Investigation*;
    *   as an hypothesis: *If the quality of supervision is good, then theses will tend to be submitted on time*; and
    *   as a thesis: *FitzGerald's Rubaiyat: a Victorian Invention* (Zare–Bentash, 1997).

2. A *thesis* (from the Greek *tithenai*: to place) is an original proposition, statement or assertion advanced and maintained by argument. A *thesis statement* in a thesis or dissertation (from the Latin *dissertare*: to discuss) will, therefore, encapsulate the central idea being advanced in a study. (Where it is not possible to encapsulate the thesis in the title it should, because of its importance, be stated as early in the text of the thesis as possible.) Whereas a *thesis* is an *assertion*, a claim vindicated by strong supporting evidence, a *hypothesis* is only an assumption, tentative in exegetic and qualitative research, less so in empirical research. (A continually supported hypothesis evolves into a theory. Theories, in turn, may bind hypotheses together to form new hypotheses or, alternatively, in empirical research a continually validated theory becomes a law.) Theses do not necessarily need to start with a hypothesis. They might, instead, investigate particular research questions as a result of which hypotheses are formulated for other researchers to investigate: *This research question is aimed at formulating a hypothesis that can then be tested by large scale research design*. The traditional model of research is, thus, turned around: hypotheses are normally inputs into research. In this case they become research outputs (Punch, 2006).

3. Questions provide focus to a thesis because they require a relevant response. The effect is apparent in the following comment by an examiner:

    A thesis which depends upon a title, rather than a question, to link all its discussions together is always hard work for the reader/examiner who is then forced to deduce the candidate's 'line' on the topic for him- or herself. Sometimes the question is there—implicitly or explicitly—a few pages in, but on other occasions it never materializes and the examiner is left deciding the extent to which this matters.

(Cited in Pearce, 2005, p.51)

Hypotheses in empirical research, though, can be more useful than questions because they provide an even greater degree of focus. This can be seen in the following comment by an examiner:

I think the thesis would have been strengthened considerably if he had been able to develop some specific hypotheses around which he could have organised his methodology rather than approaching the subject from the standpoint of broad questions.

(Cited in Anderson & Poole, 1994, p.32)

However, generating empirical hypotheses presupposes a significant degree of initial insight into the factors at play. This, in turn, implies that some hypotheses might be difficult to develop because, for example, the phenomena under investigation have not been sufficiently researched. In such cases broad research questions instead of hypotheses might be necessary.

3.4 HYPOTHESES IN EMPIRICAL RESEARCH

1. In empirical research a hypothesis is a suggested solution to a problem or an assumption tentatively advanced to account for the relationship of specified variables (Mauch & Birch, 1998). They are, thus, reductive because ideas are reduced to small, discrete sets to test. There are many types of variables: discrete, continuous, interval, ratio, ordinal or nominal, for example. But the basic types are independent, dependent and controlled. The independent variable is the variable purposely manipulated. The dependent variable changes in response to the independent variable. The variables not changed are the controlled variables. When advanced to account for the relationship between variables empirical assumptions become less tentative than those in exegetic or qualitative research: an empirical hypothesis, in other words, is not simply a suggestion to account for a relationship; it is also a suggestion that the relationship is empirically testable. This also indicates the nature of an empirical problem statement: it has more to do with what is known than with what is not known for a researcher must know enough to say what the hypothetical relations are (Van Wagenen, 1991).
2. Statistics defines a hypothesis according to the nature of that testable relationship: a *null hypothesis* conjectures that in the general population, no

relationship or no difference exists between groups on a variable. The wording, therefore, is: 'There is no difference (or relationship) between the groups' (Creswell, 2003, p.109). (When a research question is framed as a test of the null hypothesis an explicit statement will be necessary in order to indicate the confidence levels for rejecting it [Bryant, 2004].) The *alternative hypothesis*, on the other hand, conjectures either a simple association between the variables (*a two-tailed hypothesis*) or an association between the variables that has either a positive or negative direction *(a one-tailed hypothesis)*. There will be a difference in scores between Group A and Group B on the dependent variable is an example of the former. Group A will score higher than Group B on the dependent variable is an example of the latter (Creswell, 2003). One-tailed hypotheses, therefore, are expressions of what we know in substance; two-tailed hypotheses are a consequence of not knowing what the outcome will be (Van Wagenen, 1991). It might in particular cases be necessary to undertake research on an alternative hypothesis dependent for its success on acceptance or rejection of either a positive or negative direction. It is usually safer, though, to undertake research where there will be 'symmetry of potential outcomes: all potential outcomes, whether the hypothesis is accepted or rejected or where the result is inconclusive, will be equally satisfactory to the examiners' (Phillips & Pugh, 2005). (Apart from an inconclusive outcome a hypothesis cannot be proved or disproved; it can only be accepted or rejected.)

3. Both the null and alternative forms of hypothesis are not speculative but evidentially supported forms of prediction. They are only appropriate, therefore, when an explanation or theory to one degree or another, supports the hypothesis. If no prediction can be made with any degree of confidence research questions replace hypotheses: *what is the relationship between…* for example rather than *there is no significant difference between…* However, although differing in their origin 'there is no logical difference between research questions and research hypotheses when it comes to their implications for design, data collection and data analysis' (Punch, 2006, p.38).

4. Providing operational definitions frames empirical research questions or hypotheses with sufficient detail to focus the research. Although hypotheses might be formulated in a number of ways not all of them are equally useful in terms of the focus they provide. They may, for example, be formulated as a conditional statement: Quality of supervision may be a factor in the timely completion of theses. They might also be formulated as 'if, then' statements: 'If the quality of supervision is good, then theses will tend to be submitted on time'. Of the two the latter is most useful because it not only explicitly indicates the specific relationship to be examined but also, in the word 'good', suggests the nature of that relationship. An 'if, then' statement might, however, resemble a simple prediction because it is not clear what the independent and

dependent variables are. Because the direction of the relationship is indicated this problem can be overcome by use of 'related to': 'if the timely submission of theses is related to the quality of supervision then well supervised theses should be submitted on time.' (In this case 'timely submission of theses' will be the dependent variable and 'quality of supervision' the independent variable.) Presented in this way it is clear that a one-tailed hypothesis is being proposed and that the research design will be correlational. (A one-tailed hypothesis is not, though, necessarily correlational.) It also, as a result, indicates the nature of the data that will be collected and the types of statistical test that need to be applied to that data (Adapted from Cone & Foster, 1998, p.39).

5. It is usually preferable when generating an empirical hypothesis involving human participants to go one step further in the wording of the hypothesis by also indicating the nature of the population from which they have been drawn: 'If the timely submission of theses is related to the quality of supervision then well supervised theses in the humanities should be submitted on time'. It is generally better not to provide further detail because, as in the following example, the focus might be shifted towards the method of analysis and away from the relationship that is the concern of the hypothesis: 'If the timely submission of theses is related to the quality of supervision as measured by a…test then well supervised theses in the humanities should be submitted on time' (Adapted from Cone & Foster, 1998, p.39). (Discussion of the choice of statistical measures applied to test a hypothesis should be conducted in the methods section.)

6. An empirical thesis can, of course, deal with a number of hypotheses. But how many is too many? There can be no definitive answer because each research undertaking is unique. Nonetheless, it is generally better, particularly in a master's thesis, to err on the side of caution. One main hypothesis from which one or two sub-hypotheses have been generated, thus providing unity to the set of hypotheses, is generally enough. Any more will run the risk of losing focus and/or running out of space to deal with each hypothesis in adequate detail.

3.5 HYPOTHESES IN EXEGETIC AND QUALITATIVE RESEARCH

1. While empirical research is normative and nomothetic, exegetic and qualitative research is concerned with the *idiographic*: with unique social and cultural phenomena that defy objective measurement. Because exegetic and qualitative approaches cannot, as a result of their subject matter's idiosyncrasy and amorphousness, rest to the same degree as in empirical research upon a significant body of previously established knowledge and theory they tend primarily to be *exploratory* and *interpretive*. Because less clearly defined criteria

mean an increase in interpretive variation (Peck MacDonald, 1994) explorative and interpretive research is pattern and explanation seeking; theory generators rather than theory testers. The use of the word 'tend' is deliberate, for to write otherwise would imply that exegetic and qualitative approaches can only be exploratory and only generate theory and that empirical approaches are only confirmatory and theory verifying. If this dichotomy were considered absolute exegetic and qualitative approaches would be confined permanently to the preliminary phases of mixed methodology research. Nonetheless, the fact that there often is a dichotomy indicates one of the advantages of a mixed methodology approach for it enables researchers simultaneously to answer confirmatory and exploratory questions and, therefore, verify and generate theory in the same study (Teddlie & Tashakkori, 2003a).

Qualitative propositions

2. It is in the context of generally being exploratory and interpretive that qualitative research questions are liberating in the sense that they afford the researcher wide investigative latitude (Creswell, 1994). This explains why they are normally only formulated after the researcher has spent some time collecting data: guiding hypotheses are used as tools to generate questions and search for patterns (Marshall & Rossman, 2006). In this way the foci of the research emerge as preconceptions alter with the new understandings developed in the research setting (Meloy, 2002). Reflection on one's identity and assumptions in this context are key to a discussion of the researcher's choice of questions and of his or her role in the research (Marshall & Rossman, 2006). An important aspect of this discussion might be the need to change or develop research methods as a consequence of the reformulation of questions or hypotheses. The gradual metamorphosis of qualitative hypotheses also indicates their distinctiveness from empirical hypotheses. Rather than a suggested solution to a problem or an assumption tentatively advanced to account for the relationship of specified variables, they are propositions: phenomena presented for critical discussion rather than as attempts to provide explanations or show correlations (Hart, 2005). Nonetheless, it is possible for qualitative researchers to use statistical vocabulary without doing injury to the qualitative process: *I have focused on journalists at the... paper in order to explore a working discourse community and to have as few confounding categorical variables as possible.*

Exegetic propositions

3. Propositions are also at play in exegetic research. Just as qualitative researchers immerse themselves in the research setting, so exegetic researchers develop

understanding as a result of immersion in the literature. This can be seen in the thesis title *FitzGerald's Rubaiyat: a Victorian Invention* (Zare–Behtash, 1997). ('The Rubaiyat' is an epic poem composed in 12th century CE Persia by Omar Khayyam and translated into English in 1859 by Edward FitzGerald.) In the title the researcher proposes that the translation, rather than reflecting the mores of twelfth century Persia, reflects those of nineteenth century England. But, assuming that a similar study had not previously been conducted, the researcher could not have started with this proposition; it likely arose, instead, from a prolonged and detailed study of the poem. The initial research question, would, therefore, have been exploratory: 'how did FitzGerald's *Rubaiyat* differ from the original?' As the investigation proceeded along the path indicated by the question the researcher, on the basis of indicative evidence, developed a *hypothesis*: 'The impulse to translate was generated by nineteenth century cultural interests: why did this poem generated in twelfth century Persia resonate with Fitzgerald, a product of his own society?' By providing a more explicit focus the hypothesis, because it was subsequently supported by sufficient *substantive evidence*, metamorphosed from a proposition, to hypothesis, to thesis. The final result of this process, *FitzGerald's Rubaiyat: a Victorian Invention*, is, thus, both title and thesis. Exegetic and most qualitative researchers should, therefore, expect, as their research progresses and deeper understanding of the relevant issues develops, that the wording of their initial proposition will require redefinition.

4. When this takes place it indicates a reciprocal relationship has developed between research and proposition: the latter provides direction to the research while the findings of the research help redefine the proposition. The number of times such redefinition takes place will depend upon the nature of the research and the tentativeness of the initial proposition. It is important, though, to recognise that this redefinition is a natural and important element in the unfolding of the research process and serves as an indicator of a student's growth as a researcher. The process can be seen in the following explanation by a supervisor in philosophy:

> *The student is the one who drives the thing. But there is advice from members of the department; I think in the end the crunch is that people often bite off just a bit much, which doesn't help them, so the judgment of the supervisor should be respected. Philosophy being what it is, by and large you can decide to build great detail on some topic, and as you do that, the focus can change. But that's all part of the thing.*

(Cited in Parry, 2007, p.42)

5. Redefinition is not limited to propositions and hypotheses; the focus of all research projects can, and often does, alter as a consequence of insights developed

as the research progresses. An intrinsically interesting part of a thesis is, in fact, the story explaining any alteration of focus that might have occurred:

Initial exploration around the topic of the measurement of vital sign collection uncovered a cluster of issues that surround the practice. What was apparent was a strong association between the collection of vital signs and other aspects of patient monitoring usually included in the broader use of the term 'observations.' This changed the researchers' focus from vital sign collection in isolation to an investigation focusing on nursing observations inclusive of vital signs.

(Zeitz, 2003, p.2.)

Focus or foci?

6. Theses with more than one focus might provide an opportunity for enriched discussion but they can invite over-ambition. They also require not only that care be devoted to the definition of each of the foci but also to the issue of their importance relative to each other. The danger is that establishing this balance often involves a significant subjective element. In, for example, the thesis *Bernard of Cluny: the Literature of Complaint, the Benedictine Tradition and the Twelfth-century Renaissance,* it is not self-evident that each of the three contexts in which the central character is to be discussed should enjoy equal treatment. Examiners will certainly have their own opinions about the relative weight that ought to be attached to each. It is important, therefore, in cases like this that a justification has been provided for the manner in which the argument has been structured. If this is sufficiently convincing examiners will generally accept what has been done even though they might feel an alternative approach may have been better. If, though, a justification has not been provided the researcher will be left defenceless. Therefore, in all instances in a thesis where a significant legitimate difference of opinion might arise between researcher and examiners, thesis writers need to develop a habit of briefly defending the decisions they have made. Not doing so might convey the wrong impression: that they thought the decision was the only one that could have been made.

3.6 THE VALUE AND ORIGINALITY OF RESEARCH
Value

1. Research is not simply a process of filling *lacunae*, filling holes in a stationary field, the equivalent of climbing a mountain because it is there. This impression is sometimes given in policy documents which, rather than calling for new

interpretations, emphasise the need for research to fill 'gaps in knowledge' (Rowland, 2006). Instead, research must have clearly defined value and examiners ought to be able to recognise it clearly: 'The fundamental purpose of the investigation is both an interesting and an important one' (cited in Anderson & Poole, 1994, p.31). If it is not clearly recognisable questions will be asked: 'Is this a candidate whose discussions/analyses intervene in debates without necessarily taking them forward?' (Pearce, 2005, p.51). But, because defining value involves social agreement and because epistemological approaches interpret the concept differently, identifying the value of a particular research undertaking might well be a contested process. Take, for example, the following list of possible criteria (from top to bottom) for valuing empirical research. It has value when it:

- offers new, supplementary knowledge;
- solves a problem;
- brings established beliefs into question;
- articulates a problem that others should take seriously but which, until that time, has gone unrecognised (Booth et al., 2003, pp. 71 & 132).

2. The results of empirical research are directly measurable; thus their value can be expressed in concrete terms. This approach to value is apparent in the listed criteria; hierarchically organised and problem centred they implicitly reflect knowledge as a coherent body of thought. Qualitative researchers, therefore, will contest these criteria. Empirical and qualitative researchers also differ in the value they ascribe to results derived from the application of particular research methods. Empirical researchers in the medical field, for example, ascribe high value to the results of randomised controlled trials. Action Researchers, in contrast, define the value of research in terms of the extent to which outcomes are transformative. Differences in the perception of value need not, though, only be between empirical and qualitative researchers. They can be reflected within disciplines: 'One of the reasons I went into mathematics is, unlike most other subjects, the question of right or wrong is usually not an opinion...But as far as significant and non-significant [is concerned], that's still very fuzzy...' (cited in Lovitts, 2007, p.201). They can also be reflected in separate schools of thought. Take for example the concept *contributing towards progress* as the basis for assessing the value of research in the natural sciences. On the grounds that there cannot 'be any external philosophical basis for judging the success of science' (Sharrock & Read, 2002, p.18), it is possible to reject the concept of progress as meaningless by denying that progress in science is progress towards anything. Then, of course, there is the entirely practical consideration that potential employers ascribe particular value to relevant applied research. However, this type of value calls for a degree of caution. Because it tends

to be specific to a particular need the risk of failure is much greater than would be the case if an acceptable research outcome were to be more broadly defined (Phillips & Pugh, 2005). It also, of course, runs the risk of pre-emption by other researchers.

3. Irrespective of the perspective from which the study has been approached, examiners will not only expect to see an explicit statement of its value, usually early in the introduction or literature review, but will also expect to be convinced by the argument provided to support the statement: '…theory is still at the stage of development thus further work to develop more accurate theory and to unify existing theory is essential for the development of the subject.' A way to reinforce, by implication, the value of research is to indicate in the conclusion to the thesis any new avenues of investigation the findings might have made possible. What, in other words, can researchers now do that could not have been done prior to the completion of the study? When examiners are convinced of the value of what has been done appropriate praise can be expected: 'X develops an original and important argument and covers ground not previously walked by researchers' (Holbrook, Bourke & Dally, 2003, p.8). In this instance not only the importance and thus value of the research has been established but also its originality, the latter an intrinsic aspect of the value of all research. This is apparent in the following comment by a qualitative researcher:

…when we direct our work toward a particular theoretical audience, we are looking to join in, not just eavesdrop on their conversation…As researchers, we must somehow show that our work brings something new to the conversation.

(Golden–Biddle & Locke, 1997, p.11)

Originality

4. Most definitions of doctoral research contain an explicit requirement that the contribution made should be original. Most definitions of masters research do not contain this explicit requirement but do, nonetheless, generally require students 'to apply knowledge to new situations; and to engage in rigorous intellectual analysis, criticism and problem-solving…' (University of Auckland, 2001) There is an implicit requirement for an element of originality. Seen in the context of the need by universities to prevent the pursuit of trivial or ill-conceived research the explicit requirement for doctoral work to be original and the implicit expectation of an element of originality in masters research is understandable. But, while most universities trumpet '[originality] as a gold standard' (Pearce, 2005, p.37) they depend on examiners to know and recognise it instinctively. Originality might well

be definable in specific instances. For example, when it demonstrates the capacity to look at the same facts and see new explanations (Forty, 2001). However, the art historian Kenneth Clark illustrated the difficulty of defining originality generically when he said he could not define civilisation in the abstract but knew it when he saw it (Clark, 1969). Shakespeare's Hamlet is another example of an individual who has exact knowledge of experiences he cannot propositionally enunciate (Fiumara, 1995). In consequence he is left ineffectively with the question whether to be or not. Foucault, in common with other post-structuralists, added to the already lengthy list of intangibles defining originality. In, for example, *What is an Author?* emphasis is shifted away from individuals as the source of new ideas towards the societies of which they are part (Peck MacDonald, 1994).

5. If originality is difficult to define generically it is especially difficult to define in the context of a thesis, for both doctoral and masters projects are essentially *research training* processes and in this sense originality has to be interpreted quite narrowly (Phillips & Pugh, 2005). As in the case of value, therefore, originality is a problematic concept for, depending upon the definition applied, not only can it be expressed in a variety of ways, the expectation of it is greater in some disciplines, and in some individual examiners and supervisors, than in others (Tinkler & Jackson, 2004). In many of the sciences, for example a distinction is drawn between reinterpretation and new knowledge; the former often not being considered research. In the humanities, however, criticism, interpretation and reinterpretation are research activities (Rowland, 2006) and might be seen as original contributions to knowledge. In addition, for a historian 'originality' might mean quite literally 'evidence of having worked with original sources' and in the humanities in general a premium is placed on a researcher's ability to formulate interesting and original questions (Pearce, 2005). In economics it is often felt that an original contribution should have some type of practical application (Lovitts, 2007). But, although innovation is seen as a key step in the development of successful research programs in the sciences (Woods, 2006), expectation by examiners of originality in an empirical thesis might be particularly modest.

6. A number of reasons explain this. One is that much of the work is done in groups. When this is the case the research question has often already been defined when thesis writers begin their research and, particularly in regard to doctoral students, projects are often passed on from one candidate to another. In these circumstances a researcher's ability to be self-directed is often of greater value than the originality of their contribution (Pearce, 2005). But perhaps the most important reason for the modest expectation of originality in the sciences lies in the nature of empirical work. Because of the inherent idiosyncrasy of exegetic and qualitative approaches, claims of

significant originality are more frequent than in empirical research. Here, in fact, the opportunity to induce fundamental novelty is relatively rare both because originality tends to be unpredictable and because it often requires a combination of fortuitous circumstances (Sharrock & Read, 2002). This is the classical model of discovery: Columbus searched for an alternative route to India and found, in the Americas, something he did not know was there. This is serendipity, a word derived from the fairy tale *The Three Princes of Seredin* the central characters of which were always discovering things of which they were not in quest (Taleb, 2007).

7. A useful way to focus thinking about what in an academic work constitutes originality is the criterion 'potentially publishable' in a peer-reviewed journal. Because editors generally require the material in their publications to have both value and originality 'potentially publishable', particularly in regard to doctoral work, is increasingly being equated with 'originality' in research (Cryer, 2006). Nonetheless, part of the difficulty some students confront in developing a realistic understanding of what is meant by originality is their interpretation of the concept in absolute terms. Originality in a thesis should, instead, be seen as the child of a lesser god: a contribution to the incremental process of paradigm development rather than of paradigm change. Something creative, significant and original, for example, can be done with previously reported data, or research can be undertaken the findings of which suggest that further exploration might be fruitful (Mauch & Birch, 1998). This is what might be called undiscovered public knowledge: 'you can actually do lab work sitting in an armchair, just by linking bits and pieces of research by people who labor apart from one another and miss on connections' (Taleb, 2007, p.321).

8. What, though, of the case when a thesis is highly original? Two immediate subjective concerns arise. The first relates to evaluation: it is of the nature of innovation that it is difficult to evaluate until it is no longer innovative (Rowland, 2006). The second is that the thesis, by definition, will be contentious (Tinkler & Jackson, 2004). Ironically, therefore, an examiner's reputation will be at stake when a highly original thesis is accepted. It is understandable therefore that they will take great care to check the work and possibly refer the thesis back to clarify points (Cryer, 2006). There is some evidence to indicate that highly original papers submitted for publication are likely to be referred back more frequently than those less controversial (Cryer, 2006). Do not let this be a deterrent. Getting an examiner or an editor to sit back and think before they commit themselves is, in academe, the highest form of flattery and if the work survives the interrogation intact it will, in due course, receive its just reward.

9. Because it so important, because it is often so difficult to define and because it can apply to so many facets of a thesis, both student and supervisors should

from the outset of the research hold ongoing discussions about what in the thesis is original (Phillips & Pugh, 2005). The following is an indicative list of the range of definitions within which the originality of a thesis might fall:

- The method or its application is unique.
- A new synthesis of existing material has been provided.
- It has been done under a unique set of circumstances.
- The work is uniquely interdisciplinary.
- The findings are unique.
- Another researcher's original insight has been extended.
- An original contribution has been made to an ongoing debate.
- An established interpretation has been challenged. (Adapted from Murray, 2003, p.52)

Unless informed otherwise by the researcher, thesis examiners, irrespective of discipline, will tend to seek originality not only in terms of the publication potential of the material, but also in the nature of the thesis statement, in the methodology, in the modes of analysis adopted, in the depth of analysis displayed in the literature review and/or in the research outcomes (Tinkler & Jackson, 2004). Developing a clear idea of what in their thesis is original might not only allow thesis writers to develop the concept further but also to assist the examiners in their search for originality by explicitly indicating in the text where that element is considered to lie. The latter can be seen, for example, in the following thesis extract: 'The researcher collated and analysed the most comprehensive database of…yet developed. This provided greater confidence in the results because…'

3.7 JOINT PROJECTS

1. One of the reasons explaining the formation of multidisciplinary research teams is the belief that innovation is most frequent where disciplines meet (Woods, 2006). Joint projects also have an entirely practical function: funding bodies place a significant premium on collaboration (Yates, 2007). They have good reasons for doing so for, in a highly audited academic environment, enhanced productivity is an important consideration (Becher & Trowler, 2001). This is particularly the case in the sciences where the competitive nature of the disciplines encourages fast research output (Parry, 2007). This also explains why in these disciplines no time can be wasted on research topics not in line with the aims of a research group or which will not attract funding. A supervisor in experimental physics said: 'A range of available projects where the resources and equipment are available is offered, and then it is a matter of negotiation between the supervisor and the student' (cited in Parry, 2007, p.41). This explains why students in theoretical physics are less

constrained in their choice of topic than are experimental researchers in the discipline (Lovitts, 2007).

2. But, although experimental work might limit the choice of topics available and make it particularly difficult for those undertaking interdisciplinary studies to find supervisors, joint projects also have specific advantages. This can be seen in the following remark by a supervisor: 'A useful ploy is to attach a new candidate to a fairly mature research project so that they can taste the success of publication early in their candidature' (Yates, 2007, p.107). Another benefit is the personal stake supervisors have in the project. Even when appropriate, though, joint projects are not always necessarily beneficial:

Clearly, the composition of research teams and the relationship among their members are crucial. Despite the general 'multiplier effect', they might also represent constraints for certain individuals, rather than liberation. The group itself might set up its own constraining parameters…

(Woods, 2006, p.111)

3. Thus, the appropriateness of joint projects and the manner in which they function is not homogeneous. Qualitative researchers using the constant comparative method[1] might, for example, work together in joint projects because the comparative base can be substantively expanded and writer triangulation, the variety of interpretive perspectives brought to bear, increased (Woods, 2006). The number of researchers involved in these projects tends, though, to be small. This is not necessarily the case in astronomy and physics where collaborative teams numbering in the hundreds and which involve enormous logistical effort are not unusual (Becher & Trowler, 2001). But it is often the case in disciplines like these that research projects are theory driven and thus largely inseparable. It is for this reason the teams undertake large, unified operational tasks. In, for example, chemistry, the tasks are usually divisible and team members undertake smaller, diverse tasks. In terms of the appropriateness of research groups the case of mathematics is often similar to that in the humanities. In the latter interpretation, a characteristically individual process predominates. In the former the problems generally constitute organic wholes, a process that usually involves intense individual effort (Becher & Trowler, 2001). In both, though, there is generally ample opportunity for individual researchers to avoid overlap with each other. Taxonomy is an extreme example of research that is inherently individual: 'like judges, taxonomists can give opinions, but they don't give joint opinions' (Becher & Trowler, 2001, p.126).

4. From a supervisor's perspective the benefits of joint projects lie not only in the student's research contribution, but also in the extent to which it enables them

to keep control of the supervisory process: the more diverse the research of a group of students for whom a supervisor is responsible, the more difficult the process of coordinating them becomes. The corollary for the student though is that the needs of the research can take precedence over their individual need to exercise a degree of independence (Cryer, 2006). The task of a good supervisor is to prevent this from happening for there are two significant dangers if it does. In the first instance the student does not develop a sense of 'ownership' of the project. This often results in, apart from lower motivation, lack of conceptual depth: the student is simply 'carrying out tasks and seeing only a fragmented process' (Wisker, 2005, p.49). The second danger relates to the requirement that a thesis should reflect the work of an individual, albeit one who has conducted and presented the research under supervision. It can come as a shock to students involved in joint projects to discover when they are drafting their work that they are unable to delineate clearly their role in the project from that of the other members. Examiners will certainly pay particular attention to the researcher's contribution if the thesis arose from a joint project (Tinkler & Jackson, 2004). During the oral examination of doctoral candidates who were part of a large investigation examiners might well ask, for example, how the researcher was able to maintain a degree of independence (Mauch & Birch, 1998). (If a thesis writer is involved in a joint project they should test how often they can use 'I' instead of 'we' when describing their role.) Because examiners like to feel clear that what they are marking belongs to the candidate it is therefore important at the outset of all joint undertakings to identify, in collaboration with the supervisors, not only what the researcher's individual role in the joint project is to be but also the degree to which they will be free to develop that role.

3.8 FACTORS TO CONSIDER PRIOR TO DEVELOPING A RESEARCH QUESTION

1. Stamping their own identity on the research is not normally an issue for students who are expected to establish their own research question/s. This sometimes applies to empirical researchers but frequently applies to those involved in exegetic or qualitative projects. A possible exception from the norm is two-phase sequential projects where the questions for the second phase are contingent on the completion of the first (Creswell, 2003). However, because the design of most qualitative work emerges from within a predetermined context and because most empirical work develops an early focus, researchers in each of these approaches are normally exempt from the price that exegetic researchers often have to pay: that of making one or more false starts before a firm choice emerges (Mauch & Birch, 1998). But, because establishing a

research question is an intrinsic part of being an exegetic researcher this is what the process of research naturally involves. In this regard a supervisor in archaeology said:

We believe that if you give a person a PhD topic, then you're inviting the worst trouble in the world. Students have to come up with a topic and that's the very first thing. They've got to believe that even though it might get modified a lot, it's originally their idea that they're working on. And this they find enormously difficult to do…I think it is the first measure of whether they are going to be a good student or not.

(Cited in Parry, 2007, p.41)

2. There are, however, factors common to all approaches to research that might or should influence the final choice of research question/s. One good principle is to exercise caution in regard to research projects that require the application of procedures, techniques or skills that have not been exercised before (Phillips & Pugh, 2005). If this is unavoidable take every opportunity to develop the necessary experience before the project begins. This might include designing a pilot study specifically to allow a researcher to do so. Foreign students sometimes encounter difficulty when they know what problems need solutions in their own country but cannot find a supervisor who understands the problems or thinks them suitable for investigation (Mauch & Birch, 1998). A more common issue is the need for financial support. Although it is often difficult at masters level to find funding, doctoral students, particularly in the applied and natural sciences and in business, are often able to apply if they are willing to adjust their research to fit the criteria of the funding body. Care, however, will need to be exercised to ensure that the funding criteria do not bias the design of the research. It should also be remembered that applied work often involves putting all of a researcher's metaphorical eggs into one basket. (If the funding body requires a signed contract go through it with the guidance of a lawyer so that all commitments are fully understood [Marsh, 2006].)

3. It sounds mercenary but an entirely practical consideration is the undertaking of research that can be 'cannibalised' maximally in terms of the number of publications or conference papers derivable from it. This is certainly an important consideration for doctoral candidates. Masters students might want to include these attributes in a project that will also lead smoothly into doctoral research and thus, provide a significant head start when that process begins. Even if masters students do not plan eventually to undertake research for a doctorate it should always be borne in mind that once the master's thesis has been successfully completed the temptation to go on can be strong. It

often pays to prepare for this possibility by choosing an appropriate field of research at the beginning of the masters process. The successful completion of a thesis has much to do with an ability to plan ahead; this is an example of an opportunity for a student to do so.

4. More often, however, research students undertake projects they believe will provide them a stepping-stone in their future careers. If this consideration is likely to influence the choice of research question then sound advice should be sought to help make the decision an informed one. It is also useful, in this regard, to keep in mind that thesis writers will live with the title of the thesis for the rest of their life (Dunleavy, 2003) and that job applicants, among other criteria, are rarely short-listed because potential employers have read the thesis. They are, instead, usually short-listed on the strength of the title of the thesis. However, having said this, research indicates that it is probable that the topic of research will limit a researcher's employability much less than they might think (Cryer, 2006). What will tend to be of most importance are the relevant skills they have developed. This is indicated in the following statement by a supervisor in economics:

*We tend to encourage **PhD** topics that can be tailored to what's required for three years' work. Usually the student wants to take on more, but we know that they'll never work in the same field after they finish; it's more important to have skills that they can apply afterwards to other situations.*

(Cited in Parry, 2007, p.40)

3.9 IDENTIFYING THE ELEMENTS OF A RESEARCH QUESTION

1. Unlike enquiry in law enforcement, enquiry in research suggests a continuing and developing interest rather than one that becomes exhausted once the initial question has been answered (Rowland, 2006). Research, in other words, explores ideas that lend themselves to sustained exploration. There will, of course, always be constraints. Methods, for example, can influence research questions by constraining what can be studied (Punch, 2006). Some constraints are subconscious. Rational judgement is often suspended during daily life simply because it is efficient to do what others are doing instead of reinventing the wheel. But when the process leads to imitation chains it can become inefficient: 'Soon everyone is running in the same direction, and it can be for spurious reasons. This behavior causes stock market bubbles and the formation of massive cultural fads' (Taleb, 2007, p.328). It also explains the bandwagon effect on choice of research topic: everyone else seems to be doing it so I should too.

2. But, after having taken possible constraints into account thesis research should, ideally, spring from a 'topic area' that is of more than passing interest. Certainly spending an extended period of time in the company of a topic for which enthusiasm is lacking will, inevitably, affect motivation, with the additional risk that lack of enthusiasm might become evident in the text of the thesis. Even if a topic area is of interest, if it is also unfamiliar a student new to research might be placing themselves at a disadvantage for it is unlikely they will be able to develop the broad background needed to do the study well in the time available (Mauch & Birch, 1998). However, because what is of interest is also usually familiar it is usually easy to identify a suitable topic area in which to conduct research: *post-operative observations*, for example. Yet 'topic areas' encompass a wide range of research possibilities: a more refined focus may be needed. Deriving a research question from the topic area is an ideal refining process because a question enhances focus by requiring a clearly defined response: 'Post-operative observations: ritualised or vital in the detection of post-operative complications?' (Zeitz, 2003). How, though, does one go about determining a researchable question from a 'topic area'?

Exploring the literature

3. The identification of the initial elements of a research question from a topic area is usually the result of a preliminary exploration of the literature on a broad scale. In this sense searching and evaluating what has been done on a topic is, in itself, research. In this sense also the preliminary review of the literature has an 'initiating function' (Marshall & Rossman, 2006) for what is learned can subsequently be explored permitting the focus of the research to be progressively refined and the depth of the reading to increase. It is always possible of course that the search of the literature will provide the answer to the question and save the need for further work (Poggenpohl, 2000). But even when this is the case if an electronic or hardcopy 'Possible Questions' notebook is kept to record ideas as the reading progresses (Mauch & Birch, 1998) viable new questions might well emerge.

4. What, though, does 'exploration of the literature on a broad scale' mean?
   • Investigate relevant conferences, both international and local, that have recently been, or are soon to be, held. Look at the themes of each conference and, where available, the titles of the papers presented. Not only might these themes and titles indicate potential research questions they will also provide clues as to the direction in which research in the topic area is moving. Just as research and the way it was written in academic journals only a few decades ago often seems archaic from a contemporary perspective so too will current research appear to other researchers in a few decades

79

time. While the direction of movement and the logic explaining it generally become visible with the benefit of hindsight only the most perceptive can deduce them from the perspective of the present. Researchers should, therefore, make an effort to develop this perception for it might protect them from undertaking research that, though relevant now, might not be so in a few years time. Because the research in which they are involved extends over a longer period this is particularly pertinent to doctoral candidates and to most applied researchers. But, just as important to both masters and doctoral students is evidence of insight into what in the future will be at the cutting edge of research: this is something that examiners will be responsive to when they see it in a thesis.

- The 'tables of content' of as many recent and relevant refereed journals as possible should be scrutinised. This can be particularly useful when their articles contain arguments, or aspects with which the researcher disagrees. It might also prove useful to read through both the dedicated book review articles in those journals and the literature reviews that generally precede the research articles themselves for the authors of each often either point out flaws in existing studies or areas where productive research might be undertaken.

- Another strategy to apply in order to explore the literature on a broad scale is to browse through recently completed doctoral and masters' theses, both electronic and hardcopy, which are broadly related to the topic area. (Networked Digital Thesis and Dissertations is an international organisation dedicated to promoting the dissemination of digital theses. Largely as a result of this initiative the number of freely accessible online theses is growing rapidly.) Look, in particular, at the conclusion chapter in each for most doctoral theses, as will also be the case in many masters' theses too, will have a 'Suggestions for Further Research' sub-section.

3.10 DEVELOPING A RESEARCH QUESTION

1. Once, as a result of this exploration, the elements of a research question have begun to be identified they will need to be filtered and reorganised so that, together, they constitute a viable research project. The first step is to recognise that asking a question that has no known answer but is, nonetheless, answerable, is a more subtle proposition than asking a question that seeks to obtain missing information or clarification; the type of question, in other words, that is the staple of everyday social interaction (Poggenpohl, 2000). The former category tends to differ from the latter in two ways. First, as has already been established, they need to have a clearly defined societal and epistemological value. Second, their focus generally, but not always, needs

to be developed through a step-by-step iterative process. The exceptions are usually empirical or applied. These might involve the use, for example, of the PICO (Patient or Problem; Intervention; Comparison; Outcome) framework for research question development. The framework has been adopted in medicine to establish detailed and specific comparative questions for clinical research. For example: *In a paediatric patient with recurrent otitis media* (Patient or Problem) *is coamoxiclav* (Intervention) *or azithromycin* (Comparison) *more effective in reducing symptoms and signs....* (Outcome)? (ADHB, 2008). (While the PICO framework is used for specific interventions the PECOT framework, where 'E' represents Exposure or Intervention and which also includes Time as a component, has a more generic application.)

Developing an exegetic question

2. Rare exceptions, like the PICO and PECOT methods, apart, the focus of questions in most approaches to research (but particularly in exegetic research) generally develops through a step-by-step iterative, but not necessarily linear, process. This can be seen in the following where the topic area is romantic film. In order to initiate the filtering process, a broad question central to the 'topic area' is first posed in order to indicate the consequences of not finding an answer to it: 'How have romantic films changed in the last fifty years?' If this question cannot be answered then neither can the subsequent question: 'How have our cultural depictions of romantic love changed?' If, in turn, this question cannot be answered then neither can the next more fundamental question: 'How is our culture shaping the expectations of young men and women concerning marriage and families?' (Booth, Colomb & Williams, 2003, p.63). What this iterative process involves then is the identification of a specific case (cultural depictions of romantic love) from a general topic (romantic films) and then the determination of clarifying aspects about that specific case (shaping expectations concerning marriage and families).

3. This approach to question development indicates the importance of consequence to research. If there are no consequences to not doing the research why do it? An alternative approach, particularly useful in exegetic work, is first to identify the key theoretic issue: *The Rhetoric of Adolescent Fiction*. Then to establish the analytic focus: *The Pedagogy of Reading Practices*. And, finally, to define the context: *South Australian Secondary English Classes*. (Should this approach be adopted be careful not to juxtapose a broad theoretic issue with an equally broad context: *Advertising and the Internet*, for example.) The key role the *theoretic issue, analytic focus, context* format of questions like this plays in clarifying focus is clear in the following examples where the lack of explicit focus in the first is apparent when compared to that in the second: *Social*

movements in Turkey and the suppression of dissent, 1970–1975 as opposed to: *The suppression of dissent: social movements in Turkey, 1970–1975.* (If context is defined by physical or, as in this case, chronological boundaries, it is important they are not arbitrarily chosen but convincingly explained and defended as early in the thesis as possible.)

Developing qualitative questions

4. Most qualitative approaches to enquiry are uniquely suited to exploration. This demands reconciliation of contradictory elements in research questions. On the one hand there is a need for ongoing flexibility so that data gathering can respond to increasingly refined research questions. On the other the project needs to remain focused enough for it to be delimited. Achieving reconciliation is often not an easy task (Marshall & Rossman, 2006). A useful way of doing so is to begin the initial questions with 'how' and to include open-ended verbs such as 'describe' in the question: 'How do women in a psychology doctoral program describe their reentry experiences?' (Creswell, 2003). In participatory action research, the enquiry deliberately starts from specific practical questions for the sole purpose of the research is to find practical responses to those questions. But, because the approach is fundamentally interactive participants should be fully involved both in framing the questions and in gathering data (Marshall & Rossman, 2006). Autoethnography is fundamentally interactive in a different way: it is a reflexive account by the researcher who proceeds through multiple layers of consciousness to connect the personal to pertinent social or cultural events (Marshall & Rossman, 2006).

5. In mixed methodology studies a number of design options can be utilised. In an exploratory design, for example, the qualitative phase will be emphasised: 'Family portraits formed through mixed methododology: stories as standards for family relationships' (adapted from Creswell & Plano Clark, 2007, p.93). In an explanatory design emphasis will be placed on the first empirical stage for it will guide the study: 'Depression and substance use in two divergent high school cultures: an empirical and qualitative analysis'. In triangulation design the simple statement 'a mixed methodology study' is all that might need to be appended: 'Adolescent development and transitions to motherhood: a mixed methodology study' (adapted from Creswell & Plano Clark, 2007, p.93).

Seminars as 'engines for tinkering'

6. Once a potential question has begun to take shape barrage each of its elements with further questions in order to establish how they interrelate with each other and with the larger system or process. Doing so in a seminar

can be particularly useful and affording a student the opportunity to do so is an aspect of good supervision. Here, other supervisor and peer group perspectives will enrich insights and possibly also reveal unforeseen avenues of research: '…the effects of cognitive diversity on problem solving shows how variability in views and methods acts like an engine for tinkering. It works like evolution' (Taleb, 2007, p.225). A major advantage of developing a research question through an iterative process of questioning is that research rigidity is prevented because approaching a topic area with preconceived methods in mind is discouraged (Poggenpohl, 2000). Thus, although it is inevitable that researchers will approach topic areas from a particular methodological perspective, the decision as to the particular methods that are best suited to explore a question will be made subsequent to, and not prior to, the framing of the research question. This is why the next step in developing the question will be to clarify thinking by summarising, in writing, what the researcher plans to do: 'I am working in the area of…, so that I can find out…, because I want my readers to understand better…' (Booth et al., 2003, p.80). The significant advantage of writing this summary is that it will help to identify the purpose behind the question. Because purpose is central to deciding what method to adopt and because purpose is often complex the researcher will then be in a better position to identify the methods that adequately reflect that complexity (Newman et al., 2003).

3.11 RESEARCH DUPLICATION

1. Because human behaviour defies precise definition it is often necessary in the social sciences to redo reported studies with, for example, new or enhanced populations or with strengthened design and improved controls (Mauch & Birch, 1998). (The possible need to redo research might be applied in the Suggestions for Further Research section of a thesis.) The subjectivity implicit in textual interpretation and the changing contexts in which these interpretations are made imply that a significant body of exegetic research will also be amenable to useful duplication. Each qualitative undertaking is, by definition, unique. Although replication is inbuilt in empirical projects it is rarely undertaken for, in reality, the checking of other researchers' results is a haphazard process:

    …assuming that people's findings are correct and building on them until some-thing is clearly seen to have gone wrong, at which point some credit may be given for tracking down the original error.

    (Becher & Trowler, 2001, p.89)

The reason why checking the results of empirical research is haphazard is because in the natural and applied sciences there is no reward for coming second and a paper will get rejected simply on the grounds that the work has already been done (Sharrock & Read, 2002). Nonetheless, because the rewards for coming first can be significant, much of the current research being undertaken in these sciences is, in fact, broadly similar. This ought to be seen though in terms of the 'people to problem ratio'. At one end of the scale the number of researchers in some specialist fields is substantial relative to the issues being researched. At the other the number of viable questions that could be asked is infinite while the number of researchers engaged in answering them is negligible in comparison. Competition will tend, therefore, to be most intense in the former rather than the latter (Becher & Trowler, 2001, p.105). It is with these considerations in mind that once a preliminary research question has been identified empirical and to a lesser extent exegetic researchers will need to take reasonable steps to ascertain whether or not it has already been, or is in the process of being, researched.

2. The fact that a significant volume of research conducted internationally is replicated unintentionally indicates that taking these steps is not necessarily as easy as might at first appear. At least part of the reason is because searches of the literature have different levels of efficiency. Web search engines, for example, look for words, not ideas. So, if a researcher is not aware of the name given to an idea they will not be aware of its existence. But even when the levels of search efficiency are high the sheer volume of published research imposes limitations upon any individual's ability to keep abreast of it. Throughout the world, for example, some two million articles are published annually in over twenty thousand biomedical journals (Mulrow, 1994). During the 1990s the worldwide literature in the field of chemistry grew by more than half a million articles per year (Rowland, 2006) and more academic works in history were published between 1960 and 1980 than in all previous time (Becher & Trowler, 2001, p.14).

3. Very few researchers in very few fields can, therefore, claim to be fully up to date with the literature. Unless a research project has a specific local focus it might, for these reasons, be difficult to establish whether or not it has, or is being, conducted elsewhere. But, even in the natural sciences, discovering after the research has been started that it is duplicating a similar study elsewhere need not necessarily be of great concern. Replication of already published research, certainly in the case of masters' rather than doctoral theses, has obvious benefits in regard, for example, to learning particular approaches to research if the original study was well conducted. There are, in any event, likely to be at least some differences between a student's study and those that initially appeared to be identical. Nonetheless, replicating research has

the potential, if only for ethical reasons, to be problematic. So, if it arises as an issue prior to undertaking the project, the implications will need to be carefully considered by the supervisor/s and researcher before a decision is taken to proceed or not to do so.

3.12 EVALUATING RESEARCH QUESTIONS

1. Some topics are central and others peripheral; some are demanding and others comparatively tame. Each, in its own way, involves a gamble: large stakes for high dividends or low stakes for an assured return (Becher & Trowler, 2001, p.139). Like contradictory parables the following extracts indicate the difficulty of providing informed advice on this issue:
   • 'The farther you aim, the more an initial error matters' (Wenger, 1998, p.9).
   • '…our reach should regularly exceed our grasp, for if it did not it would be pointless as an inquiry' (Fiumara, 1995, p.33).

With this gamble in mind beginning researchers together with their supervisor/s will also need to evaluate additional aspects of the proposed research by addressing questions such as the following:
   • *Can it be thoroughly explored within the length, time and financial constraints?* It goes without saying that in, for example, the natural sciences a student's research may have to fit in with the availability of expensive equipment or with what other members of a research group are doing (Cryer, 2006). There are also less obvious factors that should be considered. Among these are the significant hidden costs some research entails. Postal surveys, for example, can be surprisingly expensive and, because research often takes longer than initially projected, the costs involved are often commensurately higher. The most important of the less obvious factors to be considered, however, is the most commonly misunderstood. Overawed by the imposing number of pages that need to be filled the initial temptation to which some beginning research students succumb is to be over-ambitious in regard to the amount of work they propose to undertake. They usually do this simply to ensure they have sufficient research material to cover that empty space. But, even those who do not succumb to this temptation generally find as the research progresses that their awe rapidly dissipates in the face of a more urgent problem: how to fit all they would like to write within such confining boundaries? The price of over-ambition can be high. It might, on the one hand prevent completion of the thesis on time. On the other, it might affect the way in which the thesis is written: lacking the room to be discursive, a primary requirement of empirical and exegetic theses, the writer instead will be forced to be narrative. Should this be the case the examiners of the thesis might not be as forgiving as shown in the following instance:

One drawback of the very broad scope of the thesis is that each of the topics discussed could only receive a relatively sketchy treatment. One could argue that each of the chapters could easily be a thesis topic in itself. However, it was obviously the author's choice to provide a broad overview...

(Holbrook & Dally, 2003, p.11)

All qualitative theses are implicitly narrative but phenomenological research, for example, is explicitly so. In this case narrative imposes problems of its own:

...narrative data must be voluminous if they are to make their point. They are voluminous because a story teller does not usually go straight to the point. Indeed the glory of narrative is as much in the journey as in the destination.

(Thody, 2006, p.147)

Therefore, in both discursive and narrative theses, length requirement will determine how restrictive the title ought to be. It is usual in order to determine the restrictions, and for the examiners to understand the logic explaining them, to have an explicit Delimitations and Key Assumptions section in either the introduction or methods chapter of the thesis. (Limitations are imposed by circumstance, delimitations by choice.) This section will not only define, with explanation, the nature of the delimitations applied but will also explain the key assumptions upon which the research is premised. It is of course a *sine qua non* of research that assumptions should be soundly based for all that follows in the thesis will stand or fall upon the degree to which they are valid. This is particularly the case when a thesis opens with a statement like the following: 'Based on the assumption that ... my aim is to...' If the premise for the assumption is not soundly based why should the examiners bother to read any further?

- *Is the research material accessible?* Before a research proposal is accepted the supervisor/s will need to feel confident that the information required to answer the question/s can be gathered. This aspect of research can also spring surprises on beginning researchers. Students conducting empirical research, for example, often discover to their dismay how difficult it is to get a sufficiently large sample of individuals who are willing to participate in their research. Students conducting qualitative undertakings often find it difficult to gain access to appropriate research participants. Qualitative research, in this regard, has a significant gendered component because in many research settings access is gender sensitive. Male researchers, for example, may find that their gender constrains the sensitive data that females are willing to share; female researchers may similarly find that in some cultural settings male participants are not forthcoming. In the case of both empirical and qualitative approaches gaining access to individuals within corporate structures might require a lengthy approval process involving various levels of management each of whom, if they approve the research, could make access conditional. The problems of adequate sample size and access are, in fact, so fraught that some supervisors advise students to resolve them first before deciding upon the specifics of the research project they want to undertake. A useful strategy is to read as many studies as possible which have used a research design similar to that being considered to see how other researchers overcame the associated problems. In most cases it will be found that site and sample selection were planned around the researcher's ability to fill a particular role (Marshall & Rossman, 2006).

The grim reality, however, is that many fertile fields of research are effectively closed because the relevant research material is inaccessible. This is normally, though, relatively easy to ascertain. Of greater concern, and less easy to ascertain in advance, is the role of 'gatekeepers' in research. They will always be there, supervisors, examiners, librarians and university administrators, for example, will all, of necessity, impose limitations to a researcher's freedom of action. Generally, however, their actions will be benign, regulated and predictable. The same might not be the case with those 'gatekeepers', outside the confines of the university, who control, implicitly or explicitly (as in the case of corporate management) access to the required research material. Keep in mind that the annals of research are replete with examples of researchers who have seen years of work drain away when the gate to their material has suddenly been locked. So, if gatekeepers have the power to do so or, even, to withdraw permission to use material already accessed, the risks of either or both actually happening will have to be carefully considered. Confidentiality agreements with gatekeepers also need careful consideration for they might, for example, restrict a researcher's ability to present conference papers and seminars or to publish their work. Examiners too might also be required to sign the agreement (Denholm, 2007).

- *Is the research ethical?* Ethics is a broad issue in research for it incorporates both values and morals. There is, though, no clear distinction between these two systems: values are the conceptual rules that define right from wrong while morals correspond to a society's attitude towards what is actually done in that society. In this sense values are defined internally, morals externally. It is possible, therefore, to have values and yet be considered immoral. Ethics reflect this distinction in the sense that they might be prescriptive or descriptive. The former might be defined as sets of professional values and morals codified into a formal system. All universities have these. They might apply, for example, to plagiarism and to the manner in which research involving animals or humans is conducted. Where these codes apply, ethical clearance is necessary for all research that falls within the definition provided by the university. The clearances are generally necessary irrespective of where in the world the research is to be conducted; they are not generally provided retrospectively; and neither do they exempt the researcher from any other ethics clearances that might be required from other authorities: hospitals or schools, for example. These are the researcher's responsibility to obtain and, as in the case of seeking permission to gain access to research participants, can be very time consuming. This is why, if ethics clearance is needed, every effort should be made to have the necessary clearances already in place at the start of the research project. This is another instance of the importance of long-term planning.

Descriptive ethics, on the other hand, are not codified. They are sets of understandings about what is or is not acceptable and carry with them varying levels of praise or censure. So a researcher might receive praise for asking a balanced research question. (Researchers are often socialised, for example, to ask negative questions about marginalised communities and to ignore questions that might shed more positive light [Mertens, 2003].) The same researcher may be censured for the manner in which the research literature has been treated. (It is possible, for example, to quote another researcher accurately and yet do so in a context that distorts the original meaning of the quotation.)

3.13 REFINING THE TITLE

1. There are some fundamental things a thesis title should not do. One, for example, is to be formulated in such a way as to preclude discussion: *Why private hospitals are more efficient than public hospitals.* A title like this would be acceptable, however, when qualified: *The 1995 Hospitals Act: Why private hospitals are considered more efficient than public hospitals.* But, usually only when the thesis writing process has entered its closing phase, is the wording of the title, particularly of exegetic and qualitative theses, finalised. Insights revealed as the research, and the researcher's level of expertise, develop enables finalisation (Dunleavy, 2003). Nonetheless, care with each word in each of the working titles used during this iterative process is helpful, since the working title assists the researcher to retain focus. Although the following advice applies to research questions it is equally apposite to the anchoring role of the title:

Clearly stated research questions have great value in bringing the research back on track in those situations when complications or side issues threaten to take it off course. Being able to step back from the complications and details, and to refer again to research questions, can be of great assistance.

(Punch, 2006, p.37)

The wording of the title should also assist examiners when they read it to understand accurately the thesis writer's intention. For this reason examiners will usually expect to see definitions in the text of all the key terms that appear in the title and to see those terms, as defined, frequently and coherently applied (Dunleavy, 2003). Learning that words should not be used loosely is an important aspect of the thesis writing process for a negative response from examiners can be expected if this has been done:

X cannot quite decide whether the thesis is focussing on...foreign policy, policy-making or the policy-making process. The thesis title refers to foreign policy. Chapter 1 claims that the thesis is about foreign policy-making, while throughout the thesis there is reference to the policy-making process.

(Cited in Holbrook & Dally, 2003, p.14)

This is not the sort of comment a thesis writer wants in the examiner's report so, each time the title is revised during the writing process interrogate each of the key words used: *What issues (vague) affect student (which students?) choice?(of what?)*

2. Key words are important for an additional reason. Dissertation Abstracts uses key words to index thousands of thesis titles a year. Thus, to make retrieval easier and more accurate ensure not only that the thesis title contains words other researchers are likely to use when conducting a key word search but also that words adding little to an understanding of the contents of the thesis are eliminated: *a study of,* or *an investigation of,* for example, are normally self-evident and, thus, redundant. Sub-titles also often fall into this category although it might sometimes be necessary, in order to prevent misunderstanding, to add details in parenthesis. To add clarity they are necessary, for example, in the following title: *The role of non-governmental agencies in the making of Mercosur (Brazil, Argentina, Uruguay, Paraguay).* The information in parenthesis in the title *A comparison of the discourses of religion on public health (Uganda)* indicates that similar studies have been, or could be, conducted in other countries and that this study is a particular contribution to a broader understanding of the issue under investigation.

3. In general thesis titles, in the interests of clarity, ought to be as concise as possible. Ideally, they should be defined in one line. Because of their inherent focus the titles of empirical projects lend themselves, in particular, to this type

of brevity: 'Restricted Spanning Trees and Graph Partitioning' (Lam, 1999), for example. Two or three lines might, however, be necessary to describe a particular project adequately. Notice how much information is provided (the theoretic context, the method and a specific research boundary), and how concisely it is imparted, in the following example: *Workers changing work: a cross-sectional case study analysis of workplace change at Transit Removals Limited*. Titles longer than three lines begin to run counter to the very specific purpose of a title. Although there are exceptions, particularly in fine arts for example where reference to a number of works and contexts often needs to be made, it is unusual for thesis titles to be longer than three lines. Ultimately the researcher, together with their supervisor/s, will need to decide how, within the constraints described above, they should best construct the title of the thesis.

ENDNOTE

1   Differences between individuals or groups are compared incrementally in order to develop a grounded theory.

CHAPTER 4

Supervision

Hamlet: *Do you see yonder cloud that's almost in shape of a camel?*

Polonius: *By the Mass, and 'tis like a camel indeed.*

Hamlet: *Methinks it is like a weasel.*

Polonius: *It is backed like a weasel.*

Hamlet: *Or like a whale?*

Polonius: *Very like a whale.*

(Shakespeare, *Hamlet, Prince of Denmark*, 3.3, 339–344).

4.1 INTRODUCTION

1. Supervision needs to be understood within the context of academic research communities. Features of these are self-sufficiency and self-direction but not isolation. In this sense they are communities of individuals at different levels of expertise each of whom either implicitly or explicitly, learn from each other (Conrad, 2006). Review by academic peers, for example, underlies every aspect of a research community's life (Marsh, 2006). From this perspective some of the best advice received by thesis researchers might come from within these communities. It might, for example, be suggestions made by academics at other universities in response to a candidate's conference paper, or be helpful feedback from reviewers of a journal article based upon research for the thesis (Conrad, 2006). There is, nonetheless, need for ongoing direction and support if research students (including post-docs) are to become members of and derive maximum support from their own research community. Legitimate entry is the crucial first step:

   Granting the newcomers legitimacy is important because they are likely to come short of what the community regards as competent engagement. Only with enough legitimacy can all their inevitable stumblings and violations become opportunities for learning rather than cause for dismissal, neglect, or exclusion.

   (Wenger, 1998, p.101)

This is why supervisors and the quality of the support they provide rank among the most important factors in the timely completion of a sound thesis. It is also the primary reason why each has been among the most researched aspects of the thesis production process. The results of this research indicate the nature of the relationship between student and supervisor is inherently complex because it involves interplay between distinct elements. It requires both affirmation (pastoral support and advice) and advocacy (support for funding). It also has a significant contractual aspect for the parties to the supervisory process have both rights and obligations stipulated in university policies. Perhaps most importantly, it involves a unique 'chemistry' between two or more individuals. This close, but not necessarily personal relationship is of particular importance to doctoral candidates for whom the length of the research process is more enduring than for masters researchers. However, in both cases it is clear that the necessary interplay of the elements of the supervisory relationship needs to be complementary if all of the parties are to benefit. In this sense, therefore, it is not mere participation in a supervisory relationship that counts, but the quality of the participation. It is in this sense also that the crucial difference between education and training lies. Because they do not share the use to which their actions are put trainees are not partners in a shared activity. In education, however, participants share in a common activity and have an equal interest in its accomplishment (Biesta, 2008).

4.2 DIFFERENCES IN PERCEPTION

1. At some universities the terms 'tutor', 'advisor', 'promoter' or 'mentor' are used instead of 'supervisor'; the choice of term denoting a subtle difference in the manner in which each university perceives the nature of the relationship between academic and thesis writer. For example, 'supervisor' implies a directive function. It is primarily for this reason that some universities apply the term 'supervisor' to the masters process and 'promoter' to the doctoral. In part the reason for the different usages reflects the theories of power implicit in the supervisory relationship: pedagogy understood as the active, productive power relations between student, supervisor and knowledge (Manathunga et al., 2006). From this perspective the challenge for the supervisor is to conceptualise and exercise power that is neither conflictual nor simply consensual: power that permits necessary control over a candidate but which does not unnecessarily inhibit his or her independence. Part of the challenge lies in the reconciliation of contradictory impulses. On the one hand the task of a supervisor is Socratic *maieusis*, the bringing of students' minds to birth (Aspin, 2009). On the other, one of the social functions of an intellectual position is to reproduce itself among the next generation (Mackenzie, 2009).

The relationship between teaching and supervision

2. Another and related reason for the use of different terms lies in the manner in which each university interprets the hybrid space (Tennant & Roberts, 2007) between supervision and teaching: is the nexus tenuous because supervisors should only be expected to provide guidance, or is it strong because supervision is a unique and sophisticated form of teaching? These questions are particularly pertinent at explicitly research led universities where 'research' and 'knowledge' tend to be valued above 'teaching' and 'learning' (Ferman, 2002). Not only is each set driven by different reward structures, but the former are considered fundamental to the latter. Furthermore, it does not necessarily follow that there is a positive correlation between being a good teacher and a good researcher (Rowland, 2006). Nor is it to suggest that teaching is a transmissive process, for learners do not necessarily understand what they are taught in the same way as their teachers: "'sharing an understanding" is not the same as "having the same understanding'" (Rowland, 2006, p.64).

3. A more constructive enquiry based model of learning is, in fact, appropriate in the context of supervision because much of what academic supervisors understand is tacit: they know more than they can tell. Their research experience and membership of discrete discourse communities, in other words, means the knowledge acquired is always ahead of the capability of its possessor to explicate it (Parry, 2007, p.35). Moreover, an open and obvious knowledge of rhetorical convention is not necessarily a precondition for participation in discourse. An inability by some supervisors to make explicit their knowledge of these conventions makes them inadequate to teach research students how to participate in relevant discourse communities (Lee & Aitchison, 2009). This inadequacy is serious because non-explicated discourse knowledge forms a considerable part of the cultural capital of both disciplines and of methodological approaches to research. There is an additional reason why being able to tell and being able to do are not equivalent (Wenger, 1998). As in the case of Adam and Eve after their expulsion from Paradise, supervisors cannot go back from their transformed perspective. They cannot, thus, fully comprehend the difficulties untransformed candidate researchers experience when they confront thresholds the supervisors have long since passed (Meyer & Land, 2003):

    [My] supervisor assumes that I already know [sic] what I was doing in a research environment...That I knew the administrative procedures of my new depart-ment...That I knew how to conduct a major piece of research...that I knew how to write a journal article. There was no 'apprenticeship' or coaching.

    (Cited in Manathunga, 2005, p.226)

    For this reason a supervisor who answers questions a candidate has not thought to ask (Cryer, 2006) is a treasure.

Inherent differences

4. In addition to possible differences in the interpretation of the relationship between supervision and teaching, there is also an inherent difference in the way in which candidates and experienced supervisors perceive the nature of the relationship between them. For the candidates the thesis is central to their intellectual endeavour and, to a significant extent, to their life. For supervisors, however, often with a number of students to supervise, supervision is simply one among a number of academic tasks (Soliman, 1999). This explains why some thesis writers might find the best possible support is available from other thesis writers. This applies even if each is writing on significantly different topics, for writing a thesis is immediate and central to their lives too (Conrad, 2006). There are though some supervisors for whom supervision ranks more highly among the tasks they need to perform. It is, for example, important for less experienced supervisors, normally new academics, to build a good research and publication record in tandem with a solid record in supervision (Denholm & Evans, 2007).

5. There is also often a difference in the manner in which students in the humanities perceive the student supervisor relationship from those in the sciences; the latter, unlike the former, are often surrounded by people on paper but none in actuality (Marshall & Rossman, 2006). Lacking the collegiality of a laboratory and the direct mentoring of a supervisor involved with them in a joint project students in the humanities are often envious of the quality of supervision enjoyed by students in the sciences. The following question by a doctoral candidate indicates the delicate balance often required of researchers in the humanities if they are to remain integrated with their research community: 'How can I specialize my own interests while staying generalizable enough to my peers?' (cited in Marshall & Rossman, 2006, p.216). For this reason thesis writers in the humanities often report that the extent to which they feel supported depends significantly on the efforts made by their supervisor/s (Parry, 2007).

6. However, it is also sometimes the case in the sciences that companionship is more illusion than reality (Phillips & Pugh, 2005). This is evident in the following comment by a supervisor in biochemistry:

    ...we hope that we'll have a senior PhD student or a post-doc in the lab who can nurture new ones. That's a critical issue. If you don't have that senior layer in the laboratory it can be very, very difficult for the student.

    (Cited in Parry, 2007, p.45)

    Often this difficulty is exacerbated by high staff turnover in many laboratories in consequence of unstable funding and changing priorities (Cumming, 2009). But, even when nurtured, the companionship students in the sciences enjoy comes at a price. Not only do they frequently need to take on trust findings established by their immediate predecessors (Cumming, 2009), they are also often expected to produce fast research outputs irrespective of personal considerations and are set step-by-step tasks to ensure as few errors as possible are made (Parry, 2007). Nonetheless, even in these circumstances, supervisors sometimes need to 'carry' students. This is apparent in the following excerpt where supervisors and their students had been conducting research under contract to organisations outside the university:

We know of cases where the supervisors have analyzed the data collected by the candidate and written the report required to fulfill the contract because of the candidate's failure to meet the deadlines.

(Denholm, 2007, p.75)

4.3 RESEARCH GROUPS

1. The formation of research groups is a useful way to surmount some of the obstacles research students from all disciplines might confront. In the sciences these groups are often simply the regular meetings held by a research team. In both the sciences and humanities all of the candidates of one or more supervisors might be brought together for group meetings less intense and thus often more open and facilitative than when student and supervisor meet alone (Conrad, 2007). Researchers too might form their own supportive communities. The individuals in these groups need not necessarily be in the same discipline area; more important is their willingness both to offer and receive support (Fisher, 2006):

I have [set up] a research group that is an instant source of confirmation, a source of people who are at the same stage, people to talk with … not in a competitive way but in a problem solving way.

(Cited in Manathunga, 2005, p.231)

Alternatively these communities could be virtual with thesis writers constructing a web page or blog that describes their research project and invites email contributions from researchers with similar interests (Conrad, 2006).

4.4 THE HISTORICAL CONTEXT

1. Thesis supervision is a practice that, in parts of Europe, dates back almost three centuries. It has since become the manner in which research communities reproduce their membership. In this sense, supervision is a shared history of learning. This shared history is not, though, akin to an

object handed down from one generation of researchers to the next. It is, instead, an evolving Socratic dialogue where newcomers are introduced to a version of what went before (Wenger, 1998). As originally conceived in the eighteenth century the mentor/mentee relationship central to supervision was modeled on the concept of apprenticeship where identity transformation was a consequence of the mentee's initial legitimate peripheral participation (Wenger, 1998). In the second half of the twentieth century, however, the traditional model gradually became less sustainable. The move away from the apprentice–master model of research education to one of supervision as a shared responsibility (Krone, 2006) holds significant consequence for contemporary thesis writers and explains, for example, their need to form research groups.

Increased student diversity

2. Consequent upon the post–Second World War economic recovery and 'baby-boom' in the West, the rapid expansion, during the 1960s and 1970s, in university undergraduate enrolments was a precursor to the beginning, from the 1980s, of a sustained increase in the number of postgraduate research students. (The increase was not, however, uniform. In the United States, for example, the number of doctoral completions has continued to increase while the number of males undertaking doctoral research has fallen.) By the late 1990s in the United Kingdom and United States the number of postgraduates was increasing proportionately more than undergraduates (Emilsson & Johnsson, 2007). An indication of the overall trend is apparent in postgraduate enrolments at British universities. Currently about 13 per cent of all students at these universities are postgraduate. Just prior to the Second World War the percentage was six per cent. Just prior to the First World War only a handful went beyond a bachelor's degree (Simpson, 1983).

3. The overall increase from the 1980s in the number of postgraduate research students both accompanied and precipitated other changes at universities. One was the development of research profiles in disciplines without a substantial research tradition. Academics in, for example, fine arts, have had less time than those in research-focused disciplines like medicine to develop supervisory protocols. Another change has been an increase in the diversity of the postgraduate population; a reflection of a similar change that had earlier taken place within the undergraduate body. Currently postgraduates are no longer as economically, culturally and ethnically uniform as they had been until the start of the second half of the twentieth century; they are no longer in the traditional age bracket of 18–25 years, they are no longer predominantly male and a far higher proportion are conducting their

research part-time. In the United Kingdom and Australasia for example, about half of all doctoral candidates are part-time (Evans, 2006). This dramatic change in the profile of postgraduate students has led to a greater demand for a customer orientation in postgraduate programs in general and specifically to greater sensitivity to the quality of supervision provided. In the supervision guidelines of one university, for example, the responsibilities of supervisors have trebled while those of the candidate have remained almost static (Grant & Pearson, 2007).

Fiscal constraints

4. An additional widespread change has been a tightening of the fiscal constraints within which universities operate. This tightening is a consequence of the steep rise in the cost of running universities, currently far more enlarged and technologically sophisticated even when compared to those of the early 1990s. The increased scrutiny and stringency these cost increases induced in major donors, both private and public, prompted universities to diversify their revenue base. The urgent need to do so was also a consequence of corporate and government funded agencies increasing their research output relative to those of universities. Universities, therefore, had not only lost their exceptional status but were being forced to compete with one another for funding. As a result university management gave increased attention, for example, to marketing research findings and to increasing the number of fee-paying international students. They also gave even greater attention to postgraduate students for when universities are state subsidised the subsidy received for a postgraduate is generally far higher than for an undergraduate. There are many reasons explaining the increase in the number of postgraduates at universities since the 1980s, so it would be unreasonable and excessively cynical to explain the increase in numbers purely in terms of their pecuniary value to universities. Nonetheless, by enriching and maturing the total student population through their experience and because they are major contributors to the research output of universities postgraduates also have marketing value in addition to the increased subsidy they attract.

5. Initially this subsidy tended to be granted either on the basis of the number of postgraduates registered during the course of an academic year, irrespective of whether they passed or not, or on the basis of the number who completed their degrees, only limited regard being paid to the length of time it took them to do so. The inefficiency inherent in this system led to the widespread introduction from the late 1990s of 'performance based funding' for universities. On this basis the increased government subsidy would continue

to be paid only if a recognised course was successfully completed within a stipulated time. In effect this new funding system rewarded universities for successful completions within the stipulated time and effectively punished those with low success rates (Wilks, 2006). This change introduced a new element of urgency to the student–supervisor relationship because university administrators, in addition to their moral obligation, now had a direct financial interest in the successful and timely completion of theses. The trickle-down effect was for supervisor performance to be measured by the number of on-time completions. This, in turn, drove supervisors to take on only the best candidates if they could manage to do so (Tennant & Roberts, 2007). The universities reciprocated by verging on risk analysis when selecting candidates for higher degrees (Manathunga, 2005) and by increasing turn-over time by reducing the number of years required for the completion of a doctoral thesis (Krone, 2006).

6. While these alterations to the nature of the relationship between student and supervisor were consequences of the efforts by university management to increase revenue, other changes to the manner in which supervisors and research students relate were a consequence of simultaneous efforts by management to decrease expenditure. The largest ongoing expense at universities is staff salaries. Pulled by the need to economise and pushed by the need to be flexible and competitive, university administrators have tended to adopt consistent strategies: to reduce the number of academics on the payroll relative to the number of students, to remove the implicit prefix 'life' from the definition of 'tenure' and to maintain a set ratio of academic staff members on fixed term contracts. The collective consequences for the supervisory process of these changes to university employment practice have been twofold. One has been an increase in the ratio of research students relative to the number of academic staff able to supervise them. The other has been an increased emphasis upon research output as the primary work performance indicator of academic staff. Because of a relative lack of special incentives, this development has led to a decrease in the emphasis on teaching of which supervision is an implicit part (Taylor, 2001).

7. Care needs to be taken though to understand these consequences as an overall trend rather than as universally applicable. Departments of physics, for example, have tended to be relatively unaffected by the trends, the ratio between staff and research students having remained relatively constant. The traditional mentoring approach to supervision in most departments of physics has, therefore, remained substantially in place. In addition, university enrolments, both in total and within departments, often defy overall trends by fluctuating significantly from one year to the next or cyclically over a period of years.

4.5 THE CURRENT CONTEXT

1. University administrators and academics have not been blind to the consequences of these recent historical developments upon the quality of supervision and have attempted to ameliorate the effects. One of the strategies adopted has been to improve the efficiency and effectiveness of the supervisory process by introducing formal courses on the theory and practice of supervision, academics being obliged to attend them before being permitted to become supervisors. Another stratagem has been to spread the supervisory 'load' by limiting the number of research students any one academic is allowed to supervise. The extent of the limitation varies from one institution to another; some have a maximum of three, in others it is as high as ten (Phillips & Pugh, 2005). Some also have a specific limit to the number of doctoral candidates who can be included within the overall limitation. However, these limits, as in the case of the overall trends in supervision, need to be interpreted in context. At some universities, for example, there is significant back-up support for both supervisors and research students from research tutors and other academics in service roles (Phillips & Pugh, 2005). Much also depends on what particular universities or supervisors understand as supervision. During an interview one supervisor, for example, said:

There was no student whose thesis I read in full. And I told them at the beginning. And I said I'm not going to be reading more than half of this and if you are uneasy about that, I won't supervise you. I will recommend someone else. Because…it is more than just writing a thesis. It's about learning to be independent. And I think that's one of the great things in scholarship, learning but it's tough, you've got to learn to rely on your own judgement and not to run to the supervisor for every problem that you have. And that's the test in the end. And you can fail it.

(Cited in Tennant & Roberts, 2007, p.25)

It can also be the case that limitations to the number of students an academic might supervise do not apply to the number of students they might jointly supervise. As a result of an international trend towards joint supervision of both masters and doctoral researchers, this number can be considerable. 'Loopholes' in regulations limiting the number of students any one individual can supervise has not been the only reason why the attempt to spread the supervisory 'load' has had only limited success. A common complaint by heads of department is that the same academics tend, year after year, to supervise students while others in the same department do not. The usual reasons for this are that the individuals who do consistently supervise generally have either or both of the following attributes: they have good rapport with students and/or are specialists in fields popular with researchers.

2. One of the possible consequences of the lack of spread of the supervisory 'load' is tension between those academics who have a disproportionately high 'load' and those who do not. The source of this tension lies in the nature of supervision: it is an extremely time consuming process. This is important because although the number of students successfully supervised is a valuable addition to an academic's *curriculum vitae* it is not as valuable as the number of research publications produced. While it can be argued that both supervisors and their research students author a significant body of research literature the reality is that those academics with fewer supervisory responsibilities tend to have more time to publish. Some universities have attempted to compensate the time supervisors spend on thesis writers by diminishing the amount of time they are expected to provide formal lectures in proportion to their supervisory load: five per cent less time spent lecturing, for example, per student supervised. These attempts have, however, had limited success because, in practice, the reductions have proved to be both difficult to translate into concrete terms and to implement within a meaningful timeframe.

4.6 THE DIFFICULTY OF DEFINING THE SUPERVISORY PROCESS

1. Ameliorating the effects on supervision of increased financial constraints and a rise in student numbers relative to available academic staff have placed university administrators and academic managers in an invidious position. Nothing indicates this better than the difficulties they face when attempting more clearly to define the supervisory process in order to monitor its effectiveness and ensure consistency of quality. To date, the main monitoring mechanism has been the use of research student satisfaction surveys. By nature, though, these instruments are not only retrospective but also blunt in respect to such a complex process as supervision. A more prospective approach, a formal contract between supervisor and student in which the roles, responsibilities and expectations of each are clearly delineated, also runs into similar difficulties. The nature of the supervisory relationship includes so many intangibles and unique elements that any attempt to define these roles, responsibilities and expectations runs the risk of exposing universities to extensive and expensive litigation should students perceive a shortcoming in regard to their interpretation of any one of them.

Learning contracts

2. However, an implicit contractual obligation does underlie the thesis writing process: the university agrees to support the research and the student agrees to work and remain focused (Rowarth & Green, 2006). The fact that this implicit

contractual obligation is, for all practical purposes, between student and supervisor (Cryer, 2006) is reflected in the concept of a 'learning contract'. Used in lieu of a formal contract, 'learning contracts' list broad principles to the spirit of which students and supervisors are expected to adhere. When drawn up by a student and supervisor/s together the agreement has the advantages not only of encouraging students to be more deeply involved in their own program planning (Wisker, 2005) but also of cementing more closely the relationship between the parties to it. Most universities, however, have a document indicating the responsibilities of supervisors and students. When this is the case a learning contract signed by both student and supervisor/s might simply reflect the following:

We, the student and supervisor/s, have read the document Responsibilities of Supervisors and Students. We agree with the principles in the document and will endeavour to work together in the spirit of them.

Time spent

3. In tandem with 'learning contracts' some universities have also attempted to ensure consistency in the quality of supervision by defining the number of hours a supervisor, at a minimum, should be expected to spend on each student supervised. But informal surveys of academics to establish such a minimum have produced results roughly within the range of thirty to eighty hours per annum. These results pose a number of questions. What factors, for example, explain the breadth of the range and how did those academics surveyed think the number of hours they considered appropriate ought to be distributed during the course of the year? The more important question, though, is what is meant by the term 'time spent'? Does it apply only to consultation time or does it include the time supervisors invest in reading and commenting on thesis drafts prior to consultation? Students tend to adopt the former definition, supervisors the latter. Moreover, attempts to reconcile these definitions in order to identify a standard minimum time that supervisors ought to spend on each student have confronted two immediate difficulties. First, face-to-face time for a student involved in a joint project with a supervisor or supervisors will differ significantly from that of a student involved in an individual project. Second, the quality of student writing and the degree of independence students develop varies greatly between individuals. It can also vary according to discipline:

Solving a problem in engineering often means having to build something before an experiment can be run. Consequently, even though the student may know exactly what experiment needs to be run on exactly what system, the student may 'disappear for two years' to build the system.

(Lovitts, 2007, p.78)

4.7 THE SUPERVISOR'S ROLE

1. The numerous intangibles means each party to the supervisory relationship needs to make as explicit as possible what they expect a supervisor's role to be. The student, for example, needs to ask: 'What do I want my supervisors to do for me?' (Wilks, 2006, p.17). Not only will doing so minimise misunderstanding between each party but will also prevent the dual burden that inadequately supervised researchers sometimes carry: they are inadequately supervised without being aware the supervision is deficient (Phillips & Pugh, 2005). It is only such awareness that will allow them to take action when supervisors fail to meet their responsibilities (Krone, 2006). The supervisor of a joint project will certainly need to ask: 'What do I want the student to contribute?' But, in all cases, it is of benefit to both students and supervisors if the latter provide a statement, on the web or in hardcopy, of their approach to supervision. In the broadest sense the aim of the process is to increase the knowledge and competence of a research initiate (Emilsson & Johnsson, 2007).

2. From a more detailed perspective two factors are central to the achievement of this outcome: the promptness and accuracy of supervisor feedback to students and the frequency of face-to-face meetings between them (Seagram et al., 1998). These meetings, together with, for example, email contact and seminar presentations should be a facet of 'shadowing': a sustained tracking of a research student's progress or lack thereof (Rowarth & Green, 2006). At a minimum, though, supervisors should be expected to identify three factors in a student's work: its strengths, its weaknesses and the means to address the latter. But how they should go about doing so, and to what extent they should go beyond the bare minimum, are elements in a subjective debate. Consider, for example, the following:
    *   The supervisor wants a photocopy of the texts from which all of the quotations in a thesis have been taken.
    *   A supervisor photocopies comments they have made in the margin of drafts of the thesis so as to ensure they are acted upon.

    The fact that some students and supervisors see these actions as entirely legitimate while others might consider them patently unreasonable provides some indication of the range of perceptions at play.

Interpersonal skills and self-insight

3. A question: given the choice, should a prospective research student select a supervisor who is an undisputed authority in his or her field but who has poorly developed interpersonal skills or an individual of lesser authority but whose interpersonal skills are well developed? Because each relationship has an individual chemistry it is readily conceded this question is largely rhetorical.

Nonetheless, research indicates that, for most individuals, the second option would be the wisest choice (Tennant & Roberts, 2007). Numerous reasons explain the wisdom of the choice but perhaps the most important, particularly for doctoral candidates, is the possible intensity of the student supervisor relationship: it is easy for personal issues to become confused with differences of opinion about the thesis. When this happens and the relationship is not open students, justifiably or not, often feel vulnerable because of the ease with which supervisors, subtly or otherwise, can affect progress (Krone, 2006). This type of atmosphere inhibits individual thinking and has the potential to fester relationships. This could lead to a change in supervisor. If this occurs once a student is well into the research the upheaval can make the change the academic equivalent of a messy divorce (Phillips & Pugh, 2005).

4. In fact, as in marriage, it is unusual for students during the course of their research not to have a few disagreements with their supervisor/s (Burton & Steane, 2004a). When these arise it is important that the relationship is such that the differences can be discussed and resolved. The emphasis here is on 'discussed' for even in the most open student–supervisor relationships it is rarely sensible for a student to reject criticism as unjustified (Cryer, 2006). A student's personality and degree of self-insight are, thus, also important ingredients in a supervisory relationship for they need the ability to adjust their definition of the relationship in such a way that it reflects their personal development as a researcher. If, for example, a student continues from the outset to interpret the relationship as one of dependency how can they claim the thesis as their own? This reflexiveness is also required of effective supervisors. They not only need the necessary flexibility, self-insight and ability to recognise the strengths and weaknesses of others, but also of themselves, in order to be able to adopt a variety of roles during the course of the supervisory relationship. They might on different occasions, for example, be required to cast themselves as teacher, critic, guide, supporter and, often, as examiner. Overall, surveys of research students and interviews with supervisors have indicated that the following supervisor attributes are important contributors to the personal development of research students:

    *   when they see a student as an individual whom it is important to understand;
    *   when they schedule regular meetings and appraisals;
    *   when they provide opportunities to be independent;
    *   when supportive comments are made during chance meetings;
    *   when possible problems are foreshadowed;
    *   when there is prompt feedback on written work (Conrad, 2003);
    *   when they make an effort to bring research students together;
    *   when they break down tasks into manageable steps;
    *   when they provide guidance not only in regard to the thesis but also in terms of the student's personal and professional development (Manathunga, 2005).

4.8 JOINT PUBLICATION

1. A considerate supervisor will either forgo having his or her name appear first in a joint publication or agree to not having their names appear at all when the research is predominantly the student's (Marsh, 2006). (In publications with a number of authors common practice is that the name of the primary author should be placed first in the list and that of the second author placed last.) In some circumstances supervisors share authorship of controversial papers in order to protect their students (Lewin, 2001). Such gestures are significant when it is borne in mind that the question of whose name should appear on a publication is ethically and politically loaded and can thus, become a source of ill-feeling between supervisor and student. The invention of the laser is one of the more recent illustrations of this. Charles Townsend won the Nobel Prize for the invention but was subsequently sued by his student Gordon Gould, who claimed he had done most of the work (Taleb, 2007).[1] Supervisors who do insist, either subtly or otherwise, that they should be acknowledged as co-author even when their direct contribution to a paper based upon a student's thesis research has been minimal can create the impression that their research students are mere cannon fodder to further the supervisor's own ambitions (Becher & Trowler, 2001). This is not, by the way, unknown. Nonetheless, supervisors often have an ethical basis for their insistence. They can, for example, claim that the student's association with a more prestigious author is a way of underwriting the quality of an article (Becher & Trowler, 2001). With considerable justification they can also claim it is they who have guided the research and, in the case of most group projects, it is they who initiated the project and acquired funding for it.

2. Group projects, in particular, offer singular challenges to the management of intellectual property because, unless the university already has ownership, the research is owned by several intellects (Denholm, 2007). But the same might also be said of any paper that has undergone revision after peer review. One doctoral candidate after a number of such revisions said: 'I don't think it's my paper anymore. It is group writing. I'm just one of the players' (cited in Golden-Biddle & Locke, 1997, p.100). Currently, however, good practice recognises that authorship comes with responsibilities: all share the blame should there be subsequent problems with the paper. In this light all named authors should have contributed significantly to both the writing of a publication and to the research it describes (Denholm, 2006).

4.9 MATCHING STRATEGIES

1. Institutional and departmental practices to match students who fit the criteria for undertaking a research degree with an appropriate supervisor or supervisors

vary. Student and supervisor/s might negotiate directly as a result, for example, of internal recruitment by supervisors of both masters and doctoral students. Alternatively academics in a department might meet and discuss, on the basis of a student's thesis proposal and academic record, which of them would be the most appropriate supervisor/s (Graham & Grant, 2000). In each case though, if group research is involved, the prospective student is also assessed on the basis of the extent to which they fit the research culture of the group: '…we have a lab meeting after we've all talked to the prospective student, and (we) decide whether it's going to work or not' (Parry, 2007, p.43). In each case also, it is the supervisor who makes the final decision about whether they agree to take on a particular research student. Understandably their preference, whenever possible, will be for students they think have the greatest likelihood of succeeding (Burton & Steane, 2004b).

4.10 MAKING AN INFORMED ASSESSMENT

1. In order to establish a high research profile as early as possible prospective researchers should ideally attach themselves to an appropriate high profile supervisor in the most prestigious department in their field. To the extent that the matching strategies of such departments permit prospective researchers choice in the selection of supervisor/s seeking answers to the following questions in, for example, the university calendar, departmental websites or handbooks, will assist in making an informed assessment: what are their research interests; what have they published recently and what is their supervisory experience? (Murray, 2003, p.45). In addition, potential supervisors often have theses they hold in particularly high regard, these (if recent) might include their own. Reading them will provide some insight into how the prospective supervisor thinks (Mauch & Birch, 1998). This is particularly important in those fields where research communities comprise ideologically divided cliques. A sociology professor, for example, said:

Sociology is such a diverse discipline theoretically that it really would be very problematic if you actually didn't let students make judgements about who they relate to, and which theorists they will use.

(Cited in Parry, 2007, p.86)

There are usually three factors in a successful match: the degree of alignment of a supervisor's expertise with the thesis topic; the extent to which personalities are compatible and the extent to which theoretical positions match. Research on the relative importance of these factors indicates the following:

Some supervisors and students were willing to accept a high match in two areas and sacrifice the third. The area that most supervisors were willing to sacrifice was the

match in methodology; whereas students were more willing to sacrifice the topic…
Both groups thought the match in interpersonal working patterns was critical.

(Tennant & Roberts, 2007, p.22)

2. Once a possible supervisor has been identified his or her reputation among other research students should be investigated. This should be done in awareness, though, that the chemistry of each relationship is different: a wonderful supervisor for one student might not prove so for another (Burton & Steane, 2004b). Also, particularly for masters students, assurances should be sought that the individual does not plan to be away for any significant period of time either during the actual degree period or any possible extension periods. (It is not unusual for doctoral supervisors to be away for extended periods prior to completion of the degree.) If the potential supervisor does plan to be away and a decision is made to go ahead ascertain what arrangements will be in place to ensure an interim supervisor will be available. A situation where a research student is left unsupervised for more than a few weeks at a time should, whenever possible, be avoided. (Unforeseen events do happen, a supervisor, for example, might resign and take up a position elsewhere. Should this happen beware of assurances that supervision will continue via email. Even with the best of intentions new priorities intervene and only very rarely are such arrangements satisfactory.)

3. Enquiries should also be made about the number of students already being supervised by the potential supervisor and, particularly in the case of masters research, the number of those students who plan to submit at the same time the prospective researcher intends to do so. If the number is significant students should incorporate this into the planning of the thesis by bringing their own completion date—as opposed to the university's completion date—forward. This will help prevent competing with others for the supervisor's attention at a crucial time in the thesis preparation process.

4. If English is not a student's first language there could be additional issues to consider in regard to supervision. This is both because they may require more supervision than native speakers and because, in addition to language, there might also be layers of cultural difference that contribute further challenges (Murray, 2003). The corollary is that language and other cultural differences might also arise when the student is a native speaker of English and the supervisor is a non-native speaker.

5. There also needs to be awareness of the possibility (though it is more likely to occur in doctoral rather than masters research) that the evolution of the topic might serve to make the initial choice of supervisor inappropriate. If this happens a good supervisor will help match the student with someone more suitable. Nonetheless, bear in mind that remaining broadly within the original topic area and with the same supervisor/s are significant factors in the timely completion of theses.

4.11 JOINT SUPERVISION

1. Most universities adopt a team or committee approach to doctoral supervision. This is also progressively becoming the case in regard to master's supervision. There might, though, be differences between the regulations governing supervision and what happens in practice. In some of the sciences and in, for example statistics, the names of joint supervisors might appear on official documents but only one is the *de facto* supervisor. Referring to this a supervisor in physics said: '…we have different areas, that's how we are' (cited in Cryer, 2006, p.45). In fact joint supervision is an umbrella term that describes a number of possible relationships between supervisors and student. The usual are:
   • co-supervision (50/50)—a roughly equal contribution by each supervisor;
   • primary/secondary(70/30)—primary responsibility rests with one supervisor but the other makes a significant contribution in a particular area of expertise;
   • primary/advisory (80/20)—a limited contribution by a specialist advisor; university regulations often make it possible for a suitably qualified person who is not a member of staff to act as advisory supervisor;
   • primary/ 'back-up'—the 'back-up' covers for the primary supervisor when he or she is away (University of Auckland, 2000).
   There should be a jointly agreed rationale, based upon the requirements of the research, for the type of joint supervision adopted. This rationale should be flexible enough to change should the subsequent needs of the study make that necessary.

Risks and benefits

2. The benefits of defined and substantiated joint supervision go beyond the additional expertise and perspectives to which a research student will be exposed. An expanded range of networks and resources is but one example. There are, however, also risks to joint supervision (University of Auckland, 2000). One is the impression, particularly if both supervisors are senior academics, that a student's freedom to express his or her ideas will be threatened. Much also depends on the personal relationship between the supervisors. This is particularly the case when, having been given conflicting advice, a student appears to be playing one supervisor off against the other. Conflict can also occur when theoretic perspectives differ. A philosophy student recalled:

   …we tended to have consultations together; they would sort of both be in the same room, and it wasn't working for anybody…I found that it was more productive if I saw them separately. Eventually…I had a bit of a dispute…and I had to choose.

   (Cited in Cryer, 2006, p.45)

107

There is also a particular danger to co-supervision, for a student runs the risk of being without an individual who is personally responsible for 'driving' the supervisory process. In this case having two supervisors or more is equivalent to having no supervisor. There is also the mundane but also very real problem of bringing supervisors together for a joint meeting. It can be difficult enough when each is in the same building, when in separate buildings or even campuses a joint meeting can become a major planning exercise.

The importance of protocols

3. Strong protocols are an 'insurance policy': things are less likely to go wrong if everyone knows their role and responsibilities (Krone, 2006). But, because the working relationship with each joint supervisor is likely to be different, it is normally better at the start of the research to meet each separately in order to establish individual protocols. At a subsequent 'establishment' meeting the central questions relating to how the student and supervisors will work together can then be discussed jointly (University of Auckland, 2000):

   - What will be the relative contribution of each supervisor? (Irrespective of the contribution of each, the supervisors should jointly assist and approve the initial thesis proposal so each is clear about what the research project will entail.)
   - How often meetings should be held with each of the supervisors, how many of these should be joint meetings and who should be responsible for calling them? (Aside from co-supervisory relationships, the calling of joint meetings is normally the prerogative of the primary supervisor.)
   - What should be expected of each of the supervisors and what should each expect of the student?
   - What are to be the milestones in the research? (These are important in order to assess progress.)
   - How will each supervisor be kept informed of progress between joint meetings? (Would, for example, emailed reports be acceptable?)

4.12 THE PHASES OF SUPERVISION

1. The completion rate of research degrees in general, and of research degrees in the humanities and social sciences in particular, is not high. One of the reasons is not so much that candidates fail to complete, it is because they never get started. Even in the case of many of those who do complete much of the research time is spent in aimless reading and the remainder in frenzied activity (Ingleby, 2007). The first few months of thesis research are, thus, crucial if the remainder of the time is to be put to effective use. For this reason

students in the sciences are often given close initial direction (Parry, 2007). It is also for this reason that across the disciplines some departments require research students to justify the proposed topic and methods at seminars prior to the start of the research. This ensures there is also input from experienced researchers other than the supervisors at the foundational stage of the work (Moses, 1985). Subsequently the supervisor's task will be to guide and negotiate the transition of the student from dependence to greater degrees of independence. Etienne Wenger's definition of negotiation is particularly apposite to this stage of the student–supervisor relationship:

The concept of negotiation often denotes reaching an agreement between people, as in 'negotiating a price,' but it is not limited to that usage. It is also used to suggest an accomplishment that requires sustained attention and readjustment, as in 'negotiating a sharp curve'. I want to capture both aspects at once…I intend the term negotiation to convey a flavor of continuous interaction, of gradual achievement, and of give-and-take.

(Wenger, 1998, p.54)

2. Negotiating greater independence between supervisor/s and student requires, therefore, different degrees of direction at different times and the attainment of different levels of mutual understanding between supervisor and student as the research progresses. This is the context in which the following discussion of three phases in supervision should be considered: though each phase is generally discernible, the boundary between them is necessarily indistinct and movement between each not necessarily linear. To see them as clearly structured and develop from one to another as a progressive step-like process is to consider supervision, quite unrealistically, as project management (Tennant & Roberts, 2007). Thus, on the basis that negotiating greater independence is an iterative, interactive process the initial phase generally involves the establishment by both student and supervisor/s of mutual expectations and agreed procedures. It also usually requires regular and frequent meetings between them so as to assist the student to start the research process as seamlessly as possible. (This normally translates into one meeting every two to four weeks.) The median phase is marked by the gradual withdrawal by supervisors of the scaffolding erected during the initial phase and by the concomitant sustaining by the student of a balance between support and challenge (Horn, 2005). This often involves the forging of new research identities by research students. A supervisor stated that he knew the transition was taking place when student researchers:

…begin to be the ones who retrieve relevant articles and present them to me…they know what they are looking for and they know what is relevant. Before that you

have to keep saying you should look at this piece, have a look at this, have a look at this, see if you find anything on that. There comes a time when they are coming to you and telling you this is really important.

(Kiley & Wisker, 2009, p.435)

3. In the sciences the transition often becomes apparent when the previous year's trainee now helps new trainees (Wenger, 1998). Some students, however, develop neither direction nor momentum so the supervisor's support and the additional labour involved will need to remain in place. But, even for those students who do develop the necessary confidence, there will, inevitably, be moments of self-doubt when confronting the apparent enormity of the task of writing a thesis. For this reason the pastoral element in the supervisor's role often assumes a greater degree of importance during the median phase than in either of the others. There are also sound academic reasons why some supervisors might at this stage also look, for example, at samples of the data as they are generated. This need not imply lack of confidence in the student, for doing so not only helps supervisors keep abreast of the work but will also assist them to offer more informed advice during the data analysis stage (Carson, 2007).

4. The final phase is often intense and pressured: students face a looming deadline while supervisors generally confront the demands of a number of research students each wanting 'their' supervisor's undivided assistance in order to enable them to meet that deadline. These demands can be particularly exhausting for supervisors coming as they so often do either during, or soon after, the university examination period. However, the unsettling impression some supervisors give at this stage of 'withdrawing' from the supervisory process is not only a consequence of these particular demands and pressures. Unlike students they work on an endless production line of thesis writers; as one group finishes a new group begins.

5. The duration of each of the three phases of supervision will differ according to the unique requirements of each research undertaking. It is, nonetheless, self evident that the first phase should be as brief as possible relative to the others. However, its relative brevity is in inverse relation to its importance, for the subsequent smooth development of the thesis process depends upon the effectiveness of its foundational function. This can be seen, for example, in the number of student supervisor cases mediators at universities deal with during the course of an academic year. At some institutions the numbers are considerable. Many of these disputes could have been avoided had mutually agreed expectations and open lines of communication been established at the outset.

4.13 CLARIFYING MUTUAL EXPECTATIONS

1. The first step a prospective student should take towards avoiding disputes with supervisors is to become informed of the university's regulations and policies. Just as it is a citizen's responsibility to know the law so too no research student, or supervisor for that matter, can claim ignorance of the university's regulations and policies. Therefore, despite their apparent aridity, they deserve close reading (Edwards, 2006). Upon the basis of this knowledge mutual expectations between student and supervisor/s should be clarified. Among them:

   - *How frequently will meetings take place?* This is central to a communication plan. The frequency of meetings will depend roughly upon the phase of supervision. But, despite their change of frequency during each phase, there should be explicit agreement on how often the meetings will take place. Related to the issue of frequency of meetings is the role of email. Will detailed questions emailed to a supervisor be considered as equivalent to a meeting and, if not, how many will be considered excessive? (A few comments need at this point to be made about the virtues and drawbacks of email. While they are not as intrusive as telephone calls and can be sent and accessed anywhere, adequate answers to even brief questions often require a very considerable investment of time. Even with this investment the result is generally not a satisfactory substitute for face-to-face contact where issues, far more adequately and within a briefer time frame, can mutually be developed and explored. Therefore, expectations of what can be expected of emails to supervisors should be limited. Instead of queries that involve long and detailed replies students should make them specific and easily responded to.)

   - *How long should be the wait before work submitted for comment is returned?* Learning is an adaptation system and feedback constitutes an essential element in the process. This explains why this issue, along with frequency of meetings, is the most important cause of student dissatisfaction with supervisors. Clarification of the length of time a student should wait for work to be returned is, thus, important. Because each thesis is unique it is difficult to provide a blanket figure that takes cognisance of both the varying demands of a supervisor's workload and is fair to the needs of a student. However, between two to three weeks should normally be considered reasonable. Bear in mind that if no consensus is reached between student and supervisor on this issue the former will have little leverage if, subsequently, the return of submitted work is delayed unreasonably.

   - *What are the milestones?* Because adequate thesis planning depends upon the time of intended submission this should mutually be agreed upon first. The milestones can then more realistically be established by moving backwards in time. In addition to its important administrative function a flowchart indicating agreed upon milestones provides a comforting anchor when, inevitably, feelings of drift later set in.

- *What should be the approximate word length of the thesis?* Knowing how long the thesis ought to be is crucial to planning how it will be structured and written. At some universities academic departments rather than the central administration administer masters' theses. If this is the case one should not simply assume that the word length expectation of one department applies to all other departments as well. Because departments might have specific length requirements for theses students should take particular care to establish what the department or, in the case of interdisciplinary theses, what each of the departments, expect the length of the thesis to be. As might be expected minimum thesis word length will, even at those universities where masters' theses are centrally administered, vary widely between disciplines. It is possible, for example, for an excellent thesis in physics or mathematics to be only a few score pages long while it would be almost impossible to replicate this feat in a thesis in either English or history. But generally, as a rough guide, a full master's thesis is usually about 35 000 words long and a doctorate between 80 000 and 100 000.
- *What citation system should be used?* This is an issue that can become problematic in interdisciplinary theses. It is important in such instances, therefore, that there should be joint agreement between each of the supervisors and the student at the outset on the system to be used.

2. The following will also need to be ascertained from the supervisor/s:
   - What departmental handbooks and/or other documentation should be consulted?
   - All researchers need a home base so what workspace will be provided and what access will be given, for example, to photocopiers and to computer equipment?
   - Whether a joint record of meetings will be kept and, if so, whose responsibility this should be? It is likely that supervisor/s will, in any event, maintain a personal record of all supervisory meetings so, as a useful means to prevent possible future misunderstanding about what transpired at those meetings, a joint record should be kept. The student or supervisor, for example, might agree to write notes detailing the information indicated below and then to send a copy to the other.

Supervision Meeting Record (adapted from Wisker, 2005, p.65)

Meeting between…

Date and time…

Issues discussed…

Progress made…

Agreed next steps…

4.14 SKILLS DEVELOPMENT

1. The possibility of conducting a generic (for example: time management, presentation and networking skills) and/or subject specific research skills audit can also usefully be discussed in order to identify those areas where a student feels confident and those where he or she feels less so. (It requires mention here that supervisors across disciplines often mention that assisting students appreciate the theoretical basis of their research is one of the most difficult activities involved in supervision [Kiley & Wisker, 2009].) At some universities doctoral students are expected from the outset to have advanced writing skills and the ability to work independently. A supervisor in history commented:

We expect them to work independently when we accept them. After all, if they are going to hit the wall at this stage, then there's no sense prolonging the whole thing.

(Cited in Parry, 2007, p.41)

However, many universities structure the first year of doctoral research as a confirmation of candidature: the completion of a sequence of defined tasks necessary for the successful conduct of the research. Among other discipline-specific tasks, these could include, for example, presentation of a research seminar and the completion of an acceptable proposal (Owens, 2007a, p.151).

2. In fact, doctoral candidates apart, universities are currently expected to produce graduates in general with definable skills. Skills provision requires coordinated effort by a wide range of university staff (Krone, 2006) but much also depends on the efforts of supervisor/s. Introducing graduate researchers to academic networks has, for example, long been an acknowledged task of supervisors. The acknowledgement that they also have a role to play in the structured development of transferable generic skills is related to the current emphasis at universities on the timely completion of quality research (Yates, 2007). The need for audits of research skills has been a recent development and has come to apply to both students and supervisors. In the case of the latter, for example, there needs to be an honest appraisal of their own strengths and weaknesses relative to the needs of the former (Tennant & Roberts, 2007, p.25). The audit of the student thus complements the self-audit of the supervisor/s. If the supervisor has known the student for some time the audit is usually conducted informally. If, however, each has only recently been introduced then a more formal approach, as indicated below, might be more appropriate.

Possible Items to be Included in a Skills Audit (adapted from Wisker, 2005, p.55)

Items: Confident   Less   Confident
- Project planning
- Time management

- Critical skills
- Creative thinking
- Information literacy
- Writing skills
- Understanding of relevant theory
- Research methods
- Data analysis
- Ability to use relevant computer software
- Oral presentation skills

It would be surprising, should an audit have been conducted, for no areas of lesser confidence to be identified. But some students misconstrue the audit as a threatening test of their research capabilities and feel inadequate if areas of potential weakness are identified. A good supervisor will set these fears to rest for it is better to strengthen research skills earlier rather than later.

4.15 TIME MANAGEMENT

1. The need to strengthen weaknesses applies in particular to time management. The manner in which individual researchers organise their time is both person and task dependent. In regard to the latter, for example, the seasons provide opportunities and also impose clear limitations, for many students in biology. A year's penalty might, therefore, need to be paid if a research project does not go as planned (Phillips & Pugh, 2005). Planning for a complex project like a thesis involves setting short- and long-term goals. For many students new to research the former can often be defined but because of inexperience the long-term goals often defy practical definition (Phillips & Pugh, 2005). In fact, the two are interdependent, for writing a thesis involves a series of tasks that lead to an iterative reduction of uncertainty. Supervisors, therefore, play a central role in negotiating a personal development plan for their research students. Central to this is the setting of realistic short- and long-term goals. It is in their own interests to do so for an unstructured approach will ultimately lead to greater dependence by the student on them (Phillips & Pugh, 2005). This applies, in particular, to part-time researchers for whom writing a thesis usually takes twice as long as it does for full-time students. But the process of negotiating a personal development plan for part-timers will differ from that for full-time researchers. The latter can be considered full-time employees working from nine to five, five days a week. Part-timers often really are full-time employees who have both experience and expertise in the workplace. It might for them, therefore:

…be counter-productive for a relatively junior supervisor to adopt time-management and goal-setting strategies that they may well find useful with new full-time doctoral candidates who have just completed their honours degrees.

(Evans, 2007, p.116)

2. In both cases, however, project management will be an important element in personal development planning. Important elements, in turn, of project management are Gantt charts: bar charts that indicate the start time of a project and the primary tasks necessary for on-time completion. The advantage of Gantt charts is the clarity with which the sequence of tasks, and the relation of each to time, is shown. Gantt charts, however, capture sequences and relationships as they are or are expected to be. Not only, therefore, will they require frequent revision because the unanticipated is integral to research (Cryer, 2006) but also because they rapidly become unwieldy as projects grow in size. Although in Critical Path Analysis the relation of tasks to time is not as immediately apparent as in Gantt charts its advantage is the overview it provides for the identification and sequencing of tasks in larger projects so no work is held up while waiting for another on which it relies (Cryer, 2006).

4.16 PROGRESS REVIEWS

1. Careful project management is important because formal progress reviews are generally required either annually or biannually by postgraduate deans from both supervisors and doctoral candidates. Full-time masters researchers are often assessed after six months and part-time students annually. Conducting a review has two principle aims. The first is to assess the extent to which the research is going according to plan. The present report is often compared with the previous one (Rugg & Petre, 2004). The second aim is to develop collectively a plan of action for the next six months or year to address some of the issues raised in the review (Manathunga, 2005). Apart from satisfying standard university procedure progress reports, when they are carried out well and the research is on track, can provide both candidate and supervisor a sense of achievement, a good way to start the next stage of the research process. To be carried out well, though, the review should be considered by both supervisor/s and student as a learning opportunity. For this reason the supervisor/s ought not to dominate the review and the questions asked should neither question the intrinsic worth of the research project nor be inquisitorial. Instead, developmental questions that reflect the student's level of readiness will provide both a good sense of how the supervisory relationship is functioning and an opportunity for the researcher to showcase their developing expertise (Denholm, 2007).

4.17 SUPERVISORS AND THE WRITING PROCESS

1. Nonetheless, developmental questions might well be constructively critical. While it is never easy to receive criticism, particularly when it is justified, constructive criticism should be seen in context: it is an institutionalised feature of academic life. Very few highly regarded academics have not received negative feedback on work submitted for publication. This means most articles in refereed journals have, to one degree or another been modified during the review process by a combination of authors, reviewers, and editors (Golden-Biddle, 1997). Effective writers and poets are often their own best critics. T. S. Eliot, for example, emphasised the:

   …capital importance of criticism in the work of creation itself. Probably, indeed, the larger part of the labour of an author in composing his [sic] work is critical labour; the labour of sifting, combining, constructing, expunging, correcting, testing: this frightful toil is as much critical as creative.

   (Cited in Tufte, 2001, p.100)

2. Thus a thesis writer should actively seek constructive criticism. Not only will it enrich insights, it is also the process whereby academic integrity is maintained. In a Darwinian sense supervisors and examiners are like predators in the wild: they keep scholarship healthy and make it stronger (Wisker, 2005). The simile might seem lurid but is not out of place because, between academic peers, constructive criticism tends to be shorn of its niceties. But between supervisor and student niceties constitute the traditional feedback sandwich: first what was good and why, then what was not so good and what can be done about it and, finally, a note of encouragement (Paltridge & Starfield, 2007). Criticism that cuts closer to the bone can often, thus, be a confidence builder for it indicates progress is being made toward becoming a fully-fledged researcher. In any event, by this time most students will have become so involved with their work that the need for external approval will have lessened considerably (Phillips & Pugh, 2005).

Narrative

3. Because the supervisors will continue to be a thesis writer's immediate audience they will have an important influence upon the way in which the thesis is written. There is usually, however, an initial dichotomy in the emphasis that supervisors and students place on aspects of the writing process. Those students undertaking empirical projects, for example, generally seek to write concisely, follow a prescribed format and use correct terminology. Their supervisors generally feel, however, that the primary requirements are

the need to present solid arguments supported by empirical evidence and theory and, prosaic as it might sound, to tell a coherent and compelling story. Why is this? In the West stories have a traditional narrative structure, an introduction setting the scene, a middle in which the narrative is developed and a denouement. Within this structure events are explained through the development of plots (Golden-Biddle, 1997). A comparison of the following two statements provides insight into the potency of narrative:

- The king died and the queen died.
- The king died, and then the queen died of grief.

The first statement is simply a succession of information while the second has a plot: a single piece of information in place of two. This is the strength of narrative; because it can be remembered with less effort it can be marketed effectively as a single idea (Taleb, 2007).

Facilitating improvement

4. Striking a balance between supervisor and student perceptions of effective writing might take some time (Murray, 2003) because, while supervisors can often explain what is wrong with a piece of writing, they equally as often cannot explain how to improve it (Krone, 2006). There are, however, two simultaneous ways to facilitate such improvement. One is to make writing, from the beginning, an explicitly social process. There is, for example no need to wait for the supervisor/s to critique a draft before revision is started. This is inefficient for an informal network of readers should ideally be in place to respond to the writing before it is submitted to the supervisor/s for review (Golden-Biddle, 1997). The second way to improve the quality of writing is to submit rough, but readable, drafts to the supervisor/s on the understanding that the purpose of doing so is to allow them to comment on the overall structure rather than on the detail of the writing. Understandably supervisors will set limits on the number of drafts they are prepared to comment on so the limit will need to be negotiated beforehand (Cryer, 2006).

Autonomy and dependence

5. When supervisors do comment on the way in which an argument has been constructed it is inevitable that they will, either consciously or subconsciously, tend to direct the student toward their way of thinking. This is not only a reflection of the human condition but also of one of the oldest pedagogical problems: what is the relationship between discovery and instruction? (Rowland, 2006). In the specific case of supervision this problem is most apparent in the continuous tension between autonomy and

dependence. Ideally, supervisors will, while providing direction, continually encourage autonomy by asking open questions, drawing out ideas and defining problems (Wisker, 2005). The supervisor of a student undertaking qualitative research epitomised this approach when he told her: 'Don't write for me, write to me—from you' (Meloy, 2002, p.124). When the approach works as it should thesis writers will progressively develop their own sense of narrative and structure and, thus, take ownership of what they write. Occasionally this can be taken too far:

...the major problem of these theses, it seemed to me, was not that their authors were uncritically swallowing, or being dominated by, their teachers' intellectual obsessions, but that supervisors did not feel confident, or competent, to rein in student theoretical and philosophical enthusiasms.

(Kitching, 2009, p.252)

6. A supervisor cannot, should a student object, insist that changes be made to a thesis. If they did have the authority to do so a student's claim to ownership of the thesis would be compromised significantly. But, if supervisors express concerns about aspects of the work, it would be wise for students, even when the concerns are thought unjustified, to consider carefully the grounds for them. By doing so they might well be protecting themselves from similar concerns by examiners (Burton & Steane, 2004a). Although supervisors cannot insist that a thesis should be altered it is incumbent upon them to help thesis writers deepen their thinking about issues relevant to their research projects. Occasionally roles are reversed as the following statement by a supervisor in history indicates:

It was almost embarrassing. He came to me with a draft of the dissertation. When I first read the draft I thought it was just spectacular. I said, 'Put your cover page on it and let's go.' He said, 'I want to talk to you because I'm not really happy with it.' I thought, 'This is supposed to be my role. I'm supposed to be advising him'.

(Cited in Lovitts, 2007, p.338)

7. Not all supervisors, however, will see guiding and shaping a student's writing skills as an aspect of their responsibility. But those who do, often find themselves in an invidious position for, when they devote comments to the written expression in a thesis, it is often at the expense of comment on the substance of the text. For some non-native speakers of English, in particular, this can lead to a considerable degree of frustration for they argue that they can get assistance to improve their writing elsewhere; what they most need from their supervisors, they feel, is comment on the substance of what they have written (Ridsdale, 2000).

118

Setting the bar

8. Written comments by supervisors on the contents of thesis drafts are at their most helpful when they are both clear in intent and when viable alternatives are suggested. Unhelpful comment is judgemental (*This is not what I expect of a student at masters/doctoral level!*), global *(Satisfactory)* or elliptical *(Develop, Revise* or *Expand.)* So, if unhelpful comments are made, the supervisor should be asked to clarify their meaning (Murray, 2003). There should, in any event, be an ongoing discussion about what a supervisor's expectations are in regard to the quality of the final draft of the thesis. It really is important, both in terms of a student's peace of mind and, ultimately, in terms of the success of the supervisory relationship, that a sense of proportion is kept about the entirely natural desire to write a 'perfect' thesis. Both masters' and doctoral theses are examined on a benchmarked basis of what can reasonably be expected of a student working within the constraints of the master's or doctoral thesis processes: 'the level of 'good enough' will be high, but that's different from perfection' (Rugg & Petre, 2004, p.161). Therefore, even in the case of a thesis considered to be excellent, examiners will not expect it to be perfect. The concept of 'perfection' is, anyway, inimical to the academic process for it posits an end product that cannot be improved upon. Nonetheless, because it is understandably difficult for inexperienced students to set a realistic standard for their work, 'perfectionism' is an issue commonly encountered by supervisors. When thesis writers set their own bar too high it is inevitable that both their motivation and productivity will be affected detrimentally. As an example of how insightful and understanding good supervisors can be one supervisor, who is in fact a very tidy person, deliberately keeps an untidy office in order to help break the aura of the need for 'perfection'.

4.18 MAKING THE RELATIONSHIP WORK

1. In summary, what can a thesis writer do to help make the supervisory relationship function as effectively as possible?
   - *Help the supervisor/s to be helpful.* Few things are more frustrating for supervisors than, after having spent considerable time carefully scrutinising and correcting a significantly blemished draft, to be told by a student that global comment on the structure of the argument was all that was required. When submitting a draft, therefore, assist the supervisor/s by providing a cover sheet. On this sheet provide the date, draft number or draft title (for example: Early Planning Draft or Near Final Draft), word count and purpose of the submission, together with a list of the issues about which particular comment is required (Cryer, 2006).

- *Ensure that issues the supervisor/s identified in a previous draft have been addressed.* This is one of the few things that supervisors find even more frustrating than going beyond what was required when reviewing a draft. When resubmitting drafts, therefore, the cover sheet should also indicate how previous advice was acted on. Any disagreements with aspects of the advice should be discussed with the supervisor/s; the advice should not simply be ignored nor should the passage to which it refers simply be deleted.

- *Be receptive to constructive criticism.* When, for example, extensive revision of a draft work is required the transference of blame to the supervisor/s should be resisted. Negative transfer is most common in the generally time pressured period immediately prior to final submission, the time when the supervisor/s are usually first able to see all of the thesis chapters together. It is often only at this stage that it becomes evident that revisions need to be made to allow the separate chapters to 'flow' into one another. Thesis writers should, therefore, ensure they have sufficient time to make these changes if required. This is one of the reasons why sound planning at the outset of the thesis writing process is so important.

- *Be aware of the numerous responsibilities supervisors have and of the time constraints within which they have to work.* There should also be awareness that there will be times of the year when these responsibilities and constraints might be particularly severe. These are important reasons why there should be mutual agreement from the outset both about the length of time that should be allowed to elapse before work submitted for review is returned and for the occasional need for flexibility in this regard. Unless there has been prior agreement that rough drafts will be submitted for review there should also be a general rule that all drafts submitted have been proofread. This will allow the supervisor to save time by concentrating on the substance of the text rather than on blemishes of presentation. Consideration of the constraints that confront supervisors should not, however, be taken to the opposite extreme where a student becomes apologetic for using any of the supervisor's time: having taken a student on supervision is part of an academic's job description and the student is thus entitled to a fair share of the supervisor's time.

- *Go to each meeting with the supervisor/s prepared.* This means, ideally, that each meeting will have a clear purpose or set of purposes and that this will be indicated in a written agenda submitted to the supervisor/s prior to the meeting. Only the most extreme circumstances should prevent attendance at an arranged meeting with supervisor/s. If absence is unavoidable an apology should be sent as quickly as possible. It is usually a good idea after a meeting for either the student or supervisor to send an email to the other summarising what was discussed, the agreed actions that need to be taken and the date and time of the next meeting set. Doing so provides a common record of what transpired and also provides momentum to the thesis writing process (Phillips & Pugh, 2005).

- *Be aware that the quality of a thesis will reflect not only on the thesis writer but also on the supervisor/s and the university.* It is a small world and, because they meet at conferences and read each other's work, the world that academics inhabit is even smaller. Academe is also an intensely competitive world where the reputation of a university and of the academics who work in it are hard won and easily tarnished. Because the thesis examination process is as much a test of a supervisor's expertise as it is of the ability of a student the comments that examiners make in their reports indicate how a supervisor's reputation can either be enhanced or tarnished by the quality of a thesis: 'This was (sic) a great piece of work and both the candidate and supervisors are to be congratulated' (Lovat & Morrison, 2003, p.8). 'All of the above matters should have been dealt with during the draft stages of the thesis and reflect badly on the supervisor more so than the candidate' (Lovat & Morrison, 2003, p.6).

- *Maintain absolute integrity and confidentiality.* The relationship between student and supervisor is a professional one and should be treated as such. If there are significant differences of opinion with a supervisor attempts at resolution should be made in private. Going public simply makes resolution more difficult. If the differences still defy resolution there are generally a number of individuals in the university with whom students can speak in confidence: heads of department, graduate co-ordinators, university mediators, student counsellors, tutors at student learning centres and individuals in the student union. If their assistance does not help each university, as a last resort, has formal processes in place to facilitate the resolution of disputes. The initial steps in these processes generally emphasise and attempt to facilitate mutual reconciliation. If this is not possible the steps that follow become increasingly bureaucratic and lengthy, the eventual resolution usually being achieved at a time when the origin of the differences has long ceased to have any relevance. For this reason, and because of the emotional disruption that inevitably accompanies student-supervisor disputes, it is difficult to overemphasise the importance to students of avoiding serious disputes with their supervisor/s by establishing an open and informed relationship with them from the outset.

- *Do not be reticent about raising personal issues if they are affecting the thesis.* Students are sometimes reticent about discussing personal issues with supervisor/s because they feel doing so will indicate lack of commitment to the thesis (Manathunga, 2006). These fears are rarely justified for many supervisors consider providing appropriate pastoral support to be part of their task. But even if they consider otherwise they should be kept informed of issues that are likely to affect the thesis process because it at least keeps them in the picture. There is much to be gained, therefore, and little to lose by being less reticent about raising personal issues if they threaten to delay completion of the thesis.

- *Take care to preserve all research material (usually for a minimum period of five years) so as to avoid possible disputes over ownership rights.* An individual can only claim rights to research findings if they have specific evidence to support those claims. In many instances, though, it is difficult to provide such evidence. This is particularly the case in joint projects. Avoiding contentious differences over the rights to research findings depends, therefore, upon the integrity of the individuals involved and upon the maintenance of good records. It might be necessary in some instances (where, for example, thesis research has commercial significance) to apply for the thesis to be treated as a confidential document. But, because it impedes the free exchange of ideas, universities are usually reluctant to embargo a thesis without very persuasive reasons. Even when they do agree to do so the embargo is usually for a limited time only. In those countries, such as the United States, that adhere to the Universal Copyright Convention it is necessary to register a thesis in order to claim copyright. The copyright laws of most other countries ensure that copyright comes into existence automatically on the completion of any original literary work. This normally includes a thesis but consultation with, for example, the graduate advisory service or relevant university legal advisor is, nonetheless, advisable should copyright be a concern.
- *Remain as enthusiastic as possible about the thesis.* It is entirely natural for a researcher's enthusiasm for a thesis project to wax and wane with the passage of time. If, however, lack of enthusiasm becomes a sustained feature of the process it is also entirely natural that the supervisor's enthusiasm is also likely to wane.

2. From the supervisor's perspective each of the following behaviours, or combinations thereof, will be interpreted as a warning sign that a student is at risk of not completing his or her thesis (adapted from Manathunga, 2005, pp.223–231).
   - seeks out the supervisor more than seems warranted or, alternatively, avoids the supervisor and other research students;
   - resists advice and reacts negatively to criticism;
   - avoids submitting work for review;
   - makes excuses for unfinished tasks;
   - focuses far ahead rather than on immediate tasks;
   - constantly changes topic and/or work plan;
   - procrastinates and blames others for the delay.

Students should bear in mind that supervisors have the right, should they feel inadequate progress with the thesis is being made, to withdraw from the supervisory process. It will then be up to the student to attempt the invidious task of finding a replacement. For those, the great majority, who successfully complete their thesis with the original supervisor or supervisory team in place, good practice is to acknowledge their contribution formally in the thesis and to give them a copy for their own library. It is also a nice gesture to include a hand–written note of appreciation with the copy given to them (Cryer, 2006).

ENDNOTE

1 Universities usually claim ownership of inventions made by staff members as an employer's right. Research students might assign patent rights to the university. In return for sacrificing intellectual property they receive an agreed share of any profits.

CHAPTER 5

Academic Discourses

In order to function socially we do make temporary determinations of meaning but meaning itself is never determinate.

(Meyer & Land, 2003, p.9)

5.1 INTRODUCTION

1. Just as there is no universal form of language called philosophy, so too there is no universal form of writing (Peters, 2008). Straight writing, for example, is value laden. It can be interpreted as honest, simple and trustworthy as opposed to non-straight writing: bent, distorted, perverse (Davis & Sumara, 2005). Even plain speaking:

   …is neither benign nor inert. It is, rather, an insistence that is embedded in a particular worldview. More precisely, it is a notion that is caught up in Euclidean geometry[1]—a frame which privileges not just a particular set of elements and images, but a logico-rational mode of argumentation.

   (Davis & Sumara, 2005, p.307)

   Writing is not only an inherently idiosyncratic exercise it is also epistemic. There are, for this reason, multiple approaches to learning how to write. This contrasts with a conception of writing as simply information transmitting. From this perspective writing is a process involving learning, and mechanically applying, rules. Well into the twentieth century, for example, writing in the natural sciences was often considered a non-rhetorical[2] special discourse: persuasion was not a consequence of linguistic device but of evidence and logic alone. It is this perception that best defines the changes in academic writing during the final decades of the twentieth century: it was not logic giving way to rhetoric but 'the rhetoric of impersonal objectivity being challenged by the rhetoric of reflexive self-awareness' (Dillon, 1991, p.156). The consequence has been general acknowledgement that all academic writing is rhetorical: all researchers need to construct inherently theoretical arguments to persuade their intended audience (Golden–Biddle & Locke, 1997).

From this perspective not only might a contemporary university lecture be seen as a rhetorical device in which a lecturer attempts to persuade students but the concept of a discipline might even be considered a consequence of rhetorical argument.

(Rowland, 2006, p.108)

2. Academic literacy, therefore, is an intertextual process requiring both linguistic ability and 'rhetorical insight' into a research community's ways of constructing meaning (Partridge & Starfield, 2007). An empirical approach, for example, will emphasise accuracy, objectivity and formality: 'it was found that… the data suggests that…' while a qualitative approach might be in an informal, first person, discursive style replete with quotations (Burton & Steene, 2004c). Verisimilitude, for example, is a style of writing that draws the reader into the world being studied (Angrosino, 2007). These differences arise from a conception of writing as epistemic, knowledge making and, therefore, a unique mode of learning. From this perspective reflection replaces rules: reflection, for example, on audience, modes of argument and on methodological and disciplinary genre. Each of the latter has its specialist vocabulary and means of conveying meaning. Writing in the mathematical disciplines, for example, is often unintelligible to non-specialists not only because the content is unfamiliar but also because meaning is conveyed in highly specialised, compressed codes (Becher & Trowler, 2001). Given the limited degree of standardisation possible and the ambiguity of research results, this degree of codification is less evident in the social sciences. It is evident even less so in the humanities and fine arts for each has more phenomenal layers of intermediary representation than in the sciences and, thus, multiple legitimate perspectives. This explains why students in the humanities and fine arts tend to be presented with a far greater range of competing approaches to writing than in the natural or social sciences (Peck MacDonald, 1994).

3. Nonetheless, the specialised terms that all disciplines use move in and out of favour as perspectives alter. The malleability of these vocabularies reflects not only the way in which words but also writing as a whole, evolves to suit particular purposes. For this reason the style of writing and the words used in a thesis will need to be interrogated with the same degree of intensity applied to all other aspects of the research undertaking. Researchers will necessarily bring their own constructions of writing to this process. Some of these will and some will not facilitate an alteration of interpretive horizons (Crusius, 1991). But only by deconstructing and reconstructing will a definition incrementally develop of what, in terms of a researcher's own needs, constitutes sound

academic discourse. It is the incremental, immersive nature of this process that justifies use of the term 'academic discourses', communication involving specialised knowledge, rather than the usual term 'academic writing'.

5.2 CITING WITHIN THE DISCOURSES

1. However, despite the distinctions between academic discourses, no text in any discipline is unique. It would be unrecognisable if it were (Frow, 2006). Each text, thus, rather than belonging to, participates simultaneously in several genres. They have elements, in other words, they share with all other texts. Because these elements provide context and meaning, invoking them indicates inter-relationships between texts. This is what is meant by intertextuality and it is the over seven hundred styles of citation that make it apparent (Macauley, 2006); the development of this number is indicative of the role the styles play in academic discourse. Just as writing is not neutral but reflects dominant theories and their rhetorical conventions so too are citation styles. For example, in the American Psychological Association (APA) style, the style often adopted in the more empirical of the social sciences, the in-text author, date method is applied (Stockwell, 2006) and either the past or present perfect tense used ('found' or 'has found'). (In APA a page reference should be provided for direct quotations or detailed paraphrases [Stockwell, 2006, p.34]). On the other hand, in the Modern Languages Association (MLA) style, the style often adopted in exegetic research, the in-text author page number method is applied (Stockwell 237) and the present tense used. In addition, the APA style discourages use of content footnotes or endnotes for anything other than brief statements conveying one point. The MLA style, on the other hand, is more forgiving of their use as sub-text to elaborate aspects of the primary text. Possibly the most flexible in this regard is the Chicago style. This is particularly useful in theses in history or social anthropology, for example, where footnotes (which are always single-spaced) sometimes become so extensive they consume more space on a page than primary text. Each of these differences reflects the theoretic approach upon which each style is premised. The APA style, for example, indicates the importance of linearity and recency in the social sciences: the inclusion of the date in the in-text reference indicates new findings have been layered upon a normative foundation provided by the most recent prior research. That this is a completed action is indicated by use of the past or present perfect tense. The present tense of the MLA, though, together with the omission of a date of publication in the in-text reference, indicates the subjective character of interpretive exegesis and qualitative analysis.

2. That particular systems of reference have come to be associated with particular disciplines is a reflection of the dominant theories and conventions that

have come to be associated with those disciplines: empirical in the natural and social sciences and exegetic and qualitative in the humanities and fine arts. This association between discipline and citation styles (reinforced by journal editorial requirements and occasionally by departmental regulations) has, however, often come to be applied as though the dominant theories and conventions were the only ones that could be applied in those disciplines. But this is not the case. Citation styles indicate the discourse community, not the discipline to which a researcher belongs. For example, seeking to make explicit a claim that a Darwinian approach could free literary criticism from its umbilical link to the humanities, the author of the article *Literary Darwinism: Evolution, Human Nature, and Literature* (Smith, 2006) chose to use the APA in preference to the MLA style that readers of a work of literary criticism would normally expect to see (Kelly, 2005).

3. The use of a citation style other than that to which one has become accustomed will not, thus, simply be a mechanical process of altering citation details and format. It will, instead, alter thinking and writing and the readers' response to it at a fundamental level. For this reason particular styles have the potential to discomfort supervisors who are not familiar with them (Kelly, 2005). Particularly in interdisciplinary undertakings the issue of the type of style to adopt ought to be discussed with supervisors at the outset of the research. The resulting consensus should not, however, be considered inviolate. As the research develops and evolves so too might the needs the system of citation is required to fulfil. In addition, examiners will have their own views about the suitability of particular citation styles. If the choice made has the potential to be problematic a brief explanation justifying its use should be provided in the thesis. If the system changed during the course of the research, explain why the change was necessary.

5.3 REFERENCES

1. This brief excursion into citation styles is not an attempt to complicate what, in most cases, is a straightforward decision. It is simply an attempt to provide insight into the range of options available so as to enable an informed decision to be made about what style might best suit particular research needs. But it is, nonetheless, important to point out that the term 'citation styles' can be misleading because they are, in fact, much more. They are, instead, editorial systems the requirements of which are presented in handbooks and manuals and in some cases journals specific to each. For example:
    *   *MLA Handbook for Writers of Research Papers* (2009, 7th edition). New York: Modern Language Association of America.
    *   Turabian, K.L. (2007, 7th edition). *A Manual for Writers of Research Papers,*

Theses, and Dissertations. Chicago Style for Students and Researchers. Chicago: University of Chicago Press.

- *Publication Manual of the American Psychological Association* (2010, 6th edition). Washington, D.C.: American Psychological Association (APA).

As can be expected the more empirical the research the more prescriptive the styles tend to be. This is evident, for example, in a comparison of the contents of the APA manual and the MLA handbook. Thus, while many websites helpfully indicate how to cite material in each style, few show extensively the editorial conventions specific to each. It is recommended, therefore, that a copy of the appropriate guide should be available for quick reference when writing a thesis.

Dictionaries and thesauri

2. Two additional references are essential: a good dictionary and a thesaurus. Word processing packages generally have a built in dictionary and thesaurus. These are usually useful but, at present, no substitute for the hardcopy versions. The producers of the *Oxford English Dictionary*, for example, seek to establish the meaning and etymology of every English word currently in use: a number approaching one million words if technical terms are included. They thus have a claim to be engaged in one of the greatest research endeavours ever undertaken. (The *Oxford English Dictionary* should not be confused with the *Oxford Dictionary of English*. The former is in twenty volumes, the latter in one.) In addition, with a vocabulary considerably larger than any other and because of the layered manner in which it has been historically structured, English is the only language that has, or possibly can have, a thesaurus. The title of the first edition, published by Roget in 1852, indicates its purpose: *Thesaurus of English Words and Phrases, Classified and Arranged so as to Facilitate the Expression of Ideas and Assist in Literary Composition* (Anderson & Poole, 1994).

3. However, despite the size of the English vocabulary only sixty thousand words are considered main words; of these only a few hundred constitute the bulk of writing and even fewer appear with any regularity in conversation (Wenger, 1998). Most home speakers of English, therefore, barely scratch the surface of what the language has to offer. So rare, in fact, is the use of a wide vocabulary that it is noteworthy. This is indicated in the following extract from a book review: 'If you want to meet a master in perfect control of his medium, then look no further: this is beautiful English and an unhurried display of the glorious potential of the language' (The *Economist*, 9 June 2007, p.92). Some poetry and philosophy, by its very nature, is dense. But for the audience for which a thesis is designed the writing ought usually to be as transparent as language will allow. Consciously seeking to increase ones vocabulary will assist in the achievement of clarity. There is also another important reason: we use words to conceptualise and understand

128

and it is these concepts and understandings that control our range of options. A diminished vocabulary thus limits the size of that range (Wenger, 1998).

4. Two caveats need, however, to be made in regard to the use of a dictionary and thesaurus. First, ensure the dictionary used is appropriate. The *Institute of Electrical and Electronics Engineers (IEEE) Editorial Style Manual*, for example, specifies use of the most recent edition of *Webster's College Dictionary*. Many other professional fields also have specialised dictionaries. In addition, dictionaries originating in the United States or United Kingdom provide word meanings and spellings appropriate to each country: jelly/jam and realize/realise, for example. Even dictionaries originating in the same country occasionally provide different spellings and meanings for the same word. Appendices and appendixes, are examples of the former. The same dictionary, therefore, should be used to retain consistency. The spellchecker on word processing software should also be set for the type of English the university accepts. The second caveat is that use of a thesaurus by a second-language speaker of English can be double-edged. On the one hand it is invaluable as a builder of vocabulary but, on the other, it is an invitation, because meanings might improperly be understood, to use words inappropriately.

5.4 TABLE OF CONTENTS

1. All theses need a table of contents to signpost what the contents are and where to locate them. Do not, however, leave the task of writing the table until after the bulk of the thesis has been written. One reason is that it will be among the first things the examiners will read and, particularly in exegetic and qualitative theses, get a sense of how the argument or narrative unfolds. An indication of this is provided in the following advice to examiners: 'A good test is to look over the table of contents to see how much you can anticipate about the research just by scanning the headings' (Rugg & Petre, 2004, p.101). This is also a good reason for the early construction of the table: it can be used as a 'roadmap' to assist in the initial drafting of the thesis. Its importance stems from a tendency for the purpose of chapters to become obscured by a drive to present information (Cantwell, 2006). So, irrespective of the type of research conducted, compose an outline table of contents with at least chapter titles as early as possible[3]. Once the titles have been composed, go one step further. In so far as is possible, list the headings and subheadings within each chapter. Because chapters might have several themes, word the headings and subheadings as comprehensively as possible so as to reflect the contents clearly (Cryer, 2006). (In doing so take care to use labels rather than statements.) These headings and subheadings can subsequently be changed as a stronger sense of direction develops but, in

the interim, they will assist in bringing coherence to the early drafts of the thesis. (It does not matter at this early stage if headings and subheadings are wordy; this too can be corrected later.)

2. Not all research, however, lends itself to the use of headings and subheadings. Qualitative and exegetic studies, for example, tend to be discursive and thus fragment into identifiable sections far less readily than is often the case in empirical studies. There are, of course exceptions: interpretive studies in law usually adopt subheadings to help readers negotiate thickets of legislation (Thody, 2006). But, whenever the need for them does arise, headings and subheadings should be used properly and consistently. In a minimalist sense, headings and subheadings simply indicate what lies ahead. But, when formatted properly, they not only fulfil this function but also signpost the relationship between what lies ahead and what went before. This explains why the Manual of the APA recommends the use of five levels of headings and subheadings:

Centred, Boldface, Uppercase and Lowercase (level 1)

Flush Left, Boldface, Uppercase and Lowercase (Level 2)

    Indented, boldface, lowercase paragraph heading ending with a period. (Level 3)

    Indented, boldface, italicized, lowercase paragraph heading ending with a period. (Level 4)

    Indented, italicized, lowercase paragraph heading ending with a period. (Level 5)

(Publication Manual of the APA, 2010, p.62)

3. Bearing in mind the limitations of short-term memory the use of more than five levels would make it difficult for readers to distinguish the nature of the relationships each level is intended to convey. To ease this difficulty the number of levels in most theses is limited to four. The headings and subheadings may be formatted as is done in APA journal articles but it is common in theses for them to be presented flush left. It is not normal practice to underline headings and subheadings; this is a relic of typewriters. In all instances, though, the university's formatting requirements, should there be any, must take precedence.

4. When adroitly formatted the table of contents of a thesis with numerous headings and subheadings will explicitly demonstrate the relationship between them. Note in the third of the following examples how effective the combination of indentation with numbering can be when compared to the first with neither and the second with numbering only:

Chapter Two[+]: Literature Review

5. If used as in the third example a table of contents in the final draft of the thesis will act to complement the abstract by forecasting the manner in which the argument in the thesis has been constructed. The table of contents thus becomes a rhetorical device, a useful navigational tool for the examiners. In order to reinforce the utility of a table of contents it is worth mentioning that when authors submit a book proposal to publishers they do not usually submit a draft of the entire work, merely sample chapters together with a full table of contents. It is largely on the basis of this representative material that publishers decide whether or not to proceed with the proposal.

5.5 METATEXT

1. The template chapter headings of empirical theses usually make explicit the purpose of each chapter. But, lacking these clear transition points, writers of exegetic and some qualitative theses usually need, in addition to explanatory chapter headings, a brief introductory section where the contents and relevance of each chapter to the central research issue is forecast. In doing so they also indicate that chapters do not overlap with each other (Dunleavy, 2003). This *text about the text* or metatext[5] is an overt acknowledgement by the writer of the reader. This acknowledgement might, for example take the form of an explanation as in the following book extract:

...readers will probably be annoyed that we have suspended our discussion here and may be surprised at our treatment. On the first count, this is, as we said, an introduction. Development and critique will be resumed in due course. As to the second point, we must reply that...

(Smith & Jenks, 2006, p.60)

More usually, though, it takes the form of an acknowledgement that readers need assistance to follow the organisation of an extended text. This explains one of the most significant differences between journal articles and theses: metatext is used far more frequently in the latter than in the former (Paltridge & Starfield, 2007). This acknowledgement, though, is cultural. Some languages like French, Polish and Japanese, for example, tend to be 'reader responsible'. This means readers might perceive such an acknowledgement as demeaning. But English and, for example, Norwegian, tend to be 'writer responsible'. In these languages there tends, therefore, to be a cultural expectation that writers should help guide readers through clear and well-organised text. There are, though, differences in the use of metatext between writers of doctoral and masters' theses. This can partly be explained by the length of doctoral texts relative to those of masters. But the probable primary explanation is the usual prior experience by doctoral candidates of already having written a thesis. They tend, thus, to be more sensitive than masters students to the needs of their readers (Paltridge & Starfield, 2007).

Previews, overviews and recalls

2. In both masters' and doctoral theses, however, a query by an examiner on how parts of a thesis relate to the central question or hypothesis usually indicates insufficient guidance has been provided. This might be provided in a number of ways. Most frequently used are preview, overview and recall sentences. Previews anticipate what is to follow later in the thesis or, as in the following example from a chapter introduction, later in the same chapter: *The following analysis is presented in two stages. In the first the current perspectives on... are evaluated. The second is a critical evaluation of...*Overviews may look in both directions: *In this chapter the reason for...has been discussed. In the next this discussion will be elaborated by...* Recalls look back to an earlier stage of the text: *As described in the introduction...* Preview and recall sentences should, however, be used with caution. While powerful writing should be oriented forwards as much as possible resist the temptation at the end of each chapter to pre-empt the next. For example: *The next chapter describes and discusses the approaches to...* Succumbing to the temptation diminishes the self-contained purpose of each chapter. The same logic applies to recall sentences at the start of chapters: *In the previous chapter we...*

Signalling

3. Another way in which a reader can be guided through text is the use by a writer of implicit and explicit signals. These, for example, can be brief notes inserted immediately prior to a subheading indicating that a transition is about to occur: *I will now focus on...* A signal can also be words that indicate the nature of what is to follow: *as a result*; *on the other hand* or *to conclude*. These signals can be seen in the following: *Previous studies of... provide some evidence that... On the other hand, there are studies that have not found the expected relationship.* Signals might also be individual connectives: *however, conversely, furthermore, therefore, secondly,* or *similarly.* There is also an additional function to signal words; they indicate, as in the following example that a discussion is in progress: *However some researchers (Canto, 2003; Perkins, 2005) reject the effectiveness of... suggesting instead that...is a better strategy. Friedman & Wilkins (2004) also claim that...Therefore, knowing what types of...are most effective will be helpful for...*

4. While signals indicate and chapter introductions preview what is to come, the conclusion to each chapter recalls what has been achieved. For example:

This inquiry began with an examination of the differences in how... Next, I considered how greater depth and clarity could be brought to understanding the intersection of...Finally, I introduced a process with the goal of...

(MacMynowski, 2007, p.2).

Chapter conclusions will generally need to be headed as such in order to distinguish their purpose from the preceding text. But, because there is no preceding text, the section introducing each chapter does not necessarily need a heading if double spacing separates it from the following paragraph. Take care, though, to head the conclusion 'Conclusion' and not 'Summary' (unless, of course, a summary is intended). The following, for example, was called a summary but is, in fact, a conclusion:

In summary this chapter shows that claims about the nature of... are largely based on...and are often speculative rather than being underpinned by detailed analysis. Classification of... would, therefore, benefit from more theoretically motivated and empirically supported accounts of... Most importantly, such an approach would allow finer distinctions to be made between... which preliminary research (e.g. Thorpe, 2003) indicates as being of particular importance in...contexts.

While a recapitulation merely lists the main points and a summary provides marginally more detail, a conclusion, as in the example above, provides meaning to those points by linking them to the central purpose of the thesis. How, in other words, has the chapter contributed to moving the central argument forward? A summary and a conclusion are not, though, mutually exclusive for a summary can be used to provide context to a conclusion. For example:

The three sections described above presented various ways in which… The first section argued that… The second section showed that… Finally, the last section presented cases of the… Considering these observations about how the three types of… phenomena appear, this study strongly supports Murray's (2004) claim that… is not a matter of choice but rather of degree.

However, the term 'conclusion' can be problematic in qualitative theses because it implies the research is an encapsulation rather than an exploration of a complex web of ongoing processes. While it is true that 'conclusion' is often used in qualitative theses it might, nonetheless, be more appropriate to use terms such as *reminders, implications, closing* or *epilogue* instead. Irrespective of the term used, when the draft of a chapter has been completed return to the paragraph introducing it so as to ensure what has been forecast has been fleshed out adequately (Galvan, 2004).

5.6 SENTENCE LENGTH

1. The use of metatext is a subjective cultural imperative. So too is the issue of sentence length. English is a very flexible language. 'I cup of tea would like a', for example, can easily be understood (Canter & Fairbairn, 2006, p.83). This flexibility makes sentence construction malleable but it also makes confusion easy to sow; a fault most evident in long sentences. Common to the clarity of all sentences in English is an unobstructed relationship between subject, verb and object: *The girl*—subject—*threw*—verb—*the ball*—object. The longer a sentence grows, though, the more obscure this relationship becomes: *The young, athletic girl with long, flaxen hair threw with enormous vigor the red beach ball she had been given for her birthday.* The obscuring effect is enhanced when a subordinate clause interrupts the main clause: *The young, athletic girl with long, flaxen hair, because she was feeling particularly happy, threw with enormous vigour the red beach ball she had been given for her birthday.* In addition, the longer a sentence becomes so too does the temptation increase to use ambiguous words like *it, this* and *they*.

2. So, when a sentence runs beyond 25 words, clarity is usually served by splitting the sentence in two. However, this advice is provided with two caveats. First, sentences resemble musical notation in the sense that when of equal length they make reading a tedious task. Varying sentence length, therefore, can add not only music but also drama to writing: *The landscape looked quiet and peaceful in the dappled sunlight of late afternoon. But it wasn't.* (Because they are informal, contractions of verbs and pronouns such as *can't, it's* and *they're*, should not

be used in a thesis.) Second, because they can be so rich, a good case can be made for the advantages, when appropriate, of using long sentences. Read, for example, the following:

> *Before getting to the things that Bernard–Henri Levy does well in* American Vertigo *(Random House; 308 pages), his entertaining and insightful account of how, last year, to mark the 200th anniversary of the birth of Alexis de Tocqueville— the aristocratic French author renowned for his perceptive and enduring classic,* Democracy in America—*the U.S. monthly magazine Atlantic commissioned Levy, who is perhaps the world's most famous living celebrity-intellectual, to retrace the steps of de Tocqueville's 1831–1832 ramble through the young republic, a trip that inspired Democracy, let's identify, just for the record, the single most annoying flaw in Levy's tome: overly long sentences.*

(Morrison, D., *Time*, May 1, 2006, p.62)

3. While a series of long sentences certainly can make writing unfathomable the corollary is that, because they are so laden with information, they force readers to slow down and concentrate on the meaning. That is why some authors sing the praises of long sentences. There is, in other words, nothing intrinsically wrong with long sentences as long as the syntax is correct and they are not used too frequently. The obverse also applies. Series of short sentences, as in recipe instructions, lack flow and it is left to the reader to make the necessary connections between them. The ideal sentence length for smooth reading, therefore, is between about 18 and 25 words.

5.7 VOICE AND PERSON

1. The statements *the tube was filled with water by the researcher* (past tense) or *the tube is being filled with water by the researcher* (present continuous) are examples of writing in passive voice. *The researcher filled the tube with water* (past tense) or *the researcher is filling the tube with water* (present continuous) is writing in active voice. These examples indicate that voice is not dependent on tense. The difference between active and passive voice lies, rather, in the relationship between subject and verb. Thus, in sentences written in active voice the subject (in this case, *the researcher*) performs the action whereas in sentences written in passive voice, the subject is acted upon. The use of passive voice is appropriate when the agent performing the action is obvious, unimportant or unknown. For example: *Every year thousands of people are identified as bulimic.* The passive and active voice can also be mixed: 'Attitudes towards asylum seekers were investigated via a survey of registered voters. In this article I describe the procedures by which I gathered my data…' (cited in Canter & Fairbairn, 2006, p. 64).

2. There are also instances where voice can be used creatively. The passive might, for example, be used to indicate a standard approach and the active a novel approach. For example: *Participants were organised* (passive) *into small groups in the first half of the experiment while, in the second half, participants selected* (active) *their own groups.* Be careful, though, to avoid starting a sentence in active voice and then shifting to passive: *I identified the relationship between the variables but accurate measurement was difficult.* As opposed to: *I identified the relationship between the variables but it was difficult for me to measure accurately.* What is evident, though, is when used in isolation passive voice obviates use of personal names or personal pronouns. By obscuring agency it helps create the appearance of objective presentation. This epistemological implication helps explain why nineteenth-century Positivists favoured use of passive voice.

3. But, the very reason passive voice found favour with Positivists also explains why it is currently out of favour. Because writing cannot be seen as objective or 'innocent' qualitative researchers, for example, need to indicate ownership of the views they present. The reflexive nature of their work requires, therefore, that they write in the first person, active voice and, whenever possible, in the present tense. For example: *I do not have an argument with Freudian theory per se, but will show that it is culturally inappropriate to apply to academic structure.* The avoidance of culpability in passive voice can also irritate examiners when thesis writers using other approaches to research refuse to take ownership of a statement. For example: *It is thought that Hamlet was written by Shakespeare;* as opposed to: *The overwhelming body of evidence indicates that Shakespeare wrote Hamlet.* The former example would, however, be more acceptable if it received evidential support and was, thus, provided with an owner: *It is thought that Hamlet was written by Shakespeare (Smith, p.97).*

4. Apart from the issue of ownership, there are also important stylistic reasons why the active voice, in all approaches to research, has progressively come to be the preferred tradition: whereas writing in passive can be flat and uninteresting, writing in the active permits the construction of less wordy and, usually as a result, more forceful sentences. Compare for example, the passive: *The bus was being got into by passengers* with the active: *Passengers got into the bus.* It is primarily for these reasons that the APA Publication Manual explicitly recommends (*Publication Manual of the APA*, 2010, p.77), and the MLA and Chicago manuals implicitly recommend, use of the active voice whenever appropriate to do so.

5. In fact, the APA Publication Manual not only favours use of the active voice but also its use in conjunction with the first person. It might have been noted that, although the relationship between subject and verb explains the differences between active and passive voice, no specific mention until this point has been made of the first, second and third person: first person—*I, we, our;* second

person—*you, us, your;* third person—*he/she/it, they, their.* (There is also a rarely used fourth person where, for example, one person in a group of three speaks to one in the group and refers to the other as though he or she were not present.) The reason for the omission is to avoid possible confusion between the use of voice and person. This is because, for example, active can be written in the third person: *They drew many of their ideas from earlier sources;* while the passive voice can be written in the first person: *I was hit by the ball.* Sentences written in the active or passive voice can also be written without person. For example, the passive: *A number of important issues are revealed by these findings* can be rewritten in the active voice as: *These findings reveal a number of important issues.*

6. As can be seen in these examples use of a particular combination of voice and person or the use of voice separately from person is not a question of right or wrong. Their appropriate use is dependent, instead, upon context. What, though, are the criteria for choice? First person, active voice should normally be used in the acknowledgements section of a thesis and wherever researcher-specific perspectives are being provided. But the lack of an explicit agent in the passive is useful in the methods section where the emphasis needs to be on what was done rather than upon the doer of the action. It is generally understood that in this section the researcher is the agent. There might be instances though, as, for example, in joint research undertakings, where the identity of the agent needs to be established. In this case the sentence: *the tube was filled with deionised water;* might need to be rewritten in the first person, active voice: *I (or we) filled the tube with deionised water.* (As opposed to the use of passive voice: *The tube was filled by me with deionised water.*)

7. Elsewhere in the thesis the introductory and concluding paragraphs to chapters are examples of the way in which person can be used both effectively and creatively. Because, in both instances, explicit directions or observations are being provided, it is appropriate to use the first person active voice. However, it might be appropriate because of the research approach to write the balance of the chapter in the active voice without person. In this case the introductory paragraph might, for example, have sentences that start as follows: *In this chapter I will discuss...I have structured this chapter on the basis of the assumption that...I, therefore...* The first paragraph of the body of the chapter might then start: *Recent findings relating to...reveal a number of important issues. These are...*

8. In practice first and third person is easily translated one into the other. Thus the first person: *I would argue that...* could be translated into the coy third person as: *It might be argued that...* For this reason thesis writers, when the need arises can readily move between the two. Although, in general, most theses (with the exception of the methods section if there is one) are primarily written in the active voice, there tends to be a distinction in the

use of person between exegetic and qualitative researchers on the one hand and empirical researchers on the other. The former tend to use third person frequently while in the latter first person tends to be used more frequently. The explanation for the distinction lies in the fact that exegetic and qualitative researchers usually need to analyse the thoughts and actions of others, hence the frequent need to use personal names and 'him' or 'her'. Free from the first person requirement to see things only as an observer, the third person allows writers to be 'omniscient' in the sense that they can get into the character of different individuals and, in doing so, easily include description and emotion.

9. Mention of second person has been limited. This is a consequence of its primary suitability for instructional writing—*you should do this; that applies to us*—so the need for it in a thesis rarely arises. However, as the following extract from a qualitative researcher indicates, there are creative exceptions:

    In letting go of first person and trying on second, I felt oddly free to challenge convention, to create a new authorial stance and presence. Displacing 'I' altered my perspective, gave me another view of 'self' and in its mode of direct address, drew a circle and taking the reader in.

    (Logsdon, 2006, p.163).

10. Unlike most exegetic research and some qualitative work, writers of empirical theses are the central character in the story: it is their experience and they need to tell what they did from a single perspective. This is what writing in the first person, without the need for frequent recourse to the third person, allows them to do. Their use of first person active voice, as the APA Publication Manual's endorsement testifies, makes a forceful combination. The drawback to the use of the first person, though, is constant repetition of 'I' 'our' or 'we'. For example: *In the following section of the study I discuss the ways in which the… Where possible, I also highlight the… relevance of the research. First I consider…I then focus on…I then conclude by…* Some thesis writers attempt to circumvent the problem of personal pronoun repetition by using the terms *the author* or *the researcher*. These, however, generally sound clumsy and pretentious so be wary of using them. The natural sciences, medicine and engineering are generally tolerant of the use of 'we' in place of 'I' throughout a thesis simply because so much research in these fields is conducted by teams. But a thesis is expected primarily to be the work of an individual, so there is danger in the continuous use of 'we'. Thesis writers will, thus, normally be expected by examiners to be discriminating in the use of 'I' and 'we' or 'our' and 'my'. When, in other words is 'we' 'we' and 'our' 'our' and when is 'we' 'I' and 'our' 'my'?

11. The act of making a distinction between 'I' and 'we' or 'our' and 'my' can, however, be very unsettling to students when it suddenly becomes apparent,

138

because of the limited number of times they can indisputably use 'I' instead of 'we' or 'my' instead of 'our', how significant the contribution of other researchers has been. There is no easy answer to this dilemma because it raises the subjective issue of the 'ownership' of knowledge: some examiners will accept the use of 'we' or 'our' throughout a thesis while others will consider their continuous use to be problematic. This is why it is so important when involved in a joint research project to avoid disputed ownership by staking a claim at the outset to a clearly identifiable aspect of it.

5.8 AUDIENCE

1. Undergraduate students need to display their knowledge of a topic regardless of the fact that the marker generally knows all about it. Thesis writers, however, have a more complex relationship with their audience (Paltridge & Starfield, 2007). From a metaphysical perspective philosophical discourse is oriented to truth rather than opinion: to a nominal audience, in other words, rather than a real one. A thesis, however, is a rhetorical instrument, for its focus is on the requirements of a real audience. Who, though, constitutes this audience? If the Goldilocks principle applies to theses who should they be 'just right' for? Ultimately, the intention behind the research encapsulated in a thesis is that it should, in the broadest sense, be a contribution to knowledge and understanding. But the readership that constitutes this wider audience will not accept the findings in a thesis until it has first passed through the quality control implicit in the examination process. The immediate audience, then, is the examiners. It can, of course, be argued that these examiners have been chosen because they reflect the standards and expectations of the wider audience. But, the counter argument is not only that the standards and expectations of the wider audience lack uniformity, but also that the standards and expectations of individual examiners also differ. This is why universities exercise such care in the procedures they stipulate in regard to the examination of theses and why supervisors should exercise equal care in the choice of appropriate external examiners or moderators.

2. It is a sobering thought that most theses are only ever read cover to cover by a handful of individuals. Converting the thesis into a book could alter this fate. But doing so only emphasises the importance of audience, for rewriting a thesis for publication is rarely a question of simply revising the original text. More usually it means the original is merely the basis for an entirely new work, written with a different audience in mind (Macauley & Green, 2007). Converting parts of a thesis into journal articles does not normally involve a similarly dramatic transformation. However, a distinction remains, for a thesis is written for examiners while journal articles are tailored to an audience of fellow researchers. The fact that audience has such a profound effect on the manner in which text is written indicates that

they are, in a real sense, concealed participants in the writing process and that a degree of power is being imparted to them (Golden-Biddle & Locke, 1997). This is particularly the case in fragmented disciplinary areas each with its own specialty audience. The extent of the power transferred is, thus, often inversely proportional to the size of the audience: the most powerful normally being small and relatively homogeneous; editors, moderators and examiners (Thody, 2006). This implies some masters students have an advantage over doctoral candidates for whom at many universities supervisors no longer also act as examiners. Cogent reasons have prompted this change but, nonetheless, if their supervisor is also an examiner, masters' theses writers are often in a better position to assess the needs and requirements of their immediate audience. They run less risk, therefore, of writing for an amorphous audience that defies definition.

5.9 AUTHENTICITY

1. But all writers, in addition to identifying the needs of their audience, also need to recognise that their own position in relation to that audience will be an evolving one. Thus, because writing a thesis is a process of personal growth, the perceived relationship with the audience will not be the same at the time of submission as it was at the start of the research. Certainly for doctoral candidates the final draft of the thesis will aspire to be written for an audience of equals. The need to be aware of this transition is important for it constitutes the element of authenticity in a thesis, an element that is often an explicit criterion in the examination process. Self-insight, an ancient concept dating back to Socrates' fourth century BCE admonition that an unexamined life is not worth living, is a key ingredient in developing an awareness of the transition in the relationship with one's audience. The following advice to supervisors illustrates the point:

    Most importantly, encourage your student, when examining recently submitted theses, to look out for how the writer 'talks' about his or her role in the research— to what extent is the writer 'present' in the thesis?

    (Cited in Paltridge & Starfield, 2007, p.130)

2. The final draft of a thesis cannot, of course, be entirely authentic because it needs to fulfil the cultural and administrative requirements expected of it. Authenticity in a thesis might, thus, be regarded as filtered by those requirements. Nonetheless, even though filtered, developing a reflexive insight into one's personal growth as a researcher and writer will permit the achievement of a number of key objectives. The first is an ability to pitch writing at the right level. This means an ability to 'thicken' writing with detail that assists rather than irritates readers. The second is an ability to develop an

awareness of and an informed response to the many subjective decisions that writing a thesis involves. Most important, though, it means the development of a well-grounded confidence that, in turn, translates into assertive writing.

5.10 ASSERTIVENESS

1. Assertive writers are able to infuse their writing with vigour because it enables them to do two things denied those who are hesitant and defensive. The first is the ability, because they know to whom they are writing and where they are going, to write concisely. The second is the ability to choose from a wider vocabulary. Freed from the hesitant and defensive writer's need to be only narrative and descriptive, assertive writers can also argue. When necessary, therefore, bland verbs like 'said' or 'wrote' can be rejected in favour of more forceful ones like 'overlooked' and 'criticised'; bland adjectives like 'sound' and 'good' can be replaced by more powerful ones like 'admirable', 'insightful' and 'deficient'; and weak transitional words like 'secondly' and 'another' can be substituted by those that convey an explicit opinion like 'of equal importance…', and 'in contrast to…'

2. Assertive vocabulary is not, however, the only way to focus a reader's attention on what is considered important. Exclamation marks[6] or repetition, for example, can also be used. But, one of the most effective ways to focus attention and thus indicate assertiveness is by astute use of placement. Readers, as are listeners, tend to be most heavily influenced by what comes either first or last: this applies to the thesis as a whole, to individual chapters, to paragraphs and, ultimately, to sentences also. Placement, therefore, is an element in writing that will need to be kept continuously in mind. The result, should this not be done, might be the cardinal sin of burying important points in the bowels of the text where, like a rose born to blush unseen, they will lie unnoticed.

5.11 HEDGING

1. Assertiveness should not, however, blind a thesis writer to one of the necessary conditions of academic discourse: the need to hedge, to indicate analytic uncertainty. Because no methodology or method is free of limiting conditions, because causation is problematic, it is impossible to prove anything incontrovertibly: all temporal 'proofs' are ephemeral phenomena open to disproof:

To say that 'X is true' may be misleading in a complex environment. To say 'X is true sometimes or to a degree', may be more accurate. In a complex world fuzziness may increase accuracy whilst assertive certainty may decrease it.

(Smith & Jenks, 2006, p.18)

On this basis it can be argued that no statement in a thesis should be prescriptive. Instead, modifying words such as 'suggests', 'supports' or 'reinforces' rather than 'proves' or 'shows', should be used as *hedges* in order to provide nuance. Doing so is not, however, a simple process for it involves drawing on a complex range of linguistic resources to persuade readers in a way that is concomitantly precise, cautious and appropriately humble (Paltridge & Starfield, 2007). This is the ability that lies at the core of a carefully defined argument: some evidence will support an argument more strongly than will others and this will need to be indicated. Thus, defining nuance as 'shades of meaning' implies the use of carefully chosen words in order to indicate to readers the degree to which particular evidence supports a particular assertion. 'Suggests', for example, is less strong than 'supports' that, in turn, is less strong than 'reinforces'. Hedging does not, therefore, mean a blanket hesitancy to make any commitment: defending a thesis does not mean being defensive. This does not necessarily apply, though, outside the realms of academe. For example, governors of reserve banks, in order not to commit themselves to particular policies, have become adept at delivering carefully crafted Delphic statements. Economists then, with equal poetic care, subsequently deconstruct these statements:

The tone of the statement has shifted the reserve bank away from a firm to a slight tightening bias. This is because the statement says only 'a somewhat more restrictive policy was required'. This is weaker than 'a more restrictive stance is required'.

2. There will be few, if any, occasions in a thesis where statements that a reader needs to deconstruct in order to speculate meaning will be appropriate. There might be instances in a thesis, though, where hesitancy is appropriate. In the discussion or in the conclusion there might, for example, be occasions where the evidence is merely indicative thus preventing the making of anything other than speculative statements. However, particular care should be taken to avoid sweeping statements that have no evidential support apart from an implied belief they are common knowledge: *All researchers must…* or *All research should…* Such statements might in most instances be true, but they provide an irresistible temptation to examiners to look for the exception (Burton & Steane, 2004c). The need in most cases, instead, is for the researcher to help readers comprehend meaning by making a careful assessment of the quality of the evidence used to support an argument. Note the careful blend of both humility and confidence with which Watson and Crick announced one of the most significant scientific achievements of the twentieth century, the discovery of the molecular structure of nucleic acids:

We wish to suggest a structure for the salt of deoxyribose nucleic acid (DNA)… A structure for nucleic acid has already been proposed by Pauling and Corey… In our opinion, this structure is unsatisfactory for two reasons: We believe that the material which gives the X-ray diagrams is the salt, not the free acid... Some of the van der Waals distances appear to be too small.

(Cited in Steane, 2004, p.137)

5.12 SYSTEMATIC ARGUMENTS

1. Rhetoric, dialectic, and logic respectively distinguish the process, procedure and product of argument. Rhetoric is the study of process; attention is directed to audience, purpose and occasion. Dialectic, the study of procedure, focuses on the rules for the scrutiny of evidence while, finally, logic tests the validity of the product of argument (Dillon, 1991). Arguments have two contradictory impulses: self-groundedness and self-reflexiveness. The former is a process informed by an unproblematic rationality while the latter seeks to make that rationality problematic. In this context it is possible to say that both empirical and interpretive researchers persuade by reason. Academic discourse thus entails a rotating division of labour: a speaker or writer has a vested interest in his or her assumptions while a listener or reader has a vested interest in his or her capacity to challenge those assumptions. The process, thus, permits mutual assumptions to be examined regressively (Dillon, 1991). However, as a sequence of ideas structured to support a particular position, the process need not necessarily be systematic. Systematic arguments rest on an assumption that for any significant question sufficient agreement can be found to arrive at reasoned consensus. This assumption is not, though, universally shared. Richard Rorty, for example, imagines academic discourse as conversation: an open-ended process that may be oriented towards agreement but does not necessarily produce it (Dillon, 1991). The interpretation of the nature of academic discourse depends, therefore, upon value judgements that influence our intellectual behaviour (Fiumara, 1995). Thus the statement that 'one of the most significant challenges confronting thesis writers is to argue rather than to assert or summarise' (McWilliam, 2006, p.167) ought to be interpreted in the context of a term in dispute for it embraces different sets of understandings.

2. A systematic argument is a series of propositions connected by the conclusion they claim to support. In this sense understanding the logic of an argument is based on inference: this (conclusion) for that (reason) (Barnacle, 2006). The salient attribute of systematic arguments, thus, is rationality (Dillon, 1991). The model for this process derives from Aristotle who identified four basic types of argument: abductive, analogical, inductive and deductive. Most academic work involves a continual interplay between each. In abduction,

alternatively called inference to the best explanation or hypothetical deduction, a hypothesis is proposed that, if sound, would best explain the relevant evidence. This is the type of reasoning made famous by Sherlock Holmes. It depends on the plausibility of the best explanation and operates on the surprise principle: any other explanation than that proposed in the hypothesis would be a surprise. Argument by analogy is based on an inference that if two or more phenomena are similar in some observed way they are also likely to be similar in a way not yet observed. As in the case of abductive argument the plausibility of the inference is paramount in deciding the acceptability of the conclusion. In inductive arguments the premises are believed to support but not ensure a conclusion. This is because inductive reasoning is a process where assumptions are determined by repeated observation. An inductive argument, therefore, is the formulation of a general statement from individual instances. Deductive reasoning, however, proceeds from generalisation to particular instance, the proof of the conclusion being established by the truth of the premises.

Deduction

3. The distinction between deductive and inductive arguments is made clear in syllogisms, three-step statements devised by Aristotle, in which one proposition (the conclusion) is inferred from two others (the major and minor premises). Where the inference is definitive the syllogism is deductive where suggestive, inductive. The former is indicated in the following: All humans are mortal (major premise), you are human (minor premise) therefore, you are mortal. In order to be credible, though, deductive arguments need to be both valid and true. They might, for example, be validly constructed but not true because one of the premises is wrong: All humans are happy (major premise), you are human (minor premise) therefore, you are happy. Alternatively, they might be true but, because the conclusion does not follow from the premises, invalid: All humans are mammals (major premise), most mammals live on land (minor premise) certainly therefore, humans live on land. It is, therefore, only when a deductive argument is validly constructed and has true premises that it proves its conclusion.

4. This should be borne in mind when critiquing a deductive argument: the conclusion might be true but the argument invalid. Nonetheless, the conclusion of a valid and true deductive argument provides an impression of clarity, power and persuasiveness and is particularly useful in formal logic and in the natural sciences where premises are often definitions. A definition, however, might be a dictionary definition in which case the quality of the argument will change if the definition changes. Because particular verification criteria

have been satisfied it might, though, be an empirical definition. But, even in this case, the conclusion is accepted on a conditional basis, for a deductive argument is only defined as definitive on the assumption that either or both of the premises might subsequently be proved wrong. It is also worth noting that the strength of deductive arguments comes at a price for the conclusion and, thus, new insights that might be derived from it are tightly constrained within the boundaries imposed by the premises.

Induction

5. This is not the case in inductive arguments where, even though the conclusions are less robust than in deductive arguments, they nonetheless provide better opportunities to generate new ideas. This is because inductive arguments generalise from the known in order to make inferences about the unknown. Unlike deductive arguments inductive arguments are neither valid or invalid nor true or untrue. Instead, given that the premises only support the conclusion to a degree, they are either sound or unsound. The statement *most people are happy because an opinion poll with a sample of ten indicates that is the case* is unsound. However, the statement *most people eat fish; you are a person; it is likely therefore that you eat fish* is sound. So also is the statement *many people eat lobsters; you are a person; it is possible therefore that you eat lobsters.* Note the use of 'likely' in the first statement and 'possible' in the second. Each of these words indicates the strength of the evidence relative to the conclusion reached. It is often the case in theses that such qualifiers are omitted: the use of 'therefore' in isolation leaving it up to the examiners to decide the strength of the evidence provided. But even when strong inductive, as in the case of deductive arguments, are only conditionally so for inductive arguments rest on the flaw of inductivity: no matter how many times an observation of a particular phenomenon has indicated the soundness of a conclusion, all that is needed to make the conclusion unsound is one contrary observation. The term 'black swan', for example, is derived from an ancient perception in Europe that all swans are white. The seventeenth century discovery of black swans in Australia metamorphosed the meaning of the term: it now connotes the reversal of a perceived impossibility.

Epistemic and structural problems

6. Although systematic arguments are called such because of their reliance on rational inference, rationality in contemporary terms is enmeshed in a fallibilist epistemology. In other words being rational implies acceptance of the certainty of occasional error in the procedures we adopt (Woods, 2008). We have in this sense taken to heart Oliver Cromwell's seventeenth century plea to recalcitrant parliamentarians: 'Gentlemen, I beseech thee; in

the bowels of Christ, consider that ye may be mistaken' (Allen Smith, 1994, p.127). Being rational, as Thomas Kuhn has shown, also implies rejection of the idea that sets of rules can be devised which will tell us how rational agreement can be reached between conflicting points of view (Bernstein, 1983). This is acknowledgement that participants in an argument often cannot, by logical and evidential proofs, establish the correctness of their perspective: convincing proof can only be given to someone who accepts the premises of an argument. If premises are based upon principles each contests, the participants simply talk past one another, each unable to appreciate the point of view of the other (Sharrock & Read, 2002). Therefore, apart from the epistemic difficulties deduction and induction impose the structure of systematic arguments tends to make them suitable only for isolated adversarial arguments in logic or highly mathematical disciplines (Fiumara, 1995). Otherwise interwoven complexity prevents the demarcation of both clear premises and precise conclusions. Many academic arguments tend, thus, to be by enthymeme rather than syllogism, the former a syllogism in which one or more of the premises is assumed rather than stated: *you*, for example, *are mortal because you are human.* In most other cases, however, 'arguments are buried within dense paragraphs of text containing many sub-clauses, hidden clauses, undeclared assumptions and countless assertions' (Barnacle, 2006, p.99).

Argument as warfare

7. It is because of the difficulties posed in attempting to convince another of our point of view that, in Western culture at least, argument has developed an eristic or controversial tendency. This means victory over an opponent is the primary goal rather than to understand his or her point of view. At least two features of Western culture make this evident. One is admiration for parsimony and lucidity. 'Occam's razor', for example, is a principle established by a fourteenth century English monk expressed in the law of parsimony: *lex parsimoniae.* The law requires the 'shaving off' of as many assumptions in an argument as possible without weakening the conclusion. The implication, therefore, is the possibility of objective argument where only one position can be correct. Another is the metaphoric association of argument with warfare. This is evident when a claim is 'defended, points are attacked, ground is gained or lost and arguments are won' (Fiumara, 1995, p.43). In this sense adversaries are required to attack each other for they share the assumption that only one point of view can survive (Fiumara, 1995).
8. By what process, though, is victory to be achieved? For one side to concede to the other requires a common understanding not only of what constitute sound

reasons but also the rules governing the exchange. These are explanations for the importance of disciplines in academic debate. In history, for example, each participant has a reasonably clear understanding of what arguments are clearly inadmissible and which are possibly worthy of belief (Dillon, 1991). However, in law, an adversary profession, participants are permitted, within the rules, not only to advance causes they know to be unjust but also to harm others in ways that, if not for the discipline, would be wrong. This specificity of argument implies that both reasoning and disciplinary knowledge lie at the core of rational academic argument. It also implies that this rationality is not transferable: being able to think rationally in one discipline does not guarantee the ability to do so in others (Barnacle, 2006). An additional implication is that academic arguments apply at least two models to establish their degree of credibility. One is the Anglo-Saxon adversarial legal pleading where ratified members of the disciplinary community play the role of judge and jury. The other is where the one to be convinced is the opposing party. In this case an alternation between partial and impartial stances is assumed in the hope of arriving at an eventual reasoned consensus (Dillon, 1991).

9. In each of these models, though, the vocabulary of argument-as-war needs to be transcended. Possibly the best way to do so is to show that argument-as-war is just a metaphor and can, thus, be changed: argument-as-development, for example. In this case the metaphor would be more amenable to building a discussion rather than to addressing objections to isolated parts of whatever position is opposed. Adopting the latter approach ignores the fact that claims do not exist in isolation but are aspects of integrated systems (Fiumara, 1995). In addition, from a deconstructive perspective disagreement between participants in any argument is largely relational and, thus, collaborative for disagreement can only be recognised as such against a background of broad agreement on other issues (Fiumara, 1995). So, while it might be proper to refuse to engage in argument with some individuals because the very act of doing so may concede too much (Dillon, 1991), making sense of the arguments of others requires us to find a basis of reason in them. To do otherwise simply undermines the ability to understand what it is they are being unreasonable about (Fiumara, 1995). This is why Thomas Kuhn gave the following advice to his students:

When reading the works of an important thinker, look first for the apparent absurdities in the text and ask yourself how a sensible person could have written them. When you find an answer…when those passages make sense, then you may find that more central passages, ones you previously thought you understood, have changed their meaning.

(Cited in Bernstein, 1983, p.31)

It is in this sense then that academics, when they argue, do not necessarily aim at seeking agreement with others. What they seek instead is to impinge on others, in other words, to be taken seriously by them (Dillon, 1991). This perspective is central to the thesis examination process: examiners are not looking to be convinced they are looking, instead, for an argument they can take seriously.

5.13 CASUIST ARGUMENTS

1. This was the context in which, in 1958, the British philosopher Stephen Toulmin published *The Uses of Argument* (Toulmin, 2003). A like-minded contemporary of Thomas Kuhn and precursor to Richard Rorty and Jacques Derrida, Toulmin focused in the book on the justificatory aspect of argumentation as opposed to the inferential approach of systematic arguments. Whereas the latter make inferences based on a set of principles to make a claim, Toulmin believed that reasoners first make a claim and then sift and test ideas to support it. This is most apparent, for example, in regard to moral issues. Both Plato and Aristotle were absolutists: they believed that all moral issues could be resolved by adhering to a set of universal moral principles. Toulmin, however, argued that these absolutes are usually irrelevant to the complex moral issues people confront in daily life. Rorty later illustrated this when he wrote:

> *If I am told that a controversial action which I have taken has to be defended by being subsumed under a universal, rational principle, I may be able to dream up such a principle to fit the occasion, but sometimes I may only be able to say, 'Well, it seemed like the best thing to do at the time, all things considered.' It is not clear that the latter defense is less rational than some universal–sounding principle that I have dreamed up ad hoc to justify my action.*

(Rorty, 1999, p.xxx).

Field dependence and field invariance

2. It was for this reason that Toulmin introduced the concept 'argument field': because they vary from field to field aspects of some arguments are 'field dependent' while others are 'field invariant'. It was the distinction between the types of field, Toulmin believed, that explained the discrepancy between absolutism and moral quandary. The former ignores the field dependent aspect of argument. However, making this distinction exposed arguments to relativism for Toulmin also argued that relativists overemphasised the 'field dependence' of arguments at the cost of the 'field invariant'. There would, therefore, be no basis for distinguishing moral from immoral arguments. Thus,

in an attempt to establish middle ground between absolutism and relativism, Toulmin applied casuistry or case ethics.

Individual and type cases

3. Casuistry had a long historical heritage but one which had been tarnished when late medieval clerics had used the 'field dependence' aspect of the approach to serve their own interests. Toulmin, however, argued that the problem was the abuse of casuistry not with the approach itself. Unlike both absolutism and relativism, casuistry emphasises the importance of comparison in the conduct of argument. In order to do so it employs standard principles, called 'type cases', without resorting to absolutism. In moral arguments, for example, a standard principle such as the sanctity of life is used as a point of reference. An individual case is then rationally compared with the type case. Thus, for a casuist, the circumstances of an individual case are essential for evaluating an appropriate moral response. Toulmin later used the example of Descartes to illustrate how the circumstances of his exposure to the horrors of the Thirty Years War help in understanding why he thought in the way he did:

    The war must have been a searing and indigestible kind of experience...it's under-standable that he felt an intellectual mission to create a basis for people to agree on foundations about which they need no longer fight.

    (Lifson, 1997, np)

Claim, evidence and warrant

4. However, rationally comparing individual cases with type cases is not without its difficulties. First, a type case may fit an individual case only ambiguously. Second, two contradictory type cases may fit an individual case. Third, an individual case may be so unique it has no type case with which it might be compared. In order to resolve such difficulties Toulmin developed a model identifying three of the most commonly used elements in argument: claim, evidence and warrant. A claim states a position on an issue. But, without evidential support, a claim is merely an assertion. However, the relationship between claim and evidence is often tangential or opaque. Opposing lawyers in a trial, for example, might agree on the evidence but dispute its relationship to the criminal act. One lawyer will present warrants, statements that make explicit how evidence supports a claim, while the other will provide a rebuttal: an argument that the statements are unwarranted. Because the weakest part of any argument is its weakest warrant the first lawyer might, in response rebut the rebuttal by providing further reasons, or backing, to support a warrant. Advertisers regularly use implicit warrants. They might,

for example, claim their product makes hair silky, a claim that only makes sense on the assumption that the target audience identifies with a culture that values silky hair. They also rarely make the link between product and end result explicit because if they were to do so it would often be simple to reject the warrant: an advertisement for a sports car, for example, in which a scantily clad model reclines across the bonnet. Academic arguments rarely lend themselves to such salacious warrants the nearest equivalent being the *argumentum ad vericundiam* in which the warrants a writer provides are references to individuals prominent in the field: this is impression management, since important people believe something so should we (Golden-Biddle & Locke, 1997).

Concession, refutation and irrelevance

5. Rarely, though, are warrants so blatantly presented for academics are aware that counterarguments are bound to emerge. Dealing with these proactively is, thus, an important element in building an argument. In doing so participants tend to adopt one or more of the following three approaches. The first is strategic concession. On the one hand, this frequently involves the use of qualifiers to indicate the degree to which evidence supports a warrant: 'usually', 'sometimes' or 'partially', for example. On the other, it often involves strengthening one's own position by acknowledging and incorporating part of another perspective that cannot be refuted. An argument on global warming, for example, might concede natural fluctuations of the earth's temperature but argue that these are not the only or most significant contributors to temperature increase. The second approach is refutation: an identification of a weakness in the position of the other so fundamental that the warrant ought to be rejected. The third is a demonstration of irrelevance: though aspects of the other argument might be valid, they fail to meet the criteria that define the issue.

Argument as dialogue

6. Unlike the absolutism inherent in systematic arguments, casuistry has removed the concept of conclusiveness from argument. There is no ultimate justification for a justification. In its place is commentary upon commentary: argument as open-ended dialogue (Dillon, 1991). In doing so it has allowed arguments in academic writing, as in the following example, to reflect the complexity and richness of the human condition:

Foucault is fond of transgressive poets and writers. There are at least two questions here. What is the reason for Foucault's fond interest? Why does Bataille fit the specification? There is something of a tension between the two responses. Fou-

cault's reasons can be presented as twofold, and of course they are intertwined. The first argument concerns what Foucault calls the 'tragic or cosmic experience of madness' which the rules of rational discourse exclude from literature. It is kept alive, in view, presented back to us in transgressive literature and art: Bosch, Goya, Nietzsche, Roussell, Bataille. The second is the more familiar argument that such work points back to the instability and disorder at the heart of being... The poet and the madman thus share the same dwelling and the same proximity to being in Foucault's work...

(Smith & Jenks, 2006, p.152)

ENDNOTES

1   A defining feature of Euclidean geometry is an assumption of reduction; that phenomena can be broken down into fundamental parts.
2   Basic to rhetoric is the indivisibility of means from meaning; how something is said conveys as much meaning as what is said.
3   Chapter titles in the table of contents are normally preceded by the abstract, acknowledgements and an optional dedication. Chapter titles are then followed by a list of tables and figures and by abbreviations and/or glossary if there are any.
4   There are a number of ways in which chapter headings may be numbered: titles may be preceded by Roman numerals (XI: Title) or the titles may be preceded by the word 'CHAPTER' followed by the number in words (Chapter Two: Title, the APA preference) or figures (Chapter 2: Title, the MLA preference).
5   Paratexts are external cues. A book's mere appearance, for example, creates a prior impression of it.
6   Because a thesis is not usually an exclamatory genre exclamation marks should be used with care.

CHAPTER 6

Drafting

…what really characterizes [Shakespeare's] work…is a positive and palpable appreciation of the transfixing power of language. 'A Midsummer Night's Dream' remains an enchanting work after four hundred years, but few would argue that it cuts to the very heart of human behaviour. What it does do is take, and give, a positive satisfaction in the joyous possibilities of verbal expression.

(Bryson, 2008, p.109)

6.1 INTRODUCTION

1. Drafting a thesis is a meaning making process. It is not only a complex cognitive act but also an incremental and evolving one. In this sense a thesis writer's relationship with writing will form and reform (Logsdon, 2006). For example, the style of writing adopted in each draft of the thesis will differ. This will be most apparent when the initial and final drafts are compared. The marked difference between them a consequence of maturation in understanding and skill in writing and of the different audiences for which each draft will have been written: the initial draft will be writer centred, the final draft reader centred. In most cases, though, the initial readership will be small, select, exceptionally busy and grossly underpaid for the task they are expected to perform (Cryer, 2006).

2. It is in this context that a particular reality needs to be borne in mind: writing a thesis is an examination, albeit an extended one. So, as in the case of most examinations, it is both written and marked within time constraints. The constraints for the examiners lie not only in an administrative requirement to complete the examining process as efficiently as possible, but also in the other academic and administrative responsibilities they might have. This is particularly apposite for writers of masters' theses for these responsibilities tend to weigh particularly heavily at the end and beginning of each semester, the times when masters' theses are most often examined. Nonetheless, because the examining process for all theses is likely to be both constrained and

interrupted, they should be written on the basis of a worst case scenario: that each examiner will only read the thesis twice at the most and that each of these readings will be undertaken during a number of brief, periodically interrupted sessions. This is not a likely scenario, but the dividend for writing the thesis on the basis that it might eventuate is the emphasis provided to the importance of making the text in the thesis as clear and 'reader friendly' as possible.

6.2 THE PROCESS OF WRITING

1. The key to doing so is recognition of the fundamental, interrelated principles involved in the thesis writing process (Murray, 2003, p.7):
   • Insight develops as a consequence of writing because thinking and writing are inseparable processes.
   • Clarity in writing is the end product of multiple drafts.
   • Regular writing and—just as important—reading, develops fluency.

These principles are likely to be immediately apparent to writers of qualitative theses where personal connection with both the process and product of research relate thinking and writing intimately: evocation through which readers feel present with the researcher is a prime aim. For these researchers writing, therefore, becomes an explicit part of the research process. So is it also for writers of exegetic theses for they too write their data into existence. It is significantly less apparent though to empirical researchers. This explains why they often comprehend the thesis process as a sustained period of research followed by a sustained period of writing. It is, however, an outdated approach stemming from a pre-computer age when research could not as easily be written up and amended as the research proceeded. It is also a mistaken approach because for all researchers writing is an essential means of clarifying thinking. Poor writing in a mathematics thesis, for example, not only makes it difficult for examiners to establish whether or not a proof is correct; its lack of clarity normally indicates the proof is incorrect. Delaying writing becomes, therefore, an obstacle to understanding (Paltridge & Starfield, 2007). Completion of the end product is, as a result, also delayed and its quality diminished. There is also an additional reason why delaying writing is a mistake. Writing a thesis is often similar to building a house—it will usually cost more and take longer to complete than initially supposed. There is sound historical precedent to support this view. For example Gustave Flaubert in the nineteenth century wrote: 'A good sentence can be a good day's work'; while Hemingway in the twentieth rewrote the ending of *A Farewell to Arms* thirty-nine times before he was satisfied (Woods, 2006, p.16). So, because writing the thesis will usually take longer than initially expected start writing as early as possible and take care to budget for extra time. It is possible, though, to go too far by continuing to write until near perfection has been achieved. It is important to keep a sense of perspective: because theses are written under examination conditions a compromise necessarily needs to be found between what can be produced within the constraints of those conditions and an ideal situation (Murray, 2003). It is within this context that there might be need, if they are perceived in a negative light, for a revision of attitude towards deadlines: they have the virtue of bringing a potentially endless process to a concise end.

The affective dimension of writing

2. Even with this revised attitude in place, there is no denying that while some researchers find writing a thesis an enjoyable, if not liberating, exercise some find it stressful. That there is an affective dimension to writing in addition to the intellectual is perfectly understandable. This is not only because it is a time constrained and potentially isolating process, but also because it is both quantitatively and qualitatively different from any writing task previously undertaken (Paltridge & Starfield, 2007). Writing a thesis is also threatening: it exposes the quality of one's thoughts to public judgement. But, worrying how writing and thinking might be judged focuses energy on self and derails generative thinking (Logsdon, 2006). It also fails to take into account one of the cruel ironies of life: the better the writing, the more critical attention it will receive. Learn, then, to be flattered, not threatened, by this attention because it means that what has been written is worth paying attention to (Murray, 2003).

3. This, of course, is easier said than done, so note the thinking behind the Johari Window: a mechanism for indicating levels of self-awareness and mutual understanding between individuals within a group. The 'open area' reflects knowledge common to the individual and the group. The 'blind area' reflects information others know about the individual but which is unknown to that individual. The 'hidden area' reflects what only the individual knows, while the 'unknown area' reflects the potential, unknown to all, latent within the individual.

Open area	Blind area
Hidden area	Unknown area

The trick, in so far as is feasible, is to enlarge the 'open area' at the expense of the other three. In regard to both the 'hidden' and 'blind' areas, for example, an individual might have a low estimate of his or her abilities as a writer. Others, however, might hold those abilities in high regard. This disjuncture is surprisingly common, it even has a name: the 'impostor syndrome', a feeling that one's inadequacy will eventually be revealed for all to see. Ludwig Wittgenstein, for example, was one among many gifted individuals torn between intellectual brilliance and feelings of deep personal inadequacy (Lifson, 1997). The following indicates how misplaced these feelings were. In 1929 Wittgenstein returned from the Continent to Cambridge.

He was met at the railway station by a crowd of England's greatest intellectuals, discovering rather to his horror that he was one of the most famed philosophers in the world. In a letter to his wife [John Maynard] Keynes wrote: 'Well, God has arrived. I met him on the 5.15 train'.

(Wikipedia)

4. This type of disjuncture can only be revealed if one is prepared to discuss the issue with others. Doing so will reveal a less ironic interpretation of the words from Robbie Burns' 1785 poem 'To a Louse', *Oh wad some Pow'r the giftie gie us to see oursels as ithers see us*: that another's view of us is as interesting and as revealing as our own (Fiumara, 1995). Because beginning researchers are new to the thesis writing process it is reasonable to expect the 'unknown' area to be large. However, an essential personal ingredient to enable the full possibilities of the 'unknown' area to be seized is well-developed emotional intelligence: realistic self-awareness, in other words, of one's strengths and weaknesses. This is a necessary precursor to the implementation of a personal development plan: a structured process that builds on those strengths and addresses the perceived weaknesses. An aspect of such a plan, for example, might be to establish or join a group of fellow thesis writers. When working effectively these groups are generative and reciprocal in the sense that members support as well as challenge one another. The reason they do so is enmeshed in the human condition: not only are individuals wired differently but the mere act of speaking appears to stimulate thinking. This is also why it is so important to develop the ability to give confident oral presentations on one's research.

5. Discovering and developing the necessary skills to enlarge the 'open' area will also be enhanced significantly in an emotionally comfortable writing environment. For some this might be a crowded railway cafeteria as in the case of J. K. Rowling, while for others it might be the preference of Henry Higgins in *My Fair Lady* for a study with the silence of an undiscovered tomb. Writing a thesis also has an important managerial component: research material must be appropriately organised and catalogued before writing begins. It does not matter whether a software program or index cards are used, as long as the system is efficient. If not writing effectiveness will decline because the flow of thought will continually be disturbed by the need to stop writing for extended periods in order to access material. It is for this reason important, if software is to be used, to become comfortable with it prior to writing the thesis rather than during the course of writing it.

Visualisation, memory and speech

6. Avoiding interruption of the thinking process raises the fundamental question of how we think. Although thinking and writing are inseparable processes, writing is thinking constrained by print in the sense that prose is written, not spoken: 'lacking the expressive resources of tone and gesture, it is monologic, not dialogic' (Dillon, 1991, p.116). Writing is also two dimensional and sequential. This is why it is often so difficult to translate onto paper what seems so clear in the multidimensional processes of one's mind. But, whereas prose is written, text can take many forms: diagrams, graphs and charts are a few examples. Because, unlike language, they can verbalise several things at the same time both reader and writer can visualise complex or interactive relationships that lie beyond the reach of simple sentences (Mauch & Birch, 1998). It is also for this reason that mind maps and argument maps are so useful and why diagrams might be used when appropriate in any part of all theses.

7. Diagrams play such a useful role because, in humans, spatial ability is highly developed. However, when we read and write we tend to use short-term memory, this is both asset and liability. The advantage is quick retrieval, the disadvantage is limited capacity: seven plus or minus two items. But, how do we know that the seven plus or minus two items that we currently remember are the most relevant of all the possible items? This limitation of short-term memory explains our 'bounded rationality': we are continuously swamped with information but have only limited capacity to process it (Bryant, 2004). Therefore, in order to allow us to respond meaningfully, memory has to be filtered even if the cost is loss of potentially useful information. This cost, however, is low when the fate of Funes in the short story, *Funes the Memorious*, is considered: he was condemned to forget nothing and, burdened with an accumulation of memories, lived a mercifully short life (Taleb, 2007).

8. While speaking does not release us from the limitations of memory, it does offer freedom from both the mechanics of the writing process and from consideration of the conventions and rules of writing. Release from these constraints provides the necessary freedom to concentrate on the substance of what needs to be written. Supervisors frequently comment in this regard that students who find it difficult to express a clear line of thinking on paper are often able to vocalise that line of thinking coherently when talking. This is an entirely human phenomenon. For example, a character in a novel 'felt a need of talking, so as to fix into a pattern of phrases some ideas obscurely milling in his head' (di Lampedusa, 1974, p.159). This explains why sound recording one's thoughts by vocalising and then replaying them prior to writing can be very helpful (Phillips & Pugh, 2005).

Research journals

9. Freewriting is premised on a similar principle: writing freely follows 'a stream of consciousness' directed at self as audience. A useful adjunct to this strategy is to keep a personal research journal. There are a number of advantages to doing so.

    - Ideas pertaining to the research can be entered as they occur. Because writing a thesis tends to be mind-occupying ideas will surface, without any prompting, at any time, day or night. They will tend to do so most frequently during mind-freeing activities, those akin to jogging or gardening. This indicates the importance of adequate rest because it is during this time that the brain subconsciously consolidates thoughts and memories and when, as a result, ideas suddenly occur to us. It is a romantic myth, therefore, that brilliant ideas magically appear from nowhere: a consequence of sudden inspiration. Ideas, instead, build on what went before. But, just as they arrive unprompted so too do they have an unnerving tendency to disappear in the same way. All that is then left is the agony of the memory of having a brilliant idea without being able to remember what the brilliant idea was. Not all ideas, of course, will be brilliant: creative people generally have more bad ideas than good ones. However, having ideas caged in a journal will enable them to be evaluated.

    - Because a research journal will document procedures and capture interpretations as the research and writing processes unfold it will also reflect the ongoing history of the thesis. For many researchers this will allow confidence to be gained when, looking back, it will be seen how writing and thinking skills have improved. Subjectivity, in other words, is subject to change as the research proceeds. This is why for qualitative researchers journals or more accurately in this case, research diaries, serve as an important resource for self-reflexive analysis: 'Yes, I kept a journal. It is like a diary with feelings and frustrations included in the entries' (cited in Meloy, 2002, p.135).

Fonts

10. There are other practical aspects to thesis writing that mind and argument maps, sound recorders, freewriting and research journals will do little to address. One is the need to give some thought to the font used in a thesis. Serifs are details on the ends of some of the strokes of letter symbols. A font without serifs is sans-serif. Serifed fonts like Times New Roman are used in lengthy, hard copy texts because the details on the end of the strokes make them more distinguishable to the eye and, thus, more readable. However, because they are clear cut, sans-serif fonts like Verdana are usually more

legible on computer screens. Some fonts like Palatino are proportionately spaced, the letter I, for example, taking less space than m. But, in monospaced fonts like Courier each letter occupies the same width. Because of the space differential between letters, proportionately spaced fonts are easy to skim read. But, because the eye glides over letters occupying less space, monospaced fonts are more suitable for proofreading. It is also because the human eye uses difference to position its focus that in both hard copy and electronic formats right unjustified text is easier to read than text with both left and right edges justified.

Keeping to schedule

11. A relevant aspect of the human condition is the peculiarity that most of us have particular periods during the day or night when writing either becomes easier or more difficult. What needs to be done, therefore, is to identify the times when writing becomes easier—for most of us mid-morning and early afternoon—and arrange a writing schedule around those times. Once this has been done remain disciplined and keep to the schedule. A novelist indicated how he remained disciplined: 'I write when I'm inspired, and I see to it that I'm inspired at nine o'clock every morning' (De Vries, P. cited in Dunleavy, 2003, p.148). Beyond the limits of the schedule interrupt normal life as little as possible: sleeping well and getting as much exercise as possible will be far more efficient in the long term than attempting to write to the point of exhaustion. For confirmation consider the following lines from Shakespeare's *As You Like It*: 'And so, from hour to hour, we ripe and ripe, And then, from hour to hour, we rot and rot, And thereby hangs a tale' (2.7.26–28).

Efficiency

12. However, even when starting a writing session at an optimum time, the initial level of writing efficiency will tend to be low because it takes time to develop the momentum established at the end of the previous session. Ideas that seemed permanently etched into the psyche at the end of one writing session may have completely disappeared at the beginning of the next. There are a number of strategies to help 'warm-up' and gradually retrieve them. One is to 'park writing downhill' by setting time aside at the end of each writing session to write a brief note about how the writing is to proceed at the start of the next. This strategy is particularly useful if there is to be a significant interval between writing sessions. A useful adjunct to this strategy is to conduct mental callisthenics at the start of each new session. For example, free association can be used in which, in rapid succession, one spontaneous idea is allowed to trigger another. Alternatively, do some quick

mental arithmetic. For example, complete the following in less than twenty seconds: 8 x 6; 13 − 5; 17 + 4; 9 x 4; 18 / 3; 17 − 9; 4 x 8; 7 + 4; 12 / 3; 9 x 8. Once these exercises have been completed go on to read the final pages from the previous session. Although doing so might appear to slow forward momentum two purposes are served: text can be edited because the writer is coming to it fresh and the thread of the writing can more easily be picked up from where it was left off.

6.3 MODELLING THE THESIS

1. Why is waking up in the morning not a frightening experience? It would be if no preparations for the future had been made: no shelter, no food, no money... Most of us, however, do prepare. By doing so we bring light to the frightening darkness of the unknown. Why not, therefore, adopt the same strategy when writing a thesis? Put as much 'light' in place as possible before starting so there is no need to write into metaphorical darkness. A similar strategy is applied when starting a large jigsaw puzzle. The pieces are not simply selected at random but first sorted into edge pieces and colours. The emphasis here, then, is on structure and helps combine both the strengths of serialist and holistic thought. The latter allows context to emerge gradually by completion of one part of a task at a time while the former requires comprehension of the whole task before attempting to undertake any part of it (Cryer, 2006). The emphasis researchers from different theoretic approaches place on each type of thinking will, however, differ. Empirical researchers will tend to emphasise a holistic approach while exegetic and qualitative researchers will tend to emphasise serialism.

Word limits

2. However, thesis writers in each of these approaches will be under a similar imperative: to keep within the word limits imposed by the university. Going back to as late as the nineteen sixties it is possible to find doctoral and even some masters' theses that run to two sizable volumes. The rapid growth since then in the number of postgraduate researchers and the increasing pressure to complete within a shrinking timeframe has seen increased emphasis placed on the maximum acceptable length of theses. So, far from being rewarded for going beyond the limit, a thesis is likely to be penalised or immediately returned for revision if it does. At present the average maximum length for a full master's thesis is about 35 000 words and for a doctoral thesis between 80 000 and 100 000. Footnotes or endnotes and the reference list are normally included in the total. Appendices are normally excluded. As in the

case of maximum word length normal practice might not, though, hold true at particular universities. It is also the case that there will be considerable variation in length expectations between disciplines. Theses in mathematics and physics, for example, are generally much shorter than those in history or sociology. So, one of the essential pieces of information to garner when starting a thesis is to establish from supervisors what the word length is expected to be.

The initial model

3. Once this is known an initial model of what the final draft might look like can be envisioned. Shakespeare provides the precedence:

When we mean to build,
We first survey the plot, then draw the model;
And when we see the figure of the house,
Then must we rate the cost of the erection;
Which if we find outweighs ability,
What do we then but draw anew the model
In fewer offices…

(Henry IV, Part 2, 1.3, 42–49)

In the case, for example, of an exegetic or qualitative master's thesis of 35 000 words a rough assumption can be made that each chapter will contain between 6000 and 7500 words. In the case of the former the initial model will have five chapters and in the latter four. Because it is either exegetic or qualitative the literature review is likely to be embedded in the introduction. This will leave either three or four chapters, each of which will be devoted to a major sub-theme of the central argument or narrative: this, after all, is the function of a chapter. An empirical master's thesis of similar length is likely to have a generic template: introduction, literature review, methods, results, discussion and conclusion. However, this template might be varied: while it is usual for the introduction, literature review and methods chapters to be presented separately, it is not unusual for the results, discussion and conclusions to be presented in various combinations. For example, results combined with the discussion, a combined discussion and conclusion chapter or, less usually, combined results, discussion and conclusion chapters. (Even when combined it is, nonetheless, normally essential in empirical theses to keep the results distinct from discussion of them.) At the opposite pole from an empirical template some qualitative studies might have 'messy text'. For example, in *Troubling the Angels* (Lather & Smithies, 1997), a study of women living with HIV/aids, short chapters contain interview narratives

160

interspersed with some of the women's own writings in the form of poems, letters, speeches and emails. Running across the pages is subtext commentary by the co-researchers. This format is purposive:

...fragmented and polyphonic, designed to counter the 'comfort text' producing the 'romance of knowledge as cure', the authors hoping that 'the very fragmentation of the book, its detours and delays, will unsettle readers into a sort of stammering knowing about the work of living with HIV/AIDS, a knowing not so sure of itself

(Woods, 2006, p.49).

Irrespective of the initial design chosen, knowing in advance the basic structure of the thesis will enable the various elements of a study to be organised into smaller, coherent units: a process that makes the thesis much easier to think and write about. It is important to recognise that this initial structure is not cast in stone and might well subsequently change. What is important at this stage, though, is that it provides a starting point.

Headings and subheadings

4. The generic template of most empirical theses makes the link between questions, methods, and results explicit. However, writers of exegetic theses and those qualitative theses without a generic structure need to make the central purpose of their studies explicit by the manner in which each chapter has been conceived and sequenced. That doing so is important is indicated in the following comment by an examiner:

...those of us who have supervised and examined extensively know all too well how many higher degrees there are out there which remain unclear—even unto the end—on exactly what question they are asking.

(Cited in Pearce, 2005, p.52)

This signals the importance of full and accurate chapter titles in exegetic and qualitative theses. An examiner, simply by looking at the table of contents of a thesis, should have a good idea about how the argument has been developed. This in turn, will assist them more easily to follow the gist of the argument or narrative, the essence of reader friendly writing. Examiners should, of course, also be able to look at well-formatted tables of contents of generic empirical theses and see how the argument in each has been structured. But, in such cases, they will base that insight on the subheadings that appear below the generic chapter titles. However, it is often the case in empirical doctoral theses and occasionally so in empirical masters' theses, that the generic headings will need to be remodelled because, for instance, there might be a number of methods, results or discussion chapters. For example, a methods chapter with the title 'Texture and Methods' might follow another methods chapter titled 'Cell Structure and Methods'. (Within each chapter headings and subheadings should not be essential for continuity and the first sentence following a heading or subheading should not depend on either for its meaning [Anderson & Poole, 1994].)

5.   It is not at all unusual for initial chapter titles to change as work progresses. The same might also apply to the number of chapters initially decided upon. It is, in this context, important to recognise that there is no ideal generic chapter length: it is only ideal if it best meets the requirements of a particular study. Nonetheless, there is an unspoken convention that the length of chapters in a thesis should be in rough balance. So, if in a particular thesis it is necessary, for example, to have a ten-page chapter followed by another of forty pages, it might be necessary to justify the imbalance if only to indicate an awareness of the convention.

6.4 THE THESIS STATEMENT

1.   With the length of the thesis established and its overall structure tentatively in place a thesis statement will need to be drafted that encapsulates the primary purpose of the study. This statement might, for example, be a question, an exploration, an investigation or hypothesis establishment or validation. Without it the text will meander for no coherent narrative can be built or argument constructed. No thesis, therefore, lacks purpose for without it there can be no thesis. The problem in many theses, though, lies in the lack of an explicit purpose statement:

Neither in the Summary nor the Introduction is there a clear statement indicating the author's central concern(s) or argument(s)... This is most unfortunate because large sections of the thesis provide most valuable and important information and analysis... But they are not generally related to a central theme and the thesis therefore tends to be episodic and at times disjointed.

(Cited in Anderson & Poole, 1994, p.32)

When the thesis statement is left implicit examiners may be forced to return repeatedly to the abstract or introduction in an attempt to follow the narrative or understand the argument (Pearce, 2005). Thus:

...although a 'thesis without a thesis' will not necessarily 'fail', for many examiners the lack of a clear, central research question will constitute a significant flaw or question mark that will have to be compensated for in other ways.

(Pearce, 2005, p.52)

It is for this reason that the thesis statement ranks as the single most important sentence or series of sentences in a thesis.

2. It is also for this reason important to place the statement as close to the opening of the introduction to the thesis as possible. This will benefit both the writer and reader of the thesis for each will be provided an immediate sense of direction and purpose. This is why theses are more akin to the 'why did they do it' rather than 'who did it' genre of crime mysteries. If in the case of the latter authors told their readers that 'the butler did it' on the opening page there would be no mystery. Rather than exploring all the possibilities and following all the red herrings set by the authors, readers, instead, would follow the actions of one character to the exclusion of all others. This is why a thesis is not like a mystery novel, readers need to know the equivalent of 'who did it' as early as possible in order to follow, to the exclusion of all else, the unfolding narrative.

3. As in the case of the title and structure of the thesis and of the chapter headings, the initial thesis statement will probably need to undergo revision as understanding of the issues deepens. Although the number of times such redefinition takes place will differ according to the nature of the research and tentativeness of the initial statement, the principle remains constant that ideas always incrementally build on what went before. This recursive, evolutionary process is central to qualitative research so redefinition of the thesis statement is a natural part of the process. However, some empirical and exegetic researchers are unnerved by the need to revise the thesis statement, considering it a failure on their part if they do not adhere to the original proposal. An insight into how understanding develops might help show these feelings are rarely justified.

6.5 DRAFTING THE THESIS

1. In 1956 Benjamin Bloom and colleagues created a hierarchy of six categories he considered reflected the cognitive skills involved in learning, each category in need of mastery before the next could be attained (Bloom, Engelhart, Furst, Walker, Krathwohl, 1956). The first rung is 'knowledge' (the ability to simply state or recall material but with little understanding of it). The second 'comprehension' (the ability to classify and describe the material and, to an extent, discuss it). The third 'application' (the ability to employ the material in a novel way). The fourth 'analysis' (the ability to compare and contrast aspects of the material). The fifth 'synthesis' (the ability to reconstruct those aspects in such a way as to provide new insights). The final category is 'evaluation' (the ability to weigh the importance of and apply those new insights. Both important criteria of critical thinking).

Writing as intermediate process

2. Although much revised, this still widely regarded taxonomy indicates that the development of understanding is an evolutionary and creative process involving both progress and error: 'to compose (from *componere*, to put together) is to construct and reconstruct, interpret and reinterpret' (Crusius, 1991, p.8). In 1890 the mathematician Giuseppe Peano contrived a space-filling curve; a one-dimensional line filling a two dimensional space. This dimension-fracturing geometry was later called fractal. Unlike the case in Euclidean geometry fractals are generated through recursive processes:

At each stage in a recursive process, the starting point is the output of the preceding iteration, and the output is the starting point of the subsequent iteration. Every stage, that is, is an elaboration, and such elaborations can quickly give rise to unexpected forms and surprising complexity.

(Davis & Sumara, 2005, p.309)

Understanding, therefore, because it is the result of a constant accumulation of events that trigger cascades of insights of varying significance follows power law not normal distributions. These recursive processes can be applied to the drafting of a thesis in the sense that 'any piece of writing has a life cycle. It does not come fully mature into the world, but usually emerges in a stumbling, often confused, and invariably undeveloped, state' (Canter & Fairbairn, 2006, p.ix). When only one draft of a document is written, writing is merely a means to commit an idea to paper: an end product. The fact that this can be done has, of course, considerable utility: there is often little need to revise the first draft of a simple document. A shopping list, for example, indicates a reality existing prior to the writing. However, in a thesis a reality is being provoked, produced by the writing itself (McCormack, 2008). Thus, the lengthier and more complex a document becomes the greater the need to write and revise a number of drafts. When each of these is a considered improvement on its predecessor, writing becomes a powerful, intermediate process: a process that allows relationships to be recognised and ideas tested. Thinking and writing become, in other words, negotiations between what has been done and what can be done to improve it (Murray, 2003). Unfortunately, there is no way to shortcut drafting; recursive processes, by definition, are non-compressible (Davis & Sumara, 2005). Drafting means, therefore, a struggle to come to grips with ideas. As the following extract indicates some writers invite their readers into the process:

Rather than flatly and forcefully affirming that 'paradigms are constitutive of nature', Kuhn is himself pondering what, in saying this, he might mean—and does say that he is not yet sure what he means: 'I am convinced that we must learn to make sense of statements that at least resemble these'.

(Sharrock & Read, 2002, p.50)

Defining 'foul paper'

3. What, though, constitutes a draft or 'foul paper' in Elizabethan parlance? (Bryson, 2008). Does it represent one or a number of attempts to write a piece of text? Prior to the availability of home computers, when text was handwritten or composed on a typewriter, the number of alterations that could, in practice, be made to a single draft was limited so it was relatively easy to identify what a draft was. Computers, of course, allow ongoing revisions to be made so a draft now might reflect multiple revisions. Each writer, therefore, will need to define what, for their particular purposes, constitutes a completed draft. It might, for example, be defined as text ready for critical review by a supervisor. Alternatively, it might be defined as a rough draft submitted to a supervisor for general comment on structure, rather than detail. It might also, particularly in regard to the initial draft of a chapter, be defined as such when for the first time it expresses the writer's ideas with sufficient coherence for it to be read as a blemished but narrative whole.

The first draft

4. For most thesis writers the first draft is usually the most difficult to write for prior experience has not usually prepared them to sustain such lengthy and complex text (Carson, 2007). But this is where the great virtue of drafting lies. Because the first draft is 'writer centred' it frees writers from the constraints of their internal editors. They are thus permitted to concentrate on developing a structure in each chapter capable of sustaining a coherent flow of ideas. Because the text in the first draft will have been written 'free of convention' the grammar, syntax and spelling are likely to be idiosyncratic. But, this is not a significant problem as long as the draft is readable: it is not 'bad-writing' but rough writing on the way to becoming good writing (Murray, 2003).

Reader-centred writing

5. This is the task of the subsequent drafts: to transform private into public narrative; to progressively translate author-centred into reader-centred writing. There will, though, be a difference in the manner in which writers of empirical as opposed to exegetic and qualitative theses set about this process of role reversal. Because, as has been established, the presentational format

of empirical theses makes explicit the link between question or hypotheses and results it is often possible to re-draft individual chapters to the point where each approaches the quality of a final draft. If this approach were to be adopted in an exegetic or qualitative thesis the result might be a study with internally coherent chapters but with little overall coherence. This is because in exegetic and qualitative studies the central research question/s and the responses to them usually evolve as the drafts of each chapter are sequentially written. Writers of such theses need to take care, therefore, to write the first draft of one chapter and then, instead of immediately re-drafting the chapter, move on to write the first draft of the next. When the same procedure is adopted with each of the subsequent chapters, the thesis will grow naturally as an organic whole.[1] In fact, one of the many rewards of writing a thesis is, after submission, to compare the first with the final draft. How, though, is the process of progressively translating author-centred writing into reader-centred writing to proceed?

6.6 PARAGRAPHS

1. Thus far the conceptualisation of the thesis writing process has reflected the manner in which readers coming to the thesis for the first time would see it: the larger structures first, the finer details later. On this basis decisions regarding the larger structure have already tentatively been made: the length of the thesis, the overall number of chapters, roughly how long each will be and, equally roughly, the sub-sections each will contain. Now is the time to move down to the next level of detail: the paragraphs.

Prioritising ideas

2. Paragraphs are of fundamental importance because they are the primary meaning making mechanism in written communication. The feature that provides this centrality is their power to convey, and elaborate upon, a single, controlling idea. One paragraph, one controlling idea means that the number of paragraphs at a writer's disposal limits the number of ideas that can be dealt with. How, though, in regard to the chapter of a thesis can this number be calculated? Unfortunately, there is no easy answer. However, there is a calculation that will provide a rough idea. First, though, an elaborate metaphor: paragraphs should not be pale, undernourished and despondent. Instead, they should be fat, chubby cheeked and gurgling with contentment. In translation short paragraphs generally imply an idea has not been developed: questions have not been asked, examples have not been given, comparisons have not been made and explanations have not been provided. Paragraphs, in other

words, should generally be substantial pieces of text. This requirement is one of the justifications for the need to write for a clearly defined audience: the questions they conjecturally could ask or observations they could make will help to 'thicken' writing by making paragraphs responsive to these questions and observations. In fact, a useful way to quickly gain insight into the quality of a piece of writing is to allow the pages to flick through the fingers so all that can be seen is the size of the paragraphs as the text flies past. Bear in mind examiners might well do this.

3. But if paragraphs should generally be substantial, how is substantial to be defined? Without attempting to be prescriptive a reasonably well-developed paragraph should, when the text is spaced one and a half lines apart, fill about a half to three quarters of an A4 size page.[2] On this basis a twenty pages long chapter would contain roughly thirty paragraphs. If, equally conjecturally, the paragraphs introducing and concluding the chapter are subtracted, between twenty and twenty-five paragraphs will be left. There will be space, therefore, for roughly twenty to twenty-five controlling ideas. This might seem a shocking limitation when the complexity of the issues with which the average thesis deals is considered. But keep in mind that the most effective arguments usually consist of relatively few points in support of a clearly defined argument.

4. Recognising how finite is the space available to express one's ideas acts as a forceful reminder that not everything one might like to include in a chapter can be used. This recognition, in turn, will require a number of essential tasks to be undertaken. The first is to remove all those points that do not directly contribute to the central theme of the chapter. The second is to prioritise those that remain by listing them in order of importance. The third is to decide where to draw the line: which of the relevant ideas, in other words, are to be excluded? (It might be necessary to indicate to examiners an awareness of the excluded points by providing in the text of the thesis a brief justification for their exclusion.)

Retaining coherence

5. Of course, describing these tasks as neat and linear is misleading: the sole justification for doing so is didactic. In reality presenting clear arguments, narratives or descriptions will involve considerable drafting and re-drafting. This takes us back to the metaphor of bringing light to the darkness of the unknown. Writing a draft introductory paragraph to a chapter and, if possible, a concluding paragraph is a useful means to develop a sense of direction when writing the chapter. (Because it is an initial draft the introductory paragraph will later need to be altered if it is to reflect the final form of the chapter accurately.) When the body of the chapter is subsequently written

there should be no jumping back and forth to elaborate on points discussed in earlier paragraphs. This tends to occur most frequently in complex discussions where paragraphs, instead of dealing with one controlling idea, deal with a subset of an idea: a common fault is to allow the subsets to be dispersed. The result might be a statement similar to the following in the examiners report: 'Why isn't the argument on p.41 integrated with the material on p.53?' (adapted from Holbrook & Dally, 2003, p.11). It is important, therefore, to retain coherence by clustering paragraphs dealing with related issues together. Coherence does not necessarily mean, though, that arguments, narratives or descriptions should proceed from the most important idea or cluster of ideas to the least important. Doing so can, in fact, drain vitality from text. Instead, starting and ending strongly can often be achieved by adopting an alternative strategy: start with the second most important idea or cluster of ideas and end with the most important. However, as in the case of most other writing techniques, this approach should not be adopted too often for repetition blunts the effect.

6.7 TOPIC SENTENCES

1. It is important to ensure that readers are able to follow the content of the text as it moves forward. The idea being dealt with in each paragraph must, therefore, be made as explicit as possible. It should also have appropriate weight: neither too complex to be dealt with in one paragraph nor too lightweight. These are the tasks of the topic sentence: by providing a carefully weighted topic and controlling idea it clearly indicates what the paragraph is about. A paragraph, for example, that starts with the sentence 'Look at the big picture, and company A's future seems assuredly bright', indicates to readers that the topic of the paragraph is 'company A' and the controlling idea 'an assuredly bright future'. By thus establishing the theme that is to be elaborated upon, topic sentences allow paragraphs to move from the general to the specific, a pattern that also more easily allows readers to understand what has been written. It is, for this reason, usual to place a topic sentence as close as possible to the beginning of a paragraph. It is also usual, because of their introductory function, for topic sentences not to include material that requires citation.

2. The clarity and energy of an argument, discussion or narrative will, therefore, depend significantly upon the degree to which topic sentences fulfil their function. A prerequisite, of course, is clarity in the mind of the writer of what the paragraph is about. A clear topic sentence will signal to the reader that a new stage of the argument, discussion or narrative is about to begin. An effective way to convey this signal is to pose a rhetorical question: a question

provides focus because it requires an immediate answer. This is why asking double questions can be particularly effective because they increase the degree of focus: *Why did she fall in love? What was there about him that so appealed to her?* Because it fails to provide a sense of direction, a paragraph should not ordinarily open with a factual statement. But a useful variation of the strategy of opening a paragraph with a question or questions is to base each on an opening statement or statements: *In 1955 Anne moved to the city. It was there that she met Clive. Why did she fall in love? What was there about him that so appealed to her?* The remainder of the paragraph, or cluster of paragraphs, must, necessarily, provide the answers. When cleverly and not too often used, topic sentences posed as questions can add variety and impact to writing.

Paragraph transitions

3. While topic sentences play the essential role of indicating what a paragraph is about, they do not necessarily indicate how a paragraph contributes to the evolving argument, discussion or narrative. A paragraph, therefore, might have excellent internal logic but have the logic of its contribution to the thrust of the chapter left unclear. This task often falls to the concluding sentence of paragraphs because they not only link one paragraph to the next they also provide momentum to writing. This can be seen in the following example where the conclusion of one paragraph flows seamlessly into the topic sentence of the next:

If you include Belgium, where a new government took nine months to settle and seems to have been formed with scantish reference to the poll result, you find that of 21 countries which have elected new governments in the past four months, the result of the vote itself was less than decisive in at least six.

The number seems to be rising. In 2006, four or possibly five elections fell into the 'inconclusive' category...

(*The Economist*, 5 April, 2008, p.66)

In the following example, though, the flow is interrupted with dramatic effect by a jarring transition. The paragraph opens with the topic sentence *Look at the big picture, and company A's future seems assuredly bright* and closes with a statement that *company A would seem to many a good long-term investment.* The topic sentence of the next paragraph, though, provides a very different perspective: *Look at the detail, however, and the depth and complexity of the problems company A faces are chronic.* This type of effect in writing is usually a consequence of revision, a process in which the text in each draft is refined and tightened.

6.8 REVISING

1. The process of revision, the translation of the writer-based text of the first draft to the reader-based text of the final draft is mirrored in the differences in emphasis applied when writing the earlier and later drafts. While the former will primarily be concerned with outlining the study and in establishing the basic structure of the thesis, the emphasis in the latter will be upon the finer levels of detail: of progressively strengthening and clarifying each paragraph and sentence. A usual indicator that the transition from one phase to the next has taken place is when, particularly in the case of exegetic and qualitative theses, the title of the thesis and the abstract have received their final definition. Part of the revising process will be to ensure not only that the most precise words have been used but also that the text has sufficient fluidity. That sufficient use, in other words, has been made of transitional devices: words and phrases that signal to readers the direction the writing is about to take. For example: *on the contrary, however, in contrast, besides, furthermore, in addition, also, similarly, likewise, moreover, indeed, therefore, as a result, consequently, hence, for instance.*

2. Careful judgement, though, will need to be applied for too many strong transitions ('however' and 'nevertheless'), particularly when placed at the beginning of a sentence, can impede the flow of text. Fluidity can also be impaired by the use of *e.g.* rather than *for example* or *i.e.* instead of *that is*. If *for example* is used, *etc.* (et cetera), an abbreviation that in any event should be avoided in a thesis, becomes redundant. It might also be necessary as part of the revising process to replace vagueness with precision: 'fifteen', for example, rather than 'many'; and, where appropriate, hesitancy with confidence: *I define…*rather than *I have attempted to define…* Care will also need to be exercised in the use of 'persuader' words and phrases. *Surely; plainly; obviously; undeniably*; or *naturally*, for example, might appear to readers as illicit attempts to nudge them without appropriate evidence towards acceptance of a particular perspective (Fairbairn & Winch, 1996). While the use by Shakespeare of double superlatives and double negatives—*'the most unkindest cut of all'*—provide an additional degree of emphasis (Bryson, 2008, p.110) they can just as easily confuse: *not dissimilar to*, for example. Because it often results in clumsy text avoiding gender insensitive language has the potential when revising to become problematic. Replacing generic male pronouns like *man* is usually straightforward, but the use of him and her and her and him, he/she or s/he provides examples of how clumsy writing can become (Canter & Fairbairn, 2006). Possibly the most efficient way to write gender neutral prose is to use plural pronouns like *they* and *them* or, as in the following examples, plural nouns: *Candidates should always check their work*; as opposed to: *A candidate should always check his or her work* (Garton & McFarlane, 2007, p.92).

Stripping away the scaffolding

3. The process of revision not only involves building structure and providing precision, clarity and meaning it also, in consequence, involves the stripping away of all text that impedes those outcomes. The most obvious candidate for removal apart from gendered terminology is the scaffolding that facilitated the writing of each draft. Redundant headings and sub-headings for example, or simplistic statements such as *This chapter contains a review of the literature relevant to the subject of this thesis* served a purpose only in the sense that they allowed a writer's thoughts to flow during the composition of the early drafts. They should subsequently be removed. Vague statements such as *In many countries it is believed that...*are also candidates for removal. More difficult to deal with, though, is the tendency, particularly in empirical theses, to repetition. This is most evident in the introductions to the methods, results and discussion sections where in each there is generally need to repeat the research questions or hypotheses. There is no easy answer to this dilemma other than to dilute the sense of repetition by taking care to change the wording and sentence structure in each of the introductions.

4. There is a tendency for beginning thesis writers to over-write, over-quote and to quilt (to stick and paste related segments of text together). While these would constitute problems were they to be features of the final draft, they are entirely understandable in the first drafts where both confidence and a coherent sense of direction have yet to be developed. The function of subsequent drafts, therefore, is to enable the writing to be 'tightened'. Where, though, should this process stop? Again, there is no easy answer but, in the majority of cases, what initially is considered to be the final draft of a piece of writing can be cut by a further ten per cent and emerge the better for it. This is because doing so is similar to keeping a sinking ship afloat by throwing the least valuable cargo overboard. Thus, in a thesis, the function not only of every quote and sentence, but also of every word will need to be questioned and, if found wanting, removed. This must, however, be interpreted in context. It is not an invitation to produce technical writing, writing so rigorously functional that it reflects neither the theoretic perspective nor personality of the writer. It is, instead, advice to remove text superfluous to the requirements of the discourse to which the writer belongs. This applies, in particular, to qualitative researchers where lack of focus can easily translate into flabby text. *The desirable outcome for all theses* of this process is nicely illustrated in the play *Amadeus*. Salieri is entranced by a new Mozart composition:

'Displace one note, and there will be diminishment; displace one phrase, and the structure will fall'. As he looked at the manuscripts he realized that he 'was staring through those ink-notes at an absolute beauty'.

(Cited in Woods, 2006, p.13)

5. The tightening of structure, the clarifying of meaning and the simultaneous stripping away of scaffolding from text accounts for the fact that, in general, each later draft of a thesis will tend to be shorter than the previous one. Do not, therefore, be alarmed if the early drafts of the thesis are considerably longer than the length requirement of the final draft. However, because empirical studies usually have a greater degree of initial focus than either exegetic or qualitative studies, the difference in length between each draft will tend to be less in the former than in the latter.

6.9 EDITING

1. It is only fair to warn that revising is a potentially endless process: there will always be improvements to be made. For this reason, it is useful to bear the following in mind: 'A thesis is never finished it is just abandoned at the least damaging point' (Race, 1999, cited in Cryer, 2006, p.241). But, while revision will be ongoing, there will, nonetheless come a point where a writer will become conscious that the emphasis has shifted from restructuring to making adjustments to the wording and punctuation of the text so that it reads smoothly. A transition, in other words, will have been made from revising to editing. It is at this point that the readership of the thesis draft should be extended as widely as possible. The supervisors will, of course, continue to play their role as primary readers but, by expanding the number and variety of readers, the writing will be strengthened even further. The reason in the first instance is that new readers come to the draft fresh. They will immediately see blemishes that, because of over-familiarity, neither researcher nor supervisors might see. (Keep in mind that examiners will come to your work fresh too!) Second, each reader will approach the work from a different perspective. It is important to recognise, though, that these perspectives need not necessarily be those of specialists in the field. It might, in fact, be advantageous to seek out non-specialist readers. Unlike specialists, they tend to concentrate only on the quality of expression rather than on the quality of both content and expression. In this role they will help to revise as well as to edit for they are often very adept at spotting structural deficiencies. They also pick up less obvious flaws, weasel words like 'probably' whose purpose often is to wriggle the writer out of making a commitment (Rugg & Petre, 2004), or terms that have been defined after already having been mentioned in the text.

Allusive and illusive

2. Because they do not usually understand them, non-specialist readers tend to be sensitive to allusions. Allusion is indirect reference as opposed to citation,

which is explicit reference. The mark of an allusion is that only those with prior knowledge can comprehend it. An allusion, for example, to 'the city that never sleeps' assumes the reader understands it as New York or an aside about an aspect of D. H. Lawrence's *Women in Love* assumes the reader has read the work. Academic writing, particularly in the humanities, is heavily allusive and it is generally only subject specialists, therefore, who are able to make the necessary connections. Nonetheless, some of the allusions made in a thesis draft might be so indirect that even the examiners might struggle to follow them. Thus by bringing allusions to the thesis writer's attention, non-specialist readers might help identify those allusions in need of clarification. For much the same reason non-specialists are also sensitive to elusive writing where the text is difficult to follow. Aristotle, for example, is well known for his elusive style:

For that which can foresee by the exercise of the mind is by nature lord and master, and that which can with its body give effect to such foresight is a subject, and by nature a slave; hence master and slave have the same interest.

(Cited in Fiumara, 1995, p.88)

Editing strategies

3. Nonetheless, despite the advantages to be derived by expanding the number and variety of readers, the thesis writer will need to be the primary editor of the final drafts. How then should he or she go about doing so? A useful strategy is to put a draft away for a few days. When read after this interval it will be as though a text written by someone else is being read for the first time: blemishes and opaque writing will more easily become apparent. This is why it is so important to plan the writing of the thesis in such a way that the time necessary to adopt this strategy is provided. Faults will also become apparent when a draft is read out loud, gasping for breath or pausing when no punctuation indicates the need to do so will identify where the wording of the text might need revision or the punctuation correction. In some cases an alteration to punctuation can have dramatic effect. Take, for example, the sentence: 'A woman, without her man, is nothing'. Introducing a colon and changing a comma alters the meaning completely: 'A woman: without her, man is nothing' (Garton & McFarlane, 2007, p.92). However, some faults are more insidious and defy easy recognition. Words like *knowledge* and *research* are uncountable nouns all of which take a singular verb. Apostrophes are notorious for their use is easily confused (*it's/its, you're/your*) and their placement in plural possessives fraught (Garton & MacFarlane, 2007): *peoples'*, for example, can be used but *childrens'* cannot. Spelling conventions too can be confusing[3]: centre/center; colour/color and the use of *–ize* or *–ise*.

To further complicate matters the spelling of the original must be adhered to when quoting. However, of all the tasks involved in editing the most tiresome and common is the correction of inaccurate citations (Hart, 2005). This is all the more reason to exercise due care to cite correctly from the outset of the thesis writing process.

4. While preliminary editing can be done on a computer the bulk of the finer work should be done on hard copy. This is primarily because when we read normally the eye subconsciously skims across four to six words at a time often ignoring significant blemishes in the text as it does so. Research has indicated, for example, that as long as the first and last letters of a word are situated correctly the word can still easily be read if the other letters are scrambled. It is, thus, *etrxraoridnray waht can eapsce your aetntiotn wehn you are treid and reshud.* How many times does the letter 'f' appear in the following sentence: *Finished files are the result of years of scientific study combined with the experience of years.*[4] Placing a ruler beneath each line of text on hard copy will help obviate these phenomena by forcing the eye to focus on a few words at a time. ('Intensive seeing' is a term used in the visual arts to indicate this type of focus [Gibbs, 2007].) As this is being done notes should also be written on a hardcopy writing guide to ensure, for example, that acronyms, the upper and lower case and the formats of headings and sub-headings have been consistently used and that tables have not been split. All errors can then be corrected electronically during a separate session.

6.10 PROOFREADING

1. The correction of finer detail indicates the point of transition from editing to proofreading. While both revising and editing are primarily concerned with the clear presentation of subject matter, proofreading is solely concerned with the correctness of grammar, syntax, spelling and punctuation in a final draft. Computer spelling and grammar checkers can be useful in detecting errors in these fields. However, they cannot be relied upon. Homonyms, for example, are frequently missed:

    I halve a spelling checker,
    It came with my pea see.
    It plainly marks four my revue
    Mistakes I dew knot sea.

    (Snow, nd, np)

2. The term 'proofreading' is derived from the need in the publishing industry to check the proofs of edited copy prior to printing. This understanding

174

of the term needs to be clear if a professional proofreader is engaged to check the final draft of a thesis. Ethical concerns regarding ownership of its contents are involved should proofreaders be asked to go beyond their remit by undertaking both revision and editing. It is these concerns that have prompted some universities to require that all theses checked by a professional proofreader should have a declaration to that effect, together with the name of the proofreader, included in the acknowledgements section of the thesis. With the ethical issue clarified it is, nonetheless, useful after having proofread the text carefully to have the final draft of the thesis proofed by someone unconnected with the research. This is explained by our tendency to be blind to our own mistakes. Even though the changes proofreaders can effect are limited it is important that someone with a style of writing similar to that of the thesis writer is chosen otherwise changes of voice in the text might jar. Keep in mind, though, that elements of some theses (for example, numbers in the results section) cannot be checked for accuracy by anyone other than the thesis writer. But other tasks such as checking, if specialist software has not been used, that all references have been included in the reference list and that all references in the list have been cited in the thesis must also be done by the writer of the thesis.

3. The polymath Henri Poincaré did not bother proofreading his texts since he regarded doing so a gross misuse of his time (Taleb, 2007). (He died relatively young so this was a sound decision.) Most of us, however, will need to confront the reality that proofreading is a tedious necessity. This necessity, furthermore, has to be undertaken at a time when the last thing needed is tedium. Proofreading in relatively short rather than in long gruelling sessions can mitigate tedium. The most effective antidote, though, is knowledge that the time spent proofreading is only a fraction of the time spent on writing the thesis as a whole. It is also reassuring to know that the reward for proofreading a thesis properly is out of all proportion to the time spent doing so. This is because a thesis that describes excellent research but which is riddled with minor errors will pay a heavy price: examiners are human and, as is common with the species, negative perception of a part will carry over to perception of the whole:

I give my students strong advice on how not to 'flip' an examiner from 'reasonable' to 'unreasonable' by having irritating things in the thesis such as typos and other careless textual mistakes that indicate lack of attention to detail. Once flipped (and I am aware of this happening), I am irritated and I have to work very hard at overcoming this irritation and not letting it influence my view of the thesis, although this is not easy.

(Cited in Mullins & Kiley, 2002, p.378)

ENDNOTES

1 Take care to save at frequent intervals what has been written during each writing session and make backup copies regularly. Each copy should be date labelled to prevent confusing earlier with later versions.

2 It is often easier to type drafts in single spacing because more text can be seen on the screen. It can then easily be converted to one and a half or, more unusually, double-spacing prior to submission to supervisors.

3 Correct spelling is a cultural rather than technical requirement. In early seventeenth century England, for example, spelling was luxuriantly variable: a dictionary published in 1604 spelled 'words' two ways on the title page (Bryson, 2008).

4 Six. We have difficulty processing *of*.

CHAPTER 7

The Introduction

The more accurate the map, the more it resembles the territory. The most accurate map possible would be the territory, and thus would be perfectly accurate and perfectly useless.

(Gaiman, 2006, p.xix)

7.1 INTRODUCTION

1. Even when they do not constitute separate chapters each of the structural elements constituting a thesis fulfils a particular, and essential, purpose. The explanation of the methods, for example, informs readers how the research was undertaken while the review of the literature situates the research. As the point of entry into a thesis the introduction, however, is of particular strategic importance for it fulfils a number of roles. It is here that the intention of and justification for the research is provided, where its scope, limitations, originality and significance lie and where the structure of the thesis is described and explained. Another author describes the purpose of the introduction more pithily:

   …although I have headed this first part of the thesis, 'Clearing the Ground', it may have been more apt to adduce a musical metaphor and to have titled it: 'Clearing the throat, finding voice, establishing a key…

   (McCormack, 2008, p.834)

   The introduction, in other words, is where a unique research space is created. It is this element of uniqueness that explains why supervisors, while normally generous with advice in regard to each of the other elements of a thesis, are generally more reticent in regard to the introduction and its complement, the conclusion (Mort & Holloway, 2006): these sections convey a story that only the researcher adequately can tell.

2. When the story is being told it ought, though, to be borne in mind that many examiners begin their report by writing an overview of the thesis; the ease

and eloquence with which they do so is 'sometimes in revealing contrast to the efforts of the candidates themselves' (Pearce, 2005, p.61). Indeed the overview function of the introduction is indicated in many theses by its location outside the chapter numbering system, the introduction preceding the first chapter (Paltridge & Starfield, 2007). In some empirical theses a brief account of the findings is often included in the introduction. In such cases the introduction:

...is thus at once a 'foreword' preceding the text and an 'afterword' following its completion; a curious combination of prologue and epilogue; a peculiar mix of promissory note and its redeemed cash value.

(McCormack, 2008, p.833)

3. The root of the difficulty some students have when writing the introduction is understandable because it is intrinsic. As the above extract from *Fragile Things* indicates the part cannot contain the whole unless the part equals the whole (Smith & Jenks, 2006). The preview and overview element of the introduction should not, therefore, be confused with writing a summary of the thesis. Such confusion will mean not only an inability in the introduction to do justice to the contents of the thesis but also to loss of clarity in delineating the objectives of the research.

7.2 CLARIFYING OBJECTIVES

1. All theses, irrespective of their structure or the research tradition from which they spring, need to be introduced. In regard to structure a doctoral thesis, for example, consisting of a collection of research articles, might need an overall introduction or a separate introduction to each article. Research tradition, however, will dictate whether or not the introduction should be a separate chapter or integrated with the review of the literature. As has already been established the issues investigated in exegetic and qualitative theses, unlike those in most empirical studies, are generally conceptual. Unless they have been operationalised (defined as measurable entities) discussion of them cannot, therefore, be separated from the literature in which they are embedded. This explains why most exegetic and qualitative theses have combined introductions and literature reviews while in most empirical theses these chapters are presented separately. However, even when the intention is to present the introduction and literature review separately in the final draft of the thesis, it is often useful to unite them in the initial drafts. Doing so obviates the need, when attempting to write each chapter separately, to draw a clear distinction between them. Once initial thoughts have been committed to paper the issues that naturally belong in each chapter can usually be identified easily. However, there is always a possibility, particularly in regard

to qualitative theses, that a logical and coherent narrative might have developed that defies easy separation. This might indicate a need to retain the combined chapter as it is.

2. How, though, should one set about writing the initial drafts of these combined chapters and, in addition, recognise what should belong in each when, or if, separated? Start by clarifying, in so far as is possible at this early stage, what the objectives of the research are. Irrespective of the research approach, a useful way for all researchers to set about this clarification process is to complete the following statements in writing (adapted from Murray, 2002 p.98):

   • The title of the thesis is…
   • The research question/s or hypothesis is/are…
   • The primary researchers in this area are…
   • The main themes are…
   • The consensus is…
   • But debate centres on the issue/s of…
   • There is still work to be done on…
   • My research is closest to… because…
   • My contribution will be…

3. At the outset of the thesis writing process supervisors sometimes suggest an alternative strategy to clarify research objectives. Just as examiners do not necessarily start by reading a thesis from the beginning, so chapters in a thesis are also not necessarily written in the order in which they finally appear. Particularly in regard to empirical theses supervisors might, therefore, recommend that a draft of the methods chapter be written first. This is partially because in the case of masters' theses this chapter is usually relatively brief and because in most theses it is predominantly descriptive rather than discursive. The primary reason, however, is because the chapter clearly defines what the research is about. Once this has been established it also then becomes clear what the focus of the introduction and literature review ought to be. This approach often works well in those research undertakings with a limited theoretic component. It is not advisable, though, in research where theory plays a more explicit role. This is because thorough understanding of relevant theory and of how other researchers have applied it is a necessary precursor to writing the methods chapter. Therefore, were this chapter to be written prior to the introduction and literature review it would not only be much the poorer but also shorn of context and, thus, of limited use in clarifying the objectives of the research.

7.3 WHAT AN INTRODUCTION SHOULD COVER

1. What then ought to be the next step following either the completion of the list of statements or the writing of the methods section or, if need be, of

both? After having discovered strong similarities in the manner in which empirical research in the biomedical field was introduced, Edward Swales developed a *Create a Research Space* (CARS) (Swales, 1990) introduction model for writers of empirical research essays and articles. The metaphor of a research space or niche was based on the idea of competition in ecology: researchers seeking to publish must compete for 'light and space' as do plants and animals (Paltridge & Starfield, 2007, p.87). The model, elements of which provide useful insights to writers from other research perspectives as well, is based on a sequence of three steps, the degree of focus increasing sequentially as one step follows on from another:

- Step one 'establishes territory' by providing background information about the main issue, question or hypothesis to be researched.
- Step two involves 'establishing a niche' by indicating, for example, a 'gap' in the research or by providing a statement that a particular research tradition is being elaborated.
- Step three requires the 'occupation of the niche' by outlining the objectives of the research and, as is sometimes the case in the sciences and engineering, by presenting the principal findings. An outline explaining to the reader how the essay or article has been structured is usually included in this final step.

2. This three-step sequence for introductions to essays and articles was subsequently elaborated into a six-step sequence for introducing the research focus in a thesis (Dudley–Evans, 1989, pp.72–79). Again, each step involves the establishment of a greater degree of focus:

- Step one provides the background to the study.
- Step two introduces the research topic.
- Step three provides greater definition to the topic.
- Step four defines the scope of the study by introducing the research parameters and summarising previous research.
- Step five prepares for the introduction of the research focus by indicating, for example, a gap in the research literature or by outlining previous research that is to be extended.
- Step six introduces the research focus by stating the aims of the study and the justification for undertaking it.

3. This step-by-step process not only contextualises the research focus but also assists readers to understand the rationale for its adoption: 'This is the question I posed. This is why I posed it. This is how I approached it. And here's a preview of where I think this is all going' (Lovitts, 2007, p.287). It is on this basis that the following extended list attempts to identify as many as possible of the key organising principles that can be applied in order for the introduction to a thesis to be effective. But, because the structure of each introduction is unique, the list

is not intended to be prescriptive. Individual researchers will need to decide whether or not the items on the list are adequate to the needs of their study:

- Because they immediately establish verisimilitude and atmosphere, observational data often make excellent openings to the introductions of qualitative theses (Thody, 2006). A purpose statement indicating the primary concept, the central phenomenon, which is to be described, understood, explored or developed, might follow these. This statement, in turn, might be followed by an indication of the design and methods adopted. Finally, information about the individuals or sites involved in the project will be provided. The end result, therefore, might resemble the following: 'The purpose of this ethnographic study is to explore the culture-sharing behaviors and language of the homeless in a soup kitchen in...'(cited in Creswell & Plano Clark, 2007, p.97) Even though the context in which the research is embedded will subsequently be provided, the introduction to empirical or exegetic theses can be opened with a short statement indicating what the thesis is about. For example: *The aim of this thesis is to investigate key aspects of...* or: *This thesis is part of a larger project... The premise of my work is that...* Immediate focus in the introduction will allow examiners more easily to place what follows in context. It also, as a bonus, creates the impression of a confident, assertive writer. Therefore, unless there is good reason, do not detract from this impression by opening with a weak statement: *In this work I attempt to...* Neither, in what is one of the key parts of a thesis, should confusion be sown. The likelihood of doing so is indicated in the following extracts from the opening of an empirical thesis: *The overall objective of the study was to...; The first objective was to...; The second and major objective was to...*
- Two additional features of these extracts are noteworthy. The first is the use of *objective* rather than *aim*. Although usage differs each is normally considered distinct from the other. Objectives are the tasks that need to be undertaken in order to achieve the aim of the research (Hart, 2005). A research aim is a statement or statements expressing both the purpose and methodological orientation of the research. This explains why the research aim is often expressed as a purpose statement, the statement normally being followed by the rationale for the research. When clearly expressed early in a thesis, examiners are likely to respond favourably: 'The fundamental purpose of the investigation is both an interesting and an important one' (cited in Anderson & Poole, 1994, p.31). When not clearly expressed the response is likely to be less favourable:

I thought that the problem under investigation was left undefined and vague for too long...Gradually the aim emerged as one read the thesis, but it needed to be much more explicit earlier in the study.

(Cited in Anderson & Poole, 1994, p.32)

The second noteworthy feature of the extracts is use of the past tense in preference to the present tense normally used in qualitative and exegetic opening statements. The distinction is explained by the ongoing discursive nature of qualitative and exegetic research and the need by empirical researchers to indicate that the research undertaken has been completed successfully thus permitting the nomothetic process to move forward. However, even though the active voice is generally used rather than the passive, the use of the latter rather than the former when stating the research aim in the introduction to an empirical thesis enhances the sense of completion. Compare, for example, the following statement in the past tense, active voice: *This study investigated the factors effecting…*; with the next statement in the past tense, passive voice: *The factors effecting…were investigated in this study.*

- After having indicated what the thesis is about, go on to explain briefly how the introduction chapter has been organised. For example:

This chapter consists of six sections: the background to the study, the purpose of the study, the significance of the problem, an overview of the research program, a rationale for the research and the definition of terms.

It might also prove useful, unless the structure has a self-explanatory logic, to explain why the chapter has been organised in a particular way. The frequent need to do so explains why a significant feature of this part of the introduction is metadiscourse in the form of forward references to what is to come. It also explains its use in the *Organisation of the Study* section of the introduction where the entire thesis, as indicated in the following, is previewed:

Chapter 1 surveys the extensive literature on…Chapter 2 focuses on the… Chapters 3 and 4 report on the experimental investigation conducted on… In the Conclusion it will be shown that the evidence suggests that… This indicates the importance of …

- Following the brief description of the organisation of the introduction start the discussion of the context of the research by indicating the topic area and by emphasising its current or future importance. For example: *Health, illness, and health care are important issues in contemporary… According to the Census Bureau…*; or: *Osteoarthritis is a common disease affecting millions of people around the world and is a leading cause of disability among…*; or: *Surface Engineering plays a vital role in enhancing materials applications in hostile environments.*
- At this point it will usually be necessary in explicitly theory driven studies to explain the conceptual framework. For example: *Constructivism and cognitive flexibility theory are significant concepts in framing this study for each focuses on the notion of learning as…* The explanation provided might need to include not

only a justification for the adoption of the framework but also an explanation of how it has been interpreted in comparison with others. The justification and explanation will be necessary precursors to a subsequent discussion of the reasons for the adoption of particular research methods; how the conceptual framework has been applied. In empirical theses, and usually in qualitative theses also, the justification for and explanation of the conceptual framework will be presented in the introduction and the explanation of how the framework was applied will be in the methods section. However, in exegetic theses and in some qualitative theses also, both the framework and its application are entirely conceptual and, therefore, inextricable from each other. Thus there will be no explicit methods section in these theses. Instead, the discussion of the conceptual framework and its application will take place in a combined introduction and literature review chapter. Because most approaches to qualitative research are either explicitly or implicitly phenomenological the researcher is necessarily an important part of the research process. For this reason a reflexive account might appropriately be included at this point in the introduction or, alternatively, could be included as a separate section after the table of contents. Irrespective of the option chosen be careful not to convey the impression that reflexivity is an unproblematic concept:

…when we introspect about who we really are we encounter only various unanchored descriptions. We might, therefore, have greater faith in some of them than in others but we can never claim to have found ourselves.

(Linn, 1996, p.33)

- Statements of research aims and discussions of concepts frequently contain ambiguous terms that need clear definition. This, in particular, applies to key terms or, for example, to different definitions of the variables under investigation. Bear in mind, though, that the meaning of some concepts might change during the course of the research. If so, updated definitions will be necessary. This will particularly be the case in qualitative research where the exploratory nature of the research process is sometimes emphasised by the insertion of 'tentative' prior to use of the word definition. The possible need to change definitions is indicative of a fundamental characteristic of words; they are abstractions representing classes of things. Apple, for example, can be a single apple or the apple family. A property of abstractions is that their referents undergo constant change. Cricket as it is played today, for example, differs significantly from how it was played fifty years ago and even more significantly from how it was played fifty years before then. It is only context, assumption or definition, therefore, which make the sentence *I like cricket* meaningful (Holt, 1987). Context and assumption appear less definitive than definition but definition itself represents a class of things we define as definitions. Poverty, for example, can be defined in absolute terms in the sense of having no possessions or in relative terms in the sense of lacking what others take for granted (Hart, 2005). So, to be useful, the type of definition applied needs to be defined. A descriptive definition, for example, provides the meaning of a word in general usage while a stipulative definition provides a particular meaning imposed upon a word:

Aware of the generally gender-specific nature of the term 'fraternal', I intend to use it here in a gender-neutral sense of 'sibling relationship', much like 'fraternal twins' who can be of any sex.

(Yang, 2008, p.223)

In general, therefore, descriptive definitions are contestable by comparison to usage, while stipulative definitions are not. It is the latter type of definition that is usually meant when empirical researchers need to construct precise definitions or critically evaluate existing definitions in order, for example, to avoid compromising the validity of data collection instruments (Hart, 2005, p.299). It is in this context that definitions are made operational: definable in terms of observable, identifiable, and repeatable operations (Mauch & Birch, 1998). Examiners will take critical note of the lack of such definitions if they should have been provided: *The opening argument needs to be re-argued. It needs operational definitions and critical comment on…*

• In most instances, though, there is no need to define terms in common use unless examiners need to understand them in a particular way. If this is necessary there are a number of ways of doing so. One way is to define terms in a glossary after the table of contents. This is useful if, because they are idiosyncratic, there is no need to reference the definitions. For example: *Alternative school: a public (not private or independent) school whose program is considered to be…* Another way is to integrate into the narrative of the thesis definitions that need to be referenced. For example:

There is a significant body of literature on… as a distinctive field of social science (Hudelston 1994; Patton 1990; Patton 1986; Weiss 1972). One consequence is a variety of definitions of…. Most of these definitions include both the purpose of an… and the types of activities commonly undertaken as part of it.

Definitions can also be implicit if brief detail is provided at first mention of a term. For example: *Multimedia, a process that combines two or more media such as text, video or sound, has had a great influence on…* The appropriate point in the thesis where such definitions need to be integrated with the text will depend on the needs of the narrative. Definitions might only become necessary, for example, once well into the body of the thesis. It is more usual, though, to apply them much earlier, often immediately after the statement in the introduction indicating what the thesis is about. Because all components of the research process have a history, there might be an opportunity to open the introduction with an account of a definition's history. For example:

Dyspraxia affects between 2–7 per cent of the population (Temple, 2002). Despite over 40 years of research the definition of dyspraxia remains contro-versial (Rutter, 1969; 1998)… The World Federation of Neurology (1968) developed one of the first working definitions. It defines dyspraxia as… This definition has received criticism because… Without agreement on the defi-nition, it is difficult to estimate precisely the prevalence of dyspraxia in the population. The term dyspraxia was first employed by Berlin (1872) to describe patients who… Later, Morgan (1896) and Kerr (1897) introduced…

- An historical account in the introduction that allows the narrative to flow easily to the focus of the research need not only be of a definition. It can, instead, be an account of the recent or even ancient history of the topic under discussion. This can be seen, for example, in the following excerpts each of which opens consecutive paragraphs at the opening of an introduction chapter:

This thesis examines…This thesis is primarily concerned with…The intrigu-ing subject of…has been discussed in the philosophies and sciences of many ancient and modern cultures…In 2500 BC the ancient Chinese classic on internal medicine…had identified…

In each case accounts such as these serve a dual purpose: they contribute towards an understanding of the context of the research and also introduce examiners to the field of investigation. The provision of sufficient background is, thus, an important aspect of the introduction. There is a difference, though, in the interpretation of 'sufficient' as it applies to empirical theses on the one hand and to exegetic and qualitative theses on the other. In empirical theses both the focus of the research and the context in which it is conducted can usually be provided in focused, descriptive and relatively brief accounts: *Particle flow can be subdivided into slow and rapid flows. In slow flows, particles stay in contact…On the other hand, in rapid flows each particle…*In exegetic and qualitative theses, however, a far wider initial focus is generally needed: *On the east coast of…lies a small rural peninsula named…* This is because exegetic research in general and qualitative research in particular is heavily dependent upon context. Not only therefore, will the introduction to the field of research in exegetic and qualitative theses tend to be longer than in empirical theses it will also usually require frequent reference to the literature. This is an additional reason why the introduction and literature review chapters in exegetic and qualitative theses are so often combined.

- Once the context and field of investigation have been established the aim of the research, although usually briefly introduced in the opening paragraph of the introduction, will need to be re-introduced. It is at this point that 'gap statements' become useful for they are typically presented in the form of negative evaluations. This can be seen in the following examples: 'One class of quality improvement which has not received much attention is…'; or: 'Due to the complexity of flow problems there are few analytic models…' (Paltridge & Starfield, 2007, p.87). A variation of this model is to indicate how the work of other researchers will be complemented or extended by introducing a problem into what until this point has been primarily descriptive text: *Studies designed by Holloway (1999) and Vincent (2004) to investigate…revealed that… These were surprising findings since…This study has, therefore, been designed to investigate these anomalies.* However, because the consequences of problems are not necessarily shared, their relative importance has a considerable subjective component. It is, thus, possible for beginning researchers to think there is a problem when there isn't one (Lovitts, 2007). For this reason the research problem will need to be substantiated by indicating the nature of the consequences if it is not undertaken. Do not do so limply: *This thesis has the potential to…* Instead, signalling the value and significance of the research calls for an element of confident assertiveness:

At present the…theory is still being developed. Thus, because there is no gener-ally accepted theory further work to develop the theory to the point of general acceptance is essential for the development of…

Alternatively, the aim of the research can be introduced immediately after a statement of the field's importance:

Based on the assumption that it is indeed crucial to understand the various factors that play a role in producing representations of the past my aim is to illuminate the cultural and cognitive processes involved in…

Empirical researchers, in particular, ought to bear the following in mind:

…clarity is not enough to make an introduction outstanding or even very good. To be outstanding, the introduction has to show that the problem is compelling, that something really motivates the problem.

(Lovitts, 2007, p.375)

- With the nature, aims and significance of the issue/s under investigation clearly established the primary research questions and/or hypotheses will need to be introduced. If, as is often the case, there is more than one of each they will need to be presented and discussed one after the other, the order of presentation being an implicit indicator of their order of importance: *Four hypotheses were tested in order to ascertain... The first research hypothesis was... The second research hypothesis tested... The third hypothesis tested... The fourth hypothesis was that...*

- It will then be necessary to frame the questions and/or hypotheses by defining the scope of the research. Two related issues are involved. The first will be the need to indicate precisely what is going to be done and, as is sometimes the case, what, and for what reasons, is not going to be done: *Prior work on...based on other theoretic approaches will not be presented as they lie outside the scope of the current research.* The second issue will be the need not only to delimit, but also explain what the boundaries of the research are and why they were they chosen:

Because the purpose of this study is to determine the impact of...the boundary for the research has been set at the perimeter of the plant. The transport of materials to and from the plant has, therefore, not been included.

In this example the research boundary is physical. But, depending upon the needs of particular research undertakings, it might also, for example, be chronological, theoretic, political or cultural.

- The importance of framing the research questions and/or hypotheses as precisely and clearly as possible is twofold. First, if the introduction and literature review chapters are to be presented separately, the placement of the questions and/or hypotheses at the end of the introduction will provide a clear focus for the literature review chapter immediately following. Second, it is essential that the examiners, at the end of the thesis, are accurately able to assess the extent to which the questions and/or hypotheses have been addressed adequately. It is for this latter reason also usually important to identify and briefly explain the limitations that might inhibit the ability to do so. In empirical and some qualitative theses, these factors will later be discussed in the methods section, but mentioning them briefly in the introduction will better assist the examiners to place the aims of the research in context at a much earlier point. In some empirical theses there might also, for much the same reason, be a discipline-specific requirement to indicate in the introduction what the principal findings of the research were expected to be:

If caching contributes to coexistence, we expect species within communities to differ in caching behaviour. We also expect the two communities from different desert sites to show similar patterns of interspecific variation...

(Price, Waser, & McDonald, 2000, p.98)

In such cases there is usually an expectation that the actual findings will also be indicated. Should they exist, the reasons for any significant discrepancies between the expectations and the findings will need to be indicated briefly.

4. In addition to deciding which elements from the bullet points above will be most suitable for the introduction to particular theses, a decision will also need to be made about the order in which they ought to appear. While all stories have a structure, how that structure is organised is an intrinsic part of the story telling process. The innovative French film director, Jean-Luc Godard made this clear in response to a statement that all narratives should have a beginning, middle and end: 'Yes, of course, but not necessarily in that order' (Canter & Fairbairn, 2006, p.74). With the exception of the first of the above bullet points they flow, as was the case in the CARS model, down an inverted pyramid: from the general to the specific. This is a reflection of the model's foundation in empirical linearity. It is also the reason why readers more easily follow this mode of presentation. However, the more theoretic the research the more idiosyncratic the structure of the introduction will tend to be. The following three examples are indicative of this tendency.

• The first is from an empirical thesis. The opening paragraph of the introduction provides the focus and theoretic approach of the research: *This thesis investigates why…are required by some…practitioners but not by others. It applies theory developed by Harding (1999) and Glaser (2000) about…and theory about… developed by Keen (2001)*. The second paragraph provides a brief description of each of the theories and explains their relevance to the topic. The next paragraph provides a definition of terms and then explains how these definitions affect the research question: *Deregistration occurs when there are…The question, therefore, is whether this definition is sufficient to explain why…are required by some practitioners and not by others?* The fourth paragraph provides the setting: *The setting for the study is…during the period…*The fifth paragraph indicates the intent of the research: *The intended contributions of this study are to enhance an understanding of…*The sixth paragraph explains how the thesis has been structured: *The thesis proceeds as follows…*The final paragraph concludes the introduction by indicating the strength of the relationship between the results and the research hypothesis: *The results are consistent with the hypotheses that…They are robust under alternative ways of measuring the…*

• The second example opens with the statement that qualitative research material:

  …privileges individuals' lived experience. Increasing our understanding of the views of children and adults is key to developing effective interventions… We know surprisingly little about the dynamics of school bullying relationships…

It is vital to have children's perspectives when trying to identify the processes involved in problematic peer relations.

(Mishna, 2004, cited in Marshall & Rossman, 2006, p.54)

In this extract the researcher first presents what is known then what needs to be established and then why a qualitative approach is needed (Marshall & Rossman, 2006, p.54).

- The third example is from an exegetic study of a Shakespearean play and is the most epistemic of the introductions. It begins by delineating the recurring patterns of theatricality in the play: 'Much Ado is filled with playlets, staged shows, actors, and interior dramatists'. Previous critical interpretations are then characterised: 'Much of this criticism aspires to articulate an unchanging or universal meaning for the play—a task both impossible and impossibly idealist'. The research topic is then introduced: 'Instead, I am interested in the historical contingency of meaning and want to explore Much Ado's preoccupation with theatrical practices in relationship to...antitheatrical tracts' (Howard, 1987, pp.163–4, cited in Peck MacDonald, 1994, p.124). The argument and method adopted are then specified:

I will argue that these tracts—through their discussions of theater—were a site where anxieties about a changing social order were discursively produced and managed... In contradistinction to a criticism committed to the drama's place 'above ideology' and to its aesthetic and thematic unity, a political criticism of Renaissance drama will focus precisely on the silences and contradictions which reveal the constructed—and interested—nature of dramatic representations...

(Howard, 1987, pp.163–4, cited in Peck MacDonald, 1994, p.124)

The epistemic focus in this extract on disciplinary discourse rather than on timeless text illustrates a departure between the structure of introductions to empirical and more theoretical studies. In the former the focus of the research tends to be placed first while, in the latter, the focus tends to be deferred until context has been developed (Peck MacDonald, 1994).

7.4 DEVELOPING A DRAFT INTRODUCTION

1. Deferral of focus in theoretical theses is a reflection both of the audience's need of context to situate the focus of the text and of the researcher's prior need to understand the context in order to develop a focus. For exegetic and qualitative researchers the process is necessarily incremental. This is evident in the following anguished statement by the writer of a qualitative thesis:

I understand what we mean by conceptual framework but I have such a hard time articulating that in my own work. How do I pull from disparate works to create a logical whole? At what point does the framework stand on its own?

(Cited in Marshall & Rossman, 2006, p.49)

Thus introductions to exegetic and qualitative theses cannot be drafted and redrafted to a point of near completion, as is often done by empirical researchers, before moving on to the next chapter. Each draft will, instead, need to be redrafted in conjunction with the drafting and redrafting of the remaining chapters of the thesis. In this way the introduction, as is the case in regard to the literature review with which the introduction in qualitative and exegetic theses is usually combined, will be able to grow organically with the rest of the thesis.

2. However, during the writing of the first drafts of the introduction, even empirical researchers often discover they are not yet in a position to elaborate on all of the issues that will need to be included in the final draft. So, instead of attempting to write a complete draft of the introduction at the outset the following subheadings, or variations thereof, could be used as an initial template: Purpose of the Study; Structure of the Chapter; Theoretic Framework; Definition of Terms; Context; Focus of the Research; Significance of the Research and, finally, Structure of the Thesis. The brief and tentative text on this initial template can then be altered, reorganised and elaborated when it is frequently revisited during the writing of the remainder of the thesis.

3. Once, when well into the writing process, a reasonably complete and sufficiently coherent draft of the introduction has been written, look again at the framework around which the introduction has been constructed. As in the following brief exemplar, each of the individual elements that have been included ought to be identifiable in terms of how they contribute to an overall pattern of meaning:

As we have investigated environmental threats, our understanding of many chemical processes such as acid rain and the buildup of carbon dioxide has improved, allowing us to understand their eventual effect on the biosphere. (Common ground) But recently the chemical processes that have been thinning the ozone layer have been found to be less well understood than once thought. (A problem) We may have labeled hydrofluorocarbons as the chief cause incorrectly and thus adopted inappropriate corrective strategies. (Cause of the problem) We have found that the bonding of carbon… (Response)

(Adapted from Booth, et al., 2003, p.233).

4. It is important to bear in mind two related issues when drafting the introduction to a thesis. First, the time spent revising this chapter should constitute the most important aspect of the entire revision process. Second,

the relationship between the introduction to and conclusion of a thesis is close: all of the research questions and issues raised in the introduction will need to be addressed in the conclusion:

Several examiners reported...that they read the introduction and the conclusion as if they were one document. They do this prior to reading the whole thesis. They are looking for coherence within the overall approach and argument.

(Kiley & Mullins, 2006, p.203)

The conclusion will often mirror the introduction with words like: *In the introduction I raised the question of...*; or: *In the introduction it was noted that researchers had not yet resolved the issue of...* In order to create linkages like these the final drafts of the introduction and conclusion should only be written after the final drafts of the remainder of the thesis have been completed. This is particularly pertinent in regard to the introduction, for it will generally only be towards the end of the drafting of the entire thesis that it will become clear what aspects of the research ought to be introduced and how and in what order they ought to be introduced. Once this version of the introduction is in place, and once it has been scoured for questions and issues that ought to be addressed in the conclusion the final draft of the conclusion may be written. A final revision of introduction and conclusion together will ensure that both are aligned as a frame to the thesis.

5. There is an additional important reason for sequencing the writing of the introduction and conclusion to the thesis in this way. Readers, as in the case of listeners, are most heavily influenced by what comes first and by what comes last. Examiners will not necessarily start reading a thesis from the beginning; they might, for example, start with the conclusion or with the methods section instead. Nonetheless, the introduction will retain its crucial role and ought to be written on the assumption that it will be read first. On this basis the introduction will be the examiners' first substantial contact with the text of the thesis. Their initial response will, therefore, have a significant impact on their total response to the work (Mathews, 2004). In the same vein the conclusion of the thesis will strongly influence their final impression. This explains why these sections of the thesis ought to be written last: it is at this point that writing is likely to be at its best.

CHAPTER 8

Literature Review Part One: Preparing the Ground

To be human is to persuade and be persuaded, to interpret and be interpreted—this is largely what it means to be a symbol-using animal.

(Crusius, 1991, p.57)

8.1 INTRODUCTION

1. The introduction to a thesis provides the justification for the research and the methodology adopted to investigate it. The purpose of the literature review is to complement the introduction by discussing the intellectual history of the study. This roots a thesis in previous research and, because existing knowledge has been assessed, makes possible a claim that the thesis is a contribution to that knowledge (Bryant, 2004). To this extent, the introduction and literature review, when presented either as separate chapters or as one, provide the foundation upon which the remainder of the thesis will rest. Do not, therefore, indicate a minimalist understanding of the purpose of a review in the chapter heading: *Lessons Learned from the Literature.*

2. As has already been established separate literature review chapters tend to be the norm in empirical theses while in exegetic theses the introduction and literature review tend to be combined. This is a consequence of the inseparability of the concepts with which exegetic researchers deal from the literature in which those concepts are embedded. This explains why in exegetic theses the literature not only co-mingles with the introduction but the literature also permeates all other chapters of the thesis as well. Nonetheless, exegetic theses have sufficient focus to justify a clearly identifiable section where the focus of the research is introduced, explained and justified in the context of the work of other researchers. This is not necessarily the case in qualitative theses where, because they are exploratory and thus explicitly research led, the relevance of the literature can only be ascertained as the research proceeds.

In grounded theory, as in action research, for example, the review of the literature is consciously delayed until direction emerges from the analysis of early data. This is to prevent categories and concepts used in the literature being brought to, rather than arising from, the data (Punch, 2006). Thus, when qualitative theses have a distinct review, the literature discussed tends only to revolve around methodological issues. In most cases, therefore, the literature in a qualitative thesis will either be introduced as the progress of the study brings it into relevance or will be discussed in a review towards the end of the study where the outcomes can be compared and contrasted with those of other studies. In the case of the former the review will be 'invisible' in the sense that it does not occupy a discrete niche in the thesis but runs throughout the text. In this sense they resemble exegetic theses. In the case of the latter where the literature is reviewed towards the end of the study qualitative theses resemble the structure of empirical studies: what is the discussion section of an empirical thesis other than a continuation of the literature review? What, though, is literature?

Defining literature

3. Dating roughly from the early eighteenth century the concept 'literature' is of relatively recent vintage. Its origin lies in the birth of modern democracy: the revolutionary establishment in law of the principle that anything can be said publicly (Derrida, 1997, p.80). However, that the concept is as open as the principle is indicated by the fact that there are as many versions of what 'literature' in a particular area comprises as there are people writing and reading in that area (Golden-Biddle, 1997). There are a number of explanations for this. Perhaps primary is that literature 'can be regarded as being about the reader at the moment of reading through the process of reading… texts require the act of reading in order to be complete…' (Fiumara, 1995, p.25). Readers bring attitudes, memories, and cultural influences to texts in ways that help determine their readings. Class might be one of these attitudes for published literature represents an elite perspective different from that found in the streets (Mertens, 2003). So might theoretic perspective. In fact understanding what constitutes academic discourse implies a theory of literature (Peters, 2008). The postmodern argument, for example, that there can be no definitive reading of anything diminishes the distinction between fiction and nonfiction (Taleb, 2007). It also makes explicit the perception of writing a thesis as participation in ongoing discourses. From this perspective the concept 'literature' is not only broadened to include the entire spectrum of writing and conversation (literature as both verbal and non-verbal discourse) but also to being integral, rather than monolithic precursor, to a study. In this context, the term 'literature review'

is inapplicable and the terms 'review of the discourses' or 'immersion in the discourses' are more accurate (Garman, 2006).

4. Discipline convention also influences the understanding of literature. Anecdotal accounts, for example, are not uncommon in journals aimed at practising professionals (Galvan, 2004). The following extract shows incorporation of wide-ranging sources:

In addition to typical organizational examples, this chapter uses illustrations from newspaper stories, movies, and other pedestrian sources to demonstrate the real-world pervasiveness of the difficulty of observation and measurement in contemporary social science issues.

(Dent, 2005, p.253)

A preference for books in the humanities is illustrative of fields where assumptions need to be developed *ab initio*, whereas that for article-length pieces in the natural sciences indicates much of the background argumentation has already been established as a consequence of the normative process (Becher & Trowler, 2001). An explanation also lies in advances in technology. As more academics read and publish online the boundary between what is and what is not literature becomes increasingly fuzzy and the importance of refereeing as a measure of quality assurance is also diminished (Becher & Trowler, 2001). Nonetheless, the mere inclusion of a citation in a review indicates what a researcher considers academic literature to be.

Skill requirements

5. It has thus far been established that all theses have a literature review; presented though in a manner that best suits the purpose of the research. It has also been established that 'literature' is a generic term embracing all literary productions, published and unpublished. What then needs to be established is the quality of the literary productions. Reviewing the literature or discourses thus requires researchers to exercise a variety of skills:

- First, the ability to define in relation to a particular research undertaking what the term 'literature' means. This is a necessary precursor to 'harvesting' the literature for, without such definition, how will a researcher know what to look for? This definition ought also to be made explicit in the text of the thesis for to write, for example, *there is disagreement in the literature as to the extent...* without first providing a definition of what is meant by 'the literature' indicates it is being left for the examiners to decide.
- Second, the ability not only to know where and how to access the bulk of the literature falling within the definition applied but, also, to have the

necessary creativity and determination to persist in the search for the illusive literature within that definition.

- Third, the ability to appraise the literature critically and, in doing so, to retain both the context and meaning intended by the original authors and also critique it.
- Fourth, the ability to manage and organise the material from the literature in such a way that it can be accessed easily and efficiently when the drafts of the thesis are being written and that all of the necessary referencing information is retained.
- Fifth, the ability not only to integrate the material into the text of the thesis so that continuity between previous work and the thesis study is demonstrated but also to explain and justify the study and the methodology used to undertake it.

There is, in other words, a distinction between conducting a review of the literature and writing a literature review.

The review as complement to the methods section

6. Just as the introduction and literature review complement each other so too do each of these sections, separately or together, complement the discussion of the methods which, in an empirical thesis and some qualitative theses, will be an explicit section following immediately after the review. The depth of the bond between the introduction, literature review and methods makes it sound policy to review the literature with an eye for the manner in which particular methods might have been applied and for any novel approaches. These observations can subsequently be incorporated into and enrich both the introduction to the thesis and explicit or implicit discussion of the methods.

7. The distinction between the literature dealing with methodology, methods application and content will need to be taken into account when the literature is being reviewed: the first two will justify the choice of theory and methods and the last will provide context to both the study and the findings. Moreover, in all methodological approaches to research, theory is likely to have a number of facets. In qualitative studies, for example, one body of literature might be devoted to qualitative approaches in general while another might focus on particular approaches. It is also likely that there will be a number of aspects to the content literature. When, for example, an indicative review for the research proposal is being constructed the literature relating to the topic of research will need to be identified and understood. However, once the research has developed direction and momentum the need for more clearly focused literature will become relevant.

8.2 SYSTEMATIC REVIEWS

1. Just as research literature can be categorised into that with a bias towards methodology, method and content and into sub-categories of each, so too are there broad categories of literature reviews—discursive and systematic:

   • Discursive reviews presented together with the introduction, separately, or as 'invisible' are the type generally found in research theses. Their function is to situate studies by demonstrating the relevant literature has been extensively researched, coherently organised, critically evaluated and effectively synthesised. In a mixed methodology review 'synthesis' will have an additional meaning in the sense that the review will include literature pertaining to the synthesis of the methodologies in addition to a review of the research results (Creswell & Plano Clark, 2007).

   • Systematic reviews on the other hand are generally self-contained. Their purpose is to synthesise, in a systematic manner, the findings of as many similar research undertakings as possible so as to increase the utility of these findings for application by other researchers. Thus, although developing a systematic review has increasingly come to be accepted as a legitimate way of earning a research master's degree, such reviews are unlikely to appear in most other theses. Nonetheless, the manner in which systematic reviews are conceived and presented provides useful insights into issues that ought to be considered when writing a discursive review in a thesis. For this reason a brief discussion of them has been included here.

2. Systematic review protocol emerged in the 1970s. By this time the international growth in the volume of medical research had made it increasingly difficult to make valid comparisons between research results and to draw practical conclusions from them. The growth in the volume of medical research has continued unabated. Currently some two million articles are published annually in over 20 000 biomedical journals (Mulrow, 1994). In even a single area of research it is not unusual for the number of published trials to run into hundreds. These studies, in addition, are of variable quality and many provide unclear or contradictory results. The purpose of systematic reviews, therefore, is to enable researchers and practitioners to draw meaningful conclusions from this mass of material. Although the use of systematic review methodology began in the medical field it subsequently expanded into those disciplines, criminology and education for example, where evidence-based comparisons can be made (Perry & Hammond, 2002).

3. The rationale for systematic reviews, an empirically reproducible process for comparing evidence, is grounded in the following premises (Mulrow, 1994):

   • A significant number of research findings can be generalised.

- The volume and diversity of the research reviewed provides an interpretive context not available in any one study.
- Data inconsistencies and conflicts in data can be explained.
- The research literature can be identified according to an explicit search strategy.
- The research literature to be reviewed can be selected according to defined inclusion and exclusion criteria.
- Studies can be evaluated against consistent methodological standards.

4. The template of a systematic review is typically divided into the following sections: background, review questions or objectives, search strategy, methods of study selection, quality assessment, data extraction and synthesis, results, summary of analysis and conclusion (Perry & Hammond, 2002):

- The *Background* section provides the context and importance of the investigation.
- The *Review Questions* or *Objectives* section contains carefully formulated, precise objectives and questions.
- The *Search Strategy* section indicates the databases used, the reasons for their use and the alternative words used in the key word searches.
- The *Methods of Study Selection* section provides the criteria used to either include or exclude primary studies. These might, for example, be 'publication bias' (publications in only one language might have been chosen; publications prior to a particular date may have been excluded as might all unpublished studies or those with negative results). Excluded studies are often reported in an appendix to the review for it is important for readers to know what they are.
- The *Quality Assessment* section indicates the means used to rank the quality of research findings. Because systematic review methodology is inherently empirical, masked randomised, placebo-controlled trials are usually placed at the pinnacle of a hierarchy of other research methods. These trials will then be followed in a list of decreasing importance by, for example, open randomised controlled trials, surveys and observational methods. The review will also only be comprehensive and balanced if it acknowledges controversies, unresolved questions, conflicts of interest and recent developments (Siwek, Gourlay, Slawson & Shaughnessy, 2002). The material referenced, therefore, will not only be that which supports the conclusions.
- The author/s of a systematic review, after having selected the research literature on the basis of the outlined criteria, will comprehensively examine that literature, seeking to identify, extract and synthesise all relevant information. The authors of systematic review meta-analyses, after having taken the extra precaution of ensuring that the studies included in the review are similar enough to justify combining their

results statistically, will do so using rigorous statistical analysis. After a summary of the analysis has been provided, systematic reviews usually conclude with a statement indicating that there is no conflict of interest between the reviewer and the issue/s under review.

5. Unlike discursive reviews, systematic reviews of the literature are developed through a standardised and clearly defined process. This is to ensure that as much of the relevant research base as possible has been searched, that the search has been conducted in an objective and clearly defined manner and that only original studies have been appraised and validly compared. So, in summary, what insights are provided by systematic review methodology that can usefully be applied by writers of discursive literature reviews in theses?

   • The review question/s or objectives are focused, justified and placed in context.
   • Care is taken to indicate that a comprehensive search of the primary literature has been made.
   • Studies are not simply juxtaposed without regard to quality or selection criteria.
   • Controversies are recognised and discussed.
   • Research findings are synthesised in order to reveal common features, trends and differences

8.3 THE RELATIONSHIP BETWEEN THESIS TITLE AND DISCURSIVE REVIEW

1. The establishment of the initial working title of a thesis will require the development of a preliminary literature review. This is the review that will generally be presented in the thesis proposal. Because the purpose of this preliminary 'indicative' review is usually to place the proposed study in context and to identify the primary sources, the literature it covers will be focused primarily on the topic area of the research rather than, as will later be the case, on the title. Nonetheless, and this applies to both exegetic and qualitative as well as to empirical theses, the narrower the focus of a study the more detailed the subsequent analysis will be. In any event, should the focus of the research subsequently change, the path through the literature can always be retraced (Hart, 1998). It follows that a focused and detailed review of the literature requires a research focus that has been as clearly defined as possible: *...we limit our analysis to... We also limit our review to studies of...because...* A focus too wide ranging will tend to limit discussion to the shallows. But, just as damaging, a broad focus will necessitate the need to consult a wider range of literature than would normally have been the case. Efficiency, therefore, will be reduced because research material loses its utility in proportion to the

rate at which it accumulates. So, do not be overambitious, cut down the scope of work that seems too large (Cryer, 2006). It is worth bearing in mind that the late submission of theses is often the result of thesis writers having fallen victim to the 'might be relevant syndrome'.

2. Even when there is a strong degree of focus at the outset it will still be normal for much of the initial reading to be exploratory and, thus, tangential. This even applies to those qualitative researchers who immerse themselves in a research setting and allow focus to emerge from the data: *The fact that I observed participants before I started my literature search gave me an opportunity to formulate my research question without being biased by the existing literature.* In essence this means working backwards from the data to the introduction and then to the literature review (Meloy, 2002). Tangential reading applies in particular, though, to researchers in loosely structured disciplines like history and English literature where wide reading is considered a mark of scholarship (Becher & Trowler, 2001). This is a primary reason why in these disciplines theses normally have a bibliography rather than reference list.[1] Nonetheless tangential material can give rise to a dilemma: some examiners see the inclusion of such material in the bibliography as indicative of a lack of direction while others, some of whom see spotting missing texts as one of their prime duties, see it as evidence of sound foundational reading (Pearce, 2005). Doctoral candidates, in particular, need to prepare for the dreaded and, unless a significant omission, frequently unfair statement in the oral examination: 'I was surprised not to find X listed in your bibliography' (cited in Pearce, 2005, p.77).

8.4 THE IMPORTANCE OF CURRENT RESEARCH

1. Just as in general there is a distinction in the expectation of wide reading between researchers in less structured and in highly structured disciplines, so too is there a distinction in the use of current research. What can be regarded as current is defined differently in particular disciplines but is usually regarded as research conducted within the previous five years. On this basis a dated study, but one whose findings are likely still to be current, found that on average between sixty and seventy per cent of references in journals in physics and biochemistry were to current research. However, in social science journals the percentage went down to about forty per cent, while in some journals in the humanities it dipped to below ten per cent (Peck MacDonald, 1994). Thus, while current research is apposite for all research it is of particular importance in the sciences and engineering. In these discipline areas, the extent to which the literature consulted is up-to-date is 'absolutely fundamental to the credibility of the thesis…' (Pearce, 2005, p.58). The last thing needed therefore, are terminal comments such as the following from examiners: 'Seriously outdated sources' (Lovat et al., 2002,

p.14); 'At least in this section if not throughout, updated references are required' (Holbrook & Dally, 2003, p.11). Because of the relative speed with which new research is published, some of the responsibility for ensuring that the literature cited in a thesis is current should lie with the supervisor (Pearce, 2005). Final responsibility, though, lies with the researcher. This is not to imply that older sources have no place in a thesis in the sciences or engineering. There might well, for example, be a need to provide an historical overview or it might be a landmark study. Nor is it to imply that there is not an equivalent need in exegetic and qualitative work to remain up to date. It is simply recognition, particularly in regard to the former, that older sources can still provide valuable and, therefore, current insights. It is also recognition that all thesis writers need to indicate they are aware of relevant research published up to the point of submission.

2. This raises a question of possible importance: what if research central to a study is published just prior to submission of the thesis? This, in turn, gives rise to another question: should the researcher have known about the research prior to its publication? 'Communism' in research is the paradox that priority of discovery and the professional pride that usually accompanies it can only be claimed once the discovery has been made public (Lewin, 2001). This is at least one of the reasons prompting the need by researchers to publish early. However, fear of intellectual theft or the desire to exploit new ideas fully motivates secrecy (Becher & Trowler). It is, thus, frequently possible to explain satisfactorily ignorance of newly published pertinent research. If this is the case then the appropriate response in a thesis to new sources of information depends on how much time the researcher has at his or her disposal. If very little then it might be useful to attach an addendum to the thesis briefly indicating what effect prior knowledge of the research would have had on the study. If more time is available then including similar information in the introduction might be an option. In either case examiners will understand the dilemma faced and appreciate the fact that an attempt has been made to resolve it. Only rarely will supervisors suggest that submission be delayed in order for the new research to be taken fully into account. If, however, such advice is given the researcher would be well advised to heed it.

3. The emphasis upon recency in the sources cited in much empirical work and, particularly in regard to methodological issues in qualitative work is reflected in what is often a noticeable difference between the reference lists of empirical and qualitative theses on the one hand and the bibliographies of exegetic theses on the other: the former two will tend to list fewer books and more journal articles and conference papers than the latter. This is at least partly explained by disciplinary differences. In history and English literature, for example, where long, complex narratives lie at the core of the discipline, books generally earn more prestige for their authors than journal articles. In the natural and applied sciences, however, books account for only a small minority of

publications (Becher & Trowler, 2001). The reason is most visible in chemistry where topics, in a comparative sense, are easily dissected into their component parts. This enables several authors to contribute to relatively brief articles. Ten publications a year, a staggering total for an historian or literary scholar, is not, therefore, uncommon among chemists (Becher & Trowler, 2001).

4. On the face of it, books should take longer to publish than journal articles. The publication process of journal articles, however, is subject to many variables, the refereeing process and the prestige of particular journals being chief among them. As indicative averages, though, a full journal article in physics may be delayed for nine to twelve months, in economics for nine to eighteen months and in engineering for between one and two years. History and sociology have waiting periods ranging from eighteen months to a few years (Becher & Trowler, 2001). There are, however, exceptions. Publication in less prestigious or in non-refereed journals is often a way to hasten publication. Another exception applies to fast moving sub-disciplines especially those within disciplinary areas like physics, chemistry and astronomy. Here 'discovery' papers are published with a minimum of delay at the price of restrictions on length. The overall trend, though, indicates that even recent articles in refereed journals can contain dated information. Nor are all databases or internet sites regularly updated. With the exception of recent refereed conference papers, all of this means, therefore, that a degree of caution will need to be exercised when judging how current the information in the literature actually is.

8.5 INFORMATION TECHNOLOGY

1. A number of strategies are available to assist in making such judgements. One is to conduct a 'cited reference' search. This is a useful tool for finding current research articles on a topic across disciplinary boundaries and for identifying the most important researchers in a field. Universities also make use of 'cited reference' searches when making tenure decisions about academic staff. Another strategy is to make use of the many alerting services provided by publishers and by the producers of the databases specific to the study. The most important strategy, though, is to make contact with an appropriate subject librarian as early as possible in the research process. Disintermediation is a contemporary term to describe the increasing tendency of user-friendly technology to diminish the role of intermediaries. In the specific case of information technology this has often meant a decline in the number of front-line librarians (Macauley, 2006). One of the side-effects has been to lull thesis researchers into a false sense of security regarding their levels of information literacy (Macauley, 2006): the ability to formulate an information problem and then to locate, critique and manage the information. We don't know, in other words, what we don't know. This means

that without the assistance of subject librarians many searches of the literature simply 'round up the usual suspects' (Hart, 2005, p.160). The assistance of subject librarians usually means, however, an extension of the net beyond the core texts to include the 'grey literature'. It is not only their expertise that enables them to do so; it is also because they tend to browse new additions to the library on a regular basis (Macauley, 2006). This also means that librarians can help researchers publish strategically by, for example, providing circulation rates and levels of prestige (Macauley, 2006). In addition to the wealth of other advice they might provide, subject librarians will also be able to direct new researchers to the appropriate tutorials on how best to use the facilities libraries offer.

2. If such tutorials have not already been attended the need to do so will soon become readily apparent, for appropriate databases will need to be identified and then the search strategies often unique to each learned. Articles in databases are selected, analysed and processed by subject specialists but articles published on the internet can be of variable quality. There might, therefore, be a need to attend additional library tutorials not only in order to learn the most efficient techniques for conducting internet searches[2] but also how to evaluate the quality of material accessed there.[3] While the internet can and electronic databases will prove to be invaluable, the possibility that important sources of information might lie elsewhere should never be dismissed. Many databases, for example, only reach back to the mid-1960s. There is also often a time lag between the publication of an article and its insertion into a database. In addition, no matter how well the descriptors have been selected, important material in both databases and the internet can escape detection (Mauch & Birch, 1998). So look, for instance, at hardcopy indexing journals (these indicate what has been published and where) and abstracting journals (each reference has an accompanying abstract) and scour the bibliographies and reference lists of the literature already consulted, both electronic and hardcopy, for any sources that might be relevant. This can be a particularly useful strategy if a start is made with the bibliographies or reference lists of sources initially identified as key to the research. In this way there will be gradual movement to the bibliographies and reference lists of peripheral sources. It will also be an ordered movement in the sense that the geometry of the process reflects movement from the tip of a pyramid to its base. This is useful because, if inverted, it will reflect the shape of most literature reviews: a progression from the general to the specific. The movement outwards from the tip will, in addition, also generally reflect a movement from the new to the old; a process providing additional contextual depth (Mauch & Birch, 1998).

3. It is also important to read theses with the proviso that caution be exercised: while they have been examined they have not been subject to the full rigours of wide public exposure. With this proviso in place theses can be particularly useful because, unlike most books and journal articles, they devote extensive

sections to methodology and method, and to reviews of the literature. Because there is an international trend to making them freely available online they are also becoming more easily accessible. Numerous databases also index theses (Macauley, 2006). While theses need to be treated with a degree of caution it is also worth bearing in mind that some articles in recognised journals have also not been subject to the full rigours of refereeing. For example, on the basis that early publication might indicate how valuable results might accrue from more careful work, the editors of a prestigious science journal remarked that when a significant breakthrough has been achieved 'we have found it necessary to relax our standards and accept some papers that present new ideas without full analysis...' (Becher & Trowler, 2001, p.119). Less than rigorous refereeing is also a feature in mathematics where it can be particularly difficult and time-consuming for referees to follow a researcher's train of thought. There is, in any event, no reward system for doing so. Thus, while authors take care not to make mistakes it is often up to readers to pick them up should there be any (Becher & Trowler, 2001).

4. Whenever possible consult the actual reports of research, the primary sources, because the author of a secondary source might have misunderstood the original. Every retelling of a story tends to simplify it and second or third-hand accounts, as a result, can appear more definitive than the first (Wallace & Wray, 2006). However, in practice, it is unrealistic to expect that no study in a thesis should be reported unless it has been read in the original. Instead, in consultation with the supervisors, a compromise needs to be found. In essence any study directly related to the central issues under investigation in a thesis should be read. Tangential studies can be cited but not read (Bryant, 2004). But it would also be unrealistic to assume a clear distinction between the two. In many cases it is no more than visceral: a study that initially appeared tangential makes a transition across an invisible boundary to greater importance. If, however, a source of clear importance could not be read in the original provide a brief explanatory note in the text of the thesis (Burton & Steane, 2004c). A common frustration is attempting to track down an apparently key unpublished conference paper. So, if finding an important source meant going to extraordinary lengths it might be useful to include the story briefly either in the text of the thesis or in a footnote. Not only might this be important for the examiners to know, it is also a way of personalising the work.

5. Particularly at the start, research often goes far more slowly than anticipated. A feeling of getting nowhere is, thus, to be expected (Cryer, 2006). Rest assured, though, that what appears a quagmire on one day can transform into a highway on the next. The quagmires simply have to be worked through. It is also reassuring to know that information technology has made the search of the literature far easier and more efficient than used to be the case. This is one

reason why thesis writers often find searching the literature one of the more enjoyable aspects of research. The actual reviewing, however, they often find the most difficult (Hart, 2005).

8.6 VALIDATING CLAIMS

1. The volume of research material available in the literature will, of course, vary between projects: less for some and more for others. In the case of the former, be wary of stating in the thesis that not much of pertinence to the research was available in the literature: *Despite its importance, limited information is available regarding the initiation and progression of this debilitating disease.* It is only valid to do so when convincing evidence has been provided that the search of the literature has been genuinely comprehensive and that a plausible reason for the lack of material has been provided. As in the following example, the latter can be accomplished by pointing to a methodological difficulty:

   Given the importance of… from a fiscal and monetary policy perspective, the paucity of… research on the topic is remarkable. However, the lack of research reflects more on the difficulties in modeling…rather than the level of interest in the topic.

   Alternatively, it could be argued that the research is in a newly developed field: *The term…does not appear in the research literature prior to 1980. Even during the following two decades only nine published papers contained the term. Currently, however…*Without such explanations for a lack of material it can be taken as given that examiners will make it their business to find out why.

2. If, however, the reverse is the case and an embarrassment of riches in the literature was discovered and organised, do not be afraid to say so: *I constructed the largest and most comprehensive database of…using both the published literature and unpublished records.* Although researchers arc not like roses 'born to blush unseen' caution should, however, be exercised when making such claims. Examiners of masters' theses in particular are wary of claims by students to have been, for example, the *first* to undertake a particular type of research or to be the *first* to do it in a particular way. The claims might well be justified and due credit ought to be given: this is why justified claims need to be made, not hidden. But again be careful fully to justify such claims by providing convincing evidence they are correct. As in the case of statements that there is limited material in the literature, examiners can sniff false claims in the wind.

8.7 MANAGING REFERENCES AND REFERENCE MATERIAL

1. New researchers are often surprised by the speed with which a well-planned search of the literature can yield a lengthy list of useful references. This initial

list will, of course, subsequently be extended and amended as the research progresses. Nonetheless, it is just as important to exercise control over the list from the outset, as it is to control the search process that gave rise to it. In this case exercising control means to reorganise the list in a way that is most meaningful and, thus, of greatest utility. One way of doing so, for example, is to reorganise the list alphabetically into different categories: books; conference papers; journal articles; theses and reports. This approach has a number of advantages. The references can be annotated thus enabling easy recall of the material and its relevance. It will also enable a researcher to stand back and gauge roughly how long it should take to read the material in the list and to assess progress as relevant material is consulted.

2. Another advantage of an ordered reference list is that reading becomes more purposeful because by reading the literature under topic headings derived from the list it will be easier to synthesise the material. But, in the context of the explosion in the volume of literature, reading will need to be alternated with skimming. Skimming, or pre-reading, involves first glancing, for example, over tables of content, abstracts, introductions, conclusions and figure captions in order to identify where to look for useful material. This means that switching, or 'gear changing', will continually need to be made between skimming and intensive reading (Fairbairn & Winch, 1996). If necessary, conduct an internet search using such descriptors as 'reading skills', 'scanning', 'skim reading', 'critical reading', 'rapid reading' and 'speed reading' to seek helpful advice on doing so (Cryer, 2006).

3. When cutting and pasting material from electronic sources, photocopying hardcopy material or when copying information by hand, take care to retain as much of the original context as possible. There are a number of good reasons for doing so. Although research material might be meaningful at the time when it is extracted, it will mean very little weeks later when the context has long been forgotten. In addition, as reading progresses so too will the depth and breadth of understanding. If the context of the material has been retained more meaning will often be extracted from it than was initially the case. Writing a literature review also gives rise to a number of ethical issues. One of these is the need to avoid using the ideas of others in ways not originally intended. This explains the need to retain context and is at least one of the reasons explaining the need to reference research material.

References

4. Referencing has three distinct intertextual functions: to acknowledge an intellectual debt to others whose ideas, either explicitly or implicitly, have been used; to provide evidence for specific claims; and to enable readers to locate

sources efficiently. Plagiarism is the failure to fulfil the first of these functions. Deliberate plagiarism, in fact, is a minority exercise. The bulk of plagiarism, instead, is inadvertent: a result of researchers losing track of which ideas belong to them and which to others. In fact most university regulations relating to plagiarism have rejected the notion of it as intention to deceive on the grounds that 'intention' is usually impossible to prove. The regulations focus, instead, on absent, or inadequate, referencing. The need to check for these is one of the reasons why some universities require electronic versions of a thesis to be submitted with the hardcopy (Pearce, 2005). It is also the reason why examiners normally check between ten to twenty per cent of the references in a thesis. They take particular care to check those that do not look right (Rugg & Petrie, 2004). Thus, although it is true that overzealous referencing can impede the flow of writing (Garton & McFarlane, 2007), particular care should be taken not only to reference direct quotations but also any material that is summarised or paraphrased. Keep in mind that any information in the text that is not referenced will be taken as belonging to the writer of the thesis alone.

5. Therefore, although it can seem to be a frustrating chore at the time, ensure that all citation details are entered in the reference style selected for the thesis as the research material is accessed. Doing so will obviate the possible need to reformat the references after the draft has been written. Bibliographic software will save much of the drudgery involved for citations will be stored and the reference list structured in the appropriate style as material is entered into it. Bear in mind that it is a 'rare research student who, at the time of writing up the thesis, does not bewail the wasted days of following up references that were not fully recorded earlier' (Cryer, 2006, p.61). However, the ability of some bibliographic software to import entire databases is a feature that should be exercised with care; there is no advantage to having numerous references with no specific relevance to the matter under investigation.

Organising and duplicating

6. If the organising features of bibliographic software are not used take care to store and organise research material in an orderly manner as it is collected. It is really important not to delay this process as the volume of material can build up very quickly and it is easy to lose control of where and when it was collected. How the material is ordered will depend upon the nature of the research and of the final cataloguing system planned. For preliminary storage, alphabetically listed hardcopy files, or their electronic equivalents, with individually numbered pages might, for example, be used. This will make the subsequent cataloguing of the material a lot less onerous. It can be expensive and time consuming but it is worth the trouble and expense to store a duplicate

copy of the research material (either hard copy or electronic) in a separate place from the original. Disasters do happen so this is a sensible precaution to take. The habit of storing duplicate copies of research material separately should subsequently extend to the storage of drafts of the thesis. This precautionary behaviour should extend to the actual drafting of the thesis: develop the habit of frequently 'backing up' material newly entered on a computer because the need to redo lost work can really test the limits of endurance.

8.8 EVALUATING MATERIAL FROM THE LITERATURE

1. At some point in the search of the literature the material will become progressively more peripheral. The law of diminishing returns will thus indicate the need to evolve from consulting the literature to the organisation and subsequent integration of the material derived from it. This implies that any search of the literature will be incomplete; there will always be an antilibrary of unread material (Taleb, 2007). But, because a researcher's task is to make the search as complete as possible, consulting the literature will continue as a background activity during the subsequent phases of the thesis writing process. The next will be the organising phase where material derived from the literature is catalogued so as to make it easily accessible during the writing phase. Upon what basis, though, ought it be catalogued? The answer lies in the deeper understanding of the research issues that develop during the process of reading the literature.

2. Initially the material from the literature will tend to be accepted at face value: the work of other researchers can merely be described. However, the new insights that develop as the reading progresses will enable the material to be placed in context and points of contact to crystallise: the work of other researchers can now be compared and interpreted. This, in turn, will allow the work of other researchers to be questioned and evaluated and, eventually, used as a point of departure (Flexible Learning Centre, nd). It might be found, for example, that studies supporting particular conclusions use methods different from those supporting alternative outcomes. It is only at this point that a researcher will be able to write as follows:

Hiller (2004) provides strong evidence that…Other researchers (Green, 2005; Wu, 2005; Harris, 2005; 2006) have provided support for this perspective but suggest that…All of the researchers concede, however, that little is known about… There is, though, some evidence (Holloway, 2006) to indicate…It can, therefore, be argued that…

This is a simple, linear explanation of a complex, incremental process. It will be initiated, however, during the first reading of the research material.

Despite the purpose of this reading primarily being to remove peripheral and duplicated material, memories will begin to be rekindled and new meanings and relationships will gradually become apparent.

Bringing coherence to the literature

3. The synthesis of qualitative studies is difficult because of the idiosyncrasy of each research undertaking. The review is often 'invisible', part of the fabric of the thesis, and, as the following excerpt indicates, because of the reflexive nature of the research process: '…the review summarizes both the content of what I read and thought to be most important, as well as the thinking processes I engaged in as I learned' (Meloy, 2002, p.122). It is primarily in the context of empirical and exegetic research, therefore, that literature reviews bring together diversities of meaning into a contextually supported and coherent unity. They thus resemble the functioning of language: a metabolic process at the symbolic level (Fiumara, 1995). There are, however, a number of ways in which the literature might be made to cohere. In synthesised coherence, for example, literature previously considered unrelated is brought together by an investigation that shares commonalities with each (Golden-Biddle & Locke, 1997). This can be seen in the following excerpt:

This paper is not only about boundaries; it is a boundary object. By quoting prac-titioners from healthcare, education, community development, business, and other fields, I am bringing them to the edge of the organizational domain, where their work intersects with the academic inquiry of complexity theorists.

(MacGillivray, 2006, p.92)

By dealing with recognisably related works progressive coherence, on the other hand, depicts relative consensus among researchers in a well-developed, cumulative line of enquiry. This is often indicated in empirical theses when serialised citations indicate the progress of successive cohorts of researchers (Golden-Biddle & Locke, 1997). For example: (*Collins, 1995; Dean, 1987; Harper, 1995; Meskill, 1997; Omeara, 1999; Rodney, 1995; Rubin, 2000; Snyder, 2001; Urban, 2003; Wolff, 2005.*) But, in non-coherent reviews the works cited, except in regard to agreement on the importance of the research field itself, are linked by disagreement (Golden-Biddle & Locke, 1997).

Subverting the literature

4. In each case, however, a review will subvert the literature brought to coherence. It might do so by indicating an incomplete problematisation: *These case studies support the finding that…but do not identify the source of…* Alternatively, in an inadequate

problematisation, a gap or deficiency in the literature might be identified: 'None of these studies incorporate the voices of participants. This study, therefore, seeks to address this deficiency' (Golden-Biddle & Locke, 1997, p.38). The extant literature in this case is not characterised as wrong, merely inadequate. However, when the literature is characterised as incommensurate the writer mounts a direct challenge to extant work advocating its overthrow and replacement with an alternative thesis: 'Adoption of this hypothesis will enable us to redirect our thinking so as better to explain...' (Golden-Biddle & Locke, 1997, p.46).

8.9 THE ORGANISING PRINCIPLE OF THE REVIEW

1. Literature reviews depend upon organising principles both for their coherence and the manner in which the works cited in them are discussed. A review should not, thus, simply be a list of researchers and the work they have done. In other words annotations should not simply be strung together. In the following extract, for example, no attempt was made to integrate the information in each of the four paragraphs and, thus, no indication is given of the organising principle informing the review: (Paragraph one) *Powell (2001) provided a bibliography of nearly 30 entries all of which relate to...*(followed by a précis of the entries); (Paragraph two) *Meskill and Snyder (2003)...provided a survey in the area of...*(followed by the survey); (Paragraph three) *Dunkel (2004) provided a comprehensive list of...*(followed by the list); Paragraph four: *Rubin (2005) presented 15 techniques drawn from various fields of...*(followed by a summary of the 15 techniques.) It is important, nonetheless, to recognise that the focus of the literature review and the organising principles informing its structure are two separate but complementary issues. The thesis statement will provide the focus: the primary hypothesis or the central research question of the study. The organising principles are a reflection of how discussion of the literature is structured around that focus. If this is not done examiners will be quick to note:
   - 'Surveys the field in an idiosyncratic and eclectic way' (Lovat et al., 2002, p.14).
   - 'Choice of literature was ad hoc. I've read it so I'll use it' (Lovat et al., 2002, p.14).
2. If a study reaches across disciplines a review might structure the literature separately around each discipline (Galvan, 2004). But, the structures most frequently applied tend to devolve into three categories: chronological; thematic or theoretic. In practice, however, these categories are loose. For example, a discussion structured around theory might have historical and methodological themes. The literature in a review is likely, therefore, to be structured using elements from each of these categories. They remain useful, however, because reviews are usually more heavily reliant upon one category than upon others. Chronological and thematic structures tend to be the easiest to build a discussion around because the narratives defining each are usually easy to

identify and control. This applies, in particular, to chronological structures, because not only is context and focus provided by the movement from early to later works but they also reflect the implicit linearity of empirical studies. This explains why chronological structures are frequently used as the guiding principles in the literature reviews of empirical theses: *The chapter begins with a review of historical perspectives and conceptual framework for…This is followed by a review of the literature on the study of…*

3. Exegetic and qualitative research, however, is explicitly theoretic dealing with background theory, focus theory and, in the case of qualitative work, data theory. Although engagement with other theorists is likely to run throughout theses in these approaches, a literature review structured around theory provides researchers a focused opportunity to indicate the depth of their understanding of relevant theory: *There are still debates regarding how the Internet is changing… Some researchers hypothesise that…while others feel that…* This is the primary reason why literature reviews based on theory are so difficult to write and why examiners display such a keen interest in them. Faced with this problem a thesis writer outlined the strategy he adopted in order to make the literature meaningful enough to work with conceptually:

I adopted a 'drift-net' exercise, reading anything I could find with the slightest bearing on my topic. Gradually I began to build up a picture that contributed to my understanding and that became, later, my conceptual framework.

(Trafford, 2008, p.282)

Reviews of this nature often have an additional layer of complexity because they usually also include the introduction to the thesis. For this reason the integrated chapters are generally longer than would have been the case had they been presented separately. This combination of length and complexity means that regardless of the fact that the manner in which the chapter has been structured will already have been indicated in the introduction to the chapter there will usually be need to prompt the examiners' memory by reminding them where they are in the chapter as they proceed through it: *In the following section of the literature review I discuss the ways in which…; I now highlight the…; At this point I consider…; I now focus on aspects of…*

Theoretic perspective

4. Classic or landmark studies, if they exist, should be identified in a review because they are usually pivotal in the historical development of a research field (Galvan, 2004). Because they are also often pivotal in the development of theory they might help researchers to deal with theory in ways few other researchers can imitate:

...very few people can actually take an existing theory and say, 'Well, in my special case we have to modify it this way.' That really requires command of the theory and that's going to be outstanding.

(Lovitts, 2007, p.158)

If theory is to be the guiding principle when writing a review, care will need to be exercised to explain why one perspective has been subscribed to in favour of others. Doing so will normally require that the strengths and the weaknesses of each pertinent theoretic approach should be discussed in order to indicate why the strengths and weaknesses of the theory or theories chosen outweigh the perceived strengths and weaknesses of others. This has a number of advantages in addition to providing a measured justification for one's theoretic position. On the one hand examiners will note awareness on the part of the researcher that every writer has theoretical commitments that need to identified and questioned. On the other, conceding that the perspectives not adhered to can, nonetheless, still contribute valuable insights, enhances the quality of the discussion. The examiners will have no need then to make comments such as the following:

- 'Systematic failure to consider or discuss alternate theories or ideas' (Lovat et al., 2002, p.14).
- 'Much of the argument takes place in isolation from current scholarship' (Lovat et al., 2002, p.14).

A discussion of the need to call attention in a thesis to alternative perspectives and, thus, to possible counterarguments might appear to be an obvious redundancy. However, an issue of great concern at many universities, theoretically forums for open debate, is a dynamic of 'patterned isolation'. This is clearly explained in the following extract. Although the reference is specifically to political philosophy the phenomenon described applies widely to other fields as well:

Journals in the subfield [political philosophy] have become extremely focused. Straussian journals circulate submissions among Straussians, for example, while Marxist journals send their submissions to Marxists, so that Marxists and Straussians seldom review each other's work. When the articles are submitted to the mainstream journals which cover a broader range of articles, the Straussians and Marxists frequently 'kill each other off' by critically reviewing submissions from the opposite perspective. The result is well-established little cadres of people who don't argue any more about how political theory should be done.

(Cited in Becher & Trowler, 2001, p.127)

That there is a price to be paid for this professional myopia is indicated equally clearly in the following extract:

It is unfortunate that one learns most from people one disagrees with—something Montaigne encouraged half a millennium ago but is rarely practiced. I discovered that it puts your arguments through robust seasoning since you know that these people will identify the slightest crack—and you get information about the limits of their theories as well as the weaknesses of your own.

(Taleb, 2007, p.304)

ENDNOTES

1   A bibliography categorises all the works that contributed to the text even if not cited in the text. A reference list indicates only those works cited in the text. This distinction explains why some theses have a reference list followed by a bibliography.

2   In brief, to isolate search descriptors first identify the key concepts in the research title. From these think of all the synonyms, abbreviations, alternative spellings, acronyms and broader and narrower phrases or words related to each concept. The operators NOT/AND reduce the number of references, OR increases the number. Use the descriptor 'review' to locate review articles.

3   When retrieving material from sites on the internet the address and all other relevant citation information will need to be documented; this will include the date the connection was made. Ensure, therefore, that the requirements for citing internet sources of the referencing system being used are known prior to conducting an internet search.

CHAPTER 9

Literature Review Part Two: Writing the Review

All texts are intertexts and behind all knowledge lies not physical reality but other texts, followed by other texts...

(Paltridge & Starfield, 2007, p.113)

9.1 INTRODUCTION

1. Academic norms strongly discountenance the *argumentum ad hominem*, the vitriolic personal attack. In its place is 'muted opposition':

   It is thought to be unkind and professionally unprofitable to point out another man's [sic] error in public; better simply to hint that his claims are not quite substantiated and then to give one's own more positive and correct version.

   (Dillon, 1991, p.56)

   It is this lack of open denunciation except in the most extreme cases that explains the need for rigorous screening by referees of research material prior to its publication (Dillon, 1991). Although not a cause explaining 'muted opposition' the need for it is reflected in general semantics. Developed during the 1920s its purpose is to bring to awareness the degree to which experience is filtered by the human physical and linguistic condition. Rather than understanding this sporadically, the approach argues that 'consciousness of abstracting' should become a matter of reflex. This is succinctly explained by the central premise of the approach: *The map is not the territory; the word is not the thing defined.* General semantics, therefore, denies Aristotle's assertion that a true definition provides the essence of the thing defined: because we cannot know everything the essence will always evade us. This insight is best expressed as an attitude: 'x does things that seem foolish to me rather than x is a fool' (Wikipedia). This might be a useful reflexive attitude to adopt when writing a review of the literature.

2. The review has a claim to be the most distinctive feature of a thesis: not only has it come to be expected that 'knowledge of the field' will be reflected in the review, it is also that part of a thesis usually edited out upon publication (Pearce, 2005). With this distinctiveness in mind a discursive review of the literature should, at a minimum, indicate the perceptiveness with which the literature has been selected, the strengths, weaknesses and omissions in the works cited, an understanding of the theory involved and, finally, how the literature affected the researcher's thinking. This is why a review can influence an examiner's perception of the thesis as a whole: 'It is unusual that if someone does a poor job of the literature review that they will suddenly improve, or vice versa' (Mullins & Kiley, 2002, p.377).

9.2 PARATACTIC AND HYPOTACTIC WRITING

1. Because it is a contribution to an open debate and thus, both rhetorical and analytical the writing in a literature review should primarily be hypotactic rather than paratactic. These terms are used to characterise the ways in which elements in a piece of text relate to each other hierarchically. Text consisting of free standing, parallel statements usually joined by 'and' or by commas is paratactic: *Brown (2001) said…, Gowens (2002) said…, and Rowens (2003) said…* Hypotactic text, in contrast, subordinates some elements of the text in relation to others. This subordination is often expressed in words such as 'because' or 'therefore' or in phrases such as 'in order to' or 'as a result': *Because both Brown (2001) and Gowens (2002) provided convincing evidence for…It can, therefore, be argued that…* These elements of subordination need not only apply to sentences or parts of sentences, paragraphs and chapters too, can be made subordinate to an overriding argument. Qualitative studies are multi-vocal thus rarely have overriding arguments; exegetic texts, while often supportive of overriding arguments, tend to be discursive with shifts of tone and mood. Hypotactic arguments, thus, are most clearly apparent in empirical theses where shifts in tone and mood are minimal and the text is built on the basis of subordination of each element to the needs of an overriding linear argument.

2. Much of the ability to construct hypotactic text depends upon the manner in which time is used. Time is a problematic concept: 'the future is not yet, the past is no longer, and the present does not endure' (Simpson, 2005, p.99). We can resolve the problem by categorising time into kairotic or chronological ordering. Chronos was the Greek god of time measured in mechanical intervals. Kairos was the god of right time in the sense that some periods are omitted and some detailed, some slowed down and others speeded up. In other words chronological accounts are raw material for kairotic ordering. Thus, although

kairotic time cannot be experienced directly, it offers meaning to narratives in a way that merely following the chronological unfolding of events cannot.

9.3 HOLISM

1. The necessary synthesis of historical, contextual, theoretic and methodological issues that hypotactic writing in the literature reviews of most empirical and exegetic theses and of some qualitative studies will entail gives rise, though, to an immediate problem. In many cases the research may not yet have been completed and the conceptual, methodological and writing skills necessary to compose the review will certainly not yet have reached full development. How then, at the early stage of writing a thesis, is it possible to situate one's research in relation to the work of others? (Nesbit, 2004). The answer is brief: it is not possible. So, as was the case in regard to the introduction to the thesis, writing a discursive review of the literature should not be considered a neatly compartmentalised task to be undertaken and completed at the outset of the writing process. It should, instead, be allowed to develop incrementally in tandem with the growth of the necessary research and writing skills. In this sense the process should be seen as holistic. Understanding something is a derivative process dependent upon an organised system of propositions. In this sense writing a literature review is not a brick-by-brick accumulation of individual self-sufficient pieces of knowledge, each 'a mutilated shred torn from the living whole in which alone it possessed its significance' (Blackburn & Simmons, 2005, p.9). Instead, as Wittgenstein put it, 'light dawns gradually over the whole' (cited in Blackburn & Simmons, 2005, p.9).

2. For this reason the final draft of the review should be among the last thesis tasks completed. It is at this point that the writer's relationship with his or her audience will have changed because understanding of theory will have deepened and research and writing skills will be at their best. This is important for the introduction and the review, whether presented separately or together, are among the first parts of a thesis the examiners will read and it will be upon these parts that their initial impression of the work as a whole will be based. The following comment by an examiner indicates the nature of the doubts sown when a review is completed too early:

Indeed, many of us who have examined PhDs with weighty literature review chapters will have lamented the fact that the candidate did not return to this early work and perform some excision … a long, rambling literature review might trigger warning bells: to range so widely, did the candidate have a clear sense of his or her research question when he or she was undertaking the review? More to the point does she or he have a clear sense of the question now?

(Pearce, 2005, p.57)

9.4 GIVING PRELIMINARY DIRECTION TO THE REVIEW

1. Questions are useful because they provide focus: an answer is needed. So, knowing the right questions to ask will provide a useful sense of direction when planning the review. In the first draft answers to the questions will provide a framework around which the discussion can be wrapped. Listed below are examples of some of the types of questions that might usefully be posed (adapted from Murray, 2003, p.108). Actually writing responses to the questions rather than merely thinking about them will not only elaborate the process of thought but will also provide tangible material with which to work:

   - What is the purpose of the research? *There is a pressing need to develop effective methodological approaches to allow the exploration of the boundaries between…In order to achieve this, the challenges include, but are not limited to…*
   - What specific questions or hypotheses will the research address? *Examining the determinants of formal social welfare system utilisation in … is the main focus of this thesis. In order to do so, I aim to answer three research questions. First, does…? Second, how is…, and lastly, does…?*
   - How are the key terms defined? If there is no agreed definition the most important of the perspectives will usually need to be provided and then the working definition applied in the thesis justified in the context of these perspectives. *The definition of…has proved to be controversial because… A major source of the tension is disagreement as to the nature of…*
   - What, and for what reason, is not going to be done? *The current project is focused on further development of…Prior work based on…will not be presented here as it is of little relevance to the present study.*
   - What are the boundaries of the investigation and why were they chosen? *The site of the study was limited to the children's ward at…hospital because this is the centre to which all children in the country infected with…are sent.*
   - What are the origins of the research? *This study had its origin in my involvement in a pilot project focusing on… The results of this research suggested that three particular issues warranted further exploration.*
   - Why is the research important? *A generally accepted theory that will explain… does not yet exist. In order to explore this field, therefore, it is essential to…*
   - What is the methodological approach? *By taking a multidisciplinary perspective this study was able to place particular emphasis on two research perspectives that currently dominate research in the field of … The first is… The second is…*
   - What contributions will my research make? *By identifying common factors in the life experiences of individuals who have… a more comprehensive treatment protocol can be developed than is currently in place.*
   - Why are some sources of key value? *Almost all the references in the following section are from…as it is currently the only substantial work dealing with this method.*

- What are the lacunae in the research? *…have been intensively studied due to their widespread occurrence in…and their behaviour is consequently well understood. …have, however, generated comparatively less interest because…Their behavior has, consequently, been less well explored.*
- What are the major issues and debates around the topic? *Gray (2005) argues that there is a clear disciplinary split between health psychology and sociology over methodological approaches to the disease. Goffman et al. (2006) suggest, therefore, that it would be valuable if an interdisciplinary approach were adopted.*
- What are the key concepts, theories and ideas? *Constructivism and cognitive flexibility theory provide the conceptual framework for this study because each focuses on…Among the concepts this thesis will explore will be…*

If the introduction to the thesis is to be presented separate from the literature review the first seven questions might more appropriately be addressed in the former rather than the latter. However, because the first draft of the introduction is usually brief, it is often easier to write the introduction and literature review chapters together in the initial drafts even if the ultimate intention is to present them separately. This is in line with the immediate task of the introduction: to introduce a thesis that has yet to be written. But even in this limited role it will provide some context and a preliminary focus, attributes without which a review of the literature cannot be written.

9.5 STARTING TO WRITE THE REVIEW

1. Avoid starting a review with a non-specific reference: *In recent years there has been renewed interest in…*Instead, in order to provide initial direction to the review it might prove useful to start with the obvious: *The purpose of this chapter is to…*; followed by: *It will be argued that…*; followed, in turn, by: *In developing this argument, I intend to…* (Cantwell, 2006, p.188). In order to develop the necessary coherence between the disparate elements of a review it might also prove useful to 'mind-map'. The sense of direction this provides will assist in the development of strong topic sentences. These are particularly important in a literature review because examiners will rely upon them to signal the direction in which the review is moving. Mind-mapping will also help provide an explanatory framework for the review. A qualitative researcher, for example, might decide to transport readers to the context of the study before taking them to the literature (Golden-Biddle & Locke, 1997). The initial outline pattern often changes as the writing of the thesis progresses, but providing an explanation for the outline eventually adopted will have two immediate benefits. The first will be an indication to examiners of awareness on the part of the writer of the numerous ways in which a literature review might be organised. The second will be the opportunity provided to indicate why the explanatory framework adopted is the most suitable:

This literature review is constructed in two sections. The purpose of this structure is to separate the literature produced prior to 1995, the year when…, from that produced subsequent to the event. Separating the earlier from the later literature not only permits each to be situated contextually but also enables useful comparisons to be made between them.

2. The next step is to define the terms used. This might be done explicitly as in the following example: *In quest for a broader definition the International Association redefined… as…This is the working definition applied in this study.* Or implicitly as follows: *The rapid development of multimedia, which combines two or more media such as text, video or sound, has had a significant influence on…* However accomplished, it is important to define terms as early as possible in order to ensure that what is written is not misinterpreted. It is at this point usually possible to move on to discuss the key sources, lacunae, issues, debates, theories and concepts as suggested in the questions listed above. This is when the concept 'audience' becomes particularly useful. Knowing who the writing is for will help fine tune the level of discussion: between the Scylla of irritating the examiners with too much detail or the Charybdis of assuming too much and providing insufficient description (Hart, 1998)

9.6 PRESENCE

1. Because thesis examiners take it for granted that a literature review is an expression of the researcher's own thinking it is unusual to use terms like, *I feel* or *In my opinion* when writing one. This creates a problem: how does a writer prevent his or her presence from being lost amidst the constant reference to other authors? Presence is an important issue in a thesis because a strong presence is often a harbinger of originality (Lovitts, 2007); examiners often comment they can sense a researcher's degree of confidence by the manner in which a thesis is written (Kiley & Mullins, 2006). This is why it is important to read recently examined theses to develop a sense of the extent to which researchers have made their presence felt in the text (Paltridge & Starfield, 2007). Where, for example, there are inconsistencies between the findings of a number of studies researchers have a number of options. They might state a generalisation based on the majority of the studies, or they might state a generalisation based only on those studies thought to have the strongest research designs. As long as the reasons for the generalisations are valid either approach might be acceptable (Galvan, 2004). What is important in each instance though is the felt presence of the thesis writer.

2. Three literary devices tend to predominate among those writers most successful in developing presence. Among the most difficult for thesis writers new to exegetic research in particular to control is agency. It is, for example, easier to observe that

'Shakespeare depicts' rather than the more theoretically sophisticated 'the text displaces' (Peck MacDonald, 1994, p.151). It is, in fact, the degree of sophistication indicated that locates the felt presence of the writer. The other two devices are more easily controlled. The first is the manner in which readers are oriented to the works or authors referred to in a review and the second is the type of verb used. All three devices depend, however, upon the degree of focus that has been developed in the text: there must be a clear issue or closely defined group of issues to discuss. It is logical that if this is not the case a personal presence cannot be established. A strong personal presence does not necessarily mean, though, an authentic presence. A writer's 'voice' might be strongly evident in the writing but because, for example, he or she has written what they imagine the examiners or their supervisors expect them to write rather than what they think ought to be written, their presence will not be authentic. Because 'inauthentic' elements are made more apparent, reading developed drafts of the literature review out loud and then revising them until it is felt they run smoothly will help infuse authenticity into text.

Orienting readers

3. So, on the assumption that the writer's presence in the text is authentic, he or she will help to make their presence felt if they indicate to examiners where their attention should be oriented. Particularly in the literature review, thesis writers should imagine they are stage directors moving the spotlights to where they want the audience to focus their attention. In the context of the literature review this might be on particular or no particular researcher or researchers, or on the results of the research. Paragraphs, for example, might be organised around the reports of individual researchers or they might be topical. In the case of the latter the results of a number of studies might be cited together after the logic for doing so has been outlined in the topic sentence (Galvan, 2004). If, for example, at the level of the sentence the researcher or researchers rather than the results are the most important feature then, if an in-text referencing system is being used, the name/s of the researcher/s referred to should be placed in the body of the sentence and the date and/or page reference placed in brackets. If, instead, the results are of more importance the entire reference should be placed in brackets after the statement of the results. The following examples are in APA format (Murison & Webb, 1991, p.21):
   - Strong researcher orientation: *Brown (2000) showed that minor infections are effectively treated with chloramphenicol.*
   - Weak researcher orientation: *Chloramphenicol has been shown to be effective in the treatment of minor infections (Brown,2000).*
   - No specific researcher orientation: *The treatment of minor infections with chloramphenicol is effective (Brown, 2000).*

4. Note, therefore, how the spotlights are moved by the manner in which the sources are referred to in the following extract: *A loss of commitment occurs when male…are separated from their young (Furst, 1997; Cole & Whittington, 2002; Kerr et al.[1], 1998). Further, Reynolds and Jackson (1999) in their study of… found…It can be seen, therefore, that…* Note also that the extract consists of assertions followed by a claim. The presence of a claim is important if examiner criticism such as the following is to be avoided:

When I read a literature review where most paragraphs start with the name of a scholar being quoted or cited, I usually find that I am reading a summary of someone else's scholarship, not an argument. So what if so-and-so thinks x and someone else thinks y. It is the writer who needs to show how and why this matters.

(Cited in McWilliam, 2006, p.168)

5. But, because in the early drafts of the review writers will not usually be in a position to compare and discuss particular research outcomes, the writing will tend to be narrative: 'this happened, then this, then this' (Murray, 2003). There will, as a result, tend to be a strong author orientation: each sentence, as in the following examples, beginning with the name of the researcher/s: (APA) last name + date + verb (Keys [2004] said…) or (MLA) last name + verb + page reference (Ryan writes… [45]) (Note the use of the past tense in the APA example and the present tense in the MLA example.) While the adoption of this approach fulfils the limited needs of the first drafts of a review, in the subsequent drafts writers will need to make their presence felt by integrating the researchers to whom they refer into an ongoing discussion. This can be seen in the following APA example: 'The phenomenon first came to light when Duke (2002), after reanalysing the data from earlier fieldwork (Harding, 2000), rejected the finding that…' It can also be seen in the following MLA example: 'Dean presents a persuasive argument in support of the assertion that… (74). However, other researchers (see Williams, 99–105; Farr, 80–95) reject this view pointing out instead the importance of…' (Note the use of 'see' in the MLA example. The use of this directive is more frequent in exegetic and qualitative than in empirical texts because each of the former often requires readers to consult arguments and opinions rather than explicit evidence as is usually the case in the latter.)

Verbs with value

6. It is not only the positioning of the references in these examples and the astute use of brackets that have allowed the writer's presence to be established. Of equal importance is the use of 'rejected' and 'reject': a verb with an attached value judgement. Verbs like *say, wrote, report, remark, suggest* and *claim* describe actions but ascribe only tangential value to those actions. 'Suggests' for

examples indicates tentativeness while 'claim' indicates disagreement between the writer and the researcher being referred to. Compare, for example, *Knowles (2003) suggested that…, Windsor (2002) asserted that…, Betz (2004) showed…,* with the following: *agree, challenge, question, endorse, refute, rebuff, dispute* and *disprove*. A change in the reporting verb thus changes the status of the overall statement: *Brookes supported early attempts to…*; as opposed to *Brookes championed early attempts to…* Indeed, the use of verbs with value, together with other assertive words *(paradoxically, clearly, indeed, in contrast to, of equal importance),* indicates the writer's opinion and thus presence. Strong verbs and adverbs also make writing more enjoyable to read: *Napoleon immediately embraced the imperial legacy by…* There are some words, though, that thesis writers ought to be wary of. *'Opined'* is one of these—it sounds pretentious. *'Evidently'* is another for it implies the evidence for a statement is anecdotal. Anecdotal evidence might well be appropriate in particular instances, but its use in a thesis is, nonetheless, unusual and will need to be justified: *These anecdotal accounts are included because few formal studies have been conducted in this field. Placed alongside more established knowledge they indicate innovative approaches to…*

7. No compulsion should be felt, though, to use 'verbs with value' each time another researcher's work is referred to. This is because reviews involve both narrative and discussion: *However the evidence to date remains inconclusive. While Franks (2002) and Howell (2002) suggest that…other studies (e.g. Fan, 2003; Davis, 2004; Gan, 2002) contradict their findings.*

8. Reviews also often involve attempts to explain events that have no clear explanation. In this case the use of a verb such as 'suggested' might be appropriate:

During training, student nurses often feel vulnerable in a hospital ward (Dawes & Ritter, 2001). This may be because they do not yet feel fully prepared or because they are conscious of being observed. Gardiner (2002) suggested that…

Beware, though, of writing a review consisting primarily of verbs without value because doing so generally indicates a low level of engagement and, thus, a concomitant loss of felt presence. Keep in mind, however, that examiners are sensitive to form without substance:

One may give all the stylistic indications of setting out a case in a rigorous fashion, using devices such as 'it follows from what I have said', when in fact nothing follows; 'I have argued that…' when in fact no argument has been offered; 'I refute the suggestion that…' when the suggestion is merely contradicted, not argued against; 'it has been shown that…, when nothing of the kind has been done…

(Cited in Fairbairn & Winch, 1996, p.73)

9.7 QUOTING

1. Presence in a review is also influenced by the manner in which quotations are used. Just as a writer's presence is diminished when sentences continually start with the names of other researchers so too is it diminished if overuse of quotations permits the voices of those researchers to drown the writer's own voice. This is usually less of an issue in empirical than in qualitative and exegetic research simply because value judgements, and the need to compare them, play a lesser role in empirical studies than in the others. Nonetheless, literature reviews are inherently a meeting place of voices and all researchers will need to select quotations judiciously and to integrate them into the flow of an ongoing discussion. In this sense quotations, along with footnotes and appendices are aspects of micro-rhetoric: 'the smaller acts of judgement a writer makes to enhance the reader's understanding of the text' (Dillon, 1991, p.117). This is illustrated in chapter epigraphs. Their usual purpose, to encapsulate the essence of the chapter, to create a gestalt, can be enhanced by integrating them, as in the following example, into the opening of the first paragraph:

CHAPTER 1: *Young England*

> *'O born in days when wits were fresh and clear,*
>
> *And life ran gaily as the sparkling Thames!'*

Few men could lay better claim than Chaucer to this happy accident of birth with which Matthew Arnold endows his Scholar Gypsy… Chaucer's times seemed sordid enough to many good and great men who lived in them; but few ages of the world have been better suited to nourish such a genius, or can afford a more delightful traveling-ground for us of the twentieth century.

(Coulton, 1963, p.1)

2. How, though, in regard to quotations are these 'smaller acts of judgement' to be made? When they begin, thesis writers typically overuse quotations. Their inability at this stage to paraphrase (reword) or abridge (summarise) are indicative of a lack of thorough understanding of key ideas. A writer not fully in control results, therefore, in 'lumpy text' (McWilliam, 2006, p.170). But this is understandable given beginning thesis writers have yet to find their own voice. As they progressively establish a more assertive presence, though, the use of quotations should become more discerning. The need to do so is explained by the strong presence most of the authors to which thesis writers refer will have developed in their own text: particular words used in particular ways to convey particular meanings. (On the whole, for example, Shakespeare wrote 'doth', about one time in four he wrote 'dost' and occasionally he used 'does':

these distinguishing habits are part of his idiolect [Bryson, 2008].) Therefore, because quotations retain elements of their semantic and structural autonomy (Frow, 2006), overuse permits the voice of other authors to dominate. There is thus little to be gained from quoting unless the needs of a study dictate otherwise. This is most likely to be the case in both qualitative and exegetic theses for an inherent feature of both is heteroglossia: 'the multiplicity of voices in the text permits researchers to explore links and interrelationships. From a reader's perspective this is also a feature of hypertext, its multi-linearity enabling them to become "authors of their reading"' (Woods, 2006, p.57).

3. However, writers of theses in all approaches to research might find that the specific words and meanings of authors are needed in order to differentiate perspectives. This might occur, for example, when a concept or position is defined. It could also be necessary, in the case of a controversial perspective, where it is important that the views of particular researchers are not misrepresented. An extract might also be so well formulated that it would be pointless to word it another way. A quotation also need not necessarily be actual spoken or written words: the inanimate can be personified or those like the collective unborn, unable to speak on their own behalf, given voice. A qualitative researcher might also, for example, quote a fellow researcher during the course of a narrative to indicate the points where the researchers agree or disagree with what is being written (Woods, 2006). In addition, researchers might quote their own thoughts in order to compare current thinking with that at an earlier stage. Qualitative researchers in auto-ethnographies often do this to indicate how new insights have altered perception.

4. Once a decision to quote speech or text has been taken the next will be how much to quote. Incorporating a short extract into a sentence has the effect of increasing the pace of the writing and of emphasising the particularity of the words quoted: *Rather than the conception of…as distinct from…Gordon argues for an analysis that 'acknowledges the intersection of society and culture' (2001, p.21).* If the quotation needs to be of greater length care should be taken to ensure first, that it is not left hanging but is immediately integrated into the text that follows and second, that if the quotation is forty words or over (APA) or four lines or longer (MLA) it is indented left and presented without quotation marks:

Based on the conception of…as atheoretical, Wilson (2001) claims that:

> ....
>
> ....
>
> ....
>
> ....

However, in contrast to this claim other researchers propose…

5. While there is flexibility in regard to the need to quote, stringent conventions apply to how quotations are presented. Of primary importance is the need to use the exact words, spelling and punctuation of the original. If the wording needs to be altered to change, for example, tense, in order to allow a quotation to blend with the text of the thesis or to insert a comment or name, square brackets must be used: *He [William Shakespeare]...* Sections omitted from a quotation must not alter the meaning of the original and must be indicated by an ellipsis: three equally spaced full stops (Anderson & Poole, 1994). (The more ellipses there are in a quotation the greater the degree of caution a reader needs to exercise in accepting the veracity of the implied meaning.) An error in a quotation is indicated by [sic] (Latin for *just as*) to show there has been no error in transcription. Archaisms are also indicated in this way. If there is a quotation within a quotation, the entire quotation, except in the case of an indented quotation should be enclosed within single quotation marks and the internal quotation in double quotation marks. (The reverse applies in the United States.)

9.8 THE ETHICS OF REVIEWING

1. Some ethically problematic practices in literature reviews are relatively easy to identify. Reading and making notes on only abstracts without acknowledging this has been done is an example (Ling Pan, 2003). Other problematic practices are less easy to identify. Extracted from context all quotations, paraphrases and summaries, to a greater or lesser extent, are subordinated to the intentions of a reviewer. We have all experienced our words being used out of context. Children are particularly good at manipulating their parents in this way. Care should be taken, therefore, to ensure that the meanings intended by the original authors are not altered. The ease with which subtle change can be introduced is indicated in the following extract:

    ...in Hargreaves' (1988: 63) article, he claims that 'As Sikes, Measor and Woods (1985) have found in their life history interviews with secondary teachers, many teachers regard examinations not as a constraint but as a resource for motivating pupils'. In fact, Sikes et al. had a sample of only 40 teachers drawn from science and art departments in two geographical areas. 'Some' teachers would have been a more accurate description.

    (Cited in Woods, 2006, p.66)

2. The need not to alter meaning applies, in particular, to representing the views of those with whom a researcher disagrees. Bear in mind that one of the

purposes of a review is to acknowledge that other perspectives can contribute valuable insights (Hart, 1998). It should also be acknowledged that all research, irrespective of how well it is conducted, has limitations. Because this is an inherent aspect of research only those limitations in the work of others that are significant in the context of the reviewer's own research focus and approach need to be identified (Murray, 2003). Even then, these particular limitations will need to be treated differently according to whether they were an intended aspect of the original research design as indicated by the self critiques of researchers or were a consequence of poor design. However, in the context of particular research perspectives some studies will inevitably be stronger than others and it is the thesis writer's responsibility to make such evaluations (Galvan, 2004). These evaluations should be expressed in a professional manner. For example, 'Williams did not address' is acceptable but 'Williams completely overlooked' is not (Publications Manual of the APA, 2010, p.66). It is also generally inappropriate to note every perceived flaw in the studies re viewed. Instead, note major weaknesses in individual studies and then remain alert for patterns of similar weakness across groups of studies (Galvan, 2004). Nonetheless, because all research has limitations the phrases *researchers have neglected to…* and *researchers have ignored*, should not be used flippantly for the negative implications of the words 'neglect' and 'ignored' are considerable. All researchers, therefore, need to exercise due care when exercising the right to identify weaknesses in the work of others. This applies even more to thesis writers who are candidates rather than fully fledged researchers.

3. However, exercising due care is more easily said than done. The numerous letters of complaint from indignant authors in *The Times Literary Review* and *The New York Review of Books*, each a highly regarded review, are testimony to the difficulty even the most erudite and careful of reviewers have in retaining both context and meaning. A variety of reasons explain this. One of the most important is that when we simplify anything we lose something. Another is that there is sufficient fluidity and ambiguity in any piece of text to allow its interpretation to be shaped authentically in a number of ways (Golden-Biddle & Locke, 1997). All texts are also partial: they are written from a particular perspective, with a particular focus for a particular audience. The review in a thesis should, therefore, be written with this partiality in mind: other researchers should not be criticised simply because their perspective, focus or audience is different (Hart, 1998).

4. Retaining context and meaning is also difficult because of the manner in which some reviews of the literature in theses are conducted. It is often the case in empirical research, for example, that analyses of only a limited number of studies are conducted in-depth. In order to buttress the reviewer's contentions

additional studies that have come to similar conclusions, but which have not been extensively reviewed, are often then bundled together with the reviewed studies:

Those individuals who are… receive less clinical care, less pastoral support and less financial support than those who are… (Clancey, 1996; Franks, 2001; Herron, 2000; Hubert et al., 2004; Manning, 1998; Keeler, 1999; Rivers, 2002; Secules et al., 2005; Snyder & Frank, 2004; Sudok, 2006; Urban, 2003; Wolfgram, 2001.)

It may well be that agreement among the researchers reviewed is unanimous. If this is the case the bundling is justified. It is, nonetheless, easy to make blanket statements that conceal important differences between studies in each bundle. It should be borne in mind, in this regard, that one of the cardinal features of a systematic review is the care taken to define quality and selection criteria before studies are juxtaposed. Particular care should, therefore, be taken to include as much detail as possible of each study in the review: examples are demographics, location, methods of data collection and the statistical tests applied. These are the details examiners will need in order to determine if the comparisons made and conclusions drawn are valid. A number of strategies might be applied to achieve this outcome. The first is as follows:

Of the four qualitative studies on teacher–learner interactions in the classroom (Grieve, 2001; Klug, 2004; Smith, 2004; Trent, 2005), Smith presents the most intensive long-term study. In his study of 25 students in one classroom over a year, he found that…

(Adapted from Galvan, 2004, p.45)

The second:

Numerous writers have indicated that children in single-parent households are at greater risk for academic underachievement than children from two-parent households (see Adams, 1999, and Block, 2002). Three recent studies have provided strong empirical support for this contention (Doe, 2004; Edgar, 200; Jones, 2003). Of these, the study by Jones is the strongest, employing a national sample with rigorous controls for…

(Galvan, 2004, p.69)

Finally:

The…theory has wide support, with 14 studies published within the last decade that provide supporting data (see especially: Smith, 2001; Jones, 2002)

(Ling Pan, 2003, p.104).

9.9 TENSE

1. The role of tense in writing is important because it not only helps readers to understand relationships between objects, events and issues. It also affects the manner in which text is written: past tense encourages a narrative of what happened in the past while present tense encourages discussion of what is happening at present. Although this appears to be straightforward the correct use of tense in a literature review can, however, be problematic. Part of the problem relates to the way tense is used in referencing systems. Therefore, because the literature review is usually among the most heavily referenced sections in a thesis, the use of correct tense can become a prominent issue when writing it.

2. In the MLA system, for example, all research, artistic creations and natural phenomena are assumed to exist in an eternal present. But the actions that gave rise to each exist in the past. Past and present, therefore, often coexist in the same sentence: *Using as evidence text written in 1974 Grant (45) argues that…and, as a result, suggests…* Or: *The eyewitness account was overlooked, but it is revealing.* It might, however, be necessary to privilege a researcher by indicating, for example, that the view of another is dated. *Butcher supports the argument that…but Richards rejects…* can, therefore, be written as: *Butcher supported the argument that…but Richards rejects…* In brief, if the MLA system has been adopted, the following indicates how tense ought to be used:
   - The simple present tense for an opinion still considered valid *(Case studies indicate that participants are…)*, an information based statement *(This literature review is structured in three sections…; Markham suggests that… [36])*, or when referring to anything in a text regardless of when that text was written *(In the play 'Hamlet, Prince of Denmark,' which was written between 1600 and 1602, Hamlet dies in Act V)*.
   - The present perfect when an action in the past affects the present *(Significant attention has been given to the issue of…)*
   - The simple past for historical statements *(During the Renaissance period artists were influenced by…)* or actions performed in the past *(Shakespeare wrote 'Hamlet, Prince of Denmark' in…)*.
   - The past perfect tense when referring to an event that preceded the one to which reference has just been made *(Barnes rejects the explanation that Gardiner had proposed three years before…)*.

3. In the APA system, the present tense, as in the MLA system, is reserved for views still considered to be current *(Bowring's [2003] finding is consistent with…)* and, also as in the MLA system, for objects that have a present material existence *(Figure 1 indicates…; or The specimens were chosen because they are perfectly adapted to…)* In all other cases either the simple past tense *(Hunter*

[2004] examined…) or the present perfect tense (*Freer [2004] has argued that…* or *Butler [2005] has opposed the view that…)* should be used. The present perfect tense can, however, be cumbersome so the simple past, whenever possible, should be used instead. The difference between the MLA and APA systems in the use of tense is clearly indicated in the following examples. The MLA: *This literature review <u>is structured</u> in three sections…;* becomes in APA: *This literature review <u>was</u>* or *<u>has been structured</u> in three sections…)*

9.10 CONCLUDING THE REVIEW

1. After having read the literature review examiners in most cases should be ready to pass through a metaphorical doorway into the details of the study undertaken in the thesis. In an effective review they will do so with a sound understanding of where the study is positioned in relation to the work of other researchers and satisfied that the study has been fully justified. This explains the foundational role a literature review plays in a thesis. But, in order for the review to play this role it should be understood that a literature review is an inherently complex piece of writing. Unless long, complex topics within a review have already been given separate summaries, it is for this reason that examiners will depend upon the review's conclusion to peel back the layers of discussion and evidence presented in the review to make clearly evident the context within which the central argument or narrative in the thesis has been positioned.

2. A generally effective strategy to ensure the conclusion succeeds in this task is to use the same mould usually applied when the first draft of the review as a whole is being written: a wide background to a narrow focus, in this case to the research question or hypothesis. The ability to do so is an explanation for why the final draft of the review should be left to the end of the writing process for it is here that the perceptiveness born of long experience comes into play: the ability to make distinct the wood from the trees. The following outline provides an indication of how this can be achieved: *In conclusion, <u>the trends</u> in the research literature indicate that… The literature <u>suggests overall</u> that… The literature <u>also demonstrates</u> the need to… The current study is, <u>therefore, essential</u> because…*

ENDNOTE

---

1   The first time a work is cited all authors should be listed in the order in which they appear in the original source. Thereafter, *et al.* from the Latin 'and others' should be used. Because it is plural *et al.* should always be followed with a plural verb: *Kerr et al. explain that….*

CHAPTER 10

Methods

…what avails a golden key if it cannot give access to the object which we wish to reach, and why find fault with a wooden key if it serves our purpose?

(St Augustine, cited in Willmann, 1907, np)

10.1 INTRODUCTION

1. The introduction to a thesis, in addition to indicating why a study needs to be undertaken, also indicates the methodological orientation of the researcher. It is this orientation that determines the type of research questions asked or hypotheses posed, the type of research pursued, and the methods and modes of analysis adopted. It also determines the choice of the literature reviewed and the context in which it is critiqued. This, in turn, indicates how other researchers have undertaken their work and helps to identify approaches that can either be used or adapted in a study: *The conventional strategy for…has been to…But in a recent work…an alternative version of this strategy has been proposed in which…* There is, thus, a clear link between the methodological assumptions in the introduction and the methods adopted. As a result, examiners in all disciplines expect to see a clear link between each in the methods section. In the social sciences, in particular, where more complete pictures of human behaviour need to be established, they will expect to see a self-conscious application of method (Garman & Piantanida, 2006). The following student, for example, had combed the:

…literature for information that would demonstrate his knowledge of many of the issues that would arise: The design section of the proposal was more than 60 pages long and addressed every conceivable issue. He had not attempted to resolve them all but, rather, to show that he was aware that they might arise, knowledgeable about how others had dealt with them and sensitive to the tradeoffs represented by various decisions.

(Marshall & Rossman, 2006, p.211)

Doctoral researchers, as indicated in the following example, should take particular care to show they have considered all options as defence against possible criticism they had not done so:

...during a review meeting of the author's candidature, the question was asked: 'What alternative methods might you use to produce the same results?' While pondering a response, the follow-up question was: '...and if you use an alternative research method, would your thesis title need to change?' These questions were posed by a senior academic who was in the habit of encouraging candidates to think deeply about the research process.

(Denholm, 2007, p.66)

The expectation by examiners that due care has been exercised in the choice and application of the methods adopted in a study lies in their need to be convinced that effective data for the requirements of the undertaking have been collected. It is this need that makes the use of methods in a thesis inseparable from the success of the thesis overall (Pearce, 2005). However, providing convincing evidence is not necessarily straightforward as the context of the research and efficacy of particular methods need to be taken into account. Take, for example, the difference in the manner in which the crime rate is measured by the Federal Bureau of Investigation and by the Justice Department in the United States: 'The FBI tabulates crimes reported to law enforcement agencies. The Justice Department surveys a representative sample of homes and asks them crime-related questions' (Dent, 2005, p.257).

The importance of explanation and justification

2. Each approach to research has strategies and methods that are typically applied. In qualitative research, for example, studies focusing on lived experience usually rely on in-depth interviews, those focusing on society and culture typically use case studies and those focusing on language and communication typically apply textual analysis (Marshall & Rossman, 2006). However, examiners expect that even when typically applied but particularly when applied atypically both strategies and methods will be explained fully and justified: 'This departure from accepted procedure certainly compromised the comparative value of the resulting data, but it made for unexpectedly rich results...'(Angrosino, 2007, p.25). That these expectations are not always satisfied is indicated by the problems examiners commonly identify: methods that are poorly explained, not justified, inappropriately applied and the strengths and weaknesses of each not indicated (Lovat et al., 2002). (Digressions, for example, are important aspects of open-ended interviews but not of semi-structured interviews.) A problem common to collaborative studies is a lack of clarity of the researcher's precise role in the work.

What is a method?

3. There are, though, additional issues that researchers need to consider when the methods section is being written. One is to decide what constitutes a method. A case study is not a specific method; 'it is a way of organizing social data so as to preserve the unitary character of the social object being studied' (Punch, 2006, p.144). CAQDAS (Computer Assisted Qualitative Data Analysis Systems) are not methods for analysing qualitative material but technical devices to support an analytic method; usually theoretic coding (Flick, 2007). Because, for example, there are many ways in which observation can be applied it might be better to define it as a strategy rather than a method. Each of its specialised applications, systematic or unsystematic, covert or overt, for example, can then be called methods. The term 'tool' has been used to differentiate specialised applications from their root method but, because 'tool' can also be used generically to indicate any instrument that assists the progress of a study, it is open to misinterpretation: a data base or even a librarian might be considered research tools.

Research purpose

4. Another issue is the role of the research questions or hypotheses. The selection of methods should not be made before they have been as clearly formulated as possible because it is the questions or hypotheses that drive the selection of methods. Exploring a wide range of issues implies, therefore, that a number of methods might need to be applied (Teddlie & Tashakkori, 2003c). This will quickly become apparent when a distinction is drawn between a research question or hypothesis and the purpose or purposes of a study. The following, for example, appears to be a straightforward question: Is teaching strategy A better than teaching strategy B? The question might, though, have a number of purposes: one might be to raise academic performance another might be to test the efficacy of various learning styles. Thus, without having the purpose or purposes of the research questions or hypotheses clarified the necessary links to appropriate methods cannot be developed (Newman et al., 2003). It is in this sense that the most convincing answers to 'why' questions are those that have addressed alternative approaches and, in consequence, have identified the merits of the choices made (Tinkler & Jackson, 2004). These merits are displayed most effectively when the strengths of each method complement the others and the weaknesses of each do not overlap. An example is the use of a case study in conjunction with a postal survey. The former provides depth, the latter breadth (Teddlie & Tashakkori, 2003a). When, as in this case, a number of methods are to be applied it is important to define the rationale for the design and to identify its main characteristics: the timing of the application

of each method relative to the others, for example, and the weighting given to each (Creswell & Plano Clark, 2007). It might also be useful to reassure examiners by indicating the skills the researcher might have developed in earlier multi-method studies.

10.2 'NEEDLES OF GOOD DESIGN IN HAYSTACKS OF POSSIBILITY'

(Dennet, D. cited in *The Economist*, 22 July 2006, p.82)

1. The sophistication with which the synergy between methodology and method is indicated and the insight shown in regard to the technical application of each method will indicate the level of understanding researchers have of the methodological issues central to their discipline. When these explanations are provided it is important, though, to recognise that just as there are no theories that can claim to solve all the problems they define, so no method is without limitations: 'It is acknowledged that information generated from focus group meetings is filtered experience rather than direct behaviour' (Kung, 2001, p.151). It follows, therefore, that all theories or methods are open to improvement. This, together with the fact that the range of methods that cut across methodological boundaries is limitless, means that the potential for innovation is always present in regard to the types of research methods adopted and the manner in which they are applied. As in the following example, the deeper a researcher's understanding of the theories and methods at play in their field the greater will be their ability to harness that potential:

Experiments involving drugs of any kind need to have a control—that is, an otherwise identical experiment in which something other than the drug is administered—to check that any effects are caused by the drug and not something else. Ideally, neither experimental subjects nor researchers should know who is in the control group, but for experiments involving psychedelic drugs this is difficult, because it is quickly apparent who is high and who is not.

For his control Dr... decided to use methylphenidate hydrochloride, otherwise known as Ritalin, a drug that calms hyperactive children... The choice of Ritalin was inspired. Neither the volunteers nor the experimenters could say reliably which drug was being administered on which occasion (The Economist, 15 July 2006, p.70).

Even the potential of knitting has recently been harnessed to provide new insight into the geometry of the natural world. A knitted Lorenz Manifold, for example, was the first physical model of the shape. (Lorenz Manifolds are shapes where, over short distances, curves can be treated as a flat plane.) Neither had any good physical models of a hyperbolic shape been produced until one was knitted. Hyperbolic planes are spaces of negative curvature:

While it is hard to model this using paper or plastic, it is easily replicated by simply increasing the number of stitches per row as the shape is knitted or crocheted. 'What you can do is get a tactile insight. I theoretically understand the concept, but [the model] allows me to communicate it…'

(*Yahoo News*, 9 July 2008)

2. The use of innovative and effective methods will constitute an important element of the originality that all theses ought to display. Examiners will not only reward this accordingly but will also take into account the amount of effort invested in the process: 'Perhaps the most impressive aspect of the work is the level of effort on both model development and field data collection' (Holbrook et al., 2003, p.10). They will also usually be prepared to acknowledge the initiative and effort that went into a new approach that did not subsequently prove viable: *After experimenting with a method for…it was decided against using the approach because more would be achieved using traditional techniques.* Discussion in a thesis of approaches that might have been adopted or of those that failed is recognition both of the untidiness of research and of the compromises that frequently need to be made in order to carry it out successfully. Because of difficulty in gaining access to research sites qualitative longitudinal studies, for example, often cannot be conducted. In such cases the only practical alternative is to compromise and conduct the study retrospectively:

One difficulty with the retrospective approach is that the research may be dependent partly on participants' memories. Nevertheless, it is possible to go a long way towards addressing associated issues to do with trustworthiness if sufficient data are available to facilitate triangulation.

(O'Donoghue, 2007, p.153)

10.3 VALIDITY

1. In the broadest sense any study can be considered valid, true until proved otherwise, when the research purposes, questions, and methods are mutually consistent and when appropriate evidence is used to support each finding (Newman et al., 2003). To this extent validity is a term that applies equally to empirical, exegetic and qualitative approaches. However,

in a more specific sense validity takes on particular meanings, internal and external, that apply and are understood differently in empirical and qualitative approaches to research.

2. In regard to internal validity, construct validity and its variants convergent, discriminant and nomological validity, for example, measure the extent to which an empirical study actually measures the construct it claims to be measuring. (A construct is a cognitive attribute that has been defined in theory, intelligence for example, and observed in practice.) In psychometric tests face validity (the extent to which a test appears to measure what it is supposed to measure), concurrent validity (when the results of a test correlate well with previously validated tests) and predictive validity (when there is a statistically significant correlation between the results of a test and a subsequent concrete observation) establish the extent to which particular tests actually measure what they claim to measure. In experimental research an equivalent method to establish internal validity is, for example, criterion validity: a measure of how well a variable or set of variables predicts an outcome based on information from other variables. Prior to the measurement of criterion validity, though, the existence of a cause–effect relationship between the variables needs to be established. This will also involve showing temporal precedence (that the cause preceded the effect), that there is a relationship (covariation of cause and effect) and that there is no plausible alternative explanation for the effect. But, because there are in the social sciences no pure samples, the existence of a cause–effect relationship between variables is not easily established. But even when, as in the natural sciences, pure samples can be identified, the influence of bias or confounding variables cannot be excluded entirely. Apart from controlled or experimental studies the most, therefore, that can be claimed in both the natural and social sciences is a *correlation* or *association* between variables; the greater the number of instances where this correlation or association can be indicated the higher will be the level of internal validity.

3. External validity (also called generalisability or applicability) is a measure of the extent to which research results can be extrapolated to another setting. For example, breadth (less discriminating criteria), rather than depth (more discriminating criteria) in representative samples will usually increase the extent to which research findings can be generalised. For empirical researchers the decision to go broad or deep will be influenced both by the nature and accessibility of the research samples or participants and by the purpose of the research. But, because breadth generally involves sacrifice of precision, the consequences of that decision are significant. Empirical researchers, therefore, will need to explain and justify their decision to go either broad or deep: *For the purpose of this research project, the decision to strive*

for breadth at the expense of depth was deliberate because... Breadth and depth are not, though, necessarily exclusive. Case study research, for example, can involve in-depth research of a representative case and some of the findings extrapolated to other settings. This too would need to be explained and justified in the introduction to the thesis:

This is a study of reading practices in elementary schools within the educational system of ... Despite this focus it is important to recognise, as the discussion below will indicate, that the findings are of general relevance to the educational systems of other English speaking countries as well.

Because the decision to go broad or deep is an important aspect of the design of any empirical research undertaking, examiners will assume that considerable thought has been devoted to the decision and its consequences. It might, therefore, strike them as odd, unless a valid justification has been provided, to see that decision in the research limitations section of the conclusion to the thesis identified as a major limitation: *The major limitation of this study is the extent to which the findings can be generalised beyond the products included within the parameters of the research.*

4. Reliability is the extent to which research is consistent in what it measures. This might mean, though, that a research undertaking might be reliable but also invalid if, for example, an inappropriate method has been applied. The implication is that validity and reliability are related in the sense that sound empirical research should be both valid and reliable. But, where a trade-off needs to be made, validity, because it indicates the extent to which research has achieved what it set out to do, should usually be considered the more important (Cryer, 2006). Reliability rests on the assumption of a single, observable and objective reality. From this perspective, therefore, studies might be replicated. Understandably though, the concept is problematic when applied to qualitative studies. There are, however, significant exceptions. The most important of these is provision by the researcher of precise guidelines explaining how interviews and/or conversations have been transcribed (Flick, 2007). Others are when, for example, a number of researchers have coded a transcript they might test for intercoder agreement: a comparison of their work to determine the extent to which they have arrived at the same codes and themes (Creswell & Plano Clark, 2007). Usually, however, qualitative researchers adopt the notion of dependability rather than reliability. Dependability is a measure of the extent to which a reader, on the basis of the evidence presented concurs with the findings of the research. The primary mechanism to enable them to do so is 'thick description'. The richness of this description indicates the density of the layers of meaning with which the interpretation has had to deal. (This is the primary measure of the

authenticity of qualitative research). In turn 'thick description' provides an 'audit trail' (auditability) so readers, from the outset of a study, might follow the interpretive process and understand the findings derived from it. The complement to dependability in qualitative research is confirmability: this is the extent to which a researcher's interpretation of the research material can be corroborated.

5. While exegetic and qualitative researchers need to strive for validity in a general sense, they will, because validity in its more specific applications is embedded in empiricism, aim instead to establish the credibility of their work: the extent to which research reflects the constructs of research participants or the characters in the literature and the degree to which the process revealing those constructs has been made transparent. In regard to interviews, for example, the question is whether respondents were given any cause consciously or unconsciously to construct a biased version of their experiences (Flick, 2007). Credibility in other words, is the degree of confidence that can be vested in a qualitative or exegetic researcher's findings. To the extent that credibility is broadly analogous to the empirical concept 'internal validity' qualitative researchers can challenge empirical findings using empirical terminology:

> *In my criticism of earlier psychological research studies on psychological factors and their relation to … I have argued that it is the objective, quantitative methods these studies have used which resulted in inconsistent outcomes. In other words, I have questioned the validity of these research projects.*

(Aydin, 2006, p.23).

6. Some qualitative researchers, though, do use the concept internal validity with meanings specific to the approach. Descriptive or contextual validity, for example, indicates the extent to which a qualitative research account is complete, while interpretive validity indicates the extent to which an account connects with the lived experience of the participants (Punch, 2006). Respondent validation enhances the trustworthiness of qualitative work for participants should feel a recognisable reality has been reproduced in a research account while dialogic validity means the research has the imprimatur of peer review. Action Research has particular criteria for the establishment of research quality and validity. Outcome validity, for example, indicates the extent to which issues providing the focus of the research have been addressed. Catalytic validity indicates the extent to which the research process energises participants to transform their own reality and democratic validity indicates the extent to which the research has been undertaken in collaboration with the stakeholders (Charles & Ward, 2007).

236

7. Qualitative studies tend to be rooted in phenomena that are worth knowing for their own sake rather than as a necessary step towards generalisation (Peck MacDonald, 1994). This, together with the fact that qualitative researchers generally use small samples to generate intrinsically time and context specific insights and hypotheses means external validity, for them, is a far more problematic concept than in empirical work. While some qualitative researchers argue that purposive and theoretical sampling, for example, can afford qualitative studies some degree of generalisability (Aydin, 2006), most see lack of generalisability as a necessary price for the strengths of the qualitative approach. The differences between empirical and qualitative approaches in regard to external validity might, therefore, make it appropriate in a research undertaking to use these differences to complement each other or to privilege one approach over the other: *Consistent with the theoretical framework of this study, the second quantitative phase was given primacy over the initial qualitative phase in order to support the generalisation of the results.*

10.4 TRANSFERABILITY

1. However without some form of generalisation qualitative researchers would go into new research settings without any precedents upon which to build their initial insights. This is very rarely the case. Instead of generalisability, therefore, qualitative researchers apply the term transferability. Because transferability is premised on the uniqueness rather than comparability of research settings, it permits a researcher who has read other qualitative accounts, to extrapolate and 'transfer' aspects of the research settings described in those accounts to that of their own. Transference should not, though, be interpreted in the context of isolated segments of meaning:

In our sense-making efforts, we think about the field experience in relation to other comparable situations and in relation to what other researchers and scholars have said about similar situations…We do not write up all that we saw or heard or were told. Rather, we write up what all of our thinking and comparing has led us to believe our field experience means.

(Cited in Golden-Biddle & Locke, 1997, p.7)

Qualitative researchers facilitate transferability by providing detailed descriptions of all aspects of their research ('thick description') together with a reflexive (self-analytical rather than merely biographical) account of themselves. They also facilitate the process through use of synecdoche. This is a rhetorical device where part represents a greater whole. A single case, a deprived individual for example, is studied because he or she exemplifies the greater population of individuals like them. 'Critical cases' like these explain why a great deal of qualitative research is synecdochal (Woods, 2006).

2. Thus, while empirical researchers indicate for readers the measures taken to establish the internal and, if necessary, external validity of their work, transferability is a process performed by other qualitative researchers but facilitated by the original researcher. Transferability is not, though, exclusive to qualitative approaches: all researchers might consciously design their work so as to make elements of it transferable to other settings. Among the reasons why transferability is not exclusive to qualitative approaches is that the distinction between it and external validity is not complete. This is logical not only in the sense that the external validity of research findings rests on the extent to which they are collectively transferable but also because all research and, therefore, the extent to which it is externally valid or transferable, must necessarily contain, as has already been established, elements of both subjectivity and uncertainty. This raises the question of the isomorphic relationship between external validity and transferability. Isomorphism maps the nature of complex relationships, in this case between two concepts. If they tend to reflect each other they are isomorphic. If, as in this case, they are substantively but not necessarily entirely different, they are less isomorphic.

10.5 MIXED METHODS

1. Ideally, multiple perspectives should be incorporated throughout a research undertaking, from problem identification through to the drawing of final inferences (Teddlie & Tashakkori, 2003b). But theoretically different approaches to research can only validly be combined when the logical relation between each has been established and when the criteria used to evaluate the research have been made clear (Flick, 2002). These relationships are often established and the criteria sustained by the extent to which the strengths of one approach compensate for the limitations of the other:

The two research strategies allow for the combination of the distinctive strengths of each approach. The empirical assessment allows for a multivariate analysis of...The qualitative case studies allow us to situate these patterns and explore the internal dynamics of...

This explains the purpose of triangulated research designs: to obtain different but complementary data on the same topic. It is, in fact, the complementariness of different methodologies and of different methods that constitute the fundamental principles of mixed methodology and mixed methods research. But, if no method is intrinsically linked with particular approaches to research what is the relationship between the latter and the former? In 2005 a new journal, *Journal of Mixed Methods Research*, devoted exclusively to publishing mixed methods studies and discussions about the methodology of mixed methods research was published. The journal's call for papers states that 'the definition of mixed methods is research in which the investigator collects, analyzes, mixes, and draws inferences from both quantitative and qualitative data in a single study or a program of inquiry' (cited in Creswell & Plano Clark, 2007). The key word here is 'data', no reference is made to empirical or qualitative methods. So, in terms of this definition mixed methods research validly incorporates the term mixed methodology research.

10.6 TRIANGULATION

1. Empirical research is particularly compelling when different methods and different data lead to the same result. But the combination of empirical and qualitative research will not necessarily lead to similar results. Rather than one invalidating the other they are, instead, more likely to indicate different constructions of the studied phenomenon. If this is the case criteria will need to be developed to assess the meanings of the congruences and discrepancies (Flick, 2007). Nonetheless, just as using one set of approaches to mediate others is central to mixed methods research so too is it central to research triangulation. This is no accident for it is very likely that the latter evolved from the former (Teddlie & Tashakkori, 2003b).

2. The validity of using triangulation as a metaphor for mediating research approaches depends upon a particular interpretation of it. This is because, as a research term, triangulation was derived from the practice in navigation and surveying where two precise bearings are used in order to calculate the position of a third. In this instance the two initial bearings are not used to check or verify the other but, rather, to complement each other in order to identify the particulars of the third. This, however, is not the sense in which it is generally used in research. Here the usual intention, instead, is to establish how different approaches or strategies relate to one another. Empirical researchers, for example, might seek to establish how different approaches or strategies check, validate or corroborate one another and qualitative researchers might seek to establish how they enhance understanding of, or elaborate one another (Brannen, 2005). What neither can do though is seek confirmation of what they triangulate. Any attempt to do so would be based on fallacy: A is valid because B is valid and B is valid because A is valid (Hart, 2005). The best that can be hoped for is that triangulation,

when implemented either simultaneously or sequentially, illuminates aspects of a phenomenon or indicates different frames of reference to broaden the interpretive repertoire (Hart, 2005). Triangulation might be applied within one method. In an interview, for example, each question might be directed towards providing different perspective to the issue under discussion (Schostak, 2006). But, where data from different methods are triangulated care will need to be exercised as to the appropriateness of doing so. The possible danger can be inferred from the following:

...if one person, says 'there's a dog down by the river', and a second person says 'there's a dog down by the river', and a third person says 'there's a dog down by the river', there is the chance that 'there's a dog down by the river'. However, two questions: is it the same river, and is it the same dog? Further questions, of course can be raised: what is meant by river? What is meant by dog? River might be the name of a night club and dog the name of a gang.

(Schostak, 2006, p.147)

10.7 LIMITATIONS AND DELIMITATIONS

1. Because all theories and methods are open to improvement no research project can claim to be perfectly designed. The successful implementation of even the best-designed projects usually depends, in fact, upon solving successive streams of problems (Hart, 2005). This applies to all approaches to research but is nicely illustrated in the following extract about qualitative methodologies in a workplace setting:

In the interest of capturing the lived experiences of real people in real settings, these methodologies recognize that there is a lot that cannot be controlled. It is here that workplace-based research methodologies take on a level of reflexivity.

(Hickey, 2007, p.80)

Research involves, therefore, a trade-off between the ideal and what, in practice, can be achieved. Empirical thesis researchers often do not have the resources to conduct large-scale studies. The result is studies with such limited numbers of participants that statistical significance is placed in question (Bryant, 2004). In both empirical and qualitative research potential participants have a right to say no or to impose significant conditions upon their agreement to participate. This means that representing a sufficient range of views without privileging some above others becomes difficult (Schostak, 2006). Discussion by a researcher of the necessary compromises these trade-offs involve indicates not only an awareness of the need to compromise but also implies realisation that the results of a study can only be discussed in the context of these compromises. The following account by an oral examiner shows the price a candidate can pay when the need to compromise is not acknowledged:

The candidate's reaction to critical points wasn't good. I thought on a number of occasions that she simply needed to acknowledge the weaknesses and say more about how she had coped with these, how she would improve things given a second chance. But she didn't do this, and so it was very difficult to have a conversation about the thesis which showed her as someone who had academic insight, which would have made us decide that some of the flaws mattered less. After all, nothing's perfect and the main thing is to show that you can see that and deal with it...

(Cited in Tinkler & Jackson, 2004, p.172)

2. Central to the trade-offs that need to be made are research limitations and delimitations. The former are the factors that may affect a study but are not under the control of the researcher; these are the known unknowns. A variable, for example, that affects the outcome of an empirical study but which cannot be controlled is a limitation. This explains why empirical researchers need to discuss threats to validity in the methods section. For a qualitative researcher an ideal setting 'is one in which the observer obtains easy access, establishes immediate rapport with informants, and gathers data directly relating to the research interests' (O'Donoghue, 2007, p.58). Such ideal settings, though, rarely exist so qualitative like empirical researchers need to acknowledge any limitations of significance and attempt to approximate the ideal as much as possible. Delimitations, on the other hand, are under the control of a researcher. A conscious choice, for example, to adopt a qualitative approach also usually constitutes a conscious choice for depth rather than breadth: to impose, in other words, limits on the generalisability of the research outcomes. The fact that delimitation is a matter of choice means the nature of the delimitations, the reason they were imposed, and how the advantage of doing so outweighs the disadvantages, will need to be indicated.

3. However, drawing a distinction between limitations common to all research (time and cost, for example), the effects of which are effectively indeterminate, and those that have a clearly determined influence on the findings of a study (again, time and cost, for example), is not always easy. A distinction will also need to be drawn between the significant limitations anticipated at the design stage and those that were not anticipated; the unknown unknowns. Examiners will expect an acknowledgement of the former and a discussion of how their impact was either eliminated or minimised. If significant unanticipated problems occurred during the research process the steps taken to circumvent

or minimise them will also need to be discussed. In most cases this will be done in the research limitations section of the discussion chapter. In cases where the impact was of particular significance it might, though, also be necessary to mention them in the methods section as well. Discussing the limitations that could not reasonably have been foreseen is an important and intrinsically interesting part of the story of a thesis. Examiners will not, however, take kindly to an admission of problems that should have been anticipated. Thus, except in the most extraordinary circumstances, examiner scepticism will be invited if it is indicated in the methods section that an eighty per cent response rate to a postal questionnaire was expected.

10.8 STYLE, VOICE AND TENSE

1. The intrinsic uniqueness of qualitative research makes research replication conceptually inapplicable. Instead, qualitative researchers measure the dependability of research according to the comprehensiveness of the audit trail provided. This means that, particularly in the methods section, qualitative researchers need to be explicit about the aims of the research, need to fully describe how it was undertaken, need to clearly distinguish data from interpretation and need to provide a comprehensive account of why each research decision was made. Doing so will involve the use of 'rich description' written in the first or third person, usually in the present tense in order to convey a sense of immediacy: *As a result, the research question I formulated for this study is…* The simple past tense, however, will be used to reflect, for example, decisions taken in the past: *These observations allowed me to develop my felt sense of being in the presence of…* It might also be advisable in qualitative theses containing a significant body of quotations to convert descriptive passages in these quotations into the past tense. This has the negative effect of diminishing the direct contact quotations provide (Darlington & Scott, 2002), but it does help prevent the confusion that can arise when the present tense is used to convey the reflections of a number of individuals over different periods of time.

2. While replication is conceptually inapplicable in qualitative research it is the primary measure of validity in empirical studies: other researchers ought to be able to replicate the research and arrive at a similar outcome. The methods section of an empirical thesis should, therefore, provide sufficient detail to enable them to do so. An initial temptation, though, is to write the section in an imperative 'recipe' style. This is because the present tense, active voice and strong verbs in short, imperative sentences, tell readers precisely what to do: *Use a checklist. Tick all the items. Place the list in the box.* This style, though, is stilted because single sentences are used to relate

single actions. The following examples indicate how combining sequences of actions improves clarity:

- *Use a clean, dry 50 ml test tube. Add 20 ml of distilled water.*
- *Twenty ml of distilled water was poured into a clean, dry 50 ml test tube.* (Be careful not to start a sentence with a digit. Confusion might result if the previous sentence ended with one.)

3. Use of the past tense in the combined sentence is appropriate because the purpose of the method section is to discuss decisions made and describe actions taken, in the past. For this reason, instead of the present tense of the imperative style, the simple past tense should normally be used: … *cells were washed twice with medium and fresh medium containing… was added.* The present tense, however, should be used when an observation reflects an ongoing truth: *The fish were fed copepods because they feed on plankton in the wild.* An event taking place at the same time as another will need to be described in the past continuous tense: …*was added while the sample was being dried.* The perfect tenses might be necessary to convey particular meaning. For example, the present perfect: *Researchers have used the procedure to verify…* indicates the procedure is still in use. The past perfect: *Researchers had used the procedure to verify…* indicates the procedure is no longer used. The future perfect: *Researchers will have used the procedure to verify…* is rarely necessary. Because use of tense in a thesis can be problematic it is often useful, when in difficulty, to talk to an imaginary listener. Problems are frequently resolved when what needs to be written is first spoken. When this is done the writing, as in the following example, will flow easily from one tense to another:

Features from the fingerprint images were extracted using the Plunkett algorithm [47]. In the Plunkett algorithm, adjacent data samples are combined by taking the square root of the sum of their squares. A flow chart of this algorithm is presented in Figure 45. Next, a template matching algorithm was applied to the data in order to…

(Hoover, 2004, np)

4. In the methods section emphasis should be placed on what was done rather than upon the performer of an action. This means the passive voice should be used when writing the section in preference to the active voice; the voice generally adopted throughout the rest of the thesis. Compare, for example, the active: *I heated the solution to 80°C;* with the passive: *The solution was heated to 80°C.* It is not usually necessary to write: *The solution was heated to 80°C by the researcher.* This is understood. However, omitting *by the researcher* in a sentence where the verb has no explicit subject can lead to odd statements: *Goggles are required to do the experiment.* There may be particular instances in

the methods section, though, where use of the active voice is more appropriate than the passive. For example, the active voice should be used when an action is performed by a piece of equipment: *A thermometer recorded the change in temperature*. The active voice should also be used where the passive creates the impression that participants in a study are 'acted on' rather than being actors. The active voice *the participants completed the questionnaire*, is thus preferable to the passive *the questionnaire was completed by the participants* (Publication Manual of the APA, 2005, p.65). Again, as in the case of tense, where the appropriateness of either active or passive voice in the methods section is in doubt read the sentence aloud.

10.9 THE PILOT STUDY

1. Any pilot studies conducted will also need to be discussed in the methods section. In the first instance the objectives of the pilot or pilots will need to be indicated for pilot studies might fulfil a number of roles. Common among these is the development of an appropriate research design:

   One of the shortcomings highlighted in… was a lack of rigour in previous studies. The objective of the pilot was, therefore, to develop a research design that would enable the project to measure precisely the impact of…

   Also common is the need to test the feasibility of a study, to gather data for a sample size calculation for a larger study or to anticipate problems. It is their purpose as anticipator of problems that indicates the advantage to be gained by conducting pilot studies as early as possible so any problems identified 'become obstacles to be overcome rather than impediments to completion' (Ingleby, 2007, p.50). This will hold true for qualitative researchers who develop research questions prior to going into the field. They will need to establish that the issues addressed in the questions are of significance to participants and not just of academic interest to themselves (O'Donoghue, 2007). For masters qualitative researchers, in particular, a pilot might be necessary to indicate both to them and their supervisors an ability to make the transition from data collection to interpretation and writing. A pilot study might serve an analogous purpose in empirical studies where research methods tend to require unique competence with specialised equipment (Cryer, 2006).

2. Pilot studies, according to the purpose they serve, might be 'quick and dirty' or highly controlled. In either case the data derived from pilots should be used in the service of the primary study but not in it, for the circumstances in the pilot and primary study will differ. They should, however, differ as little as possible. If the population in a pilot does differ significantly from that in the

primary study the manner in which the differences affect the utility of the pilot will need to be discussed. Once the beneficial relationship between the pilot and primary study has been established the effect of the former on the latter will need to be explained: *Based on the reaction of the participants to the questions in the guide I changed the order of three of the questions as follows… I also decided to omit two of the questions because…*

10.10 THE ORGANISING THEME

1. As an organising principle all theses should have a theme. The thesis statement or primary research question or hypothesis usually serves this purpose. The chapters or sections of a thesis, in turn, exist because they constitute self-contained sub-themes contributing to an understanding of the primary theme. The fact that the methods section requires an organising principle does not, therefore, make it distinct from any other part of the thesis. But the reason why the success of the organising principle in this chapter is of particular importance is because if the examiners are to have confidence in the validity, reliability and objectivity of empirical research or in the credibility, dependability and confirmability of qualitative studies, they need to have as clear an understanding as possible of all of the relevant aspects of the research procedures applied or strategies adopted. In qualitative theses, for example, 'Setting the Scene' is important in developing context and in empirical theses it needs to be made clear what methods are to be applied to what research question or hypothesis. Doing the latter will avoid comments such as the following from an examiner: 'It is entirely unclear what hypothesis is being tested' (cited in Lovat, et al., 2002, p.14). Another reason the organising principle is important is because in empirical theses the principle adopted in the methods section might usefully be extended to embrace the results and discussion sections as well. When possible, applying a similar pattern in each of these sections provides a template to follow when writing each of these sections and for the examiners to follow when reading them. Four patterns are generally used:
   - Logical Order. For example: theoretical framework, research design and pilot, setting and intervention, participants, procedures and data analysis.
   - Chronological order. This pattern is generally adopted in qualitative studies both because of the contiguity in qualitative research of data collection and analysis and because the approach is cyclical and, therefore, a chronologically ongoing, process. However, even in empirical theses where alternative patterns to chronological order are used, each section within the pattern should, nonetheless, be presented in chronological order so as not to confuse the examiners.

- Research question or hypothesis order. This pattern will be chronological in the sense that each question or hypothesis should be dealt with in the same order they were addressed in the research. It is also likely to incorporate elements from the logical order pattern because, for example, setting and intervention, participants, procedures, and analysis will need to be provided for each question or hypothesis.
- Research methods order. For example: surveys, case studies, observation. This pattern is most appropriate when the purpose of a study is to compare or triangulate the results derived from the application of each method.

(Adapted from Glatthorn, 1998, pp.153–156)

2. Irrespective of which pattern has been adopted examiners of empirical studies will need to be assured of the quality of the research design (particularly that potential flaws have been identified), of the quality of any instruments or procedures used and of the appropriateness of the modes of analysis applied. (If statistical the parameters for determining significance will need to be provided.) For writers of qualitative theses with a methods section the challenge in the section is to provide clarity and order and simultaneously convey 'the sense of flux, process, messiness, inconsistency and ambiguity, which is the very essence of everyday life' (Woods, 2006, p.71). Whether empirical or qualitative the appropriate means to achieve this balance is unique to each research undertaking. But it can often be achieved if the methods section rather than the introduction is used to provide the setting essential to an understanding of the study. If this approach is adopted a methods section might be divided as follows: research setting, data collection and data analysis. An alternative pattern that emphasises provision for entering the field might be: research setting, access and observation and data analysis (Woods, 2006). The following comment by an examiner indicates the importance of clarity in the methods section of both empirical and qualitative studies:

I am particularly irritated when I do not understand how data are coded and results are calculated in quantitatively based theses. Or exactly how qualitative data were collected and processed for interpretation and discussion.

(Cited in Leder & Holliday, 2006, p.196)

10.11 MATRICES AND NETWORKS

1. The purpose of ordered patterns is to provide clarity and logic to the methods section. But, particularly in complex research undertakings, clarity and logic

can be obscured by the length and complexity of the text required to fulfil the purposes of the section. Should this be the case the use of a display to visually represent the entire design of the study or only those aspects of it that require clarification should be considered. Displays generally fall into two categories: matrices and networks. Matrices (in essence tables) involve the intersection of two or more main dimensions or variables in order to indicate how they interact. They are useful when illustrating how particular methods have been applied to different populations or how methods intersect with theory. Networks, on the other hand, are a series of informational nodes connected by links. For this reason networks are particularly effective in the presentation of complex narrative or in plotting a series of contiguous events (Miles & Huberman, 1994). As with any effective illustration, matrix and network diagrams should not only be self-explanatory but also helpful. Because they require the distillation and coherent presentation of information, they help to focus and organise a researcher's own thinking as well as later helping the reader's conceptualisation. Matrix and network diagrams are of particular use in this regard when the issue of the most effective manner in which to organise research data is being considered. They are also useful at the beginning or end of a thesis because they visually create or re-create the intellectual journey (Miles & Huberman, 1994). There is a danger, though, of using matrices inappropriately; where categories, for example, are made too sharp:

An extreme example of this I saw once involved a 4 x 4 matrix where the author had felt pressured to produce a type for every square. The result was to make non-sense of the matrix, for most of the types could have gone anywhere.

(Woods, 2006, p.71)

But, when matrices or networks have been used effectively examiners will show their appreciation: 'The Research Matrix (p. 67 and Appendix 1) is a particularly impressive feature, summarising the key approaches to data gathering and analysis with exceptional clarity' (cited in Holbrook & Dally, 2003, p.13).

2. In fact matrices and networks, charts and graphs, diagrams and photographs can often usefully support many of the descriptions that are an inherent part of the methods section of both empirical and qualitative studies. It is, therefore, not only in the results and discussion sections that data or explanations might be represented visually. Because a thesis is intended for an international audience a map or maps might also be necessary to show place names mentioned in the text. (It is also because they are intended for an international audience that the use in an empirical thesis of informal terms not universally understood should

be avoided. *Take the patient's temperature right away*, for example, should read: *Take the patient's temperature immediately.* In qualitative theses local slang used by participants might need to be interpreted.)

10.12 WHAT TO INCLUDE AND EXCLUDE

1. Although it is usually necessary at the start of each chapter in a thesis to indicate how the chapter contributes to the focus of the research, it is of particular importance that the methods section is started by establishing the focus of the research as a whole: *The goal of this study is to...*If, in a doctoral thesis, there are a number of methods sections, the particular focus of each will need to be indicated clearly. This is because the sources of the data, the methods used to collect them and the types of data collected can only be justified in the context of that focus. This can then be reiterated in the conclusion to the methods section: *This chapter began with a discussion of the methodological challenges of studying...I proposed a...*It is not unusual, though, even in empirical studies, for the focus of a study to change as the research process unfolds:

   Originally this study was to be of...and the questionnaire was formulated accordingly. However, during the preliminary stages of this study...made a noticeable impact on the market... It was decided, therefore, to include them in the study and make a comparison between...and...

   The reasons for any change of focus together with the broad impact of that change should be discussed in the introduction to the thesis. A detailed discussion of the implications of the change upon the design of the research should be provided in the methods section.

2. Any aspects of the research setting that impacted significantly on the conduct of the study should also be discussed. However, in order to do so it will first be necessary to define the boundaries of the research: *The process was only considered from entry to exit...*Research boundaries need not, though, be physical they can also be theoretic, chronological or conceptual. 'Boundary elasticity' often occurs in qualitative studies. Even when physical, however, research boundaries need not be fixed. They might, for example, change from one context to another. Where this is the case the particulars of each setting and how they impacted on the research will also usually need to be discussed.

3. External examiners are 'likely to poke around in the foundations of your research' to ensure that relevant variables have been identified and that key assumptions have been addressed (Rugg & Petrie, 2004, p.163). This is why it is essential in the introduction to a thesis to identify assumptions and define terms and concepts central to the research questions or hypotheses. This also applies to

the methods section where all the core terms and concepts referred to must also be defined upon first use if there is any possibility of their being misunderstood. The following definition from an empirical study indicates this clearly:

We considered seeds left in the Petri dish to be unharvested and those scattered singly on the surface of a tile (usually near the Petri dish) to be scattered and also unharvested. We considered seeds in cheek pouches to be harvested but not cached, those stored in the nestbox to be larderhoarded, and those buried in caching sites within the arena to be scatterhoarded.

(Price et al., 2000, p.99)

The next definition is from a qualitative study:

In one sense, the group of supervisors could be described as homogeneous. They worked at the same department with comparable experiences as supervisors, and all held positive expectations concerning this pedagogical concept. On the other hand, the group could be described as fairly heterogeneous, consisting of seven individuals of both genders, with different ethnicities and personalities. What they had in common was trust in themselves, the group, the supervisor and the situation.

(Emilsson & Johnsson, 2007, p.173)

Some definitions may undergo change as the research proceeds so updated definitions and explanations for, and of the effects of, the changes will need to be provided (Anderson & Poole, 1994).

4. Establishing the focus of the research, providing the necessary particulars of the setting and defining core terms, concepts and assumptions are necessary precursors to deciding upon the degree of detail that ought to be provided in the methods section. This decision or, rather, series of decisions will involve answering two related questions. Both require the exercise of qualitative judgement. The first relates to one end of a scale: 'How much detail is too much?' The answer depends on what the examiners, at a minimum, should be expected to know. On this basis it is generally safe, particularly in the natural sciences, engineering and medicine where standard research practices and methods tend to be the norm, to assume that examiners will know the methods, materials and/or procedures standard to a disciplinary or methodological approach. Statistical treatments, for example, might not need to be explained in detail if they form part of the accepted procedure in a particular field. The exceptions are the social sciences and interdisciplinary studies where assumptions about what examiners should know become more problematic. So, if there is any doubt about what the examiners ought to know, err on the side of caution by providing more detail than would ordinarily be considered necessary. If a supervisor subsequently considers these to be superfluous they

can easily be deleted; it is far less easy to identify details that should be there but have been omitted.

5. The question at the opposite end of the scale is posed differently for empirical researchers on one hand and qualitative researchers on the other. To the former, the question is: 'What details will other researchers be required to know in order to replicate the study precisely?' To the latter it is: 'What details will other researchers require in order to audit the research successfully and to transfer elements from it?' At first sight both questions seem to be relatively straightforward for each requires the same type of answer: full disclosure. However, the degree of detail full disclosure requires is easy to underestimate. It is not necessary to understand what a 'Gaussian mixture model' is in order to sense this in the following advice of a supervisor to his students:

> ...too often I see sentences like, 'A pixel neighborhood of fixed size is used to derive a Gaussian mixture model of the local color distribution.' This seemingly straightforward sentence hides a large amount of detail and precludes another researcher from replicating your efforts. What size neighborhood is used? Is the neighborhood size important? How does a change in neighborhood size impact the results you describe? How many modes are used in the Gaussian model? How are means and variances determined? These are the types of questions that absolutely must be addressed in your thesis.

(Jaynes, 2007, np).

It is only when they come to recognise the importance of detail that some empirical and qualitative researchers make the profoundly unsettling discovery that they failed to take adequately detailed notes at the time the research was being conducted. Because researchers rarely have an opportunity to rectify errors of this type, it is essential to include adequate time for note taking in the initial study plan and then to use that time assiduously. (The need for precision explains why quantifiable rather than qualitative terms should be used in the methods section of empirical theses: *A 10 m deep trench was dug*, for example, instead of: *A deep trench was dug.*)

10.13 RESEARCH JOURNALS AND NOTEBOOKS

1. The need for detail explains why research journals are such an important feature of qualitative research and notebooks of empirical research. Qualitative researchers, sometimes during but usually immediately after each research episode, make observational and reflexive entries about the episode in their journal. It is these reflexive entries that account for the use of 'journal' rather than 'notebook': a journal that becomes a diary of the journey

(Edwards, 2006). The entries thus provide both the necessary material for other researchers to establish the credibility of the interpretations made or patterns observed and facilitate ongoing analysis. But, because perception is subconsciously revised by subsequent events, the diary aspect of the journal permits a particularly useful type of analysis to be conducted: perceptions are fixed in the journal before being revised so they can later be studied in their own context (Taleb, 2007). Empirical researchers, on the other hand, precisely detail their observations both during, and immediately after each research episode. It is these observations that constitute the raw material for subsequent analysis. In each instance the emphasis in both qualitative and empirical work is on entering observations into journals and notebooks while the details of each research episode are still fresh. This freshness is central to qualitative analysis and central to the needs of the methods section in empirical theses for only in this way can the necessary detail be provided for other researchers to replicate a study.

2. The importance of research notes to both empirical and qualitative researchers also serves to blur another distinction between them. While it is usually true that there is, in qualitative as opposed to empirical research, no temporal distinction between data collection and analysis, the distinction should not be taken too far. This is because it is often a useful strategy for empirical researchers to start writing the results section as data is collected. Doing so makes writing the section easier because the events are still fresh. It can also help make the research process more effective for the drawing of preliminary tables, charts and graphs might enable possible trends and gaps to be identified and followed up while the research is still in progress.

10.14 DEGREE OF DETAIL REQUIRED: MATERIALS

1. When research involves any non-human life form it is necessary, at a minimum, to provide the species and genus. It might also be necessary to provide details such as strain, breeding origins, collection site/s and culture conditions. The scientific name of a species should always be italicised. Bold font may also be used in addition to italics at first mention of a species. The first letter of the genus should always be in upper case, the species name always in lower case: *Laccospadix australasica*. The common name of a species can be used in preference to the scientific name only if the scientific name is given in full, together with the authority, when the common name is first used: *Laccospadix australasica* L. (Atherton palm). Even if the initialised scientific name (G. aculeatus) is used in preference to the common name it is normally useful to include the common name, if there is one, at first mention of the scientific name.

2. All non-routine materials should be described in sufficient detail to identify their type and origin: *Standard rodent food pellets (Lopis rodent mix, United Kingdom) were supplied…* This also applies to non-standard equipment:

We used a portable spectroradiometer (SPECTATOR S1000, Ocean Optics, Inc., Dunedin, Florida) to analyze color…Our spectroradiometer was interfaced with a laptop on which the C–SPEC colour-analysis software program (Ancal, Inc., Las Vegas, Nevada) was installed. An LS–1 Tungsten Halogen Light Source (Ocean Optics) was used as the standard light source during the study.

(Krupa & Geluso, 2000, p.89)

(Full descriptions can absorb a lot of space in a thesis, so it is often better to use illustrations, diagrams or photographs of specially adapted equipment to supplement textual description.) Because different models of standard equipment might perform differently, even equipment in common use might also need specific identification. Similarly standard materials should be identified where, for example, place of origin might affect performance: *Streptozotocin (STZ) (Sigma Chemical Company, St Louis, USA) solutions were prepared…* The details of how equipment was used during the data collection process will need to be detailed if there is any possibility it might be used differently during replication:

Before collection of data, the spectroradiometer was turned on and allowed to warm to a constant temperature for 3 h. The LS–1 light source pulsed light into the fiber-optic cable, and light was emitted from the end of the cable. This light was reflected off the sample's surface…at a 90° angle, absorbed by the fiber-optic cable, and returned to the spectroradiometer for processing. Resulting data were stored as a separate computer file for each…for future processing

(Krupa & Geluso, 2000, p.89).

The reasons for, and details of, any modifications made to the equipment should also be provided:

To prevent introducing…error in our study, the end of a black plastic cap from a ball-point pen was cut, leaving a 5 mm opening, and the end of the fiber-optic cable was inserted into the opposite end of the cap until it fitted snugly against sides of the cut end, which was tapered…With the cut end of the black cap touching the sample, we were confident that no outside light contaminated the sample.

(Krupa & Geluso, 2000, p.89)

10.15 DEGREE OF DETAIL REQUIRED: INSTRUMENTS

1. Supervisors will carefully scrutinise any instrument, even if already validated, before it is applied to a research population. If a purpose-designed instrument

(a test, survey or interview protocol, for example) was developed the need for such an instrument should be explained and a description provided of how it was developed and its validity and reliability established:

There is no existing instrument that provides a standard against which the present questionnaire could be compared, nor is there an instrument that covers similar concepts. Therefore, the validation procedures were focussed on content and construct validation.

(Kung, 2001, p.114)

Keep in mind, though, that instrument validation is not a task to be undertaken lightly for the process may be more involved than initially supposed (Bryant, 2004). A possible means to avoid a lengthy and complex validation process is to approach the Buros Institute, a valuable source of validated instruments. Another approach to instrument validation is the literature: using verified and published data might save a great deal of time (Mauch & Birch, 1998). In each case, though, data should be gathered in a focused and explicit way for, as when reviewing the literature, parsimony is better than drowning in a deluge of peripheral material (Mauch & Birch, 1998).

2. While all purpose-designed instruments should be piloted prior to their application in a primary study, even existing instruments might need to be piloted in order to ensure, for example, that the instructions, the questions and, if used, the scale items are clear:

Modification of the questionnaire took place after a pilot survey (see Appendix 1)… of a representative group of participants revealed resistance to questions relating to income. Further refinements were made after consultation with my supervisors.

Certainly, no instrument should be applied to a research population until it has been approved by the supervisor/s[1]. In addition to indicating how the sample for the pilot was obtained and explaining why it was considered representative of the sample in the primary study, so too will the procedures used to define and identify the sample for the primary study also need to be discussed:

To obtain a representative sample, an invitation (Appendix 3) to participate in the survey was sent to each employee on the company's mailing list. As an incentive, participation included entry to a draw for a $60 book voucher. This strategy, recommended by Fielding (2005), proved to be effective because, within five days, 205 positive responses were received… Once each participant completed the survey, a follow-up e-mail message was sent. The note, in addition to thanking each employee for their participation, asked them to forward the original invitation to a fellow employee. This snowball sampling yielded a further 50 *participants. This brought the total responses to 255 which was more than the approximately 180 out of 500 that had initially been expected.*

(Adapted from Bienvenu, 2004, p.46)

Ethics committees might consider the offer of an inducement, particularly to a materially deprived community, as problematic. Quite apart from the ethical issues involved, inducements can skew the findings of surveys. Therefore, if an inducement is offered its possible effects on the outcome of the study will need to be discussed. It will, in any event, be necessary to indicate what measures have been implemented to minimise the particular types of bias to which a survey might have been vulnerable: 'The impact of refusal bias was minimised due to the high response rate achieved' (Zeits, 2003, p.116).

3. Response rates are fundamental to the success of a survey and the reasons for the response rate, whether high or low, will need to be provided. If the response rate was low examiners will expect a detailed discussion of the implications of the low rate upon the findings of the study. Because it is unlikely they will accept a low rate was unexpected, they will also expect to see the details of the mechanisms that were put in place to overcome a possible low response rate:

The recommendations made by Miller (2005, pp.150–1) to assist in achieving a high response rate to postal surveys were incorporated into the design of the survey. These recommendations include a respondent friendly questionnaire, supported by an accompanying letter explaining the purpose of the study...

10.16 DEGREE OF DETAIL REQUIRED: PROCEDURES

1. The experimental method requires a hypothesis for a causal relationship, clear definition of key terms and variables and the elimination of as many confounding variables as possible:

In order to increase the focus of the current study, I chose to exclude those patients with previous incidence of psychological problems and substance abuse in order to reduce the effect of the confounding variables on the outcome.

Because the control of error is central to the success of experimental studies the means to measure each variable will need to be indicated and evidence that measurements are valid and reliable provided. All relevant details, therefore, will need to be included:

Chromosomal DNA was denatured by incubating the slides in 70% formamide; 2x standard saline citrate (SSC) for 2 min at 70°C and passing through an ethanol series (70%, 90%, and 100%), with the 70% at −20°C. Slides were air dried.

(Gosden & Lawson, 1994, p.935)

If controls were used they should be identified by indicating what they were controlling for: *As a control for the temperature change, we placed the same amount of solute in the same amount of solvent, and let the solution stand for five minutes.* Inadequate descriptions might elicit a comment similar to the following from an examiner: 'Has not demonstrated to me that they [sic] have sufficient understanding of experimental design' (Lovat et al., 2002, p.15).

2. Thus, in order to satisfy examiners as well as researchers who may subsequently attempt to replicate the study, a step-by-step description of the procedures adopted, together with the amount of time devoted to each, will be necessary. These steps will vary according to type of procedure but, for example, if participants are involved in a true experiment assurances will need to be provided that they have been randomly assigned to experimental and control groups. (In quasi-experimental studies, unlike true experiments, subjects either cannot be assigned randomly or control groups cannot be used.) What each group experienced during each step of the research process will then usually need to be described sequentially. In this case the description will need to start from the participants' initial contact with the researcher through to the post-experiment debriefing. Descriptions of all instructions given and documents used will also need to be provided: letters of introduction; consent forms; verbatim instructions and debriefing statements, for example. (Copies of these documents will also usually need to be included as appendices.) In most cases a justification for the protocol adopted will need to be included as will an explanation why possible alternatives were rejected. Bear in mind that self-designed procedures especially are subject to scrutiny by examiners (Rowarth & Fraser, 2006). (If accounts of particular procedures are lengthy it might be advisable to place the detail in an appendix rather than disturb the flow of the text in the methods section.)

10.17 DEGREE OF DETAIL REQUIRED: PARTICIPANTS

1. Qualitative research requires direct connectedness between the researcher and the individuals involved in a study. In action research, for example, researchers might forgo a leadership role in order to improve the quality of the bond between themselves and the research participants. For this reason the hierarchy explicit in the terms 'researcher' and 'research subject' is avoided by use of the term 'research participant'. While in experimental psychology, particularly in regard to statistical terms, the word subject is still considered appropriate (*Publication Manual of the APA*, 2010, p.73) the adoption of a more nuanced interpretation of objectivity has also led many empirical researchers to write about people involved in a study in a manner that acknowledges their participation. Sensitivity also requires all researchers to avoid the implication

of personal shortcomings on the part of research participants: *Ten participants did not complete the questionnaire*, is preferable, for example, to: *Ten participants failed to complete the questionnaire* (Publication Manual of the APA, 2010).

Sampling

2. Because, in all studies, the manner in which research participants were selected will need to be indicated, the type of random and/or non-random sampling[2] used will need to be justified. But take care to be specific when doing so. The following extract, for example, while correctly defining the nature of purposeful sampling, is too diffuse because it does not indicate which of the many types of purposeful sampling is being referred to: *The method of recruitment was by purposeful sampling, a technique that allows the selection of participants who are knowledgeable about… and are willing to share their experiences.* A more adequate description should resemble the following on theoretical sampling, the selection procedure applied in grounded theory:

In theoretical sampling the actual number of 'cases' studied is relatively unimportant. What is important is the potential of each 'case' to aid the researcher in developing theoretical insights into the area of social life being studied. After completing interviews with several informants, you would consciously vary the type of people interviewed until you had uncovered the full range of perspectives held by the people in whom you are interested. You would have an idea that you had reached this point when interviews with additional people yielded no genuinely new insights. Adopting a theoretical sampling approach facilitates the generation of the full range and variation in a category. Also, as a category is being developed in this manner it is constantly tested against new data as it is collected. A particular strategy utilized in this regard is that of seeking out negative cases in order to disprove hypotheses and thus further refine emerging theory.

(Taylor & Bogdon, 1984 cited in O'Donoghue, 2007, p.60)

Non-random sampling strategies like theoretical sampling are normally used in qualitative studies. Truly random sampling, though difficult to achieve in practice, is often an ideal strategy in empirical studies because each member of a population has an equal chance of selection. However, appropriate sampling strategy depends on the needs of particular studies. For example, because the selection of different individuals for each aspect of a mixed method study might threaten validity, a type of random sampling might be applied to the qualitative element in order to make the empirical and qualitative data more comparable (Creswell & Plano Clark, 2007).

3. While both qualitative and empirical researchers will need to provide the reasons for the sample selected: *Focusing on a small community allowed the*

researcher to…; empirical researchers will need to take particular care to indicate the measures taken to minimise sampling errors: the difference between the sample and the target population it estimates. In the following extract a journal editor criticises this element in an article submitted for publication:

It is based on a very small, and rather unbalanced, sample—only 20 per cent by my reckoning followed through to the classroom observation. This, then, may be a self-selected sample given to a certain mode of response by their willingness to contribute. Yet the authors still claim their sample to be representative of a whole population.

(Cited in Woods, 2006, p.140)

4. Bias, unlike random sampling error, cannot be estimated. Neither can an increase in sample size reduce the effect. The criteria employed to include or exclude participants will, therefore, need to be clearly presented and justified. This often means that analytic variables like age, ethnicity, gender, height, weight or class will need to be provided. Generally, though, where the sampling strategy is appropriate and properly applied the errors introduced into the sample by chance are reduced or eliminated by adequate sample size. But, bear in mind a large sample can produce statistical significance for a small effect while a small sample even with a relatively large effect may result in a non-significant finding (Creswell & Plano Clark, 2007). Data dispersion rather than numbers, therefore, is what should be noted. When measuring physical characteristics like height or weight, for example, no single instance no matter the size of the sample will significantly change the aggregate. But, when a social quality like wealth is measured one observation can disproportionately impact the aggregate (Taleb, 2007).

10.18 ETHICS APPROVAL

1. It is not only social scientists engaged in ethnographic work or researchers in other fields who deal with humans or animals to whom the requirement to work ethically applies. Exegetic researchers, for example, frequently confront ethical dilemmas when dealing with private texts never intended for publication. In fact, researchers in all fields who use respect, integrity and benevolence as guiding principles in their work (Denholm, 2006) find there is enough elasticity in the practical application of these principles to give rise to real moral difficulties. The problem, in essence, is no matter how carefully implemented some degree of harm might come to the subjects of research and all research to a degree is appropriated no matter how participatory the design. The questions then become how much harm and how much

appropriation is ethically acceptable? These are not easy questions to answer.

2. Where approval from a university ethics committee is required there might also be need for clearance from other interested bodies as well: medical health boards, ethnic communities or cultural organisations, for example. That such approvals were provided will need to be indicated in the methods section and the documentary proof will usually need to be placed as an appendix to the thesis: *Approval was granted for two experimental protocols: 1) Hormonal regulation of hepatic glucose production (Ethics approval no B24/05. See Appendix 2.)...* Universities require ethics approval irrespective of where a study is to be conducted. If, for example, research is proposed on ancient artefacts in another country ethics approval from the university in addition to approval from the relevant foreign authorities will usually be needed. When an application for ethics approval for an aspect of the study has been rejected the reasons for the rejection will need to be explained in the thesis. Do not simply write: *Ethics approval from...could not be obtained for various reasons.* Ethics approvals are not retrospective. They can also, particularly when permission is required from authorities other than the university, take months to process. The length of time it will take to receive approval should, therefore, be included in the initial planning schedule of the study. Ideally, and it can be achieved with effective forward planning, all necessary ethics approvals should be in place at the start of a research project.

3. If a study involves human participants the researcher will need, in the ethics application, to detail how and when informed consent will be obtained. In addition, copies of the relevant consent forms will need to be included in the ethics application and, subsequently, as an appendix in the thesis. (Both empirical and qualitative researchers should not consider the provision of informed consent as a single act but as a process: participants need to be reassured frequently during a study that, within a reasonable timeframe, they are free to withdraw consent.) Satisfactory evidence will also need to be provided to the ethics committee that the anonymity of the participants in the study will be preserved. Because anonymity does not necessarily prevent identification, the committee will also need to be satisfied that participants will be safe from identification. (Preventing identification can be particularly difficult when interviews are videotaped or, for example, if the setting for a study is a small, specialised hospital unit. In such cases ethics committees might reject a research application even though anonymity has been assured.)

4. An issue related to the guaranteed anonymity of research participants and to their freedom from identification, is confidentiality. An undertaking will need to be made to the satisfaction of the ethics committee, and to the participants in the research, that all information about the participants and all information provided by them, will (unless the participants have agreed otherwise) remain

confidential. (This undertaking should be provided to the participants in the consent form and generally includes a provision that all confidential material, documents, notes, tapes, videos, photographs and transcripts, for example, will remain in a secure location. The usual period they remain there is between five to six years after which time they will generally need to be destroyed by an ethics committee approved process.[3]) Be aware, though, that confidentiality is not an unproblematic issue. If, for example, research uncovers instances of mental or physical abuse or other crimes researchers may be bound ethically and legally to reveal such information to the relevant authorities. Insert a clause in the consent form to this effect should there be a possibility of such instances being revealed.

5. If fictitious names (of people, places and/or institutions) have been used in a study the choices made should not carry connotations: Mr Megaphone, for example (Woods, 2006). A statement to the effect that names are fictitious will need to be provided in the text of the thesis. However, using fictitious names for individuals before analysis and in the early drafts of the thesis can lead to confusion. Particularly in the case of qualitative studies, fictitious names can also impede analysis because substitute names tend to depersonalise people. It is often wise, therefore, only to fictionalise names in the final draft of a thesis.

10.19 QUALITATIVE ANALYSIS

1. Until about the mid-1990s qualitative theses frequently included lengthy sections explaining the nature and purpose of qualitative research. This was a lingering reflection of what, until then, had been the alterative status of the approach. Such explanations are historical curiosities and, thus, are no longer necessary (Bryant, 2004). Nonetheless, explanations of the specific steps and procedures adopted in particular approaches to qualitative research are required. There are, for example, many types of interviews and modes of interview analysis. Interviews, of individuals or of groups, can broadly be categorised as structured, semi-structured, and unstructured. In turn, each of these categories incorporates numerous subtypes. The semi-structured category, for example, includes focused interviews, semi-standardised interviews, expert interviews and ethnographic interviews. Do not, therefore, simply write in a thesis: Interviews were conducted… Instead, the types of interviews and modes of analysis adopted will need to be justified and explained.

2. In qualitative, unlike empirical research, data[4] collection and data analysis are not usually temporally discrete. Instead, as in grounded research, data collection and analysis inform one another in a cyclical process of development. Theory, in this context is emergent. So, while theory explaining the adoption of particular methods will be presented, as in the case of exegetic and

empirical theses, in the introduction to a qualitative thesis, the analysis of the research data will often not be conducted in the methods section. It will, instead, be carried out in the subsequent chapters as the exploration unfolds. Where this is the case the methods section, by explaining the theory and mechanics of the analytic process, is often used to provide an explanatory context for the subsequent analyses. However, process and analysis are also often not discrete:

…it is somewhat artificial to separate the analysis phase from the writing phase in this project. Others have acknowledged the blurred boundaries between these phases of work. It has been observed that it is often not clear when the writing of the study begins… Writing itself is an iterative process of discovery, analysis and reporting … making it inappropriate to strictly dichotomize storytelling and story analysis…

(Cited in Wall & Shankar, 2008, p.555)

But, as in the case of many mixed methods undertakings, it might be necessary to conduct the qualitative analysis in the methods section. Where, for example, focused interviews are followed by a survey, the interviews need to be analysed in the methods section because the findings will be used to guide the construction and implementation of the survey. Each research undertaking, of course, has its own requirements. However, because qualitative findings often allow mixed methods researchers to identify issues appropriate for empirical investigation, it is usual for qualitative approaches to precede the application of empirical ones. This is not always the case, though, so placing one approach prior or subsequent to another will need to be explained.

3. As in all approaches to research the explanations provided need to be as detailed as possible if comments such as the following are to be avoided:

We do not know how long the interviews lasted, where they took place, how they were recorded. There are no extracts given from these interviews… the observations are claimed to be 'naturalistic', but we do not know how long the researchers spent in the school, how many lessons were observed, and how observations were noted. There seems to be an assumption that you can walk into a lesson and observe 'natural' behaviour. Some qualitative researchers spend years gaining entry, in the interests of penetrating the outer layers of reality to the innermost meanings. There is no attempt to do that here. Validity therefore is suspect.

(Cited in Woods, 2006, p.140)

Among other relevant detail, the provision for entering the field will, therefore, need to be provided. In addition the role of key informants will need to be described: *She was very informative and comfortable with me sharing the office with her. This allowed me to construct a much clearer picture of…* The means used to record the research material together with the reasons why they were used should also be indicated: *Video cameras were used in order to go beyond the words reporting actions to allow the direct analysis of the actions themselves.* How the material was prepared should then be explained: *Full verbatim transcriptions from the video and audio-tapes were prepared for analysis.* Bear in mind that transcription of interviews from either video or audio equipment involves two levels of abstraction: that lost in the recording process and that subsequently lost in the process of transcription.

An interview is a live social interaction where the pace of the temporal unfolding, the tone of the voice and the bodily expressions are immediately available to the participants in the face-to-face conversation, but are not accessible to the out-of-context reader of the transcript.

(Kvale, 2007, p.93)

4. Moreover, except in the case, for example, of either conversation or discourse analysis it is usually acceptable to render dialects, hesitations and digressions into more easily readable text.[5] Two reasons explain why. First, verbatim transcripts can make reading difficult and tiring: *hm ... hmm ... well, you–know, yup.* Second, respondents might object to transcripts that make them appear incoherent and confused (Kvale, 2007). How readability was enhanced will, though, need to be explained. In the following extract, for example, a researcher indicates how she edited focus group transcripts:

...potentially identifying information...was altered, taken to a higher level of generality, or deleted. For readability, common but distracting components of speech such as 'ah', 'um', 'you know', 'I mean', 'I think', and 'sort of' were deleted from the quotations that appear in the text unless they were particularly meaningful. Discrepancies in grammar were not corrected. False sentence starts were frequently deleted... In most instances, ellipses (...) are not used to indicate these deletions.

(Cited in Lovitts, 2007, p.14)

5. Nonetheless, if transcripts are edited care will need to be taken for subsequent reading of the original words might allow reinterpretation of an apparent meaning into its opposite. When direct transcriptions of recordings including, for example, hesitations and increases in volume need to be made, the conventions and symbols used should be described clearly. For example: [ ] indicates overlapping speech; (0 3) pauses, in seconds; underlined words indicate stress or emotion; UPPER CASE indicates increase in volume. In most cases every interview conducted or observation made will need to be cited. For example: (Obs. 24; site 3, Sept 4, 2009) (Thody, 2006). When pseudonyms are not used the names of participants should be provided in

261

full at first mention and then only the first or surnames need to be used. To ensure polyvocality as many voices as possible should be included in the transcripts. These can mix summaries with direct and reported speech together with, for example, indications of anguish or laughter: *Greg howled out, 'Yesss!' between the laughter.* As much of the atmosphere in which the interviews or observations took place should, in other words, be conveyed: 'nothing conveys the sense of "being there" more than the actual words of the participants' (Angrosino, 2007, p.41). When reporting group interviews the opinions expressed should be summarised. However, also indicating the manner in which individuals in the group responded to opinions will help provide texture to the summaries (Thody, 2006).

6. The application of all methods in qualitative research requires reflexivity. Placing a hyphen in inter-view, for example, clearly indicates the two way reflexive aspect of interviews and why the term resonates with inter-subjectivity and inter-textuality (Schostak, 2006). But, auto-ethnographies aside, when taken too far reflexivity can result in researcher dominance[6]: the research is in 'danger of becoming more about me than about a social phenomenon of which I am part' (Thody, 2006, p.29). This is not the only careful balance qualitative researchers need to maintain. While, as ethnographers, they are not expected to renounce their own cultural affiliations they ought not to project those values onto participants (Marshall & Rossman, 2006). The analysis of research material indicates this is no easy task. Apart from discourse and conversation analysis, most qualitative research material needs to be distilled prior to analysis. Reading and rereading the material permits researchers to become intimately familiar with it thus facilitating the process of distillation (Marshall & Rossman, 2006). Nonetheless, the fact that some accounts are included, some summarised and some omitted indicates choices are being made. This implies that at least part of the analysis is of text constructed by the researcher (Punch, 2006). This is the context in which *selective plausibilization* might become an issue: the analysis of interview material rests entirely upon the evidence of carefully selected quotations but there might be a significant body of contradictory evidence in the interview transcriptions that has not been quoted. This, in turn, raises the question of the *credibility* of qualitative analyses: are the interpretations made or patterns revealed actually reflected in the research material? The answer to this question lies in the adequacy of the responses made to a number of additional questions. Can research participants identify with the analysis?[7] Have alternative explanations been explored? Have the research findings been triangulated with material from other sources? Selective plausibilization also raises the question of the *dependability* of qualitative research. Qualitative

research cannot, by definition, be replicated. Instead, making as transparent as possible the processes that allowed interpretations to be made and patterns to be revealed indicates the dependability of the analysis. (A particular problem when codes are used to analyse text is 'definitional drift'. Analytic inconsistency might result unless guarded against by constant checking against the original definitions applied [Gibbs, 2007].)

7. In empirical studies analytic categories are usually stipulated prior to the conduct of a study. Some qualitative research might reflect this approach but it is usual for patterns, themes, and categories to be discovered either during or after data collection (Marshall & Rossman, 2006). Qualitative researchers are usually, therefore, interpreters who begin the process of analysis by generating, comparing and clustering concepts through a process of constant comparison into meaningful themes. Categorisation schemes and corresponding codes are then developed from the themes so as to identify patterns between them:

The analysis consisted of two parts: first, to organise and subdivide the data into meaningful segments, and second, the interpretive process of determining the criteria for organising the data into conceptual categories, based on coding of the data through active searches for consistent patterns.

(Kung, 2001, p.151)

It is the saturation of these categories that draws the analytic process to a close: no matter how much new data is collected saturation indicates the categories cannot be developed further (O'Donoghue, 2007). In order to indicate the unfolding process leading to saturation the research material must be presented in a manner that makes clear the distinction between material and interpretation. Together, but distinct from one another, research material and interpretation, provide an 'audit trail' that explains each step of the interpretive process. By securely retaining the research material in retrievable form the dependability of the research is enhanced for the data will be available for scrutiny should there be a challenge to any part of the analysis (Marshall & Rossman, 2006). When ethical considerations allow, this can be taken a step further by including the transcriptions of the research material either in hardcopy as an appendix to the thesis or in a CD inserted into a folder on the back cover. In the latter case aspects of the material can be made more quickly accessible via hyperlinks. Finally any prior review of the study by participants, by key informants or by those funding the research will need to be mentioned if, in any way, they limited the autonomy of the researcher to present relevant material in the thesis.

10.20 STATISTICAL ANALYSIS

1. If treated statistically, empirical research data will be analysed in the methods section, described in the results section, and interpreted in the discussion section. While the manner in which the data are formatted in each of these sections will depend on the needs of the study and the requirements of the referencing system used, the measures applied to assess the validity of the research remain constant: the quality of data collection, the quality of the methods applied, the appropriateness and clarity of analytical procedures, the suitability of the parameters for determining significance and the analysis of the effects of the limitations and delimitations in the design of the study (Bryant, 2004). Care will also need to be taken to define, establish the integrity of, and specify the interrelationship between each of three categories of variable: the independent or predictor variable; the dependent or outcome variable and the control variable. In doing so possible confounding variables will need to be identified and their potential to affect the internal validity of the study assessed. But making these identifications and assessments is often a fraught and difficult task. Surmounting them requires recognition of two issues central to the successful application of statistical measures. The first is the importance of a pilot study. The second is that statistics is a discipline in its own right. This accounts for the tension between a specialist statistician's interpretation of research data and that of researchers for whom statistics is a secondary skill. It is this tension that raises the question about what skills are central to a study and which optional (Rugg & Petrie, 2004). The use of a statistical package like PASW (formerly SPSS), for example, carries with it a responsibility to explain the reasons why particular procedures were appropriate, what limits and conditions apply, how the variables relate to each other and what the results mean in real terms. But, while researchers must accept responsibility for everything in a thesis, they will not, unless in the disciplines of mathematics or statistics, be expected to trace the derivation of the formulas applied (Rowarth & Fraser, 2006). This explains why knowing that a qualified statistician had been consulted from the outset of a study reassures examiners. It also reassures those doctoral candidates undergoing an oral examination for the statistician can assist in preparing for it (Rowarth & Fraser, 2006). This assistance can be important for candidates might be asked not only why a particular analytic approach was adopted but also what the outcome might have been had another approach been used (Rowarth & Fraser, 2006). The legitimacy of these questions is rooted both in the level of expertise examiners expect of a candidate and in the fact that hypotheses may usually be tested in more ways than one. The best method will be a consequence of the details of the research design and the purpose of the study. In this context

the following applies: 'oral exams have been halted, and the candidate asked to remember, rewrite and resubmit, on the aspect of statistical analysis alone' (Rowarth & Fraser, 2006, p.214).

2. Not only thesis writers, but supervisors too might not have the statistical expertise necessary for particular research undertakings. However, one of the ironies of research is that it can be problematic for an expert to conduct the analysis: it is not possible for anyone else, irrespective of their expertise, to understand the subtleties of what a researcher is looking for in the way that he or she does (Burton, 2004). Apart from the intrinsic idiosyncrasy of individual studies, at least one of the reasons for this is that the way in which statistics are used and the manner in which they are expressed not only varies between disciplines but also between research approaches. But the primary reason why engaging the services of an expert in statistics often becomes problematic is because sound statistical analysis cannot be conducted on the results of poorly or inappropriately designed research. A frequent mistake beginning researchers make is to implement lengthy and labour intensive schemes of data collection only to discover the data are not suitable for the purposes of the study (Ingleby, 2007). Another frequent mistake, once the research has begun, is to enter data in a way that prevents effective analysis. Re-entering data correctly can be a frustrating and time consuming process. Significance levels[8] and sample sizes can also be based on mistaken assumptions. For example, while the level of acceptable significance depends on the norms of a discipline (Cryer, 2006) a low setting might indicate the hypothesis would have been rejected had it been set higher (Fairbairn & Winch, 1996). This is one of the reasons accounting for a shift in the social sciences away from emphasis on statistical significance to emphasis on reporting effect[9] sizes (Teddlie & Tashakkori, 2003a).

3. The ideal sample size will vary depending on the study type: data driven or concept or method testing. Not only will increased size not transform bad data into good, but excessively large sample sizes can, in fact, indicate poor experimental design and inadequate knowledge of statistics (Rugg & Petre, 2004). It is often possible, in fact, for an experienced statistician to work out statistically in advance how big a sample should be to fulfil the requirements of a particular study (Rugg & Petre, 2004).[10] Preventive steps could be taken to ensure a study does not fall victim to unnecessary errors in design and analysis. A three-pronged strategy will normally suffice. First, develop as much relevant statistical expertise as possible and, second, consult as many relevant, successfully completed theses as possible. Third, if available, seek informed advice from someone who has the necessary expertise in statistics and who is working in a similar disciplinary, interdisciplinary or mixed method field. If such advice can be given from the design stage of a study through to its conclusion so much the better for,

like the researcher, expert statisticians will gradually become sensitive to the particularities of a study. If that individual is also a supervisor of the study researchers are fortunate indeed. The need for this type of consistent advice from individuals who have expertise in particular fields is one of the reasons explaining joint supervision.

4. If research described in the methods section involves measurement of hypothetical constructs, happiness or depression for example, operational definitions will need to be provided to indicate how they were measured. Even when these definitions involve the use of pre-existing scales, the validity and reliability of the scales will need to be indicated. Start the analysis by re-stating the research questions or hypotheses and deal with each in turn. Doing so will provide immediate direction to the analysis and ensure that each element of the hypotheses or questions is addressed. It also helps to prevent a common cause for the delayed submission of theses: the over-analysis of data and a consequent loss of coherence (Cryer, 2006).

Programmed computers opened new possibilities, because they could execute long sequences of instructions at high speeds. Suddenly it was possible to explore models that were orders of magnitude more complex. This blessing also entailed a curse: you could run amok in detail, to the point that you would lose all possibility of uncovering overarching principles.

(Holland, 1998, p.17)

An effective antidote to over-analysis is both to define the research hypotheses and questions as clearly as possible and to write the results section during, not after, analysis. Statistical terms that might be misunderstood should also be defined: *age-specific*, for example, as opposed to *age-adjusted rates*. All hypotheses that influenced the way the analysis was conducted should be included: *Paired t-tests were used to compare … All data were normally distributed. We had a priori prediction that…. should closely match…., thus one-tailed t-tests were used with P < 0.05*. Although cautions on the interpretation of the data will normally be presented in the discussion section, they might also need to be mentioned in the methods section in order to place elements of the analysis in context: *Incidence and mortality rates have been calculated using population estimates released by the… These differ from the population estimates used in reports published prior to 2005*. Because each statistical measure has its own sensitivities and blind spots, the analytic method/s used to examine each hypothesis or answer each question will need to be explained and fully justified. But, although full details of the type of statistical analyses performed should be provided, the actual statistical analyses need only be indicated briefly. If, however, any were unusual it might be necessary to include the full analysis in an appendix. The source of any specialist computer software will need to be indicated and if software was especially developed for the study it may be necessary to include a non-rewritable CD copy of the program with the thesis. In order to allow both examiners and other researchers to verify the analysis, raw data may also need to be placed on a CD and included with the thesis. In any event the data (including the data from the pilot) should, as in the case of material secured for ethical reasons, be kept in a safe place usually for at least five years.

10.21 CONCLUSION

1. When full justice has been done to the methods section, a glowing comment like the following can be expected from an examiner:

Overall the chapter is thoroughly written and based on wide and careful study of the literature on research methodologies. All aspects of methodology and analysis are justified in depth. The care and attention to detail that went into the study are truly impressive, especially given the complex and multifaceted nature of the research.

(Holbrook & Dally, 2003, p.13)

ENDNOTES

---

1 Normally copies of all purpose–designed instruments should be placed as an appendix to the thesis, as should any modifications to existing instruments. If permission was required to use an instrument the document indicating such permission was granted should also be placed as an appendix.

2 Stratified, cluster, quota and spatial sampling, for example, in empirical research, and theoretical, extreme case, typical case and maximal variation in qualitative approaches.

3 Authors of manuscripts accepted for publication in APA journals are required to have their raw data available throughout the editorial review process and for at least five years after the date of publication. (This includes instructions, treatment manuals, software and details of procedures.) *Publication Manual of the American Psychological Association,* 2010, p.240

4 The term 'data' implies numeric outcomes. In qualitative research, however, words are central because they convey the subjective perspectives of research participants and researchers. This explains why some qualitative researchers prefer to use the term research 'material' rather than 'data'.

5 There are different levels of transcription: 'Just the gist', for example, where ellipses indicate omitted speech; Verbatim without dialect; Verbatim with dialect; and Discourse level transcription (Gibbs, 2007).

6 In most qualitative strategies and methods researchers attempt to start from a perspective as free from preconception as possible. Maintaining empathic neutrality is the process of *epoché*. In participatory action research, though, researchers are not neutral for their purpose is advocacy and social and political change (Marshall & Rossman, 2006).

7 Member checking, one of the most important techniques for establishing research credibility, has at least two versions: strong, where respondents evaluate the final report and weak where respondents comment on the accuracy of an interim document such as an interview transcript (Flick, 2007, p.33).

8 A difference is statistically significant if a test has indicated the difference is greater than might be expected by chance alone. This does not, though, mean the difference need necessarily be large. Even a small difference can be statistically significant.

9 Effect size is the size difference between groups of participants relative to the differences between individual participants.

10 On the basis of data from a pilot study G*Power freeware can be used to calculate required sample size.

CHAPTER 11

Results

It is easy to lie with statistics, but easier to lie without them.

(Mosteller, F., cited in *Time*, 7 August 2006, p.10)

11.1 INTRODUCTION

1. Raw data (statistical, textual or both) arising from research undertakings, irrespective of their methodological approach, do not possess inherent order, immediate relevance or readily apparent meaning. But the process of providing order, relevance and meaning—converting data to knowledge—does depend upon the methodological approach.

11.2 DISPLAYING QUALITATIVE RESULTS

1. In exegetic and qualitative research the distinction between analysis, description and interpretation is less distinct than in empirical studies. This distinction is evident in the difference in structure between generic exegetic and empirical theses: while the latter make explicit the distinction between method (analysis), description (results) and interpretation (discussion), the lack of a formal structure in the former represents an explicit blurring of any distinction between them. The position in regard to qualitative theses is rather more complex because they do not have a generic format. This is a consequence of 'form following function': the appropriate structure of a qualitative thesis will depend upon the methodology, substance and context of a particular study. Some qualitative theses, therefore, (particularly those conceptually driven) will have an idiosyncratic emergent design (the number of chapters being the result of, not the predestination for, the substance of the thesis) while others (particularly those more thematic) might more closely resemble the structure of empirical theses (Meloy, 2002): 'No other form made sense. I tried doing a more qualitative format but discarded it because it did not leave a sufficient "paper trail" for anyone else to follow' (cited in Meloy, 2002, p.12).

2. In terms of the results section the differences between these two approaches to structuring a qualitative thesis is a reflection of differences in the manner in which data in each are reported. Those with an emergent design have interpretive reporting: the data are interpreted at the point of presentation. But, even though this implies a results section is redundant, care is nonetheless taken to separate data from analysis in order to prevent the researcher's interpretation from becoming too intermingled with the voices of the research participants (Darlington & Scott, 2002). Qualitative theses where the data are reported without simultaneous interpretation usually resemble empirical theses and have a results section. In this case the contents of the section will generally consist of thematic selections of text. (For example, sections headed *Responses Indicating Fear, Responses Indicating Elation* and *Responses Indicating Remorse* are followed by a list of appropriate quotations. Subsequently, in the discussion section, each list is considered as a whole and then compared to the other lists.) To enhance the distinction between data in the results section from that in the discussion some qualitative researchers deliberately avoid using personal pronouns in the former. The material is presented in the results section, in other words, as though it had been collected independently (Golden-Biddle & Locke, 1997). This indicates the frequent challenge, because of the textual rather than numeric nature of qualitative material, of making distinct what should be presented in the results as opposed to the discussion section. Metaphor might assist in responding to the challenge: the interviewer as miner or traveller. The former regards interviews as sites of data collection to be analysed later while the latter sees interviewing and analysis as intertwined aspects of knowledge production (Kvale, 2007). Irrespective of the criteria applied they will need to be justified and explained:

Granted, it was initially hard to separate what needed to go into the results chapter and what needed to go into the discussion. The rule I developed was level of abstraction: That which appeared as cold, clinical description (how many said what) went into the results section; that which was more story-like was included in the discussion section. To reduce the boredom of qualitative data presented in this way and enhance believability, I used a lot of examples and quotes in results, which was a lengthy chapter.

(Cited in Meloy, 2002, p.12)

3. Wherever quotations are used in a qualitative study the following guidelines generally apply:
   - Quotes should relate directly to the text. (Either, for example, enhancing understanding of the respondent's world or of the theory under development.)
   - Quotes should be contextualised. (What question, for example, was it a response to or was it mentioned spontaneously by the respondent?)

- Quotes should be interpreted. (What points, for example, do they support or qualify?)
- Except in specific instances (phenomenological studies, for example), quotes and text should either be in balance or, if unbalanced, text should predominate.
- Quotes should be as brief as possible. If lengthy extracts are unavoidable consider the feasibility of breaking them into smaller sections linked by commentary.
- If a number of respondents make the same point use the most representative of the quotes. If there is a range of views use selected quotes to illustrate the range (Gibbs, 2007).

11.3 SEPARATE OR COMBINED RESULTS AND DISCUSSION SECTIONS?

1. Because of the complexity of the interrelationships between data elements it is rarely possible to hypothesise directly from the data. This explains the logic in empirical and in some qualitative theses of ordering and displaying the analysed data in the results section and discussing and interpreting them in the subsequent discussion section: it not only assists researchers to construct meaning but also allows examiners to understand how that meaning was constructed. In addition, the distinction between the two sections allows examiners to make their own inferences and draw their own conclusions from the data thus enabling them to judge the validity or, in the case of qualitative research, the credibility of a researcher's interpretation.

2. But this logic does not necessarily mean that analysed data should be presented in a chapter distinct from discussion of them. They can, instead, be presented and separately discussed in sub-sections within a combined results and discussion chapter. In empirical theses, for example, each sub-section might have its own tables and figures and, in qualitative studies, separate discussion sub-sections will follow thematic selections. This is often a useful strategy to adopt in empirical masters' theses with short results sections. On the other hand, the complexity of studies with mixed designs often requires a clear separation of results and discussion (Leder & Holliday, 2006). In order to decide how best to present research results in a thesis an additional strategy might also be adopted. Before an empirical researcher knows what he or she has found there will generally be an expectation of what will be found. This implies that in some studies a results section with simulated data can be written at the proposal stage of the research. When this is possible the decision about whether to present the results and discussion sections separately or together will be made much easier (Mauch & Birch, 1998).

271

11.4 WHAT TO INCLUDE AND OMIT

1. The purpose of the results section or sub-sections is to present key research results in an orderly and logical sequence. Notice the word 'key'. When researchers free themselves from the assumption that all the data needs to be selected they make it far easier to choose meaningful data (Garman, 2006). This is why clearly stating the research questions or hypotheses prior to analysing empirical data will help to control the number of analyses run. The consequent smaller volume of analysed data will simplify the organising process and help ensure that the only results presented will be those relevant to each question or hypothesis. In empirical research the presentation of key data is normally achieved using both tables and figures together with textual description. This time notice the word 'description'. The results in an empirical thesis must only be reported and described in the results section or sub-sections, not discussed, interpreted or speculated upon in any way. *I infer…* or *therefore…* usually indicate a discussion so these or similar words should not be used. It is also because a results section or sub-sections are descriptive, not discursive, that there will rarely be need for bibliographic references.

2. The empirical results described should also, with only rare exceptions, be final results. The exceptions might, for example, be single-case designs or illustrative cases. Raw data or intermediate results should be kept in secure storage or presented in appendices. This allows the text in the thesis to remain uncluttered while the subsequent discussion will not be weakened because the raw and intermediate data remain accessible (Anderson & Poole, 1994). Do not omit important negative results. They are not necessarily the consequence of poor research but, rather, often offer both valuable insights and avenues for further investigation. Not only, therefore, might omitting negative results distort the analysis but doing so might also detract from the 'story' of the research, a story that includes both successes and, if they were such, failures. (In some instances in, for example, ongoing studies it might be necessary to incorporate data from earlier parts of the study to ensure completeness of data.)

11.5 THE ORGANISING PRINCIPLE

1. Sequencing the results and discussion sections on the same basis as the methods section can, particularly in empirical theses, enhance the inherent synergy between the methods, results and discussion sections. This can be taken a step further by organising all three sections on the basis of the aims or research questions presented in the introduction chapter. The logic derives from landscape gardening: when any design element is repeated the composition as a whole is understood better. While the ideal of applying a

consistent organising principle to each of these chapters of a thesis, in practice, is often unattainable, the same organising principle should, at a minimum, be applied to both the results and discussion sections. In so far as it is also possible matching the order and wording of subheadings in each section will make it easier for both the researcher and examiners to move back and forth between them.

2. How, though, to order the subheadings? Both empirical and qualitative studies generally produce a far greater body of analysed data than will appear in the final draft of the results section or sub-sections. It is often difficult, therefore, when initially confronting the data to know where to start and easy to succumb to the temptation of trying to include as much as possible. The consequence of doing so in both qualitative and empirical theses is loss of direction. This is usually indicated in the latter by a long and confused sequence of tables and figures. What is needed, therefore, is sufficient data to provide coherence to the description provided but not so much as to disturb its clarity. Both to achieve this balance and to provide logic to the manner in which the data are ordered, a clear idea of the narrative to be presented should be developed. Only in this way will the examiners know where they are being led.

3. There are a number of ways of doing so, chronologically in qualitative studies, for example, or experiment by experiment, in empirical work. But the usual way is to state clearly at the outset of the results section all of the research questions posed or hypotheses proposed in the introduction to the thesis. Doing so has benefits beyond ensuring that each of the questions or hypotheses is addressed. Because the questions posed in joint research projects tend to be peculiar to each researcher, relating the data to each question helps to make distinct the thesis writer's contribution to a project from that of others. In addition, it enables combined results and discussion chapters to be divided into sub-sections: one section with its own heading, description and discussion for each question or hypothesis. Stating each question or hypothesis at the start of the results section will also enable the correct order finally to be established should there have been any doubt in this regard. Because the initial ordering was an implicit indicator of the relative importance of each question or hypothesis, it is disconcerting and confusing if the order is later changed without explanation. If, therefore, there is a change in the order this should be reflected uniformly throughout the thesis and the story of the need to change the order provided in the introduction.

4. At this point, once the order in which the data are to be presented in the results section has been established, it might also be necessary to provide definitions of terms and/or technical notes to assist examiners to understand the interpretation of the data: 'differences between mortality rates cited in this study and rates cited in other studies may be due, at least in part, to choice

of population estimates' or: 'Where relevant the data has been seasonally adjusted…' or: 'In the absence of better data, the flow of… is assumed to be proportional to the…' or 'Death certificates fall under the influence of diagnostic fashions prevailing at the time and place' (Tufte, 2001, p.26).

11.6 THE RELATIONSHIP BETWEEN TABLES, FIGURES AND TEXT

1. The template provided by the ordering of the questions or hypotheses in the results section will not only be mirrored in the discussion section but will also provide logic to the presentation and ordering of tables and figures in the results section itself. This means that tables and figures will need to be compartmentalised in such a way that each group applies to each question or hypothesis. Doing so might not always be possible because it may be necessary, for example, to summarise a number of hypotheses and present the results in one multiple regression. But, in most instances, presenting tables and figures specific to a single question or hypothesis will be more helpful to both the researcher and the examiners than tables and figures that apply to a number of them.

2. Once tables and figures and questions or hypotheses have been matched, the descriptive text the data in the tables and figures will illustrate can be written. There are two reasons why use of the words the data in the tables and figures will illustrate was deliberate. First, every result described in the results section and subsequently interpreted in the discussion section must appear in the tables and figures presented in the results section. Second, although the results of empirical research are primarily numerical, the results section in all theses is primarily text-based: the purpose, in other words, of the tables and figures in the results section is to illustrate the text, if they are not referred to in the text in either the results or discussion sections they should not be there.

3. However, an element of acculturation might be required to overcome, in the first instance, the perceived distinction between text and data and, in the second, to understand how words and illustrations relate to each other. In regard to the former people in contemporary Western society communicate using both words and numbers. But earlier civilisations either, as in the case of the Romans, used some letters of their alphabet to express numbers or, as in the case of the Hebrews and Greeks, gave each letter of their alphabets a numeric value. This meant that each word in Hebrew and Greek also had its own distinctive number or theomatic value. Words, therefore, could be read as numbers and numbers as words. With this in mind tables and graphs should be considered as synonymous with text-based paragraphs, as forms of explanation, and should be treated as such:

Words, graphics, and tables are different mechanisms with but a single purpose–the presentation of information. Why should the flow of information be broken up into different places on the page because the information is packaged one way or another?

(Tufte, 2001, Introduction)

It is in this sense that displays of visual information often have a narrative quality. They tell a story about the data (Canter & Fairbairn, 2006). On the other hand, though, illustrative material and words provide detailed evidence to support a position in ways that differ from and yet complement each other:

Words and images cannot deal with information in the same way; the substrates are not neutral. In many senses, one substrate deals with information that is almost impossible to convey in the other. Rather than translate they only overlap to a degree…

(Smith & Jenks, 2006, p.108)

11.7 WEAVING THE TEXT

1. It is in both senses then that when tables and figures are matched in the results section with each question or hypothesis they should, when scanned without reference to the accompanying text, provide a clear, self-sustained narrative. Examiners might well initiate the examination process by assessing whether this has been achieved. Tables and figures should, thus, be headed and labelled clearly so that examiners, when looking at them, see what the researcher wants them to see without the necessity of referring to the text. Nonetheless, because the results section is primarily textual, the text and accompanying tables and figures will need to be carefully interwoven with each other. The need to do so is to avoid the assumption that any trends, relationships or patterns, for example, indicated in tables and figures will be self-evident to an examiner. The following statement is indicative of this assumption:

    I have noticed that candidates using quantitative data tend to use a few tables in reporting their results as if they speak for themselves and are often reluctant to go back to their raw data for deeper justifications and interpretations of what they found.

    (Leder & Holliday, 2006, p.196)

2. There is a need, therefore, to make trends, relationships, patterns and comparisons explicit in the text. When doing so tables and figures should, whenever possible, run into the text to avoid use of clumsy and diverting phrases like *See Fig.2* (Tufte, 2001, p.181). (Using Fig. in place of Figure is hardly worth the three spaces saved [Tufte, 2001]). Note: (Figure 2) may appear within a sentence but (See for example Figure 2.), or even (See Figure 2.), because they

are complete sentences, should only be placed at the end of a sentence. In terms of punctuation the following is incorrect: *Thanks to remittances extreme poverty has declined despite mediocre economic growth (see Figure 2)*. The correct version should read: *Thanks to remittances extreme poverty has declined despite mediocre economic growth. (See Figure 2.)*

3. Phrases like *Table 2 shows…*, while difficult to avoid, should be used with care because *shows* might be used either to indicate or to inform. For example, *Table 2 shows the common forms of bacteria are…* and *Table 2 provides…* indicate. However, *Table 2 shows the most common form of bacteria is…* informs. *Table 2 gives, suggests, summarises or illustrates* are also informative. Notice the use in each of the active voice, present tense (*Table 2 shows…* as opposed to: *… are shown in Table 2*). This is consistent with the manner in which the results section as a whole should be presented: *In this chapter, the hydrogeological importance of aquitards is considered by…* As is usually the case, however, the simple past tense is sometimes appropriate: *The various units identified in this chapter are indicated in…* One of the stylistic difficulties when writing the results section is repetition of the same sentence format (*Table 2 suggests…; figure 1 shows…*). Although this does make tedious reading, it can be useful in order to enhance clarity to keep the same general sentence structure for all results that share similar characteristics.

4. Writing: *Table 2 shows that…* or: *Figure 1 indicates that…* runs the danger of relying too much on an examiner's ability to see what the researcher wants them to see. So instead, for example, write: *As is apparent in Figure 8 there is a strong positive relationship between number of years of tertiary education completed and income.* But going to the other extreme, by describing in detail the data presented in each table and figure, negates the purpose of having tables and figures. Instead, the text accompanying each table and figure should be limited to a description of the trends and effects, patterns and correlations embedded in each. For this reason data presented in results sections tend to have the following elements: Location and indicative summary (*Figure 3 provides the reasons for current unemployment in the … industry*); followed by highlighting statements (*However, the primary reasons for the current level of unemployment are…*); followed by the implications (*Because these reasons are structural rather than seasonal unemployment will persist for…*). Even when following this template it can be difficult, though, not to stray across the boundary between description and discussion. Ideally introduce a table or figure with text that clearly indicates to the examiners the essence of what they need to see in the data: 'Though the United States has had unprecedented economic growth in the last twenty-five years that has benefited some, most Americans have lost ground' (Booth et al., 2003, p.245). This should then be followed, as in the following, by demarcating the data in the display that provide support for the claim:

Between 1977 and 1999, the top 20 percent of wage earners increased their income by more than 38 percent, and the top 1 percent more than doubled theirs, but the bottom 60 percent of the population earned less in 1999 than they did in 1997.

(Booth et al., 2003, p.246)

This can then be followed with the concise and informative title of the table or figure: *Changes in After-Tax Annual Income 1977–1999*; followed, in turn, by the table or figure in which the results demarcated are made central to its purpose (Booth et al., 2003, p.245). (Should precise numerical values be difficult to extract from a figure they should, when necessary, be provided in the text.)

5. Because data may support or refute statements strongly or by implication the descriptive text in the results section should indicate the nature of the relationship between each statement made and the evidence used to support it. In each case the nature of the relationship should also be considered in the context of any contradictory evidence. Because all statements require at least indicative evidence, unsupported observations should not be made. It is also not usual in the results section to indicate the methods used to obtain data. On occasion, though, it might be necessary to indicate the methods used to collect particular data. If, for example, adaptations were introduced to a standard method (these will need to have been described in the methods section) the specific effects of the changes will need to be indicated in the results section and, usually, in the discussion section as well.

6. It is normally necessary, after having indicated the trends and effects, patterns and correlations that apply to each of the research questions posed and hypotheses proposed, to describe the most important of the overall features revealed in the data that were noteworthy or unexpected. It might even be necessary in some studies to report important incidental findings not immediately related to the central research questions or hypotheses. Providing these descriptive summaries is akin to what is done at the end of a literature review: the wood is distinguished from the trees by bringing to the fore the most important themes in the literature reviewed. There is normally no need, though, to place the summary of the results at the end of the results section. This summary, because of the context it provides, is usually of far more value when placed, instead, at the start of the discussion section.

11.8 NUMBERS, UNITS, SYMBOLS AND SIGNS

1. The publication manuals of, for example, the APA (American Psychological Association), the Council of Scientific Editors, the IEEE (Institute of Electrical and Electronics Engineers), the ACS (American Chemical Society) and the AIP (American Institute of Physics), or the websites of organisations like the

International Committee of Medical Journal Editors, indicate the rules or conventions that apply to their discipline areas in regard to the display of units, numbers, equations and tests. It is important, therefore, that the appropriate source of information on these matters is consulted prior to the start of the research. Because rules and conventions change, ensure that the source consulted is the most recent. (An example of convention change is use of the word data in the singular and plural. Some journal editors in the United States are now requesting this as their preferred use [Garton & McFarlane, 2007].) In the unlikely event that appropriate information about the necessary rules and conventions cannot be sourced a useful alternative is the 'Instructions to Authors' which can be found either on the websites of primary research journals or in the journals themselves. Although the institutions, societies or journals that provide publication guidelines expect their conventions to be adhered to whenever possible, they acknowledge that their conventions cannot cover all eventualities. They do not, therefore, expect slavish adherence to their requirements. What they do uniformly require, though, is consistency. This term should, in fact, become a mantra during the entire thesis writing process.

2. Consistency, however, does not mean uniformity. Take, for example, the presentation of numbers. In a textual statement the APA style as a general rule requires the use of words to express whole numbers up to 10 and numerals for numbers from 10. There are, however, many exceptions and special usages. All dates, sums of money and units of measurement, for example, should be expressed in numerals. (See *Publication Manual of the APA*, 2010, pp. 111–114.) The MLA style, in contrast, suggests that all numbers that can be written in two words or less should be written in words. But, as in the case of the APA style, there are many exceptions and special usages. (See MLA *Handbook for Writers of Research Papers*, 2010, pp. 81–85.) In both styles, though, no sentence should ever start with a number (or abbreviation) because the previous sentence might have ended with one. Dates should be written as 23 May, not 23rd May. Percentages too should also be expressed consistently. In APA style the abbreviation % (per cent) should only be used in tables and figures and in conjunction with numbers written in numerals (*Publication Manual of the APA*, 2010, p.118).

3. There should also be consistency in the use of symbols, signs and abbreviations. The APA Publication Manual provides comprehensive lists of each including statistical abbreviations and symbols (*Publication Manual of the APA*, 2010, pp.119–123). There should also be consistency in the use of units of measurement for it is not easy to make comparisons and easy to make mistakes when data are expressed in different units: *The absorption maximum at site A was at 189 nm while at site B its value was 3270 cm^{-1}*. The metric International System of Units (SI: System Internationale) is the measurement system most commonly used outside the United States. The APA style website (go to Supplemental

Material: Mechanics of Style at www.apastyle.org) provides comprehensive tables of conversion to International System equivalents. Also provided are sets of tables indicating the standardised names, symbols and expressions used in the International System. Do not, therefore, use l or 1 instead of L for litre except in the case of ml. SI units remain the same when used in both the singular and plural (1 ml and 10 ml) and are not followed by a full stop. When including a measure of variability, place the unit after the error value: 10 ± 2.3 m. Where there is a series of numbers of the same unit, place the unit after the last number: *…lengths of 5, 10, 15, and 20 m* (Bates College, 2007, np).

11.9 DESCRIBING STATISTICAL DATA

1. Because it is generally safe to assume that examiners will have a sound knowledge of statistics, there is usually no need to describe basic procedures. As the following comment by an examiner indicates there is, though, a need to indicate basic statistical information:

   I strongly urge theses advisors to get their students to use standard deviations and to show confidence limits henceforth. They should at least insist on exact p values, so that others can work out the confidence limits.

   (Lovat & Morrison, 2003, p.5)

   There might also be need to justify the appropriateness of a particular test should it have been applied in circumstances out of the usual. In the results section emphasis should fall on the descriptions provided rather than on statistical treatments. Try, therefore, to limit the number of statistical references in the text by indicating them, instead, in the legends of tables and figures. When presented in legends or in the text they should always be presented in the following order: test used; statistic-value; degrees of freedom (df) and the probability of the statistic for the df. But again, because emphasis needs to be placed on the textual description, these particulars should, whenever possible, be placed after the descriptive statement: *Female mice were significantly larger than males (two-tailed t-test, t=6.74, P<0.05).* The effect upon the placement of emphasis when statistical information is presented either first or last can be seen in the following examples. The first emphasises the statistic: When *plotted on an X-Y plot, plums from… and…are different.* The second emphasises the description: *Compositions of plums from… range from… to…, with a mean of… (Figure 2). In contrast, plums from… have compositions ranging from…* An additional way to place emphasis on the analysed data is to focus on hypotheses of substance *(species A is influenced by processes X and Y, resulting in different growth rates in habitats S and T)* rather than on statistical hypotheses such as the null hypothesis *(there is no difference in growth* *rates among populations of species A in habitats S and T)* (Lertzman, 1995). While the null hypothesis can be accepted[1] or rejected, statistical inference can only provide *support*; it cannot prove a hypothesis or explicitly answer a question. So, be careful in both the results and discussion sections to use appropriate vocabulary. If the study was a true experiment causal language should be used. If, however, it was correlational words that imply causation should be avoided and phrases such as *correlated with*, or *was related to*, used instead. Mention of non-significant findings will need to be substantiated. But, in doing so, avoid making excuses for those findings. The following, however, is not necessarily an excuse: *While the finding did not reach significance, it might have done so with a larger sample.* For example, evidence from a small sample with high individual variability might suggest that if the sample size was increased significance would be reached. Statistical significance should not, though, be confused with practical significance.

11.10 CHOOSING APPROPRIATE FIGURES

1. Because of the strength in humans of spatial perception the most effective way to explore a set of numbers is to look at pictures of them. In this sense they constitute 'cognitive art' (Canter & Fairbairn, 2006). In this sense also statistical graphics (a concept dating back to the second half of the eighteenth century [Tufte, 2001]) reveal data and are, thus, instruments to help reason about them (Tufte, 2001). What, though, are statistical graphics? As used here the term *figure* is defined as either a graph or chart. In turn, the term *chart* is defined as a graph other than a line graph: a bar chart or a pie chart, for example. Because they are usually used to present qualitative information structure diagrams like flow charts and organisation charts have been excluded from the definition of *chart*. However, depending upon the needs of particular studies, charts, graphs, maps, photographs, drawings and diagrams might all either be defined as figures or defined separately. When, for example, a thesis contains small numbers of charts, graphs, maps and photographs they might all be called figures and listed as such immediately after the table of contents. If, however, there are significant numbers of each they should be listed separately. For example, if there are 10 figures, 5 maps, and 5 photographs, there should be two lists: List of Figures (for the 10 figures) and List of Illustrations (for the 5 maps and 5 photographs) (Anderson & Poole, 1994). (Apart from exceptional cases all maps, diagrams and drawings should be professionally presented and all photographs ought to be clear. Because of the need for simplicity and clarity avoid, where possible, the use of shading in diagrams and drawings.)
2. When deciding whether or not to include maps, diagrams or drawings, and for that matter graphs, charts and tables, ask if they are absolutely necessary. If there is more than an element of doubt the usual decision should be to exclude

them. But, if tables and figures are included it must be on the understanding that poor presentation can undermine sound research. It is of fundamental importance, therefore, that the tables and figures presented in the results section appropriately and effectively organise the data and accurately emphasise the trends and patterns identified. They must, in other words, have rhetorical effect (Booth et al., 2003). In regard to figures this effect will only come into play when an informed choice is made about which type will be most effective in doing so. While it is common knowledge that graphs and charts derive their utility from their ability to represent the meanings embedded in complex numerical data, there is less knowledge of how extensive the list of graphs and charts in common usage is and even less of the list of specialised graphs and charts (polar charts, triangular charts and surface plots, for example) designed for particular types of data. There are, though, general principles that might be applied to assist in making a choice. These depend on what needs to be shown: comparisons, distributions, relationships or composition? Comparisons, for example, can either be static or dynamic. Bar charts can be chosen to represent the former. They might also be used to represent dynamic relationships but the result is an unsatisfactory jumble of bars. In this case if the data from the bars are extracted and, instead, applied in line graphs dynamic relationships will be represented more effectively. This can be seen in a time-series plot, a graph showing a set of successive observations taken at equally spaced points in time. When used with big data sets and significant variability dynamic relationships can easily be seen. The problem, though, is that in isolation passage of time is rarely causal explanation (Tufte, 2001). This does not, though, apply to relational graphics, a scatterplot for example. Because they link at least two variables they explicitly invite readers to account for the relationship between them (Tufte, 2001).

3. Just as there is often lack of awareness of how extensive the list of specialised graphs and charts is, so is there also of the ways graphs and charts can be used to complement each other. Histograms, for example, are graphical versions of tables that show what proportion of cases fall into specified categories. As such they are important exploratory tools for data analysis because they show the general shape of the frequency distribution. Frequency polygons, the straight line connecting the midpoints of the tips of the bars of histograms, take this process a step further by not only making the shape of the data distribution clearer but also in helping to compare different sets of data. In doing so, however, they make the class boundaries clearly evident in histograms more difficult to see. Histograms and frequency polygons, as in the case of other forms of visual data presentation, should, therefore, only be used when they fulfil a clearly defined purpose.

4. Representing data effectively in graphs and charts thus requires a reasonable level of knowledge of how they should best be used. This is particularly the case when it is borne in mind that the meaning and suitability of those chosen might

281

need to be explained. Although not a separate discipline in the way that statistics is, the field of visual data representation has been developed significantly since the use of such representations became widespread towards the end of the first half of the nineteenth century. Unfortunately, while referencing style manuals and Instructions to Authors in journals provide a considerable body of advice in regard to the presentation of tables and figures little attention is given to their appropriate use. So, in addition to consulting these sources, access the numerous websites devoted to the visual display of data and/or consult the work of specialists. Foremost among these is Edward Tufte.

5. Once in position to make an informed choice, the rules and conventions that apply to the presentation of tables and figures will need to be established. As was advised in reference to the display of units, numbers, equations and tests and also in reference to the presentation of statistical symbols, equations and data, ensure that appropriate sources are consulted. Cognisance, of course, will also need to be taken of university requirements governing the presentation of tables and figures in theses. It is usual, though, for the recommendations outlined below to be applied.

11.11 CONVENTIONS COMMON TO THE PRESENTATION OF BOTH TABLES AND FIGURES[2]

1. Although all tables and figures in the results section must be referred to in the text, it is important that the purpose and function of each table or figure should clearly be evident without the necessity of reference to the text. They should, in other words, be *self-exemplifying* (Tufte, 2001, Introduction). For this reason tables and figures need full, accurate and concise titles and labels and, where necessary, legends.[3] (Table titles are placed on the second line above the top line of the table. Figure titles—this also applies to diagrams, drawings and photographs—are placed on the second line below the bottom line of the figure. Table and figure titles must be single-spaced and may not extend beyond either the left or right margin or the labels of a table or figure.) Because no explanatory text can be placed in the list of tables and figures at the front of a thesis, the titles alone of each table and figure must have sufficient detail if the contents of each are to be ascertained simply by reading the list (Thody, 2006). Nonetheless, in complex tables and figures, it may be necessary to supplement the title with a brief explanatory caption. (The caption should appear at the bottom of both tables and figures.) All indicators of accuracy (standard errors, deviations or error bars, for example) should be included in tables and figures. (It was recommended earlier that tables and figures should be used as a framework around which to weave the text of the results section. Their usefulness in this role is enhanced significantly when

each table and figure is fully titled, labelled and, if necessary, captioned prior to their use in the framework.)

Table 11.1. **New Zealand Real Median Income† by Age Group: 1986 to 2006.**

Age Group (years)	Census year				
	1986	1991	1996	2001	2006
15–24	18,906	13,807	11,055	10,139	11,525
25–64	28,218	26,022	28,259	30,195	33,789
65 or over	14,836	14,182	14,750	14,952	15,636

Note. This data has been randomly rounded to protect confidentiality. Adapted from Statistics New Zealand (2010). Young people 1986–2006: Study, work and income. Wellington: Statistics New Zealand.

† Real median income includes those who reported receiving an income and excludes those who reported an income loss or receiving no income. All income medians are expressed in 2006 New Zealand dollars.

2. Tables or figures larger than a half page should be placed on a page of their own either immediately before or following the page where first referenced. On this basis two half page tables or figures may be grouped together on a separate page. (These pages should be numbered as though pages of text.) But, whenever practical, a figure or table should be less than a third of a page in size. (Although this effectively facilitates the integration of data and text the headings and captions of tables and figures should normally be separated from the text above and below by triple spacing.) Figures, in fact, can be compressed significantly and still retain meaning. An example is *sparklines*, word sized graphics that effectively integrate figures and text (Tufte, 2006, pp. 46–63).

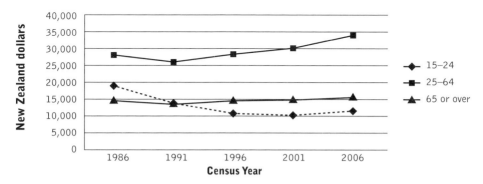

Figure 11.1. Real median income in New Zealand by age group (years) over a twenty-year period of government census.

All income medians are expressed in 2006 New Zealand dollars. Source: Statistics New Zealand (2010). Young people 1986–2006: Study, work and income. Wellington: Statistics New Zealand.

3. Separate tables or figures should not be placed side-by-side unless they share the same number and title and are used for comparison. But, irrespective of where they are placed in a thesis, tables and figures need to be numbered consecutively in Arabic numerals, and in separate sequences, in the order in which they are cited. (This explains why if they appear in the thesis tables and figures need to be cited in the text.) In Figure 1.1. or Table 1.1., for example the first numeral refers to the chapter and the second refers to the table or figure's place in the sequence. Tables and figures in appendices should be labelled as such: Figure A.2. (Figure 2 in appendix A). Only the first letter of the word 'Table' and the first letter of the main words in the title should be uppercase: Table 4.3. Rise in Public Spending on Education ($ Billion), 2002–2006. In figures only the first letter of 'Figure' and the first letter of the title and of proper names should be in uppercase: Figure 3.2. Distribution of isotherms in Crete. (In APA the title word figure is in italics: *Figure 3.2.* [*Publication Manual of the APA*, 2010, p.152]). In the text of the thesis the upper case should be used when referring to specific tables or figures: Table 4.3. or Figure 1.1. The upper case should not, however, be used when referring to elements of the tables or figures: row 2 or column 3 (Anderson & Poole, 1994). All the titles and captions of tables and figures should be in the same font and of the same size. Labels, though, may be in a different font and size from the titles and captions but they too must be consistently presented. (Although the principle of integration implies the same style of font should preferably be used for text, tables and figures the convention is to use true-spaced fonts like Arial for labels as doing so limits changes to spacing.)

4. Permission to use or adapt a copyrighted table or figure must be obtained from the copyright holder. The source must be acknowledged as a final note to the table or figure. (*Source* should be followed by a colon and the wording of the information should be as requested by the copyright holder. If a figure or table has been adapted a statement indicating this has been done must accompany the acknowledgement.)

11.12 CONVENTIONS COMMON TO THE PRESENTATION OF TABLES

1. Because comparison between data buried in text is difficult to interpret a text table is often useful (Tufte, 2001). For example: *The three groups differed in their ability to manipulate the device:*

Group A 53%	*Group B 46%*
Group B 46%	*Group A 53%*
Group C 57%	*Group C 57%*

(In cases like this where a simple data set has been presented in tabular form for ease of comparison there is no need for it to be listed as a numbered table.) In fact, when reporting sets of fewer than twenty numbers tables are normally preferable to figures for they show numbers precisely and make comparison easier. The special comparative power of figures only comes into play when large data sets are used (Tufte, 2001).

2. In essence, as a list of numbers increases so too does the need to systematise their presentation in order to allow analysis to proceed. In most cases, therefore, tables will provide the foundation upon which figures and, therefore, the description and subsequent discussion of the data will be based. Only those tables central to interpreting the results should, therefore, appear in the results section. The remainder should be appendices. (A profusion of appendices can become cumbersome when, particularly in doctoral theses, a significant number of tables need to be presented as reference material. Should this be the case a useful option is to place the tables on consecutive pages as a final chapter prior to the appendix. This chapter can be identified as a data reference chapter in the table of contents.) The best way to draw a distinction between those tables that should be placed in the results section and those in the appendix is to ensure that every table has a clearly defined purpose or, in a minority of instances, purposes. (A table whose purposes are too diffuse is generally indicated by its large size. Where this is the case consider splitting it into smaller, more focused, tables.) Clarity on the purpose of a table usually makes it easier not only to identify a direct relationship between each table and each question or hypothesis but also where each fits into the narrative of that relationship.

3. The design of each table should be as clear and simple as possible. This includes the way in which a table is oriented. Because it is cumbersome to rotate a thesis sideways, tables should ideally be oriented in portrait rather than in landscape. (If it is necessary to orient them in landscape ensure that the title is placed alongside the binding side of the page.) Irrespective of how the tables are oriented do not use vertical and horizontal lines to create *data cells;* because these are redundant it is better to use open spaces instead. (Neither should the table as a whole be enclosed in a box. Figures, however, are normally enclosed in boxes and can also incorporate grid lines to help connect the labels on the axes.) The exception to the use of lines in a table is the top row, the bowhead, where the variables (usually categories) into which the data have been subdivided are listed. This row should usually be separated from the title of the table at the top and the data below, the field, by horizontal lines. However, the variables listed on the extreme left of a table, the stub (usually items), should not be separated from the data by a vertical line.

4. The data presented in each table should be presented as cleanly and simply as possible. For this reason all labels attached to the data ($, +, % or mm, for

example) should be moved to the stub or bowheads. The data should also not include more digits than absolutely necessary. (Check on usual practice in the discipline. This is normally indicated in the editorial guidelines of appropriate journals.) In fact, if precise numbers can be rounded off without significant loss of accuracy, two digits are all that in most cases are needed:

	Exports ($m)	Imports ($m)
2006	37	54

As opposed to:

	Exports	Imports
2006	$36 742 341	$53 823 067

There might, however, be occasions when data need to be labelled or extra digits added. An asterisk, for example, indicates if data in a table are statistically significant and a negative sign in brackets (–) should follow negative numbers. In APA (2010, p.131) a zero should not precede decimal numbers less than 1.0 (.85, for example, not 0.85) but, in other instances, a zero might be required. Again usual practice should be adhered to.

5. Every row and column must be labelled in the stub and bowheads so that each element in the data field is identified. There must also be self-evident logic to the manner in which the labels are presented. For example, in a table indicating literacy levels in a number of countries, it will normally be better to order the countries in ascending or descending order of literacy rather than alphabetically. (If, however, there is no self-evident logic the labels should be presented alphabetically or chronologically. The logic explaining the ordering of labels in tables should also be applied to the bars in bar charts: whenever possible they should be grouped into related sets and arranged so as to provide an image of order [Booth et al., 2003].) Because long descriptive labels cause irregular spacing in tables, labels (particularly the bowheads) should be kept as brief as possible. For this purpose standard abbreviations (cm, min or %, for example) may be used without explanation but abbreviations of specialist terms (unless already introduced in the text of the thesis) must be explained in a note to the table.

6. When a note is needed to explain an abbreviation in a table or, for example, to describe a procedure, the word *Note* in italics followed by a full stop should be typed immediately below and flush left with the table. If a particular entry in a column requires explanation a footnote will be needed. (Wherever possible, however, avoid footnotes to a table as they run counter to the need for

clarity and simplicity.) Footnotes follow a *Note* and, because numbers might be confused with numbers in the table, should be designated by a superscript lowercase letter or a symbol next to each entry (#, +, for example). Tables are read from left to right and from top to bottom so the letters or symbols for each footnote should be presented in that order.

11.13 CONVENTIONS COMMON TO THE PRESENTATION OF FIGURES

1. Because clarity is all-important when displaying data avoid using stacked bar charts or three-dimensional charts (or, for that matter, pictograms): although they might appear impressive, they can be misleading and difficult to read. Lack of clarity is also the reason why pie charts should be used with caution. In business pie charts are popular because they quickly reveal data distribution. But, because it is more difficult to discern the relative size of a pie slice than it is to judge relative bar length, and because any data displayed in a pie chart can also be displayed in a bar chart, bar charts in some instances might be more useful than pie charts. (To overcome the problem of discerning the relative size of slices percentages or numbers can be indicated on each slice of some pie charts.) But, irrespective of the types chosen, it is likely that not all of the graphs and charts drawn during the analysis process will be required in the final results section. This will usually be a consequence of the focus that develops as themes and patterns emerge from the data. It is also likely that those finally included will have evolved with the passage of time. This is another illustration of the similarity between text and graphic representation: just as text undergoes sequential improvement with each draft, so too are graphics also improved through sequential revision and editing (Tufte, 2001). Because of this sequential development and also because constructing graphs and charts using computer software can be time-consuming, it is often more efficient to neatly draw initial graphs and charts by hand. Then, once it has been decided which ought to be included in the final draft they can be drawn properly using the appropriate software. There are numerous formats in which graphics can be stored: bitmaps, jpeg, tiff and gif, for example. Each converts data in different ways for particular purposes. Jpeg, for example, cuts data, thus producing lower quality images, in order to make the electronic file as small as possible. A tiff image, on the other hand, will be of high quality at the cost of a bigger file (Canter & Fairbairn, 2006). (When using software each graph and chart and all of the information pertaining to each should be placed in one frame to prevent separation when moved between pages. Make sure to save files of graphics as they might be needed when publishing in books or journals.)

2. As on so many occasions when writing a thesis, deciding how much data to present in a graph or chart involves walking a narrow path. On the one hand too many single purpose graphs merely serve to clutter the results section rather than clarify the data. On the other, each graph or chart, except in unusual circumstances, should serve one clearly defined purpose. To overcome this dilemma focus each figure on a particular question or hypothesis while simultaneously limiting the data sets plotted on each to four or less: lines that extend beyond continuous, dashed, dotted, dash–dot become confusing. The use of different colours in graphics can also be problematic because they do not, as do shades of grey, have a natural visual hierarchy. Up to ten shades of grey can effectively be used for the human eye is remarkably good at making distinction between shades (Tufte, 2001). Therefore, if colours are used, their meaning must be indicated clearly and the colours chosen should also cater for the colour deficient and colour blind. Most people, for example, can differentiate blue from other colours (Tufte, 2001). Nonetheless, the fact that between five to ten per cent of people perceive colour differently from the rest is one of the reasons why some universities disallow the use of colour in theses. There are other elements of the human condition that should be taken into account when preparing figures. We naturally ascribe importance to greater line weight, so thick and thin lines should have consistency of meaning when used in graphics (Tufte, 2001). Of greater importance, though, is the greater sensitivity of the human eye to deviations from the horizontal rather than the vertical. Graphic design should take advantage of this by tending towards greater length than height. If the data suggest an alternative shape then that ought to be adopted but where possible, the ideal is a graphic fifty per cent wider than tall (Tufte, 2001). It is also ideal because it has an additional advantage: by providing greater context and, thus, greater comparative value a longer horizontal allows the effects of the causal variable to be better understood (Tufte, 2001).

3. As many redundancies as possible should be removed from graphics. The bar of a bar chart is an example of redundancy for the height of the bar is indicated by each of the sides and by the horizontal line at the top (Tufte, 2001). Dark grid lines fall into the same category. While useful for initial plotting they compete for attention with the data in the final draft. Their presence, therefore, should only be implicit. Despite the need not to clutter a graphic it is, nonetheless, important that all its important attributes should be labelled with brief, legible and (where possible) horizontal text in which both the upper and lower case is used. (The y–axis should be labelled vertically; lines should not pass through any labels; units should always be in brackets and the uncertainty in the data indicated with error bars.)

4. However, if too much text is used, particularly in complex graphics, clear perception of the patterns will be disrupted. So, although in simple graphics it is

preferable to label each line individually, in complex graphs and charts as much text as possible should be placed in a legend (Booth et al., 2003). As in the case of tables, graphs and charts should have concise, clearly defined titles. But, in order to assist examiners understand particular graphics, it might be useful to elaborate the title of each by including a caption briefly indicating what has been graphed or charted and drawing their attention to the most important features in the display. If a graph or chart is to be reduced ensure that the labels as they finally appear in the thesis are a minimum size 8 font (Times New Roman equivalent) and that the lines are sharp and dark. The lines in the larger original should, therefore, be drawn thicker than would normally be the case: 3/4 pt rather than 1/4 pt, for example. A reducing photocopier is often a useful way to establish if an original can be reduced without losing clarity or looking spindly.

5. When drawing graphs and charts ensure not only that the axes are scaled regularly but also that not too much empty space is left between the scales. An irregular scale on the y–axis or a change in a regular scale from, for example, 0–100 to 0–200 or 0–60 can significantly distort interpretation by limiting or magnifying changes to the dependent variable. There might be legitimate reasons for such scales but the possible consequences for interpretation ought to be borne in mind.

6. Cautionary Note: As many informed individuals as possible should proofread the final draft of the thesis. But, when proofreading the final draft of the results section, it will be up to the thesis writer to ensure that all of the data and, for example, equations, symbols and calculations shown are correct for only he or she will be able to recognise whether or not they are.

ENDNOTES

1 A thesis examiner wrote: 'I prefer not to read that a null hypothesis had been accepted, more correctly one should say that it has not been rejected' (Holbrook & Dally, 2003, p.8).

2 See also Chapter 5, Displaying Results (pp.125–167), *Publication Manual of the American Psychological Association,* 6th edn. (2010).

3 In some disciplines the term legend not title is used for figures.

CHAPTER 12

The Discussion

Sherlock Holmes: *From a drop of water a logician could infer the possibility of an Atlantic or a Niagara without having seen or heard of one or the other. So all life is a great chain, the nature of which is known whenever we are shown a single link of it…*

Dr Watson: *What ineffable twaddle!*

(Doyle, A.C., *A study in scarlet*, 2001, Chapter 2, p.15)

12.1 INTRODUCTION

1. The *results section* of an empirical thesis indicates which results are considered relevant to the hypotheses or questions central to a research undertaking. The purpose of the discussion section (or sections in some doctoral theses) is to allow the results to be interpreted in the context of the research literature. In this section of the thesis, therefore, the extent to which each hypothesis has been confirmed, refuted, or revised will be indicated and/or the extent to which each research question has been addressed will be discussed. In order to do so all of the research objectives presented in the introduction to the thesis, regardless of whether they were successfully met or not, should also be discussed. This explains why the discussion section is that part of a thesis to which all of its constituent elements have, thus far, been directed. Its importance, therefore, should be seen in this light: it is that part of a thesis where the primary intellectual contribution is made. This also explains why it is that part of a thesis most often used for research articles and why it is the section where examiner scrutiny will be particularly intense. Their prime concern will be to ensure that the conclusions reached are a fair interpretation of the data. But they will also be looking at the degree of originality and depth of understanding brought to bear in the process. In exceptional cases examiners will pay the ultimate compliment by acknowledging that a student's interpretive skills have exceeded their own:

I thought that the interpretation of my work was very interesting as I had quite a lot of trouble digesting the data and simplifying it to explain what was happening and why. X interpretation of this and his approach … demonstrate how a fresh approach by a creative researcher … can re-interpret source data to add value and create or develop valuable new knowledge. When I think of my work now in these … terms, I find that the results become more meaningful.

(Cited in Lovat & Morrison, 2003, p.4)

2. However, two apparently contradictory impulses in both masters' and doctoral theses will be at work in this section and the comments examiners make in the final reports will be a delicate balance of each. It is in this context that the foundational importance of the methods section to the discussion needs to be recognised: data quality is a necessary condition for the quality of the inferences drawn in the discussion but is not a sufficient condition for it. In other words, the 'criteria for evaluating the quality of the data and the quality of the inferences are not the same' (Teddlie & Tashakkori, 2003c, p.696). On the one hand, therefore, examiners will expect to see displays of insight and originality in the discussion. On the other, their concern, irrespective of the conclusions drawn in the thesis, will be the extent to which the research as a whole was a meaningful learning experience for the student:

… supervisors need to emphasize to their candidates that examiners focus on the 'how' of research because this is counterintuitive for many doctoral candidates who are often more concerned about the significance of the conclusions of their research.

(Ingleby, 2007, p.48)

The discussion, therefore, needs to be written in a manner that not only facilitates a sound understanding of how the conclusions to the research were reached but which also easily allows the examiners to reach their own conclusions about the process and the product of the research as a whole. The key to this outcome is the manner in which the discussion is organised: 'Outstanding analyses make the reader feel like they are in the company of a good guide, like you've got a good bus driver on this trip' (Lovitts, 2007, p.350).

12.2 ORGANISING THE DISCUSSION

1. Because of their mutual interdependence, the sequential pattern of the discussion should (where the results and discussion are presented as separate sections) mirror that of the results section. As has already been established, the logic of the research questions/hypotheses will in most cases define the manner in which each of these sections is organised. Nonetheless, the

discussion will require elements additional to those found in the results section. The discussion will usually need, for example, to be introduced with a summary of the results, followed by a discussion of the results in the context of the literature and concluded with sub-sections dealing with the limitations of the research, with the conclusions/findings and with suggestions for further research. A discussion section might, therefore, be organised as follows:

- summary of the results in relation to each research question or hypothesis;
- the integration of the results for each question/hypothesis with the literature;
- the limitations of the research;
- the conclusions and/or implications of the findings; and
- recommendations and/or suggestions for further research.

2. However it has been presented, the theme around which the discussion section has been organised will, as in the following example, need to be made explicit at the outset:

In the first section below, I summarise the reasons for the choice of the theoretical framework of this study. The second section presents the aims of the study and the third section presents the main findings in relation to the literature. A statement of the limitations of the study and suggestions for further research follow.

What is not needed in the section of a thesis read just before examiners write their final report is justification for a comment similar to the following by an editor about a substandard research article:

Organization of the article is also suspect. There is no sectioning, with clearly identified themes, which increases the sense of it being rather a rambling discourse. I was left wondering what the aims of the article were, and what the author was trying to achieve. The abstract was no help in this respect.

(Woods, 2006, p.142)

12.3 INTRODUCING THE DISCUSSION

1. Before a discussion can begin the nature of the issues to be discussed and the context within which it will be conducted need to be established. So, to establish the former start the section with a brief descriptive (therefore textual, not numeric) summary of the results. Establish context by organising this summary around either the extent to which each set of results did or did not support each research hypothesis or the degree to which answers were provided to each research question. A supervisor in sociology wrote:

'The findings are "staged" or put together in a coherent way, usually starting with descriptions and becoming more analytic and more theoretical as the analysis proceeds' (cited in Lovitts, 2007, p.291). Alternatively, context can be established by first presenting the questions/hypotheses in isolation: *The culmination of the theory and methods described and applied in the preceding chapters must be addressed with reference to the aims stated in the overview of this project. These were…* These can then be followed by a textual summary of the results as they relate to each question/hypothesis. Do not, though, in the introduction to the discussion, simply state whether or not hypotheses were confirmed or that the questions were answered. Briefly point out, instead, any similarities to, or differences from, what had initially been expected: *Strong support is found for the first hypothesis though not the second hypothesis, and there are also some unexpected results.* A brief statement of the extent to which the findings of the study were consistent with findings discussed in the literature review might also be included at this stage.

2. Important equivocal and/or negative results should not be excluded from the introduction to the discussion if they are pertinent to a full understanding of the findings: not only might they demonstrate how research difficulties were confronted but, in well-designed studies, equivocal and/or negative outcomes can contribute as much to the discussion as any other relevant result. What, though, is the position in regard to well-designed studies whose results are predominantly negative? This outcome is more likely in doctoral than masters studies because original research by definition means a higher level of non-predictability: 'surprising outcomes happen only when the situation is prone to, or capable of, generating that outcome… It is the number of active variables, interactions and possibilities that cause non-predictability…'(Smith & Jenks, 2006, p.5). When, for example, a new type of nanoglue was recently developed researchers accidentally discovered that when heated it became better glue: 'That was something we hadn't bargained for' (*Yahoo News*, 16 May 2007). In this instance the research outcome was both positive and useful but negative outcomes might also make a useful research contribution in the sense that they help identify research approaches that appeared to be promising but were, in fact, not so. If this is the case it will be necessary, in the discussion section, to explain why the results were negative and to discuss what can be learned from the experience (Mauch & Birch, 1998). In other words examiners are not only interested in what is reported but in how, and with what insight into the realities of the research process, it is reported: '…reflexivity on this matter is regarded by many examiners as a quality, rather than a defect, in a higher degree' (Pearce, 2005, p.53). Disciplinary particularities need, though, to be taken into account. Engineers, for example, typically value the outcome of research more than the process. In consequence research degrees in

    engineering and its affiliated disciplines are not typically awarded for negative results or for disproving hypotheses (Lovitts, 2007).

3. Nonetheless, in all disciplines negative outcomes do not normally dominate the discussion sections of well-designed studies. An impression to the contrary might be created, however, if negative results of limited importance are included in the introduction to the section. For this reason it is generally better to put these results in proper perspective by placing them, instead, towards the end of the discussion section under 'research limitations'. This also explains why the limitations of a study are discussed towards the end of the discussion section and not at the beginning: because valid and reliable results are a consequence of sound research, the strengths of the research design must first be established in the introduction in order to provide a foundation of confidence upon which the subsequent discussion will be built: *A number of design features of the study added to the reliability of the data and hence gave the project's findings credibility. These were…*; or: *The pilot study was important because it exposed areas of the proposed survey that were unlikely to succeed. This enabled us to strengthen the…* Discussing the limitations of the research towards the end of the discussion will, therefore, allow context and nuance to be provided to the findings without undermining the credibility of what has already been established as sound research.

4. However, having established this, it might be necessary to include warnings on interpretation in the introduction to the discussion. These are limitations necessary to the immediate interpretation of the data and, therefore, which examiners should know about:

At a regional level, data limitations have restricted our analysis somewhat. We model prices in each region relative to… We find that these models capture the broad trends in … although they obviously miss many of the region-specific factors that have no doubt been important.

(O'Donovan & Rae, 1996, p.4)

Because the interpretation of statistical results depends on the way variables are defined, definitions will need to be provided together, if necessary, with cautionary notes:

One of the most-cited measures of prosperity, household income, is misleading over time because household sizes have changed. In 1947, the average household contained 3.6 people. By 2006, that number had dwindled to 2.6.

(*The Economist*, 26 May 2007, p.22)

Any key terms not already defined will also need definition. If these are not adequate examiners will usually take note:

Much more definitional work needs to be done. For example, it is not clear what is meant by 'structure'. In one place, social class is offered as an example, elsewhere a school or university; and later, reference is made to 'macro'. There seems to be some conceptual confusion here.

(Cited in Woods, 2006, p.141)

12.4 THE DISCUSSION AS LITERATURE REVIEW

1. As already indicated, the purpose of the discussion is to allow the results to be interpreted in the context of the research questions raised, or hypotheses formulated, and of the pertinent research literature: *Although Meyer et al. (2009) reported a change in protein x, we were unable to confirm the change. This was possibly due to...* The discussion should, therefore, be seen as a continuation of the review: 'references to primary and secondary sources give the reader a sense of interplay between data and argument—an almost literal sense of tension as the reader's eye moves constantly between the one and the other' (Becher & Trowler, 2001, p.115). If not treated in this way examiners will be quick to take note:

    ...the candidate did not integrate his findings into the existing literature, and did not provide much of his own analysis. Linking the findings into the literature situates them in their scholarly traditions, and demonstrates their wider applicability.

    (Cited in Holbrook & Dally, 2003, p.11)

    So, while the organisational structure of the discussion will closely resemble that of the results section, the manner in which much of the discussion is written will more closely resemble that of the richly referenced literature review. Therefore, before writing the discussion, the most recent draft of the literature review should be read. This will allow both re-familiarisation with the style of writing in the review and attention to be focused on what might be relevant there to the discussion of the results. Not only will the latter serve to deepen and extend the interpretation of the results they will also provide a sense of continuity and authorial control to the thesis as a whole.

2. Because it is a continuation of the review after the research has been conducted, there will be one significant difference between the review of the literature in the discussion and the earlier review: while the latter indicates what was known prior to the conduct of the research, the former provides the opportunity to show how the results have extended those boundaries. This is where the value of the review in the discussion lies: new theory is a consequence of the interaction of new data and existing literature. The distinction between the

reviews will, in the first instance, mean there will be frequent need to cite references not already cited in the original review. In the second, it means that new sets of questions will need to be addressed.

12.5 QUESTIONS TO BE ADDRESSED

1. The first set of questions around which the body of the discussion might be built relates to the relationship of the results to the research questions and/or hypotheses first presented in the introduction to the thesis:
   - What trends, patterns and/or relationships are revealed in the data in regard to each question and/or to what extent are the hypotheses supported?
   - What explains each trend, pattern or relationship and/or to what extent is the degree of support for each hypothesis provided?
   - What are the exceptions to each of the above and which results are contradictory or unexpected?
2. The second set of questions relate to the relationship of the results to those of relevant studies in the research literature:
   - To what extent are the results corroborated by other researchers?
   - To what extent do the results clarify, contribute towards or contradict the findings of other researchers?
   - What is the significance of the corroboration, clarification, contribution or contradiction?
   - What, in the results, is new and/or surprising? *This was a surprising finding since… A closer examination of this data revealed that…*
   - What were the strengths and weaknesses of the study in relation to the strengths and weaknesses of other studies?
   - What generalisations/assumptions/predictions/recommendations can be made in the light of the responses to each of the above?
3. The third set of questions relate to the manner in which the results are discussed:
   - Has each question and/or hypothesis been addressed in the same order in which they were presented in the introduction to the thesis?
   - Has sufficient evidence supporting each argument been provided?
   - Has each question and/or hypothesis been dealt with clearly and fully prior to moving on to the next?

12.6 ADDRESSING THE QUESTIONS

1. In addressing these questions only the data that have already been reported in the results section should be used. (This applies irrespective of whether the sections are presented together or separately.) Nor should there be any

reference in the discussion to tables and figures in the results section. It might, though, for comparative purposes be necessary to include in the discussion particular tables and figures from the results section and/or from the research literature. Because the results presented in some completed theses have not been published, and thus exposed to wide academic scrutiny, supervisors and examiners might be reluctant to accept the inclusion of tables and figures from other theses in a thesis discussion section. The differences between published and unpublished thesis material can be gleaned from the following comment by a doctoral candidate: 'I have had to redo all of the statistical analyses to meet the requirements of journal reviewers: what my committee accepted is not accepted by others' (cited in Meloy, 2002, p.39). Should the need to include such tables and/or figures arise, the wisdom of doing so should first be discussed with the supervisor/s. Qualitative researchers should also seek advice from their supervisors if they intend to use data from another thesis to make theoretical points in their own study for, unless care is taken, contamination from a different setting is a likely outcome (Golden-Biddle & Locke, 1997).

2. A common fault in the discussion section of empirical theses is to provide description rather than explanatory commentary: to merely translate, in other words, the numerals in the results section into text in the discussion. Qualitative research, on the other hand, is descriptive by definition. But it is description of a particular kind: theoretically informed description. It is this that turns qualitative intelligence gathering into research (Phillips & Pugh, 2005) and what makes under-theorised qualitative description the equivalent of empirical commentary. But qualitative description is also of a particular kind because it is multi-vocal. It can for this reason 'point to one of a number of possible theoretical explanations and thus have implications for a number of theoretical conversations' (Phillips & Pugh, 2005, p.103). To establish a firm linkage between data and theory in a qualitative study the two must be tightly coupled and yet, simultaneously, differentiated from one another. This calls, on the one hand, for showing and, on the other, for telling: a smaller font for the former might, for example be used to distinguish it from the interpretation of the latter (Golden–Biddle & Locke, 1997). Failure to establish these linkages might prompt comments from examiners similar to the following by a journal editor:

The paper is weak theoretically. Presumably the subject is teacher culture, but there is no discussion of this concept. There is no recognition that there can be a dialectical relation with a culture, whereby individuals both contribute to and draw from a culture, and that it is a dynamic, living, processual thing. The data might contribute to an interesting discussion along these lines, but fall well short of it.

(Cited in Woods, 2006, p.141)

3. Notice the wording of the subheading above: it is not 'answering' but 'addressing' the questions. This distinction is intended to indicate to all researchers the need to discuss a range of possible alternative responses to each question rather than simply to provide one unproblematic answer. The explanations provided when the results of the research are compared and contrasted with those in the literature are often likely to be rooted in differences in methodological approach or in identifiable methodological weaknesses. It is in this context that thesis writers in the social sciences in particular will use attitude markers such as *unfortunately, surprisingly,* and *interestingly* and self mentions such as *I, we, my* and *our* (Paltridge & Starfield, 2007). But, irrespective of the reasons for any differences, take care when providing explanations to also provide examples from the literature and from the research data, for doing so allows explanations to be far more easily understood. Explanations are also more easily understood when structured in parallel: if, for example, reasons x, y or z are proposed as possible explanations for a particular result and are then dealt with in the order y, z, x examiners are likely to be both confused and irritated.

4. Unless due care is exercised discursive texts tend to become wordy and repetitive. Reflecting the frustration that a lack of due care can provoke a supervisor was quoted as saying:

They'll include every regression equation, including ones that have no pertinence to the topic at hand, or inconclusive results, or no significance … so [it's] kind of information overkill; losing the significant and important findings in the midst of endless discussions of insignificant findings.

(Cited in Lovitts, 2007, p.291)

So another common error should also be avoided: discussion sections that are too long and verbose. The need, instead, is to focus on the specific requirements of the primary research hypotheses and/or research questions. To do so the inclusion/exclusion criteria that apply to each ought to be kept firmly in mind. Another means to retain relevance and focus is to desist from the temptation to indulge in unwarranted speculation.

12.7 MAKING WARRANTED ASSERTIONS

1. Those aspects of discussion sections that examiners often criticise are claims that 'go beyond the data'. Stating 'this clearly shows…' on the basis of results that explain five per cent of the variance is an example (Lovitts, 2007, p.292). Nonetheless, at first sight this criticism by examiners appears quixotic in the sense that if research were dependent for its progress solely upon explicit evidence, progress would indeed be slow. In fact the nature of research itself

dictates that more often than not evidence is suggestive rather than definitive. (In this regard a senior researcher wrote that he was not 'personally or professionally opposed to speculation, even wild speculation, since I am becoming more and more convinced of a serious failure of the imagination on the part of many scientists and mathematicians' (Goldstein, 2008, p.129). On condition they do not dominate, it is on these grounds perfectly acceptable and often necessary in discussion sections to make tentative and sometimes, speculative statements based upon indicative rather than direct evidence. This reality points, therefore, to an origin different from the mere act of speculation for the criticism that examiners make. It is more likely that its origin lies in a failure to indicate the quality of the relationship between a speculative statement and the evidence upon which it is based. There are, in other words, degrees of speculation ranging from the firmly based to the virtually baseless. Where the line on this continuum is crossed from acceptable to unacceptable speculation is both subjective and context dependent. To this extent speculation tests the limits of generalisation: where it does or does not apply. But it is impossible for either the thesis writer or the examiners to know whether or not the line has been crossed unless the quality of the evidence upon which the speculation relies has been indicated. Without evidence speculation is mere guesswork. In fact, indicating the strength of the evidence upon which any significant statement is predicated—providing, in other words, a warranted assertion—is fundamental to the credibility of the entire discussion section of a thesis.

Establishing warrants in qualitative research

2. It is for this reason that some qualitative researchers explicitly assess the strength of their data. For example, they categorise data according to whether it is 'strong,' 'modest' or 'weak' (Golden-Biddle & Locke, 1997, p.77). The quantifiable preciseness of doing so, understandably, is controversial but the reason for proceeding in this way, in order to make warranted assertions, is also understandable. However, most qualitative researchers overcome the problem of establishing warrants by becoming very close to their material. This involvement is essential as it is the psychological basis that gives researchers the ability to see the data from different angles and in terms of different theories (Phillips & Pugh, 2005). Qualitative researchers also expand the number of eyes looking at the data: 'Constructing meaning is almost always a richer process when it accommodates multiple understandings' (Bryant, 2004, p.121). It is these strategies that allow credible discussion of qualitative data to be built and sustained: discussions where transcripts are linked to the text, where unwarranted assumptions are avoided and where mimesis, a realistic representation of the research setting, a 'painting from

life', can be produced (Schostak, 2006, p.145). These strategies also allow a balance between the voice of the researcher and those of the participants to be established. On the one hand the researcher needs to intervene to comment on the validity of the data (Frow, 2006) and, on the other, the participants need to speak through the data without the presence of the researcher being too clearly evident (Woods, 2006). These strategies can be applied equally as well to mixed methodology studies where, for example, comparisons are made in the discussion section between empirical and qualitative data. Here, descriptive or inferential statistical results can introduce, or follow qualitative material so each can nuance the interpretation of the other (Creswell & Plano Clark, 2007).

Exploring statistical data

3. Just as qualitative researchers need to interpret data so too do empirical researchers. Indicating, for example, that a relationship exists between variables is usually straightforward; the difficulty instead usually lies in interpreting the nature of the relationship (Punch, 2006). Thus, integrating and interpreting complex data from, for example, a multivariable correlational survey involves describing emerging interpretations in a manner reflecting qualitative data analysis (Punch, 2006). Because, in other words, most statistical data do not come in black and white they need to be explored and talked about. This includes findings of significance and of non-significance (Bryant, 2004): '...99.9 percent of all species that have ever lived are now extinct... To a first approximation all species are extinct' (Lewin, 2001, p.64). A common flaw, in fact, in both reviews of the literature and in discussion sections is to treat statistically significant differences or relationships between studies as being equal in magnitude (Ling Pan, 2003). Remember too that statistics can make trivial findings seem important or important findings seem trivial and that results of statistical significance might have no practical significance. Also bear in mind that although statistical results might appear stark and unemotional much can be concealed by that appearance. For example, Stalin reportedly said: 'One death is a tragedy; a million is a statistic' (cited in Taleb, 2007, p.80). Also read W. H. Auden's poem *The Unknown Citizen: To JS/07M/378 This Marble Monument Is Erected by the State* (Thody, 2006, p.120).

He was found by the Bureau of Statistics to be
One against whom there was no official complaint,
And all the reports on his conduct agree
That, in the modern sense of an old-fashioned word, he was a saint
...
Was he free? Was he Happy? The question is absurd:
Had anything been wrong, we should certainly have heard.

There is also the problem of silent evidence: the confusion of absence of proof with proof of absence (Taleb, 2007). Two thousand years ago Cicero told the following story:

One Diagoras, a nonbeliever in the gods, was shown painted tablets bearing the portraits of some worshippers who prayed, then survived a subsequent shipwreck. The implication was that praying protects you from drowning. Diagoras asked, 'Where are the pictures of those who prayed then drowned?'

(Taleb, 2007, p.100).

Because we are not necessarily aware of the equivalent of the missing pictures we are not aware of what we don't know. All statistical outcomes, therefore, need to be discussed with the possible effects of this ignorance in mind. Because factors like these deepen and enliven the interpretation of statistical results there is no place in a discussion section for bland statements: *The large difference in mean size between population C and population D is particularly interesting.* It is in this context that a supervisor in economics wrote: 'If the dissertation does not address the economic meaning of the results, if it focuses only on the statistical value, then it's a failure. They need to do better than that' (cited in Lovitts, 2007, p.238). Thus, what specifically is significant or of interest needs to be shown and explanations, with whenever possible appropriate examples, provided: *While the mean size generally varies among populations by only a few centimetres, the mean size in populations A and B differed by 10 cm. Two hypotheses, each supported by evidence collected from disparate locations, could account for this...* If there is insufficient evidence to discriminate between different explanations this too can be discussed: *There is, frankly, no good explanation for these results at the moment. Grey (2009) suggests that part of the answer may lie in a...* Cases like this can also be included in the 'suggestions for further research' section of the discussion. It can sometimes be difficult for examiners to make comparisons across studies when statistics on an issue are dispersed throughout either the literature review or the discussion. Often, therefore, presenting values in table format makes it easier for both reader and writer to make comparisons. As an additional benefit it also allows the latter to highlight points on the table without necessarily having to repeat the statistic in the narrative (Ling Pan, 2003).

Explaining causal connections

4. Experimentation has long been a design preferred by empirical researchers: by systematically eliminating rival hypotheses a reasonably secure basis for inferring causal relationships between variables is offered (Punch, 2006). But the possible effects of confounding variables can rarely be discounted and causation itself is not a reductionist, billiard ball hits billiard ball process. This is why

causation can often only be inferred and why the word 'cause' needs to be used with a degree of caution (Punch, 2006). Explaining causal connections, therefore, usually demands both complex reasoning and elements of persuasion. It also often requires a transformation of outlook for in general humans are biased to look for confirmatory rather than disconfirming evidence. It is on this basis that the discussion of research results can be deepened by using warranted assertions to explore all possible explanations and to provide multiple hypotheses in order to draw warranted conclusions: conclusions that the evidence, on the balance of probability, supports. It is also on this basis that terms such the following will dominate the discussion: *contributed to…; was probably a major cause of…; was one of the causes of…; might have been a small factor in…; the most likely explanation for these results is…; it is probably safe to say…*

12.8 WRITING THE DISCUSSION

1. There will be need, when writing the discussion, to refer back to earlier chapters in the thesis. It is probable, particularly in the literature review that instances will be found where the findings of the study reinforce or contradict those of other researchers using similar methods or where researchers using different approaches have arrived at similar conclusions. Such instances can be used for a variety of purposes. They might, for example, help place the findings of the research in context or show how the theoretic perspective applied provided particular and valuable insights. Most important, though, is the extent to which each instance can be used to justify the decisions taken when designing the study. There are also important additional advantages to scanning back through the thesis to revisit, for example, questions raised, problems encountered and unresolved controversies identified. On the one hand doing so will help deepen and elaborate the discussion and, on the other, will enhance the sense that the writer is exercising control over the entire thesis and not simply over the interpretation of the results: *As I discussed in Chapter 4…* It often helps once the results have been interpreted in the context of both the literature and the issues raised when scanning through the thesis, to step back from the work for a few days. Doing so will provide the necessary distance for the details of the writing to be placed in perspective so insights can be developed to help fit the findings of the study into a wider context.

12.9 LIMITATIONS OF THE STUDY

1. Methodology and method require that choices are made. Because these choices are central to what it means to be a researcher it is natural to expect

that a thesis will contain a section where an open discussion takes place about what did or did not work and what changes had to be made (Pearce, 2005). There is also another important reason for the section. Significance cannot be attributed to findings if there is doubt about their veracity (Bryant, 2004). Because no method or methodology is without flaws a sub-section in the discussion entitled 'limitations of the study' will, thus, always be necessary to provide context against which the value of the research findings can be assessed. For this reason writing the sub-section should not be considered an exercise in apologetic self-criticism. Because it indicates an ability to anticipate what questions examiners might have about the findings of the study, it should, instead, be seen as an opportunity to show perceptiveness. The confident tone of the writing should reflect this: ...*the abovementioned problems ... have resulted in uncertainty regarding the interpretation of some of the data. Thus in the instances indicated the interpretations provided are necessarily tentative.* However, one of the problems, as is so often the case when writing a thesis, is recognising where to draw the line between limitations of little, and of significant, consequence. Key research limitations can generally be identified as those that have exerted a clear constraint. Groping hesitantly to find a significant consequence of a particular constraint normally indicates where the line needs to be drawn.

2. Once identified, key limitations usually fall into three categories. The first two: those recognised and catered for during the design stage and those that arose unexpectedly during the conduct of the research; will generally be accepted by examiners as a normal and necessary part of the research process. The exception, of course, is where the limitations are of such significance that they partially or totally invalidate the findings. Do not, therefore, send the wrong signal to an examiner by introducing relatively benign limitations with vocabulary alarming enough to imply the opposite is the case: *There are some significant limitations to this study. A major limitation on the data collection method was...* However, the third category: those limitations that have had a negative impact on the research and that should have been foreseen at the design stage will be considered by examiners to be far more problematic.

3. Irrespective of the category into which they fall, though, the consequences of the limitations for the findings must be discussed. So evaluate and, if absolutely necessary, speculate informatively on the effect of each of the significant limitations on the study. Then take one further step: discuss what might, in retrospect, have been a better approach to the study as a whole. Doing so means the sub-section is enriched by critical reflection. It also means the research as learning experience benefits other researchers.

12.10 CONCLUSIONS AND IMPLICATIONS

1. The introduction to an empirical thesis places the research questions and/ or hypotheses in context by moving from a wide to a specific focus. This specificity is retained in the thesis until the conclusion. It is at this point, when the results are placed into a broader context, that the focus once again becomes wider: rather 'than "wrap things up," outstanding conclusions "open things up"' (Lovitts, 2007, p.319). In alternative theses, most of which are qualitative rather than exegetic, there is often no conclusion. It is up to readers to form their own opinion. Phenomenological studies reproducing entire conversations or narratives might also not have a conclusion (Thody, 2006). In many other qualitative studies terms like *closing*, *reflections* or *epilogue* are used in place of *conclusion*. This might be because *temporary resolution* rather than the implied permanency of *conclusion* is more appropriate. More usually, however, the subjective 'situatedness' of qualitative studies makes the concept conclusion problematic: 'I cannot say in "conclusion," because I am probably at yet another beginning, laden with some thoughts that had not occurred…' (Meloy, 2002, p.183). It is also logical, therefore, that the term findings should also be problematic: 'We avoid using the notion of "findings" in our dissertations since the studies are centred on enlarging understandings, not proving specifics' (Garman, 2006, p.1).

2. In most empirical studies the focus in the discussion on the interpretation of the results 'means that the bigger picture questions about the underlying framework of the research program might receive less and less intellectual space' (MacMynowski, 2007, np). Writing the conclusion, therefore, permits a researcher to step back and place the findings in a broader context. The extent to which the design of a study permits findings to be generalised and/ or transferred will already have been discussed in the methods section. (Was the study, for example, wide or deep?) But placing the findings into a wider context in the conclusion often allows new associations, applications and conceptual possibilities to emerge. While qualitative and exegetic researchers might avoid use of 'conclusion' for theoretic reasons, empirical researchers should beware the danger of confusing examiners if the conclusion is not called 'conclusion': 'Sometimes it's not even called a conclusion, it's called an epilogue or a final thought or something like that. So I don't know what happened to the conclusion…' (cited in Lovitts, 2007, p.351). In particular instances it might also be wise to draw a distinction between the types of conclusion being made: 'The final chapter did not distinguish between factual and conceptual conclusions which could easily have been drawn from the findings and this has sub-optimised the potential of the research itself' (Trafford, 2008, p.277).

The distinction between findings, conclusions and implications

3. What, though, is the distinction between findings and conclusions? The former are the things that are now known and understood that were not known or understood prior to the completion of the study. The latter are the judgements that can reasonably be made on the basis of the findings. These judgements revolve, essentially, around two issues: how substantive and/or original is the new knowledge and sets of understandings? This is the reason why, despite sharing the characteristic of containing no new information, a summary of findings is not the same as a conclusion. While the former are statements of what was found; the latter are statements indicating the significance and value of what was found (Paltridge & Starfield, 2007). Statements of the significance and value of aspects of the study will, either implicitly or explicitly, already have been provided in the text of the discussion. But the discussion as, logically, was the case in regard to the literature review, is an inherently complex piece of writing. So, despite the argument in the discussion having been structured around clearly identified questions and/or hypotheses each conclusion will need to be extracted from the complexities of the interpretation.

4. However, the process of doing so, as is the case with the interpretation of the results themselves, often involves degrees of speculation. This can be seen in the process of generalisation where the broader the generalisation the more likely it is to be at a higher level of abstraction (Wallace & Wray, 2006). It is the speculative element in many of the wider interpretive statements made in the conclusions to theses that requires a clear distinction to be drawn between the actual findings (and the conclusions that can be drawn from them) and the implications of those findings. If, for example, a boxer falls and lies prone in the ring during a fight the referee will take the boxer's pulse, check eye movement and breathing. These are the findings. Together these findings might indicate the boxer is unconscious. This is the conclusion. The implication: the fight is over. There might also be many other implications. The fact that the fight is over is considered the most important is explained by context. In the same way the implications of a study flow from the original purpose as expressed in the introduction chapter. This example explains the distinction between conclusions and implications and the fact that the latter must always follow from the former. But, despite the distinction, each in its own way draws meaning from the findings of a study. It is, therefore, in the conclusion and implications section of a thesis that the primary intellectual contribution of a well-designed and conducted study is situated. For this reason, it is here that the value of the research will be judged. Whether or not the conclusions and implications is made a subsection of the discussion

or presented as a separate chapter is up to the thesis writer to decide. In doctoral studies they generally constitute a chapter of their own and, as such, indicate their importance. But the relative brevity of the conclusions and implications in some masters' theses often necessitates their insertion instead in the discussion chapter.

Making developed statements

5. Because of the key role played in a thesis by the conclusions and implications section it should not consist of bland undeveloped statements: *The techniques and understandings resulting from this study contribute to the development of... and have both scientific and applied significance.* Neither should each conclusion and implication be removed from discussion by being presented in a series of bulleted points. (Bulleted points can be effective, though, when used to introduce discussion of them.) Because the examiners, instead, will be looking for a synopsis, the section, as in the discussion itself, should be presented as a series of narrative statements providing reasoned judgements, supported by evidence. For example: *The main findings are considered seriatim...* (point by point in regular order). Examiners will, in particular, criticise conclusions and implications if they are not explicitly related to the research questions, are not adequately discussed and areas of agreement/disagreement with other researchers established: *My findings conflict with those who argue that... However, on the basis of the evidence provided it can be seen that... In addition, I directly challenge the argument that...* As in all other parts of the thesis the structure informing this discussion will also need to be indicated: *The significance of these findings will be discussed here in two contexts. First, the practical applications of the findings for...will be presented. Second, the findings will be discussed in terms of the theoretical implications for their contribution to...* It is statements like these that help make distinct the difference between 'good' and 'poor' theses, a characteristic of the latter being an inability to explain in the conclusion what had been argued in the thesis (Tinkler & Jackson, 2004) or, in the case of some qualitative theses, narrated. The trick then is not to have the body of the thesis 'richer and smarter' than portrayed in the conclusion (Lovitts, 2007, p.351).

6. In order to provide the necessary richness of texture to the conclusions and implications section it is useful to keep a separate 'conclusions' file at hand during the drafting of the thesis. As points arise that might appropriately be included in the conclusion they can first be included in the file. In this way a substantial body of useful material can be accumulated and tackling the conclusion and implications section becomes a less difficult task (Woods, 2006). It is also useful when writing the conclusions and implications

section to visualise the thesis as consisting of only the introduction, literature review and discussion sections. The conclusions and implications, as a result, will be seen not only as a direct response to the discussion but also to each of the other two sections as well. To this extent just as the examiners should gain from the abstract and the introduction the purpose and structure of a thesis, so too should they derive this information from a reading of the conclusions and implications section. This is important because examiners generally start writing their reports soon after reading the final chapter. The conclusion and implications section should be written with a view to facilitating their task (Owens, 2007b). Judicious phrasing is a means to do so:

If you use phrases such as 'this extends the classic work in this area by Smith and Jones (2002) by applying rough set theory' then the 'originality' bit is pretty clear... If you use phrasing such as 'these findings have significant implications for research in this field, which has typically viewed the topic as of comparatively minor importance' then the 'contribution to knowledge' bit is also pretty clear.

(Cited in Rugg & Petre, 2004, p.97)

Relating the conclusion to the introduction

7. In this vein the section should start with an assertion of the study's most important achievement: *The results contribute to existing literature by demonstrating that...* The assertion should be confident. Compare, for example, the start: *This study was centred on... and in some ways held a focus that was narrow, giving little attention to... It was, however, productive resulting in...*; with the following: *This project had two main aims. The first was to... The second was to... The achievement of the first aim allowed the development of a template that for the first time allows...* This positive introductory statement will, of necessity, need to be in reference to the main research question or hypothesis. Introduced in this way a sense of balance is created in the thesis: just as the main research question or hypothesis was the primary focus of the introduction, the answer or validation will be the primary focus of the conclusion:
   - Primary research question: 'An understanding of the factors that influence people to change their diets in a positive direction may provide us with some insights that are useful for the design of effective nutrition education and counselling programs.'
   - Primary research conclusion: 'The results of this study of adult supermarket shoppers suggest that studying those who have voluntarily changed their diets in a positive direction is a fruitful approach to the study of influences on dietary change. The information obtained in such an approach is also

useful for designing nutrition education and counselling programs.'
(Contento & Murphy, 1990, cited in Murison & Webb, 1991, p.69)

8.   The relationship between the introduction and conclusion can then be deepened by dealing, in turn, with each of the other questions or hypotheses. This not only ensures that each has adequately been addressed but it also creates an impression that the thesis has been brought full circle. By 'closing the loop' examiners are figuratively helped to see the conclusions and implications not merely as a separate section but as reflection on the thesis as a whole (Bergquist, 2004). But, in doing so, two important considerations will need to be borne in mind. First, there should be no disjuncture between the questions and/or hypotheses presented in the introduction and those discussed in the conclusions and implications section. If changes were made as the research progressed, the introduction will need to be modified appropriately and the consequences of the changes discussed in the conclusions and implications section. Second, it is unlikely that all of the research questions will be answered or all of the hypotheses validated with the same level of confidence. The difference in confidence levels will also, therefore, need to be discussed in the conclusions and implications section in the context of the strengths and limitations of the study.

Cautionary notes

9.   It might, in particular instances, be necessary to provide cautionary notes in order to nuance individual conclusions: *The assessment based on this data is only suggestive and serves merely as an indicator of a potential resource for future researchers.* If this is the case be as explicit as possible: *The findings support the need to consider...* There might also, in addition to showing why particular approaches were justified, be a need to show why particular approaches were not adopted: *Because mathematical models are less likely to be accurate when used in such areas, this study utilised these models minimally.* Even if issues like these were discussed in the methods section they ought briefly to be mentioned again both in order to jog the examiner's memory and to substantiate the wisdom of the decisions taken when the study was first designed. Because the evidence from other researchers that provided meaning, context and relevance to the results has already been provided and cited in the body of the discussion, careful thought will need to be applied to the wisdom of including the opinions of other researchers or results from their work in the conclusions and implications section. Because the purpose of this section of the thesis is to highlight the outcome of the study the spotlight should not normally be shared with anyone else.

12.11 SUGGESTIONS FOR FUTURE RESEARCH AND/OR RECOMMENDATIONS

1. Among the most useful ways to provide evidence to substantiate the value of a study is to show what can now be done that could not have been done prior to the study. This can be shown by doing either or, if appropriate, both of the following: indicating the avenues for future research the findings of the study have made possible and/or providing recommendations for improvements to, or the retention of, current practice. Recommendations constitute a powerful link between research and practice and, of all the contributions by a study tend to make the strongest claims to knowledge (Wallace & Wray, 2006). For this reason, though, care needs to be exercised when making them for each must clearly be supported by the data (Bryant, 2004). Recommendations should also be realistic in the sense that immediate linkages between research results and policy decisions are relatively rare (Thody, 2006). In some theses the recommendations made and avenues for future research suggested could, with only a limited degree of conjecture, have been made before the research was undertaken. So the latter, as in the case of the former, should also be firmly grounded in the findings of the study. Suggestions for future research can also, for example, be justified by suggesting the research be extended:

   This study improves the original work of…in that it takes into account … However, the results have been obtained by imposing the assumption that the… Because only a limited amount of information can, therefore, be extracted from the results the ultimate goal would be to…

2. Specific suggestions on how other researchers might apply the findings can also be made: *This study has shown that … theory is useful to capture certain phenomena… Therefore this method should enable further studies to compare…* The research might also be applied with refined instruments and different samples in another locale: *While the results of this study are consistent with… this outcome might not apply to other settings.* This is an indicator of the importance of replication in empirical research: the literature is replete with studies of significance but whose limitations minimise the generalisability of their findings. Suggestions might also be made that do not arise directly from the findings but from elsewhere in the thesis: *Another gap and therefore potential object of investigation that emerged in the literature review was the issue of…* Suggestions should be explicit if they are to have any impact. Do not, therefore, simply provide hints: *As suggested earlier, there are many more aspects to look at which this research was not able to investigate. Hence this study gives rise to more questions than solutions.* To be explicit suggestions need to be developed. Instead of writing for example *…it would also be interesting to study…*, explain why it would be interesting. Because they need to be developed bullet pointed

suggestions should be avoided. They can, however, be numbered or considered seriatim as this has less effect on the free flow of discussion: *Listed here, in order of importance and achievability, are possible directions for future investigations stemming from this work.* But, however avenues for further research are presented, avoid platitudes like *…more research is needed…* or *…this study has generated boundless possibilities for further investigation.*

3. Go back, after the section has been completed, and, despite fatigue, reread the introduction chapter to ensure that it is a foil for the conclusions, suggestions and recommendations. In this way the thesis becomes an encapsulated whole. This desirable outcome reiterates the importance of adequate planning at the outset of a study: despite the centrality of the conclusion to a thesis students are often left with insufficient time or energy to write it properly.

CHAPTER 13

Examining the thesis

The quality of mercy is not strained.

It droppeth as the gentle rain from heaven

Upon the place beneath. It is twice blest:

It blesseth him that gives and him that takes.

(Shakespeare, *The Merchant of Venice*, 4.1.179–182).

13.1 INTRODUCTION

1. A university's function is not only to produce and disseminate knowledge, but also to legitimise those who have met its academic and institutional norms (Garman, 2006). The examination is central to the process of legitimising a thesis. This seems clear enough, but in practice the process is not as straightforward as the statement suggests. The reason is best expressed in the following question posed by an examiner: 'It was clear that this was a weak thesis; the question was how weak can it be and still pass?' (cited in Tinkler & Jackson, 2004, p.119). There is no definitive answer for it is person, time, place and discipline dependent. What is clear is that the criteria constituting an acceptable thesis, be it a master's or doctorate, encompass a broad range of standards. Richard Rorty summed up the difficulty this broad range imposes:

   The trouble is that intersubjective agreement about who has succeeded and who has failed is easy to get if you can lay down criteria of success in advance... But intersubjective agreement is harder to get when the criteria of success begin to proliferate, and even harder when those criteria themselves are up for grabs.

   (Rorty, 1999, p.180)

2. At least part of the reason explaining the range of standards is lack of consensus about what a master's or doctoral thesis is. This has implications for the examination process: lack of consensus makes it difficult to define if a candidate has met the requirements for the degree. The implication, therefore,

is that definition and examination of a thesis are inextricable from each other (Tinkler & Jackson, 2004). This explains why thesis examinations are often conceptualised and performed in different ways (Paltridge & Starfield, 2007). These differences can become such significant aspects of the examination process, that although ostensibly so, it no longer constitutes an examination. This is apparent, for example, in the manner in which some *viva voce* (living voice) examinations are conducted. Not only are some successful candidates informed of the examiners' decision at the start of the *viva*, thus undermining the explicit purpose of the oral, surveys also indicate that in many other cases the final outcome of the examination has already been decided prior to the *viva* (Tinkler & Jackson, 2004). When neither of these instances apply the *viva*, nonetheless, introduces an important new element into the examining process for, where there is no *viva*, writing skills alone are examined, but with a *viva* the candidate's verbal skills are also implicitly assessed (Tinkler & Jackson, 2004).

3. The difference in the manner in which the oral examination is conducted is indicative of the importance of the need for thesis writers to become fully cognisant of the policies and criteria pertaining to the examination of theses at their university. Because these policies and criteria are subject to change only the most recent information should be accessed. Particular note will need to be taken of how the university defines masters' and doctoral theses for these definitions will be the touchstone upon which the criteria for their acceptability will have been based. But the interpretation of criteria has a subjective element, so gaining insight into how examiners proceed and what their expectations generally are is also important for they ought to influence the manner in which the thesis and the research it describes are both conceived and brought to fruition.

13.2 THE EXAMINING PROCESS

1. Universities administer theses differently. Some administer both masters' and doctoral theses centrally while others, particularly in regard to masters' theses, lay down basic criteria but leave the imposition of specifics to faculties or academic departments. The differences in the manner in which theses are examined are often reflections of these administrative differences. The required number of thesis examiners, for example, differs between universities. Some require two examiners for doctoral theses while others require three. In the latter case the identification of 'outrider' examiners is often made easier. Normally two examiners are required for masters' theses (Bourke, Holbrook & Lovat, 2007). In the interests of academic rigour at least one of the examiners of both masters' and doctoral theses will normally be external to the university.

Externals are usually chosen from other universities although, in exceptional circumstances, they might be specialists not employed by a university. In the case of interdisciplinary theses an additional external or internal examiner might be included. At some universities two internal examiners can be appointed if the preferred internal examiner is too inexperienced to act as sole internal examiner (Tinkler & Jackson, 2004). In the case of masters' theses supervisors can usually also be examiners of the thesis but, at most universities, supervisors of doctoral candidates have been excluded from examining the theses of their own students. In each case examiners are normally expected to act independently. In order to ensure this is the case a common practice is not to supply the names of each examiner to the other/s until the examination of the thesis has been completed (Bourke et al., 2007). There are, though, exceptions. In fine arts, for example, a common practice is the examination of a doctoral candidate's work at an exhibition. When the candidate accompanies the examiners to discuss the work the examination also constitutes a specific type of viva (Bourke et al., 2007). As in all other cases, though, each examiner submits a confidential report to an assessor.

2. Because they are expected to act as independent arbiters the role of assessor is usually filled by academics other than the examiners external or internal to the university. In the case of the latter, the assessor is often the dean of the faculty or the head of department. The role of assessor is to ensure that the evaluation process and the evaluation reports are fair. The assessor's task is also to reconcile differences between examiners in cases where their assessments differ. Each university has sets of procedures in place should the assessor be unable to reconcile these differences. Only rarely would this involve re-examination of the thesis by another examiner. Also rare is provision for an oral examination of masters candidates where the assessor is unable to reconcile differences between examiners. Common to all these cases though is the nature of the examiners' recommendations: they are just that, for it is normally a university committee acting on the basis of the recommendations that makes the final decision whether or not to accept a thesis (Bourke et al., 2007).

3. Doctoral theses, subject to the recommendation of the examiners, can be resubmitted for examination but universities differ in regard to the resubmission of masters' theses. Some merely request examiners to accept or reject the thesis and, if the former, to judge the quality of the pass. This is often the case at large, research-driven universities where the expense and administrative burden of resubmission would be considerable. Some universities, however, allow examiners of masters' theses the same degree of latitude as when a doctorate is examined. At either extreme this latitude permits examiners to either pass a thesis without amendments or to fail it outright. Between these extremes

lies a wide range of options. Normally, however, examiners may recommend that a thesis be accepted subject to the completion of alterations. Whether these alterations are to be judged as adequate by the principal supervisor or by the examiners is also usually left to the examiners to decide. In addition, examiners may recommend resubmission of a thesis for examination; they do this in full knowledge of the amount of work such a recommendation will impose on themselves, the supervisors and the candidate.

4. When examiners are provided wide latitude very few masters' or doctoral theses pass without amendment. Even fewer theses fail:

> *All PhDs are not equal and yet most get through. You form an impression that it is OK but not dazzling. This is often when the student applies standard theories in a rather pedestrian way. It's not wrong, and you can't fail it, but it's not dazzling.*

(Cited in Mullins & Kiley, 2002, p.380)

In the case of failure the appeals process and even the right to appeal differs both between masters' and doctoral theses and between universities. The ultimate appeal is to the law. But where this is the case the usual matter in contention is the placing of blame and the possible award of damages, not whether the degree should be awarded (Phillips & Pugh, 2005).

13.3 SELECTION OF EXTERNAL EXAMINERS

1. The criteria used by universities to select external examiners vary widely: some have formal requirements in terms of the qualifications, research and supervisory experience examiners should have in the area of the study; others have few formal criteria beyond expertise in the discipline (Mullins & Kiley, 2002). Heads of department or principal supervisors often approach potential candidates informally a few months prior to submission of the thesis to invite them to become an examiner. Because the examination process might include a need to comment on the quality of the supervision provided, external examiners are only rarely chosen if they are less experienced than, or junior to, the principal supervisor. Upon acceptance of the invitation, an official letter is sent confirming the appointment. Together with the title of the thesis the letter also usually contains the thesis abstract. Ideally, though, the invitee should receive the abstract prior to his or her official appointment in order to assist them to decide if they have sufficient expertise to do justice to the task (Tinkler & Jackson, 2004). In either event the letter constitutes the first meeting between the thesis writer and the external examiner. The importance of first impressions, in addition to the fact that the reports of external examiners normally carry more weight than those of internal

examiners, should provide incentive enough to ensure the title of the thesis is well worded and the abstract properly done well before final submission of the thesis itself.

2. External examiners are paid a mere honorarium to undertake work that is not only time consuming but which also needs to be undertaken in addition to the often considerable administrative, teaching and research commitments they already have. As a result the examining process is often done under pressure and at the last possible moment (Bergquist, 2004). So why do they do it? Primarily because it is usually part of an academic's job description and, together with supervision, a criterion in contract renewals and promotion applications. It also carries a degree of prestige because invitations to examine imply acknowledgement by his or her peers of an individual's ability. It is also a means not only of keeping abreast of research being conducted at other universities but also of benchmarking the standards of an examiner's own students. There is an additional, entirely pragmatic reason. The ranks of potential examiners are usually thin relative to the number of theses being produced so there is a mutual expectation of reciprocity among supervisors at different universities: we will examine your theses if you examine ours. A doctoral supervisor indicated this when he said: 'I have eight students at the moment which means I need 16 examiners soon…so I need to reciprocate' (cited in Mullins & Kiley, 2002, p.375).

3. How are external examiners chosen? The principal supervisor in consultation with the head of department generally makes the choice. The basis for the choice differs from one context to another because related factors like expertise, reputation, experience and publication profile all play a role, as do personal friendships and methodological congruence (Bourke, Scevak & Cantwell, 2001). Certainly if they do not already know the individual most supervisors attempt to find out as much as they can about them as human beings. This is implicit evidence of the significant subjective element inherent in the thesis examination process (Pearce, 2005). Related to this is the need for the external examiner either to be a user of the same broad theory and methods as applied in the thesis or flexible enough to understand and appreciate the value of different approaches (Tinkler & Jackson, 2004). The latter is generally the case with experienced examiners who, rather than adhering to a particular perspective, seek consistency in the thesis instead:

I try in my reading of theses to understand where the student is coming from. Even if I don't agree with the perspective they have, or if there are gaps, I try to see it from their eyes and whether they have been true to what they set out to do.

(Cited in Mullins & Kiley, 2002, p.375)

Thus, as in the case of refereed journal articles the examination of a thesis rests on the notion of evaluation by one's peers (Cryer, 2006). However, while it is accepted as fundamental that an external examiner should have expertise in the same research field as the thesis study it is often not possible to have an ideal match. This is particularly the case in the humanities where research tends to be more idiosyncratic than in the natural and social sciences and in interdisciplinary research where the examiners are frequently discipline based (Cryer, 2006).

4. Entirely practical factors such as convenience also play a role in the selection of external examiners: if the first or second choice of examiner is not available then the third or fourth might have to be approached. The end result might be incompatible examiners. This is why it is important that the process of selecting an external examiner, or examiners, should be started well before submission and not left until the last moment. The following extracts from two examiner reports on the same master's thesis are examples, albeit extreme ones, of what can happen when incompatible examiners are chosen[1]:

   • Examiner A: *It is rare to be invited to examine a thesis which proves pleasurable as well as interesting to read, but Ms. X's work prompted both responses. It is very impressive and shows an immensely thorough knowledge of the texts under discussion, while drawing on a widely varied range of scholarly background material in support of its arguments... Ms. X has succeeded admirably in the task she has undertaken. I strongly commend her thesis and hope very much she will publish her findings either in the form of a book or of journal articles.*

   • Examiner B: *As I cannot give a positive reply to any of the questions listed under (1) on this form, I believe I have no choice but to recommend that the candidate be not awarded this degree. This is the first time I have ever made such a recommendation—I am not prepared, however, to see the thesis awarded a master's degree... I have several pages of detailed notes but I do not believe this thesis can be revised. I am therefore not going to waste any further time writing these out. There is nothing here fit for publication and no evidence of original or independent thought.*

(Cited in Kamler & Threadgold, 1996, p.2)

The extremes of judgement displayed in these reports are unusual for there is normally a significant level of consistency between examiners in the strengths and weaknesses they identify in a thesis. Differences normally tend to become most clearly apparent in their decisions about what should happen as a result. In essence then, the comments that examiners make in their reports do not necessarily provide clear guidance to what the final outcome of the examination will be (Bourke et al., 2007).

5. Some universities require candidates to be consulted on the selection of external examiners. In practice, this usually means the principal supervisor asking a

candidate if they have a preference for particular individuals or if there are any they would not want as examiners (Bourke et al., 2007). In this case attendance at conferences is an excellent way to identify individuals who might be appropriate. However, some universities expressly forbid consultation with candidates on this matter. Nonetheless, even when it is forbidden to do so, some supervisors, when they feel it is warranted, sometimes, and in confidence, do ask candidates for an opinion. Some later regret having acted on that input for the candidate's choice of external examiner can be ill advised (pers. comm.). Take care, therefore, if asked for an opinion, to lean heavily on the supervisor's experience and advice.

6. Disciplinary rigour, personal integrity and oversight by colleagues and university committees generally ensure that the commonalities between examiners in terms of perceptions and standards are greater than the differences. Nonetheless, differences exist, for examiners come to the examining process with different sets of understandings and expectations and different levels of confidence and tolerance. These differences are not only evident between but also within individual examiners: an examiner who, for example, tolerates a degree of ambiguity in one thesis might not tolerate it in another (Lovat et al., 2002).

13.4 ASSESSMENT CRITERIA

1. Supervisors are often required to attend courses on best practice in supervision. There are no equivalent courses on thesis assessment. Many academics, in fact, would find the notion they need training to examine a thesis in their own specialism absurd (Pearce, 2005). But adopting this attitude ignores some substantive issues in thesis examining that lie outside the disciplinary arena. Obvious examples are interdisciplinary and/or mixed method studies; another is the criteria that ought to be applied when deciding whether to accept or reject the role of examiner of particular theses, another is the significant ambiguity of 'publishability', a criterion often applied to doctoral theses (Pearce, 2005). Yet another is the level of seniority of the examiner. The pressure on internal examiners, for example, to pass a thesis against their better judgement is often heavier than on external examiners, particularly where the internal examiner is junior to the candidate's supervisor (Lovat, Holbrook & Hazel, 2001). These are a few of the reasons explaining why generic guidelines for examining theses have been developed in some countries and why a number of disciplines, mainly in the natural sciences, have also developed guidelines. In all cases, though, the guidelines are not obligatory, simply checklists of good practice (Kiley & Mullins, 2006). Much the same could be said of university guidelines to examiners.

2. While masters' and doctoral theses differ from each other and may be written differently in different disciplines and methodologies, universities, apart from an emphasis on originality in doctoral theses, typically apply similar criteria

to the examination of both. This is done, insofar as possible, to standardise the examining process and, thus, to promote fairness. These criteria are usually sent in a covering letter to the examiners with a copy of the thesis to be examined. Together with the criteria these 'Instructions to Examiners and Assessors' also usually explain how the examination process is to proceed and provide an expected time frame within which the process should be completed. This is normally about six weeks but, because examining a thesis is sometimes given a lower priority than many of the other tasks confronting academics, there is little in practice a university can do if an external examiner takes longer. This explains at least one of the reasons why some students receive the examination result sooner than others who submitted at the same time.

3. The assessment standards provided by universities to examiners are, necessarily, not precisely defined. Normally they require masters' and doctoral theses, if they are to pass, to demonstrate: evidence of independent thought; originality; confident use of appropriate theory; ability to evaluate and critically discuss the literature; ability to engage in rigorous analysis and problem solving; and mastery of the conventions of the discipline/s. Individual departments also usually suggest particular areas they wish examiners to comment on: the contribution of the study; the authenticity of the study; the rationale for the study; the persuasiveness of the argument; the internal congruence; and the presentation and format. The inclusion of presentation and format indicates the explicit editorial element in the examination process (Pearce, 2005). There is, though, a caveat to this list of criteria: they are not a rubric.

Experienced examiners take a holistic approach to the process of making judgements, in the way they consider the whole thesis document and judge the quality of its various aspects as they relate to one another, rather than as stand-alone qualities. Therefore, while it was possible to list a number of characteristics of a passable thesis... it is not possible to 'mark' each one out of 10, total the results, and declare a thesis passed or failed.

(Cited in Mullins & Kiley, 2002, p.383)

Failure to recognise the holistic and relational nature of the examining process explains why some candidates consider the examination of a thesis as summative only: passing, failing or grading. Examiners, on the other hand, usually consider the process to be both summative and formative: in addition to assessing them, giving feedback to assist candidates to develop their work further (Mullins & Kiley, 2002). Examiners also seek indeterminate qualities, qualities that can be recognised but not itemised or precisely articulated.

These qualities include such things as intellectual grasp, coherence, and critical thinking. They are things that are believed to be 'caught' rather than 'taught'. In other words, possession and display of appropriate indeterminate qualities are part of the candidates' cultural capital and reflect their tacit knowledge of disciplinary and academic culture.

(Lovitts, 2007, p.7)

4. Examining a thesis would be relatively straightforward if the requirement was simply to pass or fail (Tinkler & Jackson, 2004). Not only, though, can examiners impose conditions on a pass some universities also require theses to be graded along a continuum. It is the imprecision of this process that explains the request for a grade rather than a percentage mark and also explains why grade or mark descriptors often accompany the assessment standards. For example:

   • A+ (91 to 100 per cent) Exceptional content, presentation and originality and excellent in analysis and degree of understanding displayed.
   • B+ (75 to 79 per cent) Polished, comprehensive coverage showing clear understanding of procedures and concepts.
   • C+ (60 to 64 per cent) Adequate understanding, mediocre analysis and presentation.
   • D+ (45 to 49 per cent) Inadequate understanding and poor presentation.

   These grades, marks and descriptors might vary not only between universities but also, though usually only slightly, between departments within a university. The latter, in particular, can be disconcerting to students but there are grounds for the discrepancies. Would it be fair, for example, to examine a thesis in English literature against the same set of criteria applied when examining a thesis in physics? It might well be but, because the issue is subject to debate, universities continue to adopt different policies on the issue.

5. However, the degree to which examiners adhere to the assessment standards provided by universities varies between individuals. Most experienced examiners write their reports in the manner requested by the university

   …but, when it came to the point of making a judgement, they regarded themselves as the arbiters of an acceptable thesis: 'No first rate researcher is without a belief that they understand the standards in that field and can recognise excellence in that field. So if you ask me to examine, you are going to get [my] standard.'

   (Cited in Mullins & Kiley, 2002, p.380)

   In general, the less experienced the examiner the more attention they pay to the standards. This, however, does not appear to effect materially the chances of their being either more lenient or more demanding (Holbrook et al., 2003). Despite the fact that some examiners rely more on their own internalised standards than on those supplied by the university it remains, nonetheless, advisable for thesis writers to become acquainted with the list of university criteria to ensure their thesis responds to each of the requirements (Rowarth & Fraser, 2006).

13.5 EXAMINER REPORTS

1. In the case of doctorates universities vary as to whether an independent report must be submitted formally before a viva. (If one is to be held.) They also differ in the matter of student access to the reports after the examination process has been concluded and the result released. In most cases examiners are asked to indicate whether they are prepared to have their name released to the student and whether their report too may be released. Most accede to both. In this case it is usually up to the principal supervisor to decide upon the wisdom of releasing the reports in full or, instead, to provide a digest. In highly negative reports the latter approach is normally adopted (Pearce, 2005). In particular cases, though, it might also be adopted when the reports are primarily positive. The reason lies in the nature of the reports. Unless a candidate has been exposed to the type of comments referees sometimes make of articles submitted for publication they will very likely never before have been exposed to the type of critical edge critique that is the hallmark of examiner reports (Pearce, 2005). The reports also have particularly disorienting features. A frequent one is the inverse relationship between the extensiveness of examiner comment and the quality of the thesis. Many candidates expect a poor thesis to elicit extensive comment; usually however it is the good ones that do (Kiley & Mullins, 2006). Another disorienting feature is the apparent inconsistency of simultaneous praise and criticism. This is explained by the perception of most examiners of the report as both an exercise of a pass/fail judgement and as an educational and developmental process (Kiley & Mullins, 2006). In this latter regard the reports are often cast prospectively indicating what could be done to improve the thesis (Pearce, 2005). In this sense the reports are both summative and formative. Because examiners are such because of their expertise in the area of the thesis most feel a need to make their knowledge and experience visible in the reports (Pearce, 2005). This consciousness that their own reputation will be judged through the quality of the report (Mullins & Kiley, 2002) explains why many reports are excellent pieces of writing and why candidates, despite the mixed feelings they induce, stand to gain much by reading them.

13.6 HOW EXAMINERS PROCEED

1. Examiners have no standard method for reading a thesis: manner, place and time taken vary between them. It also varies between disciplines, a short

though equation-heavy physics thesis, for example, might take longer to examine than a lengthier thesis in another discipline. Quality is an additional factor; a poorly presented thesis often requires more time and attention than a well-written one (Tinkler & Jackson, 2004). Listing required corrections in a poor thesis can, in fact be a significant undertaking: 'Indeed, examiners to whom this task falls are liable to swear that they will never accept the invitation to examine a PhD again!' (Pearce, 2005, p.101). Quite apart from the ethical need to do so threat of litigation also requires that corrections need to be detailed precisely. Explicit explanations, therefore, need to be provided for the failure of a thesis or, alternatively, explicit instructions provided on what needs to be done to allow a thesis to be accepted (Pearce, 2005). This means that although examiners might skim read a thesis to become acquainted with its contents, skim reading is not an option when an examiner's report is being prepared. This, in turn, means that simply close reading a doctoral thesis takes a minimum of eight hours, many more when note taking, report writing and the viva too are taken into consideration (Pearce, 2005).

2. Apart from personal acquaintanceship there is no way to predict how individual examiners might start the examination process. Some, for example, might start with the results and conclusions section, others might first look at the tables and figures while others, particularly in the social sciences, might start with the appendices. Here, poorly designed questionnaires and briefing sheets, for example, are likely to reflect poorly on the thesis as a whole (Rugg & Petre, 2004). The uncertainty about where examiners will begin, together with the likelihood that the thesis will be read by them in interrupted sessions, points to the need to construct the thesis so that it retains coherence irrespective of where the examiners begin (Kiley & Mullins, 2006). Nonetheless, the manner in which most examiners start the process tends to fall into two categories: those who read the thesis first and then, on the second reading, proceed to take detailed notes, and those who start a detailed analysis during the first reading. The former is preferable for it enables holistic judgements to be made in the context of the thesis as an entirety, not simply in the context of what has been read up to a particular point (Pearce, 2005).

13.7 EXAMINER COMMENTS
Intellectual endeavours

1. The comments that examiners make of theses also tend to fall into two categories. The first is 'intellectual endeavours'. Does the researcher, for example, display critical understanding of the topic? Has the literature been critically appraised? How explicit are the links between the literature and

the methodology? Has the research design been adequately justified? Have the results been rigorously analysed and interpreted, and have the research limitations been identified and adequately taken into account? (Murray, 2003). This is where the publication of aspects of doctoral research in refereed journals can be especially beneficial: 'Publications lighten the burden for the examiner as other reviewers have said that it is OK… If there is nothing published you think "That's interesting!"' (cited in Kiley & Mullins, 2006, p.202). At some universities the criterion of 'publishable quality' applies to the award of a PhD. Publication, thus, demonstrates fulfilment of the criterion (Tinkler & Jackson, 2004). An expectation of actual publication tends, though, to be discipline specific. In the natural and social sciences, for example, papers in high impact journals make a post-doctoral position following graduation more likely (Pearson et al., 2009. In the humanities, however, pre-publication is not usually a significant consideration as it is not common practice in these disciplines (Mullins & Kiley, 2002). There are, however, two related issues in regard to 'intellectual endeavours' about which examiners are particularly sensitive. The first is disjuncture between the thesis statement and the argument: 'The major weakness in the thesis is not in what it does, but in what it purports to do but does not in fact do' (cited in Holbrook & Dally, 2003, p.14). The second is lack of clarity: 'It is entirely unclear what hypothesis is being tested' (cited in Lovat et al., 2002, p.14). In the social sciences in particular, an inadequate theoretical framework will draw criticism that the research is 'merely descriptive' or 'no more than a data collecting exercise' (cited in Kiley & Mullins, 2006, p.204). On the whole, however, examiners tend to be tolerant of the research approach adopted as long as it is well argued and consistently applied (Kiley & Mullins, 2006).

2. Originality is another quality of 'intellectual endeavours' that, understandably in doctoral theses, receives frequent comment. Reports on outstanding theses, in fact, contain significantly less comment on minor inaccuracies and a significantly greater proportion about the originality and significance of the research than do average theses: 'X has been able to generate extensive and important new information that complements existing theoretical data' (cited in Holbrook et al., 2003, p.8). A doctoral thesis, even when it constitutes a significant body of well-written work, passes or fails on the strength of its originality: 'The thesis is a well-constructed body of substantial work but it has to meet the criterion in the schedule of "original and significant contribution" for a degree at this level' (cited in Lovat et al., 2002, p.11). Masters' theses are expected to contain elements of originality and examiners will expect to find them. What will need to be done, therefore, in both masters' and doctoral theses is that originality as it applies to the study in the thesis will, in most cases, need to be both defined and readily identifiable (Pearce, 2005).

3. Once the issue of originality has been satisfactorily put to rest the other qualities that examiners frequently acknowledge in the category 'intellectual endeavours' are the amount of hard work involved and the degree of difficulty intrinsic to particular research undertakings: 'This is a very impressive and thorough piece of work which tackles difficult issues which often prove hard to research' (cited in Holbrook et al., 2003, p.10). Examiners also acknowledge the commitment and effort involved in simply completing a thesis (Holbrook & Dally, 2003). This explains why they are prepared to accept work that is merely adequate:

The thesis indicates that [X] is sufficiently familiar with, and understands, the relevant scientific literature on [the specific area]. To a major degree, the thesis provides a sufficiently comprehensive investigation of... On the whole, the results are suitably set out and accompanied by adequate exposition and interpretation. The conclusions and implications have been appropriately developed and clearly linked to the nature and content of the research framework and findings.

(Cited in Holbrook & Dally, 2003, p.14)

Communicative aspects

4. The second category into which the comments of most examiners fall is 'communicative aspects' (Murray, 2003). To what extent, for example, is the explanation of the research logical and coherent, the writing clear and error free and the thesis as a whole 'user-friendly?' The latter, for example, might apply to the effectiveness of the table of contents and headings and subheadings and to whether tables and figures have been suitably presented and located (Murray, 2003). In terms of the text, long, convoluted sentences that obscure rather than clarify meaning are among the faults examiners find most irritating (Bergquist, 2004). Once annoyed by easily avoidable blemishes they tend to become very 'picky' about the remainder of the thesis (Kiley & Mullins, 2006). When well written and presented, though, examiners across the disciplines use artistic terms and metaphors to describe a thesis: 'creative', 'elegant' and 'well sculpted' are a few examples. The use of these terms and metaphors indicate that excellent theses have 'indeterminate qualities which examiners can recognize but not itemize precisely because, by their very indeterminacy, they are resistant to precise explication' (Tinkler & Jackson, 2004, p.120).

5. Within reason a well-researched thesis is unlikely to fail because of poor presentation. As a category, therefore, 'intellectual endeavours' ranks more highly than 'communicative aspects'. They are, nonetheless, related. Sound research and good presentation complement each other, while poorly presented work causes a loss of confidence by examiners in the work as a whole (Murray,

2003). In this sense, as mentioned earlier, the expectations of the examiner of a thesis are no different from those of other readers: they might be experts in their field but they also want to read well-presented, interesting and enjoyable material (Murray, 2003). This explains why well-researched and well-written theses usually receive high praise:

The… most perfectly written dissertation [sic] I have come across in my academic career. As in a perfect piece of prose, where the reader is pulled into the plot on the first page, this scientific treatise arouses your interest immediately in the intro-duction and continues to do so till its last page. The clarity of the exposition is outstanding, and one would like to see textbooks written in such an illuminating fashion. The examples used are a perfect demonstration of how to reduce complex-ity without becoming trivial. On the other hand, the scientific content is impressive.

(Cited in Holbrook & Dally, 2003, p.13)

6. It is, therefore, on the basis of both 'intellectual endeavours' and 'communicative aspects' that examiners, in the concluding comments to their reports, make clear the distinction between poor and good theses:

    *   *I have major difficulties with this thesis. The major weaknesses are that the contents are not well linked to the research literature and the research component is relatively small and appears to have been used to justify more than it deserves. Indeed, most of the conclusions are based more on findings from previous studies than on the author's own research… While the central idea is sound, the thesis reads like several poorly-connected small studies that have been put together post-hoc, with poor connection to the academic literature, inadequately thought-through and applied methodology, and poor linkage back to the real world.*

        (Cited in Lovat et al., 2002, p.20)

    *   *There are several strengths of this thesis. Firstly, it is extensively referenced and makes critical use of relevant local and international literature. Secondly, the sampling was designed meticulously to ensure that the information collected would be amenable to statistical evaluation and address the questions posed. Thirdly, a very large amount of effort went into the fieldwork (some [thousands of]… hours) to ensure accuracy of the data obtained. Finally, the thesis is well-written and produced, with relatively few minor errors. Difficulties and biases are acknowledged, such as the limited replication that was available, and the candidate has been careful not to draw conclusions that depart too far from what the results allow. The thesis overall makes a substantive original contribution to knowledge, and provides recommendations both for future… management and further research.*

        (Cited in Holbrook & Dally, 2003, p.13)

13.8 EXAMINERS AND SUPERVISORS

1. The examination of a thesis is as much a test of the supervisor/s as it is of the student. This explains why those invited to become external examiners are usually of equal or higher rank than the principal supervisor. There is, though, discrepancy in the manner in which judgements are made. Where praise is given it is usually offered to the candidate and the supervisor/s together:

    *   *...I believe that the student and supervisor should be congratulated for bringing together an excellent examination of this very sensitive area.*

(Cited in Lovat & Morrison, 2003, p.7)

    *   *This was a great piece of work and both the candidate and supervisors are to be congratulated.*

(Cited in Lovat & Morrison, 2003, p. 8)

Criticism, however, tends to be allocated separately. Although the candidate is usually held responsible for a blemished thesis, the hierarchy implicit in the examining process is made evident when, on a few occasions, the supervisor is held responsible. Some of the comments can be particularly cutting:

I note that the candidate has not had the benefit of direct supervision by an expert in the field and therefore believe that responsibility for the ultimate product does not solely lie with the candidate.

(Lovat & Morrison, 2003, p.6)

On rare occasions candidates receive sympathy while the supervisors are criticised:

...I describe earlier a concern regarding supervision; it seems remarkable that such a vivid imagination as is described here and such a capacity for the construction of narrative was not given guidance to reach the potential of this research...

(Lovat & Morrison, 2003, p.6)

To be discussed fully by the examiners, the question of whether or not it is fair to penalise a candidate for a failure of supervision requires the absence of the supervisors. This explains why they have been excluded from the doctoral examination process and why they are also progressively being removed from the examination of masters' theses as well. Where it is patently clear that an able candidate has suffered to the point of failure as a consequence of poor supervision resubmission tends to be the norm (Phillips & Pugh, 2005).

13.9 THE VIVA VOCE: INTRODUCTION

1. At some universities, primarily in Europe and North America, *viva voces* are *de rigeur*. In some others, those in Australia (but not in New Zealand) for example, they have to all intents and purposes been abandoned. In yet others they have either never been held or exist on paper only.[2] Not only tradition but also the expense of vivas in terms of both money and time explain this discrepancy. Where they are held the reasons for using them vary. In rare instances they might be applied to masters candidates where an examiner has raised particular concerns about the thesis. More usually, though, in regard to masters' theses, they apply to candidates who wish to convert to a doctorate. In the United States they might be applied at the proposal stage of a doctoral dissertation (in which case they are termed a prospectus[3]), after the submission of the dissertation, or on both occasions[4]. Where both are held the examiners will be looking for 'congruence between the promises made in the proposal and what appears in the final draft of the study' (Mauch & Birch, 1998, p.252). This type of background information is apposite for those candidates who face the prospect of a viva for it means not all supervisors or even examiners have experienced a viva themselves (Fraser & Rowarth, 2007).

Variability

2. When vivas are held the manner in which they are implemented also differs. At some universities, particularly those in continental Europe, they are formal, almost ritualised, public occasions. At others they are more private and range from the formal to the informal: 'Candidates' descriptions of their experience of the viva range from a pleasant after-tea chat to a persecutory inquisition' (Phillips & Pugh, 2005, p.178). It is the more private of the vivas to which most of what follows applies. But even in this limited sense vivas are highly variable. It is this, not knowing what to expect, that explains the fear often experienced by some candidates about to undergo a viva (Tinkler & Jackson, 2004). It also explains the primary reason for this section: to provide some indication of what to expect. But the advice needs to be applied flexibly and in the context of sometimes department-specific regulations and traditions. It has also been written for those candidates, both masters and doctoral, who will not undergo a viva. Those who do have a viva have a significant advantage over those who do not: the viva personalises the examination process. It is, therefore, even more incumbent upon those thesis writers who will not have a viva to make their presence felt in both the text and organisation of the thesis. Examiners at a viva can also ask for parts of the thesis to be clarified, those not having a viva have only one chance to be

clear. All thesis writers, though, should pay particular attention to the types of question examiners ask at vivas and those aspects of theses they are most likely to probe.

The function of vivas

3. The origin of vivas lies in antiquity and the reasons for the longevity of the tradition numerous. But, in contemporary terms, vivas fulfil a number of specific and important functions. Perhaps most important is the platform they provide for authenticating a thesis. It is here where examiners can establish the extent to which a study is indebted to supervisors or technical assistants (Rowarth & Fraser, 2006). This is a powerful reason why examiners should not release a provisional decision at the start of the viva even when the thesis is considered excellent (Tinkler & Jackson, 2004). Another important function of a viva is to test how responsive candidates are to suggestions for change and improvement (Pearce, 2005). The viva, in other words, is an examination with a didactic purpose. At a more mundane level and in a minority of instances, the outcome of a viva can decide borderline cases or confirm a fail and explore why the failure occurred (Tinkler & Jackson, 2004). The viva, when properly conducted, also fulfils an important psychological function: a good viva is not necessarily an easy viva. Intensive probing and wide ranging questions might be exhausting but they bring with them a satisfying sense of closure (Tinkler & Jackson, 2004).

The process

4. Where a preliminary decision is not released at the start, there are usually five steps in a viva. The first is a meeting between the examiners immediately prior to the viva to decide upon procedure. The second is the discussion of the thesis with the candidate. The third is when the examiners alone meet to discuss their final recommendation. The fourth is when the candidate is invited to return to the room to be informed of the recommendation. (This step is sometimes omitted at some universities; the candidate, instead, is informed by letter.) The fifth is when the examiners, either individually or collectively, draft a report indicating their recommendations in detail together with the reasons for them. This report is then submitted to the appropriate university committee and, upon its confirmation, the candidate is officially informed of the outcome (Tinkler & Jackson, 2004). Only occasionally do the second and fifth steps resemble those of Ludwig Wittgenstein at Cambridge in 1929 where his *Tractatus Logico–Philosophicus* was examined by the most esteemed British philosophers at the time, Bertrand Russell and George Moore:

…at the end of the thesis defense, Wittgenstein clapped the two examiners on the shoulder and said, 'Don't worry, I know you'll never understand it.' Moore commented in the examiner's report: 'In my opinion this is a work of genius; it is, in any case, up to the standards of a degree from Cambridge' (Wikipedia)

13.10 PREPARING FOR THE VIVA

1. Because they often work in research teams and regularly discuss the research with each other and with supervisors, doctoral candidates working in the natural sciences, engineering and medicine usually feel more confident about the viva than do lone researchers in the humanities (Pearce, 2005). Nonetheless, for researchers in all fields the waiting period between submission of the thesis and the viva is likely to exceed three months (Tinkler & Jackson, 2004), sometimes considerably so. Generally, however, the usual minimum notice indicating when the viva is to be held is only two weeks. During this time of intense anticipation researchers generally have a valid claim to be a leading expert in their particular field. What never ceases to amaze, though, is how quickly research, even in the humanities, becomes dated. Thus, because examiners will expect candidates to know their thesis in detail and because it is likely that aspects of the thesis will be forgotten in the time leading up to the viva, the thesis will need to be read and reread until it is at the candidate's fingertips: 'The candidate had a very clear view of what was where in the bound document so that flow was never interrupted by any pauses' (cited in Tinkler & Jackson, 2004, p.147). There will be no need to tremble at the prospect of reading the thesis yet again for it will be discovered that reading it after submission is an entirely different experience from reading it prior to submission (Tinkler & Jackson, 2004). Having a thesis at one's fingertips does not, however, mean that examiners will expect candidates to answer from memory. For this reason they will generally specify with a page reference the passages they wish to discuss and will provide time for the candidate to read them (Cryer, 2006). But because examiners will, nonetheless, expect the candidate to quickly find their way around the thesis methods need to be adopted to facilitate the process.

2. A particularly effective way is to annotate the thesis with stickers. Another is to divide a maximum of three sheets of ruled paper with a vertical line. Then on each horizontal half-line on either side of the vertical write a précis of each page of the thesis and number each accordingly. Not only does this encourage a close reading of each page of the thesis and allow each part to be located precisely, it also enables final revision without reference to the thesis itself (Phillips & Pugh, 2005). The danger of this method, however, is the emphasis given to knowing one's way around the thesis at the expense of understanding what has been written and why (Tinkler & Jackson, 2004).

This is why emphasis should be given to reading the thesis at regular intervals during the entire waiting period, not a few days prior to the viva. If the latter is the case there will be little time to reflect on the possible questions that might be asked and overloading and anxiety might result (Tinkler & Jackson, 2004). Instead, the readings should be unhurried and purposeful. A number of reading sessions, for example, could focus on weaknesses and contentious points in the thesis while others could focus on key stages in the development of the argument. Doing so will enable a candidate during the viva to reflect on aspects of the thesis with the examiners by, for example, indicating how thoughts about issues have changed and how parts of the thesis, as a result, could be improved. Reflection, bear in mind, is a key purpose of the viva.

Keeping abreast of the literature

3. To reflect adequately on exegetic and empirical material means going beyond the thesis. This means keeping abreast of and being able to cite the literature published since submission, particularly the literature that challenges the argument adopted in the thesis (Tinkler & Jackson, 2004). A useful way of doing so is to scan reviews and abstracts and to read a few directly relevant articles in research journals (Tinkler & Jackson, 2004). In addition, candidates should get as much experience as possible at responding to questions: 'In retrospect, further experience of fielding questions following the oral delivery of a paper would have helped my viva performance' (cited in Tinkler & Jackson, 2004, p.49). This aspect of the preparation for the viva should, therefore, begin during the conduct of the research for the thesis: candidates should actively seek out opportunities to access research cultures by, for example, tutoring and publishing and by presenting papers at conferences. Even simply attending a conference can be important for it will not only help to situate the thesis in a broader context (Tinkler & Jackson, 2004) but the sorts of questions asked will provide a basis for anticipating the questions that might be asked during the viva (Rugg & Petre, 2004). If permissible, also try to attend the viva of other candidates. There are two useful adjuncts. One is to write a book proposal based on the study in the thesis. Publisher's guidelines for prospective authors in particular fields can easily be downloaded from the web. This exercise is an interesting way of focusing on the specifics of the thesis: its originality and contribution (Tinkler & Jackson, 2004). A second adjunct is to arrange a mock viva.

Mock vivas

4. These can be conducted with fellow candidates and/or with supervisors. A degree of creativity might at times be required, a candidate reported: 'I did my mock viva over the telephone with one supervisor' (cited in Tinkler & Jackson,

2004, p.129). Mock vivas can be useful not only because they might expose candidates to questions they had not been expecting but also because they might make explicit those question that most frighten the candidates. It also enables different ways of responding to questions to be tried experimentally (Rowarth & Fraser, 2006). The net result is usually an ability to provide thoughtful answers during the actual viva (Mauch & Birch, 1998). There are, however, dangers to a mock viva. The greatest is the possibility of a wide divergence between the mock and actual viva in both atmosphere and in the type of questions asked. In regard to the latter, for example, a post-viva candidate commented:

Well, for example, personally I was expecting questions such as: What are the main findings of the study? What do you see as the main contributions of your study? Would you do anything different now? How do you see things five or ten years from now? They did not ask many questions that examined my knowledge. They were interested to find out more about the methodology and procedures. I expected something about that, but not for it to be the main content of the viva.

(Cited in Tinkler & Jackson, 2004, p.61)

The questions asked of a candidate with a good thesis might also be very different from those asked of a candidate with a borderline thesis (Cryer, 2006). This is where knowing who the examiners will be is helpful for becoming familiar with their relevant publications will help anticipate the type of questions they might ask (Rugg & Petre, 2004).

Supervisors and the viva

5. Supervisors will also usually be able to assist in the process of anticipating possible questions but they, in turn, will be assisted in doing so by the willingness of the candidate to hold a completely open discussion about the strengths and weaknesses of the thesis (Mauch & Birch, 1998). Bear in mind that for a candidate to fail a viva is rare. But, where this is the case it is usually attributable to two factors: failure to access research cultures and thus the opportunity to expose work to scrutiny and failure to listen to the advice of supervisors when preparing for the viva (Rugg & Petre, 2004). Thus, in addition to meeting supervisors while preparing for the viva, a meeting between candidate and supervisor should also take place shortly before the viva to ensure the former is clear about the procedures to be followed (Tinkler & Jackson, 2004). By this time the principal supervisor should also have been informed of any special equipment that the candidate might wish to use during the viva in order for the permission of the examiners to be requested. Supervisors will not normally attend the viva but it is usual for

them to shepherd the candidate by escorting them to the room where the viva is to be held and to greet and debrief them afterwards (Pearce, 2005). The debriefing is important. In most cases theses are passed subject to correction and amendment. But even when minor the need for these changes might appear to taint the pass. It is here where the supervisor might help to place the need for the changes in a positive light. Even when the need to do so is not necessary, the debriefing at least provides an opportunity to clarify the nature and extent of the changes and to provide encouragement for the completion of this final task.

Examiner preparations

6. Examiners too need to prepare for a viva for, despite having prepared reports they will, nonetheless, need to refresh their memory of a text possibly read weeks before. They also need to ensure that the questions they propose to ask are valid. It is in this context that an experienced examiner advises what examiners should do in the days immediately prior to the viva:

Return to those sections of the thesis which seem to be the most weak or controversial and make absolutely sure that what you are 'accusing' the candidate of is credible. Another trick is to return to the abstract and/or introduction and consider, afresh, to what extent the thesis achieves what it sets out to do. Similarly, take a further long, hard look at the conclusion and use that to direct you to the more obvious gaps in what has been presented.

(Pearce, 2005, p.78)

Examiners generally meet just prior to the viva to compare the recommendations in their preliminary reports. The fact they do not confer earlier is important: it ensures the candidate's interests are protected because the examiners will have genuinely independent opinions to fall back on should the outcome of the viva divide opinion between them (Pearce, 2005). This too is indicated in the following advice to viva examiners:

Being clear what you think about the thesis, and preparing a written account of your position, is vital to good preparation as a professor of history explains: 'I've learned over the years to be very clear about my judgement before the viva, even when this is necessarily provisional, depending in part on how the student responds to questions in the viva'.

(Tinkler & Jackson, 2004, p.122)

The implication is that examiners should be prepared, after the viva, to have an open discussion of the relative merits of the candidate's work in the thesis and in their performance during the viva. But where the preliminary reports indicate fundamental disagreement between examiners based on contrasting value systems, and should the assessor not have addressed these disagreements, then the viva should either be cancelled or university officials informed of the differences prior to the viva going ahead. Only in this way might another examiner subsequently be brought into the process to ensure a fair decision is finally reached (Pearce, 2005). However, such differences rarely occur if appropriate examiners have been chosen. The more usual situation is for the preliminary recommendations of the examiners to be in relatively close accord. When this is the case the function of the viva can then be determined: to confirm an impression where the recommendations concur or to determine an outcome when recommendations are close but on either side of a borderline (Pearce, 2005).

7. It is usual for the external examiner/s to play the lead role in both the agenda-setting meeting prior to the viva and during the viva itself. Thus, although as the discussion progresses each examiner may contribute widely or merely focus on specific topics (Phillips & Pugh, 2005), it is usually the external examiner who has first choice of questions and it is also usually he or she who determines which questions should have the most time devoted to them (Pearce, 2005). Unless carefully managed though the leading role played by the external/s can place significant pressure on less experienced more junior examiners whose opinions on a candidate's work might be overturned prior to the viva even having taken place (Pearce, 2005).

13.11 THE EXAMINATION

1. There is no common rule dictating how long vivas should last but one to three hours generally define the limits. There are, though, disciplinary differences. Vivas in the natural sciences, for example, tend towards the outer limit while those in the humanities and the social sciences towards the lower (Tinkler & Jackson, 2004). In regard to the humanities this tendency might be explained by the perception of examiners that it is the candidate and her/his potential that is being examined, not the thesis document alone (Mullins & Kiley, 2002). This reflects the more-process-than-product nature of most theses in the humanities: 'It's an idea that is in process and will often continue to be in process after they've graduated...' (Lovitts, 2007, p.301). There are also disciplinary differences in the manner in which theses are discussed at vivas. In some of the natural sciences, for example, a page-by-page or even line-by-line approach to sections of the thesis might be appropriate (Tinkler & Jackson, 2004). However if either of these approaches were to be adopted by an examiner in the humanities the viva might legitimately be seen as a nit-picking exercise demeaning the purpose of the process (Pearce,

2005). In addition to disciplinary differences there are also differences in the regulations, both written and unwritten, governing the conduct of vivas. There is, for example, no common rule prescribing who may or may not attend a viva. At some universities it is a public defence, at others attendance is limited to the candidate and the examiners. At a few universities an independent chairperson may adjudicate the viva. When supervisors are permitted to attend many candidates prefer them not to for their presence can be inhibiting (Cryer, 2006).

2. There are, though, a few pieces of advice that apply to most vivas. Apart from any other supporting material necessary for the conduct of particular vivas, candidates should at least have with them an annotated copy of their thesis and a pen and paper. Research notebooks and/or research diaries, annotated if necessary should also, if applicable, be taken. Even when the viva is informal smart clothing should be worn to acknowledge the importance of the event. Clothing that might become uncomfortably hot and thus impair thinking should not be chosen. When entering the room candidates should act with composure, greet the examiners and, in most cases, say no more until spoken to (Cryer, 2006). If, at previous vivas candidates had been told the outcome of the thesis examination at the start of the viva, silence on this matter by the examiners should not be interpreted bleakly (Tinkler & Jackson, 2004). It simply reflects the taking by them of a procedural decision.

The opening

3. A viva normally opens with the chairperson making the introductions and asking the candidate to provide a short presentation of his or her work. One purpose of asking a candidate to do this is to check both the authenticity of the work and his or her understanding of it (Cryer, 2006). However, the primary purpose of doing so is to allow everyone involved, but the candidate in particular, to settle in. It can, in fact, be quite disconcerting if the examiners decide to forgo this opening. For this reason advanced warning should be given if this decision has been taken. In the normal run of events though, the presentation will be between ten to thirty minutes long. Again the candidate needs to be provided beforehand with an indication of the length expected. The length will determine the degree of detail but at this stage of the viva fine detail is superfluous for the examiners have already read the details. What is needed, instead, is an astute précis of the research: why the work was required, the main line of argument, the strengths and important limitations, the primary findings and the conference presentations and publications emanating from the study. No emphasis at this stage needs to be placed on those aspects of the research that went wrong or were unexpected and the candidate should not

be put off if the examiners appear to be distractedly reading the thesis rather than listening to the presentation. They are able to do both. Examiners do not normally ask questions during this preliminary presentation, these usually follow immediately thereafter.

Answering the questions

4. Examiners will not expect all their questions to be answered clearly and unambiguously. This is a reflection of both their expertise as researchers and their experience as examiners. In the first instance they acknowledge that research by its nature is imperfect and frequently ambiguous. In the second they recognise the viva is an inherently stressful event complete with its own fallible mythology. Neither should questions that indicate examiner concern with aspects of the research necessarily be interpreted negatively. Questions should, however, be answered directly, succinctly (usually 2 to 3 minutes at the most) and with reference to the text of the thesis (Cryer, 2006). This is of particular importance in empirical work where questions focused on the reliability and validity of the data must be convincingly answered if doubt is not to be cast on the results (Rowarth & Fraser, 2006). If there is doubt the examiners will usually delve deeper in order to discover the reason for the inability to provide convincing answers (Mauch & Birch, 1998). Often the reason is simply lack of clarity on what is being asked: 'There were some questions that I simply couldn't answer, and with hindsight now I wish I'd said, "Can you rephrase that because I simply don't understand the question?"' (cited in Tinkler & Jackson, 2004, p.171).

5. When a question is rephrased it is often not only clarified but also simplified (Rugg & Petre, 2004). An alternative is for the candidate to rephrase the question and to ask, 'Is that what you mean?' In fairness to the candidate examiners should generally avoid multi-part questions but they do, nonetheless, ask them. If this is the case the questions should ideally be written down by the candidate and dealt with one by one. Again, if a candidate gets lost when doing so they should not hesitate to ask for clarification. This is far preferable to providing an irrelevant soliloquy. It is also useful in this regard to develop a skill fundamental to effective presentation: the ability to use silence. Awareness, in other words, that skilled presentation does not involve filling every moment with sound. It is, therefore, perfectly acceptable to pause for a few moments before delivering an answer. This can also be done during delivery of the answer. Not only does it help to make the answer more lucid but also indicates the question was worth thinking about. There is also another presentation skill that should be applied: do not only speak to the examiner asking the question, include the entire panel in the answer by

looking at each of its members; not at the ceiling, the distance, or the floor. What examiners ideally want are clear, concise answers delivered personally to each of them.

Defence vs defensiveness

6. A candidate should never interrupt an examiner when a question is being asked but should, instead, indicate they are listening attentively. This indicates the importance of posture in nonverbal communication. For this reason candidates should adopt the advice given to television presenters: lean slightly forward and assume an air of relaxed alertness (Tinkler & Jackson, 2004). In the context of the viva this attitude reflects competence, cautious confidence and non-defensiveness (Rowarth & Fraser, 2006). This is why the term 'thesis defence' is prone to misinterpretation: it implies the thesis will be attacked. When seen from this perspective defensiveness precludes developmental discussion:

I treated each question or observation as potentially hostile, playing very safe and proper and consequently missed the opportunity to discuss my research with willing and interested experts in my field.

(Cited in Tinkler & Jackson, 2004, p.164)

In the same vain an examiner commented:

I think that the oral as a means of giving the student feedback is an essential part of good teaching, but it is almost impossible to get students to see it as anything other than an examination.

(Cited in Mullins & Kiley, 2002, p.383)

Instead, when defence is not confused with defensiveness, valid points in the study can be defended against criticism and valid criticism can be accepted and used as a point of departure for constructive discussion. This can be particularly useful when discussing how the study might be developed further for publication (Cryer, 2006). Even when a candidate feels that an examiner is being unreasonably critical there should, therefore, be no need to become heatedly argumentative: undertake to reconsider the point and move on.

13.12 POSSIBLE QUESTIONS

1. By the time individual examiners, prior to the viva, have written their reports they have gone through several stages of an extended evaluative process and made a number of important judgements about the thesis. Not all of these will

necessarily be included in the reports (Mullins & Kiley, 2002). It is often these excluded judgements that either form the basis of, or at least influence, the questions they ask.

2. Opening questions tend to be general in order to put candidates at ease: 'What did you most enjoy about your work? What would you do differently if you were to start again? How did you come to study this topic? What is important, new and good in the thesis?' (Tinkler & Jackson, 2004, p.152). Two cautionary considerations, however, need to be borne in mind. The questions may appear simple pleasantries but might also mask probing into how well candidates can appraise their own work (Cryer, 2006). Examiners might also cut immediately to the quick: 'I was expecting more general questions instead but almost immediately they went straight into the details' (cited in Tinkler & Jackson, 2004, p.165). Detailed questions, of course, are specific to particular studies but some useful advice can, nonetheless be provided. First, although they might occasionally move backwards and forwards from one part of the thesis to another, examiners on the whole tend to move sequentially through a thesis. This makes mental preparation for the next question achievable from the context of the previous. Second, it is a useful strategy to start a file of anticipated questions from the outset of the research, important elements in this file should be any contentious statements made in the text of the thesis. Part of the task of a supervisor should be to assist in the identification of such statements. To avoid being flustered by errors of calculation in the thesis check each again in the period immediately prior to the viva. There are also some tricky questions like the following that are worth either preparing coherent answers to or at least mentally preparing for (adapted from Glatthorn, 1998, pp. 186–188):

* Why is the research question phrased in this way?
* Why are X's research conclusions different from yours?
* I feel the findings of Y's study may in your thesis have been misrepresented. Would you please review what you think the study showed?
* Can you clarify how the methods chosen relate to the central problem of the study?
* The results cited on page 60 appear to be in conflict with the results cited on page 92. Can you explain the discrepancy?
* I am not persuaded that the findings support the conclusions. Would you explain specifically how this conclusion derives from the results of the study?
* In what other way might this research have been undertaken?

Just as there are usually general questions at the start of a viva, so too are there often general questions to wind the proceedings down: *What do you intend to do with your research now that you have completed it?* Occasionally examiners will also ask candidates if they have questions to ask of them. Because supine candidates do not impress it is worth preparing at least one question, possibly relating to research relevant to the thesis published by one of the examiners, even if it is unlikely to be asked (Tinkler & Jackson, 2004).

13.13 CLOSING THE VIVA

1. At the end of the examination the candidate and all observers are usually asked to leave the venue while the examiners confer privately. Under the leadership of the chairperson the examiners work as a group and arrive at a consensus acceptable to all (Mauch & Birch, 1998). The fact they are able to do so is a consequence of the broad agreement arrived at during the pre-viva meeting. This is why if such agreement could not be achieved the viva should not go ahead. If, as is the usual outcome, a decision is made after the viva to pass the candidate the practical impact of the viva is alteration to the provisional list of changes that examiners might have required prior to the examination (Rugg & Petre, 2004). At some universities the examiners make no announcement of the outcome of the viva. Instead, the candidate is informed by post shortly after the relevant university committee has approved the examiners' final report (Tinkler & Jackson, 2004). More common, however, is for the candidate to be invited back to the venue where he or she is told by the chairperson what the examiners' recommendations are and what, if anything, needs to be done and by when to make the thesis acceptable to them. If needed the changes might range from insignificant to substantial but if not failed outright, an extremely rare occurrence, or required to be resubmitted for examination, a pass is a pass and formal congratulations are usually given to confirm the fact.

2. Whatever the outcome accept the recommendations graciously and thank the examiners for their efforts. This might be difficult to do in the event of failure or resubmission but it is a necessary part of the culture of research. At the other extreme, where only relatively minor changes are required, avoid the 'I can fix that easily' response for it trivialises the examiners' efforts (Rowarth & Fraser, 2006). Once any required changes have been made within the stipulated time and have received the approval of the supervisor/s whose task it normally is to oversee any changes, the candidate should write a covering letter detailing what has been done. This letter will make it much easier for the main supervisor to assure the examiners that the required changes have been made or, where the examiners themselves have requested to see the changes, to check that they are satisfactory (Rugg & Petre, 2004). (After a thesis has been examined the only changes permitted are those required by the examiners. The opportunity for substantive change lies in subsequent publication/s.)

ENDNOTES

1   Referees' reports on journal articles also at times reflect significant differences of opinion. Referee A: ...as this manuscript is purely subjective in nature I consider it to be totally unsuitable for publication... Referee B: ...ACCEPT –it's a delightfully off–the–piste piece, beautifully written... (Chanock, K. cited in Davies, 2010, p.6)

2   Nonetheless, even at universities where there is no viva, annual reviews of the work of doctoral candidates often require them to respond orally to complex questions.

3   Acceptance of a proposal, both within and outside the United States, is usually called 'confirmation of candidature.'

4   On each occasion the defence should be before a committee composed, in so far as is feasible, of the same individuals.

Afterword

> *...there ain't nothing more to write about, and I am rotten glad of it, because if I'd a-knowed what a trouble it was to make a book I wouldn't a-tackled it, and ain't a-going to no more.*

(Twain, M., *The Adventures of Huckleberry Finn*, Chapter 43)

One of the insights provided by quantum mechanics is the impossibility of total knowledge. There is, therefore, always more to write about. Why then has the book been brought to an end? The answer is the law of diminishing returns. Frustrated by the limits of his knowledge, Goethe's Faust was prepared to sell his soul to extend those limits. Publishers, however, are conscious that most people will draw a line at their soul and opt for a lower price. Thus, from a publisher's perspective the final length of a book is a fine calculation of the point where the utility of its contents parts company with the rise in its cost of production. The length of this book is a reflection of that calculation. Like theses, therefore, books are written within constraints. This requires that choices be made between what to include and exclude. Because the contents of this book are a reflection of those choices it is, inevitably, partial: a contribution to a conversation, not the conversation. Undeniably, the book has prescriptive potential but bear in mind that external imperatives doom an ability to think critically (Rowland, 2006). This explains the purpose of the book, simply to assist informed reflection about the processes involved in writing a thesis.

The decision as to whether or not a book or a thesis, at the end of the day, was worth the trouble is subjective and, because of the exploratory nature of producing each, is a decision, fortunately, that can only be made retrospectively. In each case, though, completion is the culmination of a major intellectual event (Garman, 2006). As such, whatever trouble there might have been is mitigated. This implies, of course, that the processes of writing a thesis or a book are comparative. In the case of this book I would argue they are, for the similarities are greater than the differences. Differences are evident, for example, in the audience for which each is written. Thesis writers too are generally spared the fulfilling process of compiling an index. But, the similarities between this book and both exegetic and qualitative theses in particular are significant for, as is the case in each, content and structure evolve.

The book had its origin five years ago while I was presenting seminars for thesis writers from diverse disciplinary backgrounds and with equally diverse theoretic approaches. That each could be expected to write and structure their thesis differently had long been established. Less clear were the choices involved and the decisions made that explained those differences. The subsequent journey to seek clarification resulted in moulding and remoulding an evolving manuscript. The acceptance by publishers of a proposal outlining the contents and structure of a book often precedes the actual writing of the book. Ignorance of this book's final contents and structure precluded that approach. This was both advantage and disadvantage. The disadvantage lay in anxiety whether any publisher would accept the manuscript when it was finally ready to be peddled. The advantage was the freedom provided for the manuscript to beat its own path. Four years later my uncertainty was allayed upon acceptance by ACER Press of the first of the drafts suitable for public exposure. (One must admire the courage of a publishing house that agrees to publish a book the first line of which contains the words 'this book is necessarily ephemeral'.) Acceptance, however, was a process not an event. As in the case of any thesis the draft had to be examined, in this case by a panel of referees. Acceptance of their recommendations and those of the team subsequently assembled to bring the book to production was a condition of publication. The final draft of the book, a team effort as in the case of a thesis, thus differs from that originally submitted.

The latter was some twelve thousand words longer than the former, the preface was embedded in the introduction, two chapters were devoted to interdisciplinarity, there was an additional chapter on mixed methods and the Title Development chapter (the chapter that posed the greatest organisational difficulty) contained a section on medieval universities. I thought the additional material interesting but had to agree that wading through it was enough to test the resolve of even the most committed thesis writer. Moreover focus, as in any thesis, was paramount. So, the section on medieval universities was excised, some of the mixed methods chapter was excised, part was incorporated in the Methods chapter and the remainder continued life in a subsequently published paper (White, 2008b). One of the chapters on interdisciplinarity, that dealing with the origin of disciplines, was also excised and subsequently published elsewhere (White, 2010). On one occasion the process was reversed: a published paper (White, 2008a) preceded and helped crystallise thinking about the role of metaphor in interdisciplinary research. As might be expected of exploratory work, the present title was only decided upon, again as a team effort, right at the end. For most of its life the manuscript was simply known as *Thesis Guide*.

I farm land some distance from the campus of my university. This was a contributory factor to the book in its final form. Apart from the sweated labour involved, digging does not require significant cognitive engagement. This explains why much of the thinking involved in writing the book was done behind a spade. My daily commute to work involves two hours on a bus. Over a period of a week this amounts to more than an eight–hour day. This is when much of my reading was done and where the writing was revised. There is a message here for thesis writers.

Some four hundred years ago Sir Francis Bacon wrote, 'Some books are to be tasted, others to be swallowed, and some few to be chewed and digested (Bacon, *The Essays*, 'Of Studies')'. My hope is you consider his final category appropriate to this book.

References

Ackroyd P. (2002). *Albion: the origins of the English imagination*. London: Vintage, Random House.

Alhadeff–Jones, M. (2008). 'Three generations of complexity theories: nuances and ambiguities'. *Educational Philosophy and Theory*, 40(1), pp. 66–82.

Allen Smith, J. (1994). 'Review of dictionaries, the "Bon Mot" and the "Mot Juste"'. In *Cardozo Studies in Law and Literature*, 6(1), pp.123–131.

Anderson, J., & Poole, M. (1994). *Thesis and assignment writing*. Brisbane: John Wiley & Sons.

Angrosino, M. (2007). Doing ethnographic and observational research. In U. Flick, (ed.), *The SAGE qualitative research kit*, vol.3. London: Sage Publications.

Aspin, D. (2009). 'Introduction to a "round–table review" of Gavin Kitching's "The trouble with theory"'. *Educational Philosophy and Theory*, 41(3), pp.233–240.

Auckland District Health Board (ADHB). (2008). *The clinical question*. Retrieved 25 May 2008 from http://www.library.auckland.ac.nz/subjects/med/healthcare/ebm/ebm_practice2.htm

Aydin, Elvin. (2006). 'Subjective experiences of life events in breast cancer (female patients with invasive ductal carcinoma): a psychoanalytic qualitative study'. Unpublished PhD, University of Essex.

Bargar, R. & Duncan, J. (1982). 'Cultivating creative endeavour in doctoral research'. *Journal of Higher Education*, 53(1), pp.1–31.

Barnacle, R. (2006). On being a critical researcher. In C. Denholm, & T. Evans (eds), *Doctorates downunder: keys to successful doctoral study in Australia and New Zealand* (pp.95–103). Camberwell: ACER Press.

Bastalich, Wendy. *Methodology*. University of South Australia. Retrieved 20 June 2008 from http://www.unisanet.unisa.edu.au/learningconnection/student/research/methodology.asp

Bates College, Department of Biology. *The structure, format, content, and style of a journal style scientific paper*. Retrieved 25 May 2007 from http://abacus.bates.edu/~ganderso/biology/resources/writing/HTWsections.html

Becher, T., & Trowler, P.R. (2001). *Academic tribes and territories: intellectual enquiry and the culture of disciplines*. Buckingham: The Society for Research into Higher Education and Open University Press.

Benton, T.H. (2005, April 29). 'Life after the death of theory'. *The Chronicle of Higher Education*.

Bergquist, P. (2004). Advice from the examiners. In Burton, S., & Steane, P. (eds). *Surviving your thesis*. London: Routledge.

Bernstein, R. J. (1983). *Beyond objectivism and relativism: science, hermenuetics and praxis*. Philadelphia: University of Pennsylvania Press.

Bienvenu, Beth. (2004). 'Opinions from the field: graduate assessments of the value of masters' degrees in arts administration'. Unpublished PhD, University of Oklahoma.

Biesta, G. (2008). '"This is my truth, tell me yours": deconstructive pragmatism as a philosophy for education'. *Educational Philosophy and Theory*. Oxford: Blackwell Publishing. Early view retrieved 6 June 2010 from http://www3.interscience.wiley.com/cgi-bin/fulltext/120120246/PDFSTART

Blackburn, S. (2005). *Truth: a guide*. Oxford: Oxford University Press.

Blackburn, S., & Simmons, K. (eds), (2005). *Truth*. Oxford: Oxford University Press.

Bloom, B.S. (ed.), Engelhart, M.D., Furst, E.J., Walker, H.H., Krathwohl, D.R. (1956). *Taxonomy of educational objectives, the classification of educational goals. Handbook 1 Cognitive domain.* New York: Longmans.

Booth, Michael, Rodgers, Steven & AgInsight. (2000). 'Interdisciplinary research methodologies in natural resource management'. *Report to LWRRDC*, Social and Institutional Research Program Institute for Sustainability and Technology Policy, Murdoch University.

Booth, W.C., Colomb, G.C. & Williams, J.M. (2003). *The craft of research.* Chicago: University of Chicago Press.

Bourke, S., Holbrook, A., & Lovat, T. (2007). Examiners and examination outcomes. In C. Denholm, & T. Evans (eds). *Supervising doctorates downunder: keys to effective supervision in Australia and New Zealand* (pp. 234–242). Camberwell: ACER Press.

Bourke, Sid, Scevak, Jill & Cantwell, Robert. (2001, December 2–6). 'PhD examination and examiner characteristics', paper presented at the Association for Active Educational Researchers, Fremantle, Australia.

Bowker, G. C., & Star, S. L. (1999). *Sorting things out: classification and its consequences.* Cambridge, MA: MIT Press.

Brannen, Julia (2005). 'Mixed methods research: a discussion paper'. Economic and Social Research Council, National Centre for Research Methods Review Papers. Retrieved 5 May 2010 from http://www.ncrm.ac.uk/publications/documents/MethodsReviewPaperNCRM-005.pdf

Bryant, M. T. (2004). *The portable dissertation advisor.* California: Corwin Press.

Bryson, B. (2008). *Shakespeare.* London: Harper Perennial.

Burton, S. (2004). Quantitative research and analysis. In S. Burton & P. Steane (eds), *Surviving your thesis* (pp. 138–158). London: Routledge.

Burton, S. & Steane, P. (2004a). Common problems and potential solutions. In S. Burton & P. Steane (eds), *Surviving your thesis* (pp. 195–206). London: Routledge.

Burton, S. & Steane, P. (2004b). Choosing and working with a supervisor. In S. Burton & P. Steane (eds), *Surviving your thesis* (pp. 30–45). London: Routledge.

Burton, S. & Steane, P. (2004c). Writing the thesis. In S. Burton & P. Steane (eds), Surviving your thesis (pp. 178–194). London: Routledge.

Canter, D., & Fairbairn, G. (2006). *Becoming an author: advice for academics and other professionals.* Maidenhead: Open University Press.

Cantwell, R. (2006). Thinking and writing for your thesis. In C. Denholm, & T. Evans (eds), *Doctorates downunder: keys to successful doctoral study in Australia and New Zealand* (pp. 182–190). Camberwell: ACER Press.

Carroll, L. (2007). *Through the looking glass and what Alice found there.* Scituate, MA: Digital Scanning, Inc.

Carson, E. (2007). Helping candidates manage their candidacy. In C. Denholm, & T. Evans (eds), *Supervising doctorates downunder: keys to effective supervision in Australia and New Zealand* (pp. 54–61). Camberwell: ACER Press.

Ceroni, K.M. (2006). Coming to know through the text of talk: from interviews to inner views storied to interpretation. In N. B. Garman & M. Piantanida (eds), *The authority to imagine: the struggle toward representation in dissertation writing* (pp. 113–126). New York: Peter Lang Publishing, Inc.

Charles, Liz, & Ward, Neil. (2007). 'Generating change through research: action research and its implications'. *Centre for Rural Economy Discussion Paper Series No. 10.* University of Newcastle upon Tyne.

Clark, K. (1969). *Civilisation.* New York: Harper & Row.

Cone, J.D., & Foster, S.L. (1998). *Dissertations and theses from start to finish: psychology and related fields.* Washington: American Psychological Association.

Conrad, L. (2006). Countering isolation—joining the research community. In C. Denholm, & T. Evans (eds), *Doctorates downunder: keys to successful doctoral study in Australia and New Zealand* (pp. 34–40). Camberwell: ACER Press.

Conrad, L. (2007). Developing the intellectual and emotional climate for candidates. In C. Denholm, & T. Evans (eds), *Supervising doctorates downunder: keys to effective supervision in Australia and New Zealand* (pp. 36–44). Camberwell: ACER Press.

Conrad, Linda, M. (2003, July 6–9). 'Five ways of enhancing the postgraduate community: student perceptions of effective supervision and support', paper presented at the 26th Annual Higher Education Research and Development Society of Australasia Conference, Christchurch, New Zealand.

Coulton, G.C. (1963). *Chaucer and His England.* London: Methuen & Co.

Craig, Robert T. (2003, November 21). 'Discursive origins of a communication discipline', paper presented at the National Communication Association, Miami Beach, Florida.

Creswell, J. (1994). *Research design: qualitative and quantitative approaches.* Thousand Oaks: Sage Publications.

Creswell, J.W. (2003). *Research design: qualitative, quantitative, and mixed methods approaches.* Thousand Oaks: Sage Publications.

Creswell, J.W., & Plano Clark, V.L. (2007). *Designing and conducting mixed methods research.* Thousand Oaks: Sage Publications.

Crusius, T.W. (1991). *A teacher's introduction to philosophical hermeneutics.* Urbana: National Council of Teachers of English.

Cryer, P. (2006). *The research student's guide to success,* 2nd edn. Maidenhead: Open University Press.

Cumming, J. (2009). Representing doctoral practice in the laboratory sciences. In D. Boud, & A. Lee (eds), *Changing practices of doctoral education* (pp. 113–125). Abingdon: Routledge.

Dall'Alba, G. (2009). 'Learning professional ways of being; ambiguities of becoming'. *Educational Philosophy and Theory,* 41(1), pp. 34–45.

Darlington, Y., & Scott, D. (2002). *Qualitative research in practice, stories from the field.* Crows Nest: Allen and Unwin.

Davies, M. (April, 2010). 'Thoughts of a special issue editor', *Higher Education Research and Development Society of Australasia News.*

Davis, B. (2008). 'Complexity and education: vital simultaneities'. *Educational Philosophy and Theory,* 40(1), pp. 50–65.

Davis, B., & Sumara, D.J. (2005). 'Challenging images of knowing: complexity science and educational research'. *International Journal of Qualitative Studies in Education,* 18(3), pp. 305–321.

Davis, B., & Sumara, D. (2006). *Complexity and education: inquiries into learning, teaching, and research.* Mahwah: Lawrence Erlbaum Associates.

Dawkins, R. (2005). *A pilgrimage to the dawn of life: the ancestor's tale.* London: Phoenix.

Denholm, J. (2006). On being an ethical researcher. In C. Denholm, & T. Evans (eds), *Doctorates downunder: keys to successful doctoral study in Australia and New Zealand* (pp. 104–111). Camberwell: ACER Press.

Denholm, C. (2007). Conducting reviews of candidature. In C. Denholm, & T. Evans (eds), *Supervising doctorates downunder: keys to effective supervision in Australia and New Zealand* (pp. 62–70). Camberwell: ACER Press.

Denholm, C. & Evans T. (2007). Introduction. In C. Denholm, & T. Evans (eds), *Supervising doctorates downunder: keys to effective supervision in Australia and New Zealand* (pp.1–4). Camberwell: ACER Press.

Denscombe, M. (2001). *The good research guide for small–scale social research projects*. Buckingham: Open University Press.

Dent, E.B. (2005). Challenges surfaced by complexity theory. In K.A. Richardson (ed.), *Managing the complex, vol.1. Managing organizational complexity: philosophy, theory, and application* (pp. 253–268). Connecticut: Information Age Publishing.

Derrida, J. (1997). Remarks on deconstruction and pragmatism. In C. Mouffe (ed.), *Deconstruction and pragmatism* (pp. 77–88). London: Routledge.

di Lampedusa, G. (1974). *The leopard*. London: Fontana/Collins.

Dillon, G.L., (1991). *Contending rhetorics, writing in academic disciplines*. Bloomington: Indiana University Press.

Doyle, A.C. (2001). *A study in scarlet*. London: Penguin Classics.

Dudley–Evans, T. (1989). An outline of the value of genre analysis in LSP work. In C. Laurén, & M. Nordman (eds), *Special language: from humans thinking to thinking machines* (pp. 72–79). Clevedon: Multilingual Matters.

Dunham, Penny. (2005). *Technology and interdisciplinary calculus: three challenges for educators*. Muhlenberg College, Allentown. Retrieved 31 August 2005 from http://www.dean.usma.edu/math/activities/ilap/workshops/1999/files/dunham.pdf

Dunleavy, P. (2003). *Authoring a PhD: how to plan, draft, write and finish a doctoral thesis or dissertation*. Hampshire: Palgrave Macmillan.

Edwards, B. (2006). Map, food, equipment and compass—preparing for the doctoral journey. In C. Denholm, & T. Evans (eds), *Doctorates downunder: keys to successful doctoral study in Australia and New Zealand* (pp. 6–14). Camberwell: ACER Press.

Emilsson, U.M.,& Johnsson, A. (2007). 'Supervision of supervisors: on developing supervision in postgraduate education'. *Higher Education Research and Development*, 26(2), pp. 163–179.

Emmeche, C., Kóppe, S., & Stjernfelt, F. (1997). 'Explaining emergence: towards an ontology of levels'. *Journal for General Philosophy of Science*, vol.28, pp. 83–119.

EPA STAR Water and Watersheds Research Program. (2001). *Managing interdisciplinary research: lessons learned. Workshop summary*. US Environmental Protection Agency, National Center for Environmental Research. Washington, D.C. Retrieved 25 July 2007 from http://66.102.7.104/search?q=cache:HiGYvPqjjewJ:es.epa.gov/ncer/publications/workshop/pdf/water_watershed_lessons2001.wpd+interdisciplinary+difficulties&hl=en

Evans, T. (2006). Part-time candidature-balancing candidature, work and personal life. In C. Denholm, & T. Evans (eds), *Doctorates downunder: keys to successful doctoral study in Australia and New Zealand* (pp. 136–142). Camberwell: ACER Press.

Fairbairn, G.J., & Winch, C. (1996). *Reading, writing and reasoning: a guide for students*. Buckingham: Open University Press.

Ferman, Terrie. (2002). 'The knowledge needs of doctoral supervisors', paper presented at the 2002 Annual Conference of the Australian Association for Research in Education. Retrieved 25 June 2006 from http://www.aare.edu.au/02pap/fer02251.htm

Fioretti, G., & Visser, B. (2004). 'A cognitive interpretation of organizational complexity'. *Emergence: Complexity and Organization*, 6(1–2), pp. 11–23.

Fisher, K. (2006). Peer support groups. In C. Denholm, & T. Evans (eds), *Doctorates downunder: keys to successful doctoral study in Australia and New Zealand* (pp. 41–49). Camberwell: ACER Press.

Fiumara, G.C. (1995). *The metaphoric process: connections between language and life*. Routledge: London.

Flexible Learning Centre, University of South Australia. *Organising your ideas, critical analysis*. Retrieved 4 April 2006 from http://www.unisanet.unisa.edu.au/Resources/research-Education/research%20education/researchwrite/Conceptualising

Flick, U. (2002). *An introduction to qualitative research.* London: Sage Publications

Flick, U. (2007). Managing quality in qualitative research. In U. Flick, (ed.), *The SAGE qualitative research kit*, vol.8. London: Sage Publications.

Foder, J. (2009, February 12). 'Where is My Mind?' *London Review of Books.*

Forty, R. (2001). *The Earth: an intimate history.* London: Harper Perennial.

Fraser, G., & Rowarth, J. (2007). Preparing candidates for oral examination. In C. Denholm, & T. Evans, (eds), *Supervising doctorates downunder: keys to effective supervision in Australia and New Zealand* (pp. 243–250). Camberwell: ACER Press.

Frow, J. (2006). *Genre.* Abingdon: Routledge.

Gaiman, N. (2006). *Fragile things: short fictions and wonders.* New York: Harper Collins.

Galvan, J.L. (2004). *Writing literature reviews, a guide for students of the social and behavioural sciences.* Glendale: Pyrczak Publishing.

Garman, N.B. (2006). Imagining an interpretive dissertation: voice, text, and representation. In N. B. Garman & M. Piantanida (eds), *The authority to imagine: the struggle toward representation in dissertation writing* (pp. 1–18). New York: Peter Lang Publishing, Inc.

Garman, N.B. & Piantanida, M. (2006). Preface. In N. B. Garman & M. Piantanida (eds), *The authority to imagine: the struggle toward representation in dissertation writing.* New York: Peter Lang Publishing, Inc.

Garton, A., & McFarlane, J. (2007). Editing and proofreading skills. In C. Denholm, & T. Evans, (eds), *Supervising doctorates downunder: keys to effective supervision in Australia and New Zealand* (pp. 87–94). Camberwell: ACER Press.

Gibbs, G. (2007). Analyzing qualitative data. U. Flick (ed.), *The SAGE qualitative research kit*, vol.6. London: Sage Publications.

Gilbert, Lewis.E. (March, 1998). Disciplinary breadth and interdisciplinary knowledge production. *Knowledge, Technology and Policy*, vol.11, pp. 4–15. Columbia Earth Institute, Columbia University. Retrieved 14 September, 2005 from http://www.isse.ucar.edu/extremes/papers/gilbert.PDF

Glatthorn, A.A. (1998). *Writing the winning dissertation.* California: Corwin Press.

Golden-Biddle, K., & Locke, K.D. (1997). *Composing qualitative research.* Thousand Oaks: Sage Publications.

Goldstein, J.A. (2008). 'A review of "Reinventing the sacred; new view of science, reason, and religion" by S. Kauffman'. *Emergence: Complexity and Organization*, 10(3), pp. 117–132.

Gosden, J., & Lawson, D. (1994). 'Rapid chromosome identification by oligonucleotide-primed *in situ* DNA synthesis (PRINS)'. *Human Molecular Genetics*, 3(6), pp. 931–936.

Graham, Adele, & Grant, Barbara. (2000). *Guidelines for Negotiating Supervision.* Centre for Professional Development, University of Auckland. Retrieved 25 May 2007 from http://www.waikato.ac.nz/sasd/files/pdf/postgraduate/form_12.pdf

Grant, B., & Pearson, M. (2007). Approaches to doctoral supervision in Australia and Aotearoa New Zealand. In C. Denholm, & T. Evans (eds), *Supervising doctorates downunder: keys to effective supervision in Australia and New Zealand* (pp. 11–18). Camberwell: ACER Press.

Greene, J. C., & Caracelli, V. J. (2003). Making paradigmatic sense of mixed methods practice. In A. Tashakkori & C. Teddle (eds), *Handbook of mixed methods in social and behavioral research* (pp. 91–110). Thousand Oaks: Sage Publications.

Grubs, R.E. (2006). Reimagining grounded theory: moving toward an interpretive stance. In N. B. Garman & M. Piantanida (eds), *The authority to imagine: the struggle toward representation in dissertation writing* (pp. 81–96). New York: Peter Lang Publishing, Inc.

Hart, C. (1998). *Doing a literature review: releasing the social science imagination.* London: Sage Publications.

Hart, C. (2005). *Doing your masters dissertation: realizing your potential as a social scientist.* London: Sage Publications.

Hawking, Stephen. (nd). *Public lectures: Does God play dice?* Retrieved 26 April 2007 from http://www.hawking.org.uk/lectures/dice.html

Hersch, M., & Moss, G. (2004). 'Heresy and orthodoxy: challenging established paradigms and disciplines'. *Journal of International Women's Studies*, 5 (3), pp. 6–21.

Hickey, C. (2007). Supervising workplace–based research. In C. Denholm, & T. Evans (eds), *Supervising doctorates downunder: keys to effective supervision in Australia and New Zealand* (pp. 79–86). Camberwell: ACER Press.

Hird, Lee, D. (1997). 'What is the nature of the flow field between two eccentric rotating cylinders in the presence of a slotted sleeve?' Unpublished PhD, Curtin University of Technology.

Holbrook, Allyson, Bourke, Sid & Dally, Kerry. (2003, August 26–30). 'How examiners describe quality in the doctoral thesis', paper presented at the Investigating Doctoral Assessment Symposium at the European Association for Research on Learning and Instruction, Padova, Italy.

Holbrook, Allyson & Dally, Kerry. (2003, August 26–30). 'Emphases in 603 doctoral examination reports', paper presented at the Investigating Doctoral Assessment Symposium at the European Association for Research on Learning and Instruction, Padova, Italy.

Holbrook, Allyson, Dally, Kerry, Cantwell, Robert, Scevak, Jill, Bourke, Sid & Lovat, Terry. (2003, July 7–9). 'Doctoral examiners as supervisors', paper presented at the Higher Education Research and Development Conference, Christchurch, New Zealand.

Holland, J.H. (1998). *Emergence: from chaos to order.* Massachusetts: Helix Books.

Holt, R.C. (1987). *Clear thinking: a short course in everyday logic.* Melbourne: Pitman.

Hoover, Keith. (2004). *Tenses.* Retrieved August 2008 from http://www.rose-hulman.edu/gradstudies/ThesisTenses.pdf

Horn, J.K. (2005). Parameters for sustained orderly growth in learning organizations. In K.A. Richardson, (ed.), *Managing the complex: vol.1. Managing organizational complexity: philosophy, theory, and application* (pp. 473–491). Connecticut: Information Age Publishing.

Howard, J.E. (2005). Renaissance antitheatricality and the politics of gender and rank in *Much Ado About Nothing*. In J.E. Howard, & M. O'Connor (eds), *Shakespeare reproduced: the text in history and ideology* (pp. 163–187). Abingdon: Routledge.

Ingleby, R. (2007). Helping candidates form their research question. In C. Denholm, & T. Evans (eds), *Supervising doctorates downunder: keys to effective supervision in Australia and New Zealand* (pp. 45–52). Camberwell: ACER Press.

Jaynes, Carol. (2007). *Writing a successful thesis.* Metaverse Lab., Center for Visualization and Virtual Environments. Retrieved 25 May 2007 from http://www.metaverselab.org/personnel/jaynes/thesis-advice.pdf

Kamler, Barbara, & Threadgold, Terry. (1996, November 25–29). 'PhD examiner reports: discrepant readings, conflicting discourses', paper presented at the Association for Active Educational Researchers Conference, Singapore. Retrieved 17 August 2005 from http://www.aare.edu.au/96pap/kamlb96110.txt

Kelly, Frances. (2005, November 15-17). 'Writing in the frame lock: authority and disciplinary citation', paper presented at the ATLAANZ Conference, University of Otago, Dunedin, New Zealand.

Kerwin, A. (2008). 'Reflective Practice Then and Now'. *HERDSA*, 30(3), pp. 11–12.

Kiley, M., & Mullins, G. (2006). Opening the black box: how examiners assess your thesis. In C. Denholm, & T. Evans, (eds), *Doctorates downunder: keys to successful doctoral study in Australia and New Zealand* (pp. 200–207). Camberwell: ACER Press.

Kiley, M., & Wisker, G. (2009, August). 'Threshold concepts in research education and evidence of threshold crossing'. *Higher Education Research and Development*, 28(4), pp. 431–441.

Kitching, G. (2009). 'The trouble with theory: some elucidations'. *Educational Philosophy and Theory*, 41(3), pp. 251–255.

Krone, M. (2006). Managing the relationship with your supervisor(s). In C. Denholm, & T. Evans (eds), *Doctorates downunder: keys to successful doctoral study in Australia and New Zealand* (pp. 23–32). Camberwell: ACER Press.

Krupa, J.J., & Geluso, K.N. (2000). 'Matching the color of excavated soil; cryptic coloration in the plains pocket gopher (*Geomys bursarius*)'. *Journal of Mammalogy*, 81(1), pp. 86–96.

Kung, Francis T. (2001) 'Chronic Pain in Older People'. Unpublished PhD, University of Melbourne.

Kvale, S. (2007). Doing interviews. In U. Flick (ed.), *The SAGE qualitative research kit*, vol. 2. London: Sage Publications.

Kwa, Chunglin. (March, 2002). 'Does interdisciplinarity really exist?' The European Association for the Study of Science and Technology Review, vol.21 (1/2). Retrieved 15 September 2008 from http://www.easst.net/review/march2002/kwa

Lakatos, I. (1978). *Philosophical papers. Vol. 1: The methodology of scientific research programmes*. J. Worral & G. Currie (eds). Cambridge: Cambridge University Press.

Lam, Bee K. (1999). 'Restricted Spanning Trees and Graph Partitioning'. Unpublished PhD, Curtin University.

Land, R., Meyer, J.H.F., & Smith, J. (eds), (2008). *Threshold concepts within the disciplines*. Rotterdam: Sense Publishers.

Lather, P.A., & Smithies, C.S. (1997). *Troubling the angels: women living with HIV/AIDS*. Oxford: Westview Press.

Leder, G. & Holliday, L. (2006). Research skills and writing a thesis. In C. Denholm, & T. Evans (eds), *Doctorates downunder: keys to successful doctoral study in Australia and New Zealand* (pp. 191–198). Camberwell: ACER Press.

Lee, A., & Aitchison, C. (2009). Writing for the doctorate and beyond. In D. Boud, & A. Lee (eds), *Changing practices of doctoral education* (pp. 87–99). Abingdon: Routledge.

Lertzman, Ken. (1995, June). *Notes on writing papers and theses*. School of Resource and Environmental Management, Simon Fraser University. Retrieved 3 June 2006 from http://aerg.canberra.edu.au/pub/aerg/edulertz.htm#nine

Levine, L. W. (1993). *The unpredictable past: explorations in American cultural history*. New York: Oxford University Press.

Lewin, R. (2001). *Complexity, life at the edge of chaos*. London: Phoenix.

Li, You–Zheng. (1995). 'Epistemological and methodological problems in studies of traditional Chinese ethical scholarship'. *New Literary History*, 26(3), pp. 519–536.

Liang, Weifa. (1997). 'Designing Efficient Parallel Algorithms for Graph Problems'. Unpublished PhD, Australian National University.

Lifson, Amy (1997). 'A conversation with Stephen Toulmin'. *Humanities*, 18(2). Retrieved 24 September 2008 from http://www.neh.gov/news/humanities/1997-03/toulmin.html

Ling Pan, M. (2003). *Preparing literature reviews: qualitative and quantitative approaches*. Los Angeles: Pyrczak Publishing.

Linn, R. (1996). *A teacher's introduction to postmodernism*. Urbana: National Council of Teachers of English.

Logsdon, M. B. (2006). Writing essays: minding the personal and theoretic. In N.B. Garmen & M. Piantanida (eds), *The authority to imagine: the struggle toward representation in dissertation writing* (pp. 155–166). New York: Peter Lang Publishing, Inc.

Lovat, Terry, Holbrook, Allyson, Bourke, Sid, Dally, Kerry & Hazel, Gavin. (2002). 'Examiner comment on theses that have been revised and resubmitted', paper presented at the Annual Conference of the Australian Association for Research in Education (AARE), The University of Queensland, Brisbane. Retrieved 20 November 2005 from http://www.aare.edu.au/02pap/lov02282.htm

Lovat, Terry, Holbrook, Allyson & Hazel, Gavin. (2001, December 2–6). 'What qualities are rare in examiners reports?' paper presented at the Annual Conference of the Australian Association for Research in Education (AARE), Fremantle, Australia. Retrieved 20 November 2005 from http://www.aare.edu.au/01pap/lov01589.htm

Lovat, Terry & Morrison, Kellie (2003, August 26–30). '"Ways of knowing", styles of assessment and the supervisory role in the doctorate', paper presented at the Investigating Doctoral Assessment Symposium at the European Association for Research on Learning and Instruction, Padova, Italy.

Lovitts, B.E. (2007). *Making the implicit explicit: creating performance expectations for the dissertation*. Virginia: Stylus.

Macauley, P. (2006). The librarian—the candidate's forgotten friend. In C. Denholm, & T. Evans (eds), *Doctorates downunder: keys to successful doctoral study in Australia and New Zealand* (pp. 50–58). Camberwell: ACER Press.

Macauley, P., & Green, R. (2007). Supervising publishing from the doctorate. In C. Denholm, & T. Evans (eds), *Supervising doctorates downunder: keys to effective supervision in Australia and New Zealand* (pp. 192–199). Camberwell: ACER Press.

MacGillivray, A. (2006). 'Learning at the edge – Part 1: Transdisciplinary conceptions of boundaries'. *Emergence: Complexity and Organization*, 8(3), pp. 92–104.

Mackenzie, J. (2009). 'Kitching's Trouble with theory: "The tree is known by its fruit"'. *Educational Philosophy and Theory*, 41(3), pp. 240–244.

MacMynowski, Dena P. (2007). 'Pausing at the brink of interdisciplinarity: power and knowledge at the meeting of social and biophysical science'. *Ecology and Society*, 12(1):20 Retrieved 24 September 2008 from http://www.ecologyandsociety.org/vol12/iss1/art20/

Manalo, E., & Trafford, J. (2004). *Thinking to thesis: a guide to graduate success at all levels*. Auckland: Pearson Education.

Manathunga, C. (2005). Early warning signs in postgraduate research education: a different approach to ensuring timely completions. *Teaching in Higher Education*, 10(2), pp. 219–233.

Manathunga, C. (2006, December). 'Detecting and dealing with warning signs in postgraduate research supervision'. HERDSA News.

Manathunga, C., Lant, P., & Mellick, G. (2006). 'Imagining an interdisciplinary doctoral pedagogy'. *Teaching in Higher Education*, 11:3, pp. 365–379.

Marsh, H. (2006). University–industry links—the big picture. In C. Denholm, & T. Evans (eds), *Doctorates downunder: keys to successful doctoral study in Australia and New Zealand* (pp. 60–67). Camberwell: ACER Press.

Marshall, C., & Rossman, G.B. (2006). *Designing qualitative research*. Thousand Oaks: Sage Publications.

Mason, M. (2008). 'Complexity theory and the philosophy of education'. *Educational Philosophy and Theory*, 40(1), pp. 4–18.

Mathews, J. (2004). Responding to criticism. In S. Burton & P. Steane (eds), *Surviving your thesis* (pp. 220–231). Abingdon: Routledge.

Mauch, J.E., & Birch, J.W. (1998). *Guide to the successful thesis and dissertation: a handbook for students and faculty*. New York: Marcel Dekker, Inc.

McCormack, R. 'Philosophical writing: prefacing as professing'. *Educational Philosophy and Theory*, 40(7), 2008, pp. 832–855.

McWilliam, E. (2006). Argumentation. In C. Denholm, & T. Evans (eds), *Doctorates downunder: keys to successful doctoral study in Australia and New Zealand* (pp. 166–174). Camberwell: ACER Press.

Meloy, J.M. (2002). *Writing the qualitative dissertation: understanding by doing*, 2nd edn. Mahwah: Lawrence Erlbaum Associates.

Mertens, D.M. (2003). Mixed methods and the politics of human research: the transformative–emanicipatory perspective. In A. Tashakkori & C. Teddlie (eds), *Handbook of mixed methods in social and behavioral research* (pp. 135–166). Thousand Oaks: Sage Publications.

Meyer, Jan & Land, Ray. (2003). *Threshold concepts and troublesome knowledge: linkages to ways of thinking and practising within the disciplines.* Enhancing Teaching–Learning Environments in Undergraduate Courses, Occasional Report 4. School of Education, University of Edinburgh.

Miles, M.B., & Huberman, A.M. (1994). *Qualitative data analysis.* California: Sage Publications.

Mishna, F. (2004). 'A qualitative study of bullying from multiple perspectives'. *Children and Schools*, 26(4), pp. 234–247.

MLA handbook for writers of research papers, 7th edn. (2009). New York: Modern Languages Association.

Moisio, O. (2007). 'What it Means to be a Stranger to Oneself'. *Educational Philosophy and Theory*, 41(5), pp. 490–506.

Morrison, K. (2008). 'Educational philosophy and the challenge of complexity theory'. *Educational Philosophy and Theory*, 40(1), pp. 19–34.

Morse, J.M., & Richards, L. (2002). *Read me first for a user's guide to qualitative methods.* Thousand Oaks: Sage Publications.

Mort, P., & Holloway, L. (2006). Supporting the PhD: genre and moves in engineering thesis introductions. In G. Grigg & C. Bond (eds), *Supporting learning in the 21st century*, refereed proceedings of the 2005 Association of Tertiary Learning Advisors of Aotearoa New Zealand Conference (pp. 192–204). Auckland: ATLAANZ.

Moses, I. (1985). *Supervising postgraduates.* HERDSA Green Guide no. 3. HERDSA, University of New South Wales.

Mullins, G., & Kiley, M. (2002). '"It's a PhD, not a Nobel Prize": How experienced examiners assess research theses'. *Studies in Higher Education*. 7(4), pp. 369–386.

Mulrow, C.D. (1994, September 3). Rationale for systematic reviews. *British Medical Journal*, 309:597-599. Retrieved 25 October 2005 from http://www.bmj.com/cgi/content/full/309/6954/597

Murison, Elizabeth & Webb, Carolyn. (1991). *Writing a Research Paper.* Learning Assistance Centre, University of Sydney.

Murray, R. (2002). *How to write a thesis.* Maidenhead: Open University Press.

Murray, R. (2003). *How to write a thesis.* Maidenhead: Open University Press.

Nesbit, P. (2004). The motivational journey. In S. Burton & P. Steane (eds), *Surviving your thesis* (pp. 97–109). London: Routledge.

Newman, I., Ridenour, C.S., Newman, C., & DeMarco, G.M.P. (2003). A typology of research purposes and its relationship to mixed methods. In A. Tashakkori & C. Teddlie (eds), *Handbook of mixed methods in social and behavioral research* (pp. 167–188). Thousand Oaks: Sage Publications.

Oakley, A. (1999). People's ways of knowing: gender and methodology. In S. Hood, B. Mayall & S. Oliver (eds), *Critical issues in social research: power and prejudice* (pp. 154–170). Buckingham: Open University Press.

O'Donoghue, T. (2007). *Planning your qualitative research project: an introduction to interpretivist research in education.* Abingdon: Routledge.

O'Donovan, Brendan & Rae, David. (1996). *New Zealand's House Prices.* Financial research paper no.5. The National Bank of New Zealand Limited, Economics Division.

Owens, R. (2007a). Valuing international research candidates. In C. Denholm, & T. Evans (eds), *Supervising doctorates downunder: keys to effective supervision in Australia and New Zealand* (pp. 146–154). Camberwell: ACER Press.

Owens, R. (2007b). Writing as a research tool. In C. Denholm, & T. Evans (eds). *Doctorates downunder: keys to successful doctoral study in Australia and New Zealand* (pp. 175–181). Camberwell: ACER Press.

Paltridge, B., & Starfield, S. (2007). *Thesis and dissertation writing in a second language: a handbook for supervisors.* Abingdon: Routledge.

Parry, S. (2007). *Disciplines and doctorates.* Dordrecht: Springer.

Pearce, L. (2005). *How to examine a thesis.* Maidenhead: Society for Research into Higher Education and Open University Press.

Pearson, M., Cowan, A., & Liston, A. (2009). PhD education in science. In Boud, D., & Lee, A. (eds), *Changing practices of doctoral education* (pp. 100–112). Abingdon: Routledge.

Peck MacDonald, S. (1994). *Professional academic writing in the humanities and social sciences.* Carbondale: Southern Illinois University Press.

Perry, A., & Hammond, N. (2002). 'Systematic reviews: The experiences of a PhD student'. *Psychology, Learning and Teaching*, 2(1), pp. 32–35.

Peters, M.A. (2008). 'Academic writing, genres and philosophy'. *Educational Philosophy and Theory*, 40(7), pp. 819–831.

Phillips, E.M., & Pugh, D.S. (2005). *How to get a PhD: a handbook for students and their supervisors*, 4th edn. Maidenhead: Open University Press.

Poggenpohl, Sharon, H. (2000, July). 'Constructing knowledge of design, part 2: questions—an approach to design research', paper presented at the Second Doctoral Education in Design Conference, La Clusaz, France.

Price, Kay. (2000). *Exploring what the doing does: A poststructural analysis of nurses' subjectivity in relation to pain.* Unpublished PhD, University of South Australia.

Price, M.V., Waser, N.M., & McDonald, S. (2000). 'Seed caching by heteromyid rodents from two communities: implications for coexistence'. *Journal of Mammalogy*, 81(1), pp. 97–106.

Princeton University. *Applied and computational mathematics.* Retrieved 24 August 2005 from http://www.pacm.princeton.edu/undergrad.html

Publication manual of the American Psychological Association, 5th edn. (2005). Washington, DC: American Psychological Association.

Publication manual of the American Psychological Association, 6th edn. (2010). Washington, DC: American Psychological Association.

Punch, K.F. (2006). *Introduction to social research.* London: Sage Publications.

Race, P. (1999). *How to get a good degree.* Buckingham: Open University Press.

Reason, P. (2003). 'Pragmatist philosophy and action research: readings and conversation with Richard Rorty'. *Action Research*, 1(1), pp. 103–123.

Reynolds, Teri, A. (2001). *Case Studies in cognitive metaphor and interdisciplinary studies: physics, biology, narrative.* Unpublished PhD, Columbia University.

Richardson, K.A. (2005). Introduction: using complexity theory. In K.A. Richardson, (ed.), *Managing the complex, vol.1. Managing organizational complexity: philosophy, theory, and application* (pp. 391–396). Connecticut: Information Age Publishing.

Ridsdale, M.L. (2000, November 27–28). 'I've read his comments but I don't know how to do': International postgraduate student perceptions of written supervisor feedback. In K. Charnock (ed.), *Sources of confusion: refereed proceedings of the national language and academic skills conference held at La Trobe University* (pp. 272–282). Melbourne: Language and Academic Skills Units of La Trobe University.

Rorty, R. (1999). *Philosophy and Social Hope.* London: Penguin Books.

Rowarth, J., & Fraser, G. (2006). Oral examinations. In C. Denholm, & T. Evans, (eds), *Doctorates downunder: keys to successful doctoral study in Australia and New Zealand* (pp. 208–216). Camberwell: ACER Press.

Rowarth, J. & Green, P. (2006). Sustaining inspiration and motivation. In C. Denholm, & T. Evans (eds.), *Doctorates downunder: keys to successful doctoral study in Australia and New Zealand* (pp. 112–120). Camberwell: ACER Press.

Rowland, Stephen. (2002, September 12–14). *Interdisciplinarity as a site of contestation.* Draft paper presented at the annual conference of the British Education Research Association, University of Exeter. Retrieved 23 August 2005 from http://66.102.7.104/search?q=cache:iD7OSChJhFoJ:www.ucl.ac.uk/cishe/seminars/interdisciplinarity/contestation_paper.doc+interdisciplinary+difficulties&hl=en

Rowland, Stephen. (2003). *Seeing things differently: the challenge of interdisciplinarity.* Interdisciplinarity Study Group, University College London. Retrieved 14 September 2005 from http://www.ucl.ac.uk/cishe/colloquium/papers/rowland.html

Rowland, S. (2006). *The enquiring university, compliance and contestation in higher education.* Maidenhead: Society for Research into Higher Education and Open University Press.

Rugg, G., & Petre, M. (2004). *The unwritten rules of PhD research.* Maidenhead: Open University Press.

Rumana, R. (2000). *On Rorty.* Belmont: Wadsworth.

Sawyer, K.S. (2005). *Social emergence: societies as complex systems.* New York: Cambridge University Press.

Schoenberger, E. (2001). 'Interdisciplinarity and social power'. *Progress in Human Geography* 25(3), pp. 365–382.

Schostak, J. (2006). *Interviewing and representation in qualitative research.* Maidenhead: Open University Press.

Seagram, B.C., Gould, J. & Pyke, S.W. (1998). 'An investigation of gender and other variables on timely completion of doctoral degrees'. *Research in Higher Education*, 39, pp. 319–335.

Sharrock W., & Read, R. (2002). *Kuhn: philosopher of the scientific revolution.* Cambridge: Polity Press.

Sheard, S. (2006). 'Complexity theory and continental philosophy: a hermeneutical theory of complexity'. In *Emergence: Complexity and Organization*, 8(1), pp. 50–66.

Simpson, B. (2005). Advancing complexity theory into the human domain. In K.A. Richardson, (ed.), *Managing the complex, vol.1. Managing organizational complexity: philosophy, theory and application*, (pp. 93–106). Connecticut: Information Age Publishing.

Simpson, R. (1983). *How the PhD came to Britain: a century of struggle for postgraduate education.* Guildford: The Society for Research into Higher Education.

Siwek, J., Gourlay, M.L., Slawson, D.C., Shaughnessy, A.F. (2002, January 15). 'How to write an evidence-based clinical review article'. *American Family Physician*, 65(2), pp. 252–8. Retrieved 15 July 2005 from http://www.aafp.org/afp/20020115/251.html

Smith, J. (2006). 'Review of Literary Darwinism: evolution, human nature, and literature by Joseph Carroll'. *Victorian Studies*, 48(3), pp. 573–574.

Smith, J., & Jenks, C. (2006). *Qualitative Complexity.* Abingdon: Routledge.

Snow, Martha. (nd). *Spell Chequer.* Retrieved 25 June 2009 from http://www.davidpbrown.co.uk/poetry/martha-snow.html

Soliman, Izabel. (1999). *Postgraduate supervision.* Teaching and Learning Centre, University of New England. Retrieved 17 January 2005 from http://www.une.edu.au/tlc/staff/publications/postgraduate.pdf

Sperber, Dan. (2005). *Why rethink interdisciplinarity?* Retrieved 29 August 2005 from http://www.dan.sperber.com/interdisciplinarity.htm

Stabile, M. (2006). Problematizing educational inclusion through heuristic inquiry. In N. B. Garman & M. Piantanida (eds), *The authority to imagine: the struggle toward representation in dissertation writing,* (pp. 35–48). New York: Peter Lang Publishing, Inc.

Stanford encyclopedia of philosophy. Retrieved 18 September 2008 from http://plato.stanford.edu/entries/platonism/

Steane, P. (2004). Fundamentals of a literature review. In S. Burton & P. Steane (eds), *Surviving your thesis* (pp. 124–137). London: Routledge.

Swales, J. (1990). *Genre analysis: English in academic and research settings.* Cambridge: Cambridge University Press.

Taleb, N. N. (2007). *The black swan: the impact of the highly improbable.* New York: Random House.

Taylor, J. (2001). 'The impact of performance indicators on the work of university academics: evidence from Australian universities'. *Higher Education Quarterly,* 55(1), pp. 42–61.

Teddlie, C., & Tashakkori A. (2003a). Major issues and controversies in the use of mixed methods in the social and behavioural sciences. In A. Tashakkori & C. Teddlie (eds), *Handbook of mixed methods in social and behavioral research* (pp. 3–50). Thousand Oaks: Sage Publications.

Teddlie, C., & Tashakkori A. (eds), (2003b). Preface. *Handbook of mixed methods in social and behavioural research* (pp. ix–xv). Thousand Oaks: Sage Publications.

Teddlie, C., & Tashakkori, A. (2003c). The past and future of mixed methods research: from data triangulation to mixed model designs. In A. Tashakkori & C. Teddlie (eds), *Handbook of mixed methods in social and behavioural research* (pp. 671–702). Thousand Oaks: Sage Publications.

Tennant, M. & Roberts, S. (2007). Agreeing to supervise. In C. Denholm, & T. Evans (eds), *Supervising doctorates downunder: keys to effective supervision in Australia and New Zealand* (pp. 20–27). Camberwell: ACER Press.

The Royal Society. (nd). *Individual disciplines and interdisciplinary activities.* Education, training and career development: group 7. Retrieved 26 August 2005 from http://www.royalsoc.ac.uk/downloaddoc.asp?id=1314

Thody, A. (2006). *Writing and presenting research.* London: Sage Publications.

Thompson, Susan, J. (2002). 'Knowledge and vital piety: Methodist ministry education in New Zealand from the 1840s to 1988'. Unpublished D.Phil in Theology, University of Auckland.

Thompson Klein, J. (2004). 'Interdisciplinarity and complexity: an evolving relationship'. *Emergence: Complexity and Organization,* 6(1–2), pp. 2–10.

Thompson Klein, Julie. (1994). *Notes toward a social epistemology of transdisciplinarity.* Retrieved 22 August 2005 from http://nicol.club.fr/ciret/bulletin/b12/b12c2.htm

Tinkler, P., & Jackson, C. (2004). *The doctoral examination process: a handbook for students, examiners and supervisors.* Maidenhead: Society for Research into Higher Education & Open University Press.

Toulmin, S.E. (2003). *The uses of argument.* Cambridge: Cambridge University Press.

Trafford, V. (2008). Conceptual frameworks as a threshold concept in doctorateness. In R. Land, J.H.F. Meyer, & J. Smith, (eds), *Threshold concepts within the disciplines* (pp. 273–288). Rotterdam: Sense Publishers.

Tufte, E. R. (2001). *The visual display of quantitative information,* 2nd edn. Connecticut: Graphics Press.

Tufte, E.R. (2006). *Beautiful evidence.* Connecticut: Graphics Press.

University of Auckland. (2000). *Guidelines for good practice of joint supervision.* Retrieved 12 June 2004 from http://www.auckland.ac.nz/uoa/cs-postgraduate-supervision-tools

University of Auckland. (2001). *Administration of research in masters' degrees.* Board of Graduate Studies Policy.

University of Auckland. (2004a). *Academic plan, 2005–7.* Retrieved 16 August 2008 from www.cad.auckland.ac.nz/file.php/content/files/apg/academic_plan_senate_1104.pdf

University of Auckland. (2004b). *Effective teaching at the University of Auckland.* Retrieved 15 September 2005 from http://www.auckland.ac.nz/uoa/fms/default/uoa/about/teaching/policiesprocedures/docs/effectiveteaching.pdf

Van der Hoeven, Sieta. (2002). 'The rhetoric of adolescent fiction: the pedagogy of reading practices in South Australian secondary English classes'. Unpublished PhD, University of South Australia.

Van Wagenen, K. (1991). *Writing a thesis: substance and style.* New Jersey: Prentice Hall.

Wall, S., & Shankar, I. (2008). 'Adventures in transdisciplinary learning'. *Studies in Higher Education,* 33(5), pp. 551–565.

Wallace, M., & Wray, A. (2006). *Critical reading and writing for postgraduates.* London: Sage Publications.

Wenger, E. (1998). *Communities of practice: learning, meaning and identity.* Cambridge: Cambridge University Press.

Wenger, E., McDermott, R., & Snyder, W.N. (2002). *Cultivating communities of practice: a guide to managing knowledge.* Boston: Harvard Business School Press.

White, B. (2008a). 'Metaphor: a tool for developing a community of "knowing" between asymmetric disciplinary cultures'. In Proceedings of the 31st Higher Education Research and Development Society of Australasia (HERDSA) Annual Conference, Rotorua, 1–4 July 2008, pp. 371–389.

White, B. (2008b). 'Teaching postgraduate researchers: The concept "mixed" in the context of methodology, methods and disciplines'. In *Walking a Tightrope: the balancing act of learning advising,* Refereed proceedings of the 2007 International Conference of the Association of Tertiary Learning Advisors of Aotearoa/New Zealand, Auckland, 21–23 November 2008, pp. 211–226.

White, B. (2010). 'Comprehending the always becoming and never is: the concept 'discipline' in re'. In *Shifting Sands, Firm Foundations,* Proceedings of the 2009 Annual International Conference of the Association of Tretiary Learning Advisors of Aotearoa/New Zealand, Massey University, Auckland, 18-20 November 2009, pp. 147–156.

Wilks, S. (2006). The process of supervisor selection. In C. Denholm, & T. Evans (eds), *Doctorates downunder: keys to successful doctoral study in Australia and New Zealand* (pp. 15–22). Camberwell: ACER Press.

Willmann, O. (1907). The seven liberal arts. In *The Catholic encyclopedia.* New York: Robert Appleton Company. Retrieved 21 May 2008 from http://www.newadvent.org/cathen/01760a.htm

Wisker, G. (2005). *The good supervisor.* Basingstoke: Palgrave Macmillan.

Woods, John. (2008). *Eight theses reflecting on Stephen Toulmin.* Retrieved 24 September 2008 from http://www.johnwoods.ca/Eight_Theses_Reflecting_on_Stephen_Toulmin.pdf

Woods, P. (2006). *Successful writing for qualitative researchers.* Abingdon: Routledge.

Yang, A.S. (2008). 'Matters of demarcation: philosophy, biology, and the evolving fraternity between disciplines'. *International Studies in the Philosophy of Science,* 22(2), pp. 211–225.

Yates, B. (2007). Integrating doctoral candidates into research teams. In C. Denholm, & T. Evans (eds), *Supervising doctorates downunder: keys to effective supervision in Australia and New Zealand* (pp. 105–112). Camberwell: ACER Press.

Zare–Behtash, Esmail. (1997). 'FitzGerald's Rubaiyat: a Victorian invention'. Unpublished PhD, Australian National University.

Zeitz, Kathryn, M. (2003). 'Post-operative observations: ritualised or vital in the detection of post-operative complications'. Unpublished PhD, University of Adelaide.

Index